Murder in Aubagne
Lynching, Law, and Justice during the French Revolution

This is a study of factions, lynching, murder, terror, and counterterror during the French Revolution. It examines factionalism in small towns like Aubagne near Marseille, and how this produced the murders and prison massacres of 1795–1798. Another major theme is the convergence of lynching from below with official terror from above. Although the Terror may have been designed to solve a national emergency in the spring of 1793, in southern France it permitted one faction to continue a struggle against its enemies, a struggle that had begun earlier over local issues like taxation and governance. This study uses the techniques of microhistory to tell the story of the small town of Aubagne. It then extends the scope to places nearby like Marseille, Arles, and Aix-en-Provence. Along the way, it illuminates familiar topics like the activity of clubs and revolutionary tribunals and then explores largely unexamined areas like lynching, the sociology of factions, the emergence of theories of violent fraternal democracy, and the nature of the White Terror.

D. M. G. Sutherland received his M.A. from the University of Sussex and his Ph.D. from the University of London. He is currently professor of history at the University of Maryland, College Park. He is the author of *The Chouans: The Social Origins of Popular Counterrevolution in Upper Brittany, 1770–1796* (1982), *France, 1789–1815: Revolution and Counterrevolution* (1985), and *The French Revolution, 1770–1815: The Quest for a Civic Order* (2003) as well as numerous scholarly articles.

Murder in Aubagne

Lynching, Law, and Justice during the French Revolution

D. M. G. SUTHERLAND

University of Maryland, College Park

CAMBRIDGE UNIVERSITY PRESS
Cambridge, New York, Melbourne, Madrid, Cape Town,
Singapore, São Paulo, Delhi, Tokyo, Mexico City

Cambridge University Press
32 Avenue of the Americas, New York, NY 10013-2473, USA

Published in the United States of America by Cambridge University Press, New York

www.cambridge.org
Information on this title: www.cambridge.org/9781107404281

First published 2009
First paperback edition 2011

A catalogue record for this publication is available from the British Library

Library of Congress Cataloguing in Publication Data
Sutherland, Donald (Donald M. G.)
Murder in Aubagne : lynching, law, and justice during the French Revolution /
D.M.G. Sutherland.
p. cm.
Includes bibliographical references and index.
ISBN 978-0-521-88304-7 (hardback)
1. Aubagne (France) – History – 18th century. 2. Justice, Administration of – France –
Aubagne – History – 18th century. 3. France – History – Revolution, 1789–1799 –
Atrocities. 4. Justice, Administration of – France – History – 18th century. 5. Aubagne
(France) – Social conditions – 18th century. 6. Violence – France – Aubagne – History –
18th century. 7. Lynching – France – Aubagne – History – 18th century. 8. Executions
and executioners – France – Aubagne – History – 18th century. I. Title.
DC195.A77S88 2009
944´.91 – dc22 2009000948

ISBN 978-0-521-88304-7 Hardback
ISBN 978-1-107-40428-1 Paperback

Additional resources for this publication at www.cambridge.org/9780521883047

A simple tic makes us insupportable to those who see us close up every day, not counting the thirst for independence and superiority, this incurable social wound.... Domestic quarrels, face-to-face disagreements, village antipathies all come from that.... Now these hatreds, so to speak, are endemic to small places and they doubled with intensity when the revolutionary wind fueled them. That is easy to understand: in the village, people are as narrow as their space. All Provence was thus infected in the wink of an eye; the most humble church tower had its club, its sedition mongers [*boutefeux*] and its victims.

– Laurent Lautard, *Esquisses historiques: Marseille depuis 1789 jusqu'en 1815; par un vieux Marseillais*

Contents

List of Figures

Preface

When I discovered the *grande affaire d'Aubagne* in the archives in Paris and Marseille, I thought this was a perfect opportunity to explore a genre I had admired for a long time, the microhistory. The *affaire* recounted a series of sensational revenge murders in the small town of Aubagne (population between seven thousand and eight thousand) near Marseille in 1795. The documentation in the trial dossier was huge. Two of the three major criteria of the genre, an event with a powerful narrative element and abundant sources, could be satisfied. Meeting the third criterion, the transition from the narrative to reflections on the broad significance, was another matter. The story of the murder gang in Aubagne was obviously about violence and mayhem in the French Revolution, but how it fitted with the larger picture was problematic. Concentrating on a single series of murders in one town at a particular time left a lot out. As I explored from the murders of 1795 backward into the town's earlier history and outward into the Department of the Bouches-du-Rhône and to Provence, the projected book began to turn into something else. A great deal of Aubagne's history is incomprehensible without an understanding of the broader context of the town's history and its relation to its region. The murder gang of 1795 turned out to be the end result of a factional struggle that began with the Revolution itself in 1789. Moreover, the gang was a retaliation for a particularly extreme form of Jacobinism that was ubiquitous throughout the Midi.

This changed the format of the book from microhistory to something more like the traditional regional monograph. But the context required some revisions to the traditional format of the monograph. The central problem in the history of the French Revolution in the Midi emerged as the nature of local Jacobinism. However, the evidence pointed away from the standard interpretations of extremist Jacobinism. These represent Jacobinism as a product of the radicalism of the Enlightenment or as a response to the twin crises of war and internal insurrection. For all that the Jacobins of the Midi considered themselves as belonging to a national and international movement, local, not generic, factors gave their political culture its specific shape.

Examining Jacobinism raises another problem, that of the crowd. Crowd action here did not fit any of the existing paradigms either. Subsistence issues were not so central as taxation, hope, hatred of enemies, vengeance, preemption, and punishment. The Revolution in this region drew a lot of its support from peasants and from urban working people, yet the common explanations of ordinary people's politicization did not work. Here were peasants who were not particularly antiseigneurial (although they certainly hated aristocrats), and here were artisans who were not obsessed with the rising price of bread. Jacobins and ordinary people were drawn into politics in other ways. The breakdown of the old order in 1789 allowed ordinary people to express age-old peasant ideals of a just community. At first, they demanded a more equitable tax system. But, because taxes were closely linked to local political structures, they simultaneously challenged the authority of the elite families. Once the Constituent Assembly adopted representative forms of local government and guaranteed freedom of assembly and petition, old ideals acquired the more modern-sounding language of Jacobin rural democracy. Ordinary people stayed in politics because the Revolution opened up political spaces that allowed these groups to raise their sights and expectations of what the outcome of Revolution could be. Jacobin utopianism was a product of success. Rising expectations produced an extraordinarily violent politics, one in which fears of foreign enemies definitely mattered, but in which the relationship of external crisis to violent action was much more complicated than an older literature generally allows.

The models of the relations between crowds and political leaders that are part of the literature do not fit either. Although interpretations vary, many historians argue that the crowd imposed violent policies on otherwise-reluctant Jacobins who went along to forestall an even worse violence.[1] This assumes that crowds and Jacobins were different people. The experience of Aubagne and many larger centers shows, however,

---

[1] Roger Dupuy, *La république jacobine: terreur, guerre et gouvernement révolutionnaire, 1792–1794, Nouvelle histoire de la France contemporaine*; 2 (Paris: Seuil, 2005), 301–302.

that the composition of each group overlapped considerably. Jacobins and crowds were aspects of a common movement. Some members of that movement held formal office, but their public positions did not tame them. Urban and small-town elites were divided here as bitterly as they were anywhere, but one of the defining characteristics of the elite who endorsed the Jacobins was the attitude to violence. Such individuals could be ambivalent, apologetic, or even enthusiastic supporters, but in the end, they were never willing to suppress this expression of the popular will. By the time of the Terror, violence was no longer even an episodic occurrence, to be tolerated so long as it remained in the past. Instead, it was a strategy to annihilate an enemy who blocked the construction of a tranquil community in the future. Presenting the leadership as reluctant to embrace violence is, therefore, misleading. Although the leaders' attitudes varied with time, revolutionary institutions, the press, the clubs, and even official and terrorist organs of government frequently exalted in their violent rhetoric and action. Examples of Jacobins reluctant to practice violent politics are very hard to find in big cities like Marseille and other regional centers. A common assumption in the literature that a penchant for violence correlates with social class or degrees of wealth is also unworkable. Middle-class Jacobins could be as extremist as anyone could imagine. By the time national politics had embraced the concept of revolutionary government, in the autumn of 1793, the parameters of permissible violence were very wide indeed.

Justifications for violence as the vengeance of the people emerged early here, as they did among extremists in Paris.[2] Yet, the violence of the murder gangs and the killers of prisoners in 1795 and after worked in a comparable fashion. Revenge and punishment in the name of a ruptured community was an uncanny echo of Jacobin justifications of violence.

These considerations of how the national, regional, and local revolutions interacted affected the decisions about how to present the material. The narrative oscillates back and forth from the history of Aubagne to that of the region. Sometimes, the regional has to be examined in depth before returning to the particular, and, sometimes, the struggles in a small town have to dominate.

---

[2] Colin Lucas, "Revolutionary Violence, the People and the Terror," in *The Terror*, ed. Keith Michael Baker, *The French Revolution and the creation of modern political culture* (Oxford: Pergamon Press, 1994), 57–79. See also his "The Crowd and Politics between 'Ancien Regime' and Revolution in France," *Journal of Modern History* 60, no. 3 (1988), 421–457, which emphasizes the crowd's role in imposing community norms. My argument relates to the crowd as an expression of faction.

If Aubagne was not very different from other places in terms of its extremism, it follows that an understanding of its factionalism throws light on factionalism elsewhere. A thorough prosopography of the factions is only possible in one place, not because these relations are so complex, but because it is very time consuming to uncover them. Linking various bits of biographical data about hundreds of individuals requires a thorough soaking in the local archives. Extending that to other small towns and cities would be a vast enterprise.

Moreover, the results of this minute research showed that other explanations that social-cultural historians frequently deploy must be laid aside. A working hypothesis in the historian's toolbox is that social structure determines consciousness. Another is that preexisting cultural predispositions or heritages determine action. Social and cultural issues certainly matter, but it is impossible to see how they matter without having a clear idea of what we are trying to discover. Thus the importance of establishing a clear narrative. Thus the importance too of connecting the small spokes of Aubagne to the large wheels of Marseille, the Bouches-du-Rhône, and even Provence.

Acknowledgments

Many friends and colleagues have helped make this book better by reading all or part of the manuscript. Howard Brown and his students at State University of New York, Binghamton, read the entire manuscript and gave me many useful suggestions. Tim Le Goff as always clarified my ideas and prose. Tim Tackett reminded me to bear the big picture in mind and made many helpful suggestions about the book's structure. So did Jack Censer and Alan Tulchin. Many thanks to Stephen Clay for tips on sources and archives. Without Rafe Blaufarb's suggestions, the provincial tax system and the banalities would have remained a mystery. Robert Forster gave many helpful comments on social structure and the use of tax rolls to depict it. I have also benefited from feedback in several seminars: the Baltimore-Washington Old Regime Group, the University of Delaware, the History Center at the University of Maryland and the Violence and the French Revolution Conference at College Park in October 2001, two *journées d'études* in 2001 and 2002 in Aix-en-Provence, as well as the Colloque international de Rouen of January 2007.

The generosity of colleagues and friends in France continues to be a tribute to international scholarship. Jacques Guilhaumou has shared many ideas and his abundant knowledge of the Marseille and the region. Michel and Monique Vovelle have provided hospitality, ideas, and debate from the beginning of this project.

I would also like to thank the staff of numerous libraries and archives on both sides of the Atlantic: the Library of Congress, the McKeldin Library at the University of Maryland (and especially Yelena Luckert), and the New York Public Library; the municipal librarians in Aubagne, Marseille, Arles, and Avignon; the departmental archives of the

Bouches-du-Rhône, Gard, and Vaucluse; and the municipal archives of Aubagne (especially Mme Zito and Mme Sandra Rouqueirol), Salon-de-Provence, Auriol, Aix-en-Provence, Tarascon, Toulon, and Marseille.

And, of course, my gratitude for the patience and support of my family, and, because I forgot the last time, to my daughter Jeannie, who kept me company into the small hours.

Abbreviations

AC	Archives communales
AD	Archives départementales
ADBR	Archives départementales des Bouches-du-Rhône
AhRf	*Annales historiques de la Révolution française*
AM	Archives municipales
AN	Archives nationales
AP	*Archives parlementaires*
Aulard, *RACSP*	F.A. Aulard, *Recueil des actes du Comité de Salut public*
BM	Bibliothèque municipale
CSP	Comité de Salut public
JdM	*Journal des départements méridionaux*
NYPL	New York Public Library
Rf	*Révolution française*
SP	Société populaire

Aubagne

An Introduction to the Problem

There were three bodies altogether. The first two lay close to each other, facedown. The third, the youngest of the three, lay apart, on its back, staring straight up into the pale afternoon sky. All three of them had been murdered. The justice of the peace knew very well the first steps he had to follow whenever a body had been found. He began to dictate the preliminaries of his report: "The third year of the French Republic, 3 [M]essidor (21 June 1795) at six o'clock in the afternoon, I... *juge de paix de ce canton de Roq^re* [Roquevaire]," he called out. The secretary began to scribble. He too knew the routine. No one else was there except his assistants, the medical examiner, and the scribe. He continued, "On hearing a rumor, we went... to the path going to Aubagne, *quartier de la côte de nerf.*"

He went on to describe the bodies. Two of the victims' faces were horribly disfigured from the severe beatings. All three had been shot several times. The first two, men of around sixty and forty years of age, wore very shabby, olive-colored clothes. The third was a young man of about twenty-six. He was missing several fingers on his left hand from an old accident. The clothes of all three and the ground around them were covered in dried blood.

The report concludes, without any commentary, that besides the unspeakable violence all three victims had been subjected to, the older and younger men had each had an ear cut off.

This document from the justice of the peace of Roquevaire is the first in the file relating to what contemporaries called the *grande affaire d'Aubagne.*[1] The events involved the prosecution of sixty-seven people, two of them women, from the town of Aubagne, near Marseille, and its immediate region, for having murdered, assaulted, or robbed forty-five or more of their neighbors from in and around the town over a three-year period, from 1795 to 1798. The trial itself examined the testimony of a hundred witnesses. It took a very unusual seventeen days in the early summer of 1801 to hear all the pleas and to examine all the evidence. It was one of the biggest and longest trials of the decade.

No one knew the three victims. At least that is what the report of the justice of the peace and the medical examiner claims. Yet this is implausible, because as local men, both officials ought to have known whom they could have called upon to identify them. It is significant that no one volunteered to identify the bodies, not even family members, friends, or employers. All we can infer from this document is that the three were poor working people. Also, many assailants must have attacked the victims with uncontrolled ferocity. Beyond that, there is silence.

In fact, many people knew exactly who the victims were. They also knew not only why they had been murdered but also who did it. This came out during the investigations into the *grande affaire* that began three years later. The investigation was possible only because of the coup of 18 Fructidor, year V (4 September 1797) in Paris. This led to the purge of those who had protected the killers locally and to the restoration of Jacobins to power. The complexities of the case were very confusing to judicial authorities. It took them another three years to bring the accused to trial. Even then, the victims' families must have felt cheated because the outcome was so ambiguous. The Special Tribunal acquitted many accused, and most of the others remained at large.

The victims' family name was Jullien, and they were a father and his two sons. They were laborers, but more than that they were Jacobin militants who had fled Aubagne for their own safety. One son may have been a member of the Aubagne National Guard that ravaged the château of Velaux, north of Marseille, in April 1792. The guards suspected it was a lair of counterrevolutionaries. The assailants had joined their comrades from the National Guard of Marseille to suppress the counterrevolutionaries in Arles. The attacks on Velaux and Arles were two of the many trouble spots that invited such interventions, including one in Aubagne itself during its time of troubles a few months earlier. Such adventures

---

[1] ADBR, L 3049, "Procédures contre les auteurs de vols, assassinats, attroupements, etc., d'Aubagne, Cassis, Roquefort, et leurs environs, de l'An III à l'an VI."

were preludes to the grandest expedition of all, the march on Paris to overthrow the monarchy in July and August 1792.

Local people already knew Jullien senior well. A municipal officer during the Terror, Jullien's militant activity had begun much earlier. He was involved in the most spectacular incident in the local revolution: the lynching of a former process server named Joseph Jourdan in September 1792. Perhaps the murder of the Julliens was retaliation for the murder of Jourdan three years before, but because those responsible for Jourdan's murder were never convicted, it is impossible to say.

By the time authorities began investigating the Jullien family's murder in the autumn of the year VI (1797), the democratic upsurge of 1792 was a distant memory. Yet the region was still suffering the consequences. One of these was the White Terror, a wave of mayhem, murder, massacre, robbery, and vandalism that wracked the southeast of France in the closing years of the Revolution. The White Terror is usually presented as a direct reaction to the much better known Terror of 1793–4. Nor is this view wrong, as revenge inflicted on the former Jacobin terrorists was essential to the White Terror. Nevertheless, it was not solely a reaction to the Great Terror either, because its roots go back further to an earlier phase of the Revolution. Many members of the murder gang who so cruelly maimed the Julliens had been active in town politics before the Terror. Their sponsors, men who were known but who managed to hide solid evidence of their complicity, had been too. Thus, the White Terror was one event of several that tore Aubagne apart during the emergence of democratic politics in 1792. These politics were enormously turbulent and fractious. The town witnessed two lynchings, an insurrection against the Jacobins, and a local terror as brutal as any that occurred elsewhere. The medical officer's report, therefore, is only a starting point for unraveling the *grande affaire d'Aubagne*.

The silences surrounding the medical report do point us in a certain direction. These were not ordinary murders. The deliberate mutilations, the terrifying refusal of witnesses to come forward, the anonymity of the victims themselves – all this is out of the ordinary and so, as negative evidence, shows something about what an extraordinary place Aubagne had become. As the investigations of the Year VI revealed, the Julliens were murdered in public. Witnesses saw an armed gang leave Aubagne, go to the small town of Brignolles in the nearby Department of the Var, seize the victims, rope them together, and then murder them near the Pont de l'Etoile on the path leading from Roquevaire to Aubagne. The murderers continued their spree off and on for another three years, intimidating everyone into silence. Nevertheless, everyone knew their names: Mathieu Rousserie and his sons, café owners; Joseph Guillermy, a mason; Laurent Jauffret, a cook to the retired parish priest Pierre Martinot, who himself allegedly gave the killers money and who celebrated the killings afterward in Rousserie's café; Jean-Baptiste Barthélémy *dit* La Machine, an innkeeper; Antoine Michel *dit* Calade, a baker; and several others who will appear often in this story. Men like these, in an earlier time and in another place, could have been village sansculottes.

The murder gang was thus composed of men who in the standard historiography of the Revolution opted for the wrong side. So too did their sponsors. The anti-Jacobins of Aubagne were not nobles and priests for the most part. Nobles played a very small role in local political life, and while the place had many resident priests, few involved themselves in politics. To be sure, the retired curé Martinot was deeply compromised. Nevertheless, Martinot was prominent, rich, and well connected, the opposite of the contemporary ideal of the cleric distant from his flock. He was a typical son of the local elite. Furthermore, the bourgeoisie of Aubagne as a whole not only opposed the Terror, which many of their counterparts did elsewhere, but also vigorously opposed the democratic upsurge of 1792. Professionals like them frequently supported the Revolution in other parts of the country. In Aubagne, the professional classes were almost universally hostile.

Although the term is an abused cliché, *Jacobinism* in Aubagne, and probably throughout the Midi, was a popular movement. Jacobinism in Aubagne attracted very humble men, and some committed women, overwhelmingly. Peasants were the major source of Jacobin support. Nor was their intervention episodic. We are used to images of peasants burning châteaus in 1789 or demolishing them in 1792, marching off to defend the frontiers throughout the period, petitioning higher authority, and so on. However, in Aubagne and no doubt throughout the Midi, Jacobins and peasants contested for power on a daily basis from the beginning. First in Marseille in early 1790, then at various points including Aubagne in late 1791, Jacobins took power. Their tolerance or sponsorship of violence earned them countless enemies. These turbulent democrats eventually became terrorists. They organized a vigorous purge of their local enemies and enforced the most radical aspects of the Revolution. Unfortunately, for them, their purge was not thorough enough, and it was in this context that the murder gang began its operations.

Some gaps in the record relate to the unfortunate history of the Archives Départementales des Bouches-du-Rhône or with the history of the municipal archives of Aubagne itself. The very uneven survival of club proceedings, the papers of the *comités de surveillance*, and many financial records is very disappointing. The vicissitudes of municipal budgets and the transfer of archives from the *mairie* of Aubagne to the delightful local library named after Marcel Pagnol, and back again, have destroyed the wonderful balance of the inventory someone drew up in 1950. Nevertheless, even if archivists at various epochs and in various jurisdictions had done all they could for someone looking to crack the *grande affaire*, the reality is that no one at the time confessed to murder. So an element of mystery about the *grande affaire* will always persist. Even if we had all the documents we might have wished for, we still would not have enough to answer all our questions.

It is tempting to explain the characteristics of the *grande affaire d'Aubagne* by invoking the received wisdom even contemporaries shared about Mediterranean cultures. The extreme violence, the cult of silence, the refusal to cooperate with government that ordinary people consider primordially and viscerally alien, the assertion of machismo values – even though a few women participated in the *grande affaire* – all this invites an explanation based upon inherent characteristics. Somehow or other, Mediterranean culture produced these murders.[2] Yet dismissing such obviously extravagant behavior as part of the passing scene would be too simple. In fact, the 1790s were unique in the history of Aubagne. The place appears to have been tediously peaceful before 1789, and after the *grande affaire d'Aubagne*, it slipped into an untroubled slumber.

The fact that the extreme violence in Aubagne was specific to a particular time in the town's history is one reason to reject an explanation based upon inherent characteristics. Another reason for doubting it is that contemporaries, however much they believed that the men and women of the Midi were exceptionally violent by nature, also believed that what had happened in Aubagne was particularly horrible. Even by the dismissive and casual standards of Mediterranean violence, this was a special case. And that is saying something. For anyone coming to the Midi after having studied other regions in France during the same period, regions that have the justifiable reputation of having been extraordinarily violent, the Midi is in another register. The Chouans and the Vendéens of the West were killers, no doubt about that, but their operations were normally part of a broader military strategy; in the Midi, no military strategy justified the killings.

[2] Colin Lucas, "The Problem of the Midi in the French Revolution," *Transactions of the Royal Historical Society*, 28 (1978), 23–5, gives a handy summary of these stereotypes.

The killing was on a brutal scale. Consider the *barbets* who operated in the hills above Nice. They had their own ideas about having been incorporated into *la grande nation*. To show their repugnance, they not only murdered those who collaborated with the French but also decapitated their victims. Often the head was never found again, or they tossed it into a nearby pigsty, where the animals devoured it.[3]

Or consider the appalling prison massacres in the Midi after the fall of Robespierre in 1794. In Lyon in May 1795, a mob of thousands believed that the Jacobins who had ruled the city so brutally during the Terror were going to be let off, or else were going to break out of the prisons and slaughter peaceful citizens with multibladed guillotines. To prevent these nightmares, the mob set fire to the prisons, forced all the prisoners onto the roofs, and then selectively culled the most notorious former terrorists. They killed only the terrorists and left ordinary convicts to their own devices.[4] A very similar event occurred in Marseille the next month. The mob burst into the prison at Fort Jean and murdered about a hundred Jacobins.[5] Almost simultaneously, assailants butchered nearly fifty people in two massacres at the prison in Tarascon. These atrocities shared the same motives: panic and anger at the attempt of the Jacobins in Toulon to march to the rescue of their friends in the Bouches-du-Rhône; and exasperation at the slowness of the regular courts trying former terrorists.[6] The massacre at Marseille was the worst single

---

[3] AN BB[18] 117, "Extrait du registre des jugements du tribunal de première instance de l'arrondissement de Puget-Theniers", n.d. The verbal violence of the *barbets* could be just as chilling: one named Constatin Cognoli, "bragged [*s'est flatté publiquement*] on many different occasions of having murdered [*assassiné*] a considerable quantity of French soldiers, up to 150 at least . . . , and of having eaten the liver of several of them and of having eaten bread covered and soaked with the blood of another soldier." Cognoli and his men also extorted money by threatening to bury their victims alive (ibid., BB[18] 118, "Acte d'accusation contre Constatin Cognoli, Vincent Penchinat . . . etc.," 13 Brumaire An XI – 3 November 1802). On the origin and operations of the *barbets*, see *Inventaire sommaire des archives départementales des Alpes-Maritimes. Série L.*, ed. Henri Moris and Robert Latouche (Nice, impr. et papeterie H. Ventre fils 1924), 133–41. Michel-André Iafelice, "Les 'Barbets' des Alpes-Maritimes. Origines et caractérisation du Barbétisme," François Lebrun and Roger Dupuy, eds. In *Les Résistances á la Révolution: Actes du Colloque de Rennes, 17–21 Septembre 1985* (Paris: Imago, 1987), 126–32.

[4] Renée Fuoc, *La réaction thermidorienne á Lyon (1795)* (Lyon: IAC Les Édition de Lyon, 1957), *passim*.

[5] Stephen Clay, "Le massacre du fort Saint-Jean: Un épisode de la Terreur blanche à Marseille," in *Le tournant de l'an III: Réaction et terreur blanche dans la France révolutionnaire*, ed. Michel Vovelle (Paris: Éditions. du CTHS, 1997), 569–84.

[6] AN F[7] 7130, Procureur-syndic du district de Tarascon to Comité de sûreté générale, 8 Messidor An III – 26 June 1795. Ibid., F[7] 7171, General Mille, "Tableau de la situation des Bouches-du-Rhône," n.d.

atrocity of the White Terror, but it was far from unique. Although no one has ever paid much attention to them, prison massacres also occurred at Aix-en-Provence, Bourg, Montbrison, Lons-le-Saulnier, Saint-Etienne, and Nîmes. Various authorities managed to cover up still others, including several at Aubagne, for many years.

After the Terror, the nation witnessed thousands of freelance murders, stagecoach robberies, pro- and anti-Jacobin insurrections, brigandage, and endless disorder. Yet within these numbing reports, the Bouches-du-Rhône stood out for its exceptional partisanship. According to one evaluation, the Bouches-du-Rhône "has been one of the most agitated in the Republic, one of those where the revolutionary tyranny made the most victims and where the reaction has been the most bloody."[7]

Contemporaries convinced themselves that what had happened in Aubagne was exceptionally ghastly. General Bon in 1798 called Aubagne "uniquely infamous because of the atrocities committed there."[8] General Willot claimed Aubagne had been "for a long time, the most turbulent commune in the département of the Bouches-du-Rhône."[9] One local official told the minister of police that everything the minister had heard about Aubagne was true. "Theft, murder, rape, forced contributions, devastation of property, crimes of any sort" were the order of the day.[10] According to the moderate faction in the town, "Until 9 Thermidor [i.e., the fall of Robespierre], every inconceivable horror had afflicted Aubagne. After that, the unfortunate influence of personal vengeance spread."[11] The administrators of the department of the Bouches-du-Rhône claimed Aubagne was one of those communes "of the Midi where royalism has committed the most crimes, that the soil itself is still red with [R]epublican blood that has spilled in great gobs. Reviving public opinion is

---

[7] AN F¹ᶜ III Bouches-du-Rhône, 6, Anon., "Département des Bouches-du-Rhône. Esprit publique, no. 8." The department made a similar comment: "The Revolution gave birth to factions aggravated by hatreds that acted on everyone. The greatest calamities have afflicted this region.... Every family is in mourning." ADBR, L 173, f. 33, Department to Minister of Justice, 2 Thermidor An IV – 20 July 1796.

[8] AhG, B¹³ 71, Gen. Bon to Gen. Pille, 29 Vendémiaire An VI – 20 October 1797.

[9] AN F7 7170, Gen. Willot to Jourdan 7 Pluviôse An V – 26 January 1797. See also his assessment to the Directory in his letter of 24 Brumaire An V – 14 November 1796: "the commune of Aubagne, incessantly troubled by agitators," which in Willot's case was a code word for *Jacobins* (AN F7 4444ᴬ).

[10] ADBR, L 245, p. 180, Commissaire du directoire exécutif du département des Bouches-du-Rhône to Ministre de Police générale, 23 Brumaire An VI – 13 November 1796.

[11] AN F¹ᵇ II Bouches-du-Rhône 11, Officiers municipaux de la commune d'Aubagne suspendus de leurs fonctions...to Ministre de l'Intérieur, n.d. (After 22 Pluviôse An IV – 10 February 1796).

essential, to chain all the passions and have all the citizens submit to the laws."[12]

Aubagne was thus a violent place. Whether it was unusually violent, as some contemporaries asserted, is another matter. Nonetheless, concentrating on the history of a small town can throw some light on violence in the Revolution overall. This inquiry then leads to others, into the nature of provincial Jacobinism, and then into the different and competing visions of informal and retributive justice that underlie the violence of the period.

A common approach divides the French Revolution into two periods: a heroic, running from 1789 to the fall of Robespierre on 28 July 1794, and a second depressing slide into reaction and corruption running from 1794 to the final arrival of Bonaparte. The theme of the first period is Jacobin ascendancy, the most creative and exciting period of the Revolution. The theme of the second is despair at the defeat of the popular movement.

Such a binary categorization makes sense for the national, parliamentary scene, but provincial history responded to different rhythms. Nor is it difficult to show that the rhythm of events differed throughout France as a whole. More interesting is the emergence of a different kind of Jacobinism in the Midi. Standard histories treat the Jacobins on their own terms, as exemplars of all that was best and noble in the Revolution. They saved the country in its most perilous moments from treasonous domestic counterrevolutions and dangerous foreign invasions. Yet, attractive as many of them were as individuals, external circumstances cannot explain or excuse the relationship of the Jacobins to violence. As we will see, the Jacobins of Aubagne and practically everywhere in the Bouches-du-Rhône succumbed to the temptations of a politics of violence very early, well before these perils had arisen.

The Jacobins were a faction in local politics before anything else. The support they received from their brothers in Marseille and elsewhere permitted them to use institutional and legal weapons against their enemies that rendered the struggle hopelessly uneven. The Jacobins would argue that their enemies' failure to accept the logic of the democratic politics of the early years of the Revolution justified an aggressive response. Nevertheless, the consequence of that vigorous response was to render local and regional politics seriously unhealthy. The Jacobins not only initiated violence but also, by the end of 1792, accepted and quietly condoned vigilante justice against their enemies. Moreover, vigilantism and its mutation

---

[12] AC Aubagne, registre des délibérations, f. 231, "Extrait de l'arrêté de l'administration du département des Bouches-du-Rhône du 22 pluviôse An IV (22 February 1796)."

into the Great Terror of 1793–4 would be extremely difficult to suppress. Whatever their enemies said about the Jacobins being an unrepresentative cabal, the local clubs attracted huge support from ordinary people. Because the clubs were also shameless and belligerent partisans in local politics, they provoked concomitant countermobilizations of all those whom the club threatened. High attendance at meetings and demonstrations, vast numbers of signatures for petitions, and of course occasionally high turnouts for elections were all signs of this.

Healthy politics soon gave way to murder and fear of violence. So long as one side feared that the other could organize massacres, counterviolence, not electoral politics, was a necessary act of self-defense and a preliminary to wreaking vengeance. This could have gone on forever. General Willot pointed to this stasis when he wrote, "The factions that succeed each other have become irreconcilable and aspire only to the destruction of the other side."[13]

Still, if Willot and many other observers were correct, one wonders why the seesaw killing did not evolve into a classic Mediterranean vendetta with one generation taking up the cudgels to avenge the injuries done to its predecessors. The trial of the *grande affaire d'Aubagne* did not end the vicissitudes because it convicted so few of the killers. Anti-Jacobin violence might have returned as a result. This did not happen. The killings stopped not because one side imposed justice on the other, but because of the exceptional justice of the Second Directory and the ruthlessness of the Bonapartist dictatorship. Untidy as the results of the trial were, the elimination of the feuding parties from government, the incarceration of even those whom the courts had declared innocent, the keeping up of the hunt for those who escaped, and the holding of the threat of arrest over the violent men who remained until, one by one, they died quietly in their beds, broke the cycle.

Violent politics has a structure. For Aubagne, this structure was a reflection of a culture of retributive justice. One strategy of understanding this culture would be to examine the received opinions about the Mediterranean vendetta. The hypothesis would be that the groups that killed one another so unhesitatingly had always hated one another. Thus,

---

[13] AN F⁷ 7197, letter to Ministre de la Police Générale, 4 Brumaire An V – 25 October 1795. He used the same phrasing in his letter to the department of 3 Brumaire An V – 23 October 1795 (ADBR, L 135 f. 83v) and went on to describe Aubagne as dominated by "agitators who have no other way to maintain their domination than through trouble and disorder. These men who earlier could only subsist by a painful and laborious work have become well off by pillage . . . , passing their time in the cabarets."

the Revolution provided merely the pretext for these ancestral hatreds to manifest themselves. Although the exercise in comparative history can be useful, unfortunately, the relationship between violent politics and vendetta was not direct. One might have expected contemporaries to have said more about it. Yet they said practically nothing. Although their explanations of how they found themselves in their dreadful situation are often quite naive in retrospect, they never cite long-standing feuds. When we compare what happened in Aubagne with other Mediterranean societies that were based on vendetta, we can see that the dissimilarities were clearly all important. In nineteenth-century Corsica, for example, the absence of a well-defined property law explained the endemic violence. In Montenegro, a clan-based honor system substituted for an impartial system of institutional justice.[14] Needless to say, nothing that happened in Aubagne resembled this kind of semistructured lawlessness.

Anthropologists have shown that vendetta and feuding are highly developed forms of vengeance.[15] Vendetta focuses on the possession of something tangible, like women or animals; is often based on kin; is usually multigenerational; and is often resolved by temporary and frequently insincere ceremonies of reconciliation.[16] In Aubagne, the object in dispute was political power; the struggle was short-lived; other forms of association in addition to kin were involved; and there never was reconciliation so much as a fight to the finish.

The *grande affaire d'Aubagne* most closely resembles the sort of intraurban rivalry that erupted from time to time in Mediterranean Europe

[14] On Corsica and Montenegro, see the two very fine monographs by Stephen Wilson, *Feuding, Conflict, and Banditry in Nineteenth-Century Corsica* (Cambridge: Cambridge University Press, 1988) and Christopher Boehm, *Blood Revenge: The Anthropology of Feuding in Montenegro and Other Tribal Societies* (Lawrence: University Press of Kansas, 1984).

[15] Julian Alfred Pitt-Rivers, *The People of the Sierra* (Chicago: University of Chicago Press, 1971), 89–92. Rudolph M. Bell, *Fate and Honor, Family and Village: Demographic and Cultural Change in Rural Italy since 1800* (Chicago: University of Chicago Press, 1979), 105–6.

[16] Philippe Descola, *The Spears of Twilight: Life and Death in the Amazon Jungle* (New York: New Press, 1996), 61–2, 277, 291–4. Marshall David Sahlins, *Islands of History* (Chicago: University of Chicago Press, 1985). Marshall Sahlins, "The Return of the Event, Again: With Reflections on the Beginnings of the Great Fijian War of 1843 to 1855 between the Kingdoms of Bau and Rewa," in *Clio in Oceania: Toward a historical Anthropology*, ed. Aletta Biersack (Washington, D.C.: Smithsonian Institution Press, 1990), 67–78. John A. Davis, *Conflict and Control: Law and Order in Nineteenth-Century Italy* (Atlantic Highlands, NJ: Humanities Press International, 1988), 88–90. Jacob Black-Michaud, *Cohesive force: Feud in the Mediterranean and the Middle East* (New York: St. Martin's Press, 1975), 13–14.

before 1789. Even these cases are weakly related, however. One startling example of intraurban violence was the long-standing fighting between neighborhoods for control of the city's dozens of bridges in early-modern Venice. But this was a permissible violence that local elites encouraged to keep martial spirit high. Other types of violence involved the feuds of elite families that dragged ordinary people along in their wake.[17] Nothing like this occurred in Aubagne.

The *grande affaire d'Aubagne* thus fits awkwardly into the standard models of Mediterranean violence, the vendetta or the intraurban brawl. Nonetheless, we can still take some valuable suggestions from an examination of the historical and anthropological literature on vendettas and fighting. The importance of neighborhood allegiances; the complicated social alliances that transcend class; the prior relationships among the warring factions, in this case kin and godparent relationships; and the importance of reciprocity – all these are important clues to look for.

The most common element that violence in Aubagne shares with the historical and anthropological cases, however, is the weakness of the state. Italian-style feuding emerged because in Venice, authority temporarily withdrew its support for law and order. In the case of Venetian Friuli, violence was endemic because the city never had a strong institutional presence in the remoter hinterlands of its own territories. The weakness of the state and especially of judicial institutions in Corsica or in the Ottoman Mediterranean or elsewhere in the world left communities to regulate conflict informally. The result was vendetta. Aubagne's experience of weak legal institutions was so brief that vendettas never developed. Nevertheless, huge resentments did build up with no institutional means of satisfying them. During the Revolution, authorities were unable or unwilling to deploy the judicial apparatus impartially, or even at all. The desire to use the judicial apparatus of government for political ends in the French Midi, or the failure to intervene to regulate venomous conflicts or to impose restitution, produced truly tragic consequences. The resultant lack of public confidence in authority to mete out justice as ordinary people understood it was a precondition to vigilante justice.

---

[17] See Robert C. Davis, *The War of the Fists: Popular Culture and Public Violence in Late Renaissance Venice* (New York: Oxford University Press, 1994). Edward, Muir, *Mad Blood Stirring: Vendetta and Factions in Friuli during the Renaissance* (Baltimore: Johns Hopkins University Press, 1993), *passim*. For a general overview that argues for a conflict between the establishment and new men, see Lauro Martines, "Political Violence in the Thirteenth Century," in *Violence and Civil Disorder in Italian Cities, 1200–1500*, ed. Lauro Martines (Berkeley: University of California Press, 1972), 331–53.

Aubagne exemplifies the vast and murderous fighting within the large and small cities of Languedoc and Provence during the French Revolution.[18] For many people, the Revolution's doctrines of popular sovereignty extended to the application of justice. Popular sovereignty permitted them to bypass legal procedures and the rule of law to punish their enemies directly. When institutional means failed, they, like the kings of old, could reclaim the right to administer justice. Jacobins and anti-Jacobins alike could invoke this right. The hangings of 1792 and the murder of the Julliens thus became thinkable. A special kind of democracy explains why the Revolution was so violent and tragic here.

[18] The only general treatment is Colin Lucas, "Themes in Southern Violence after 9 Thermidor," in *Beyond the Terror: Essays in French Regional and Social History, 1794–1815*, ed. Gwynne Lewis and Colin Lucas (Cambridge: Cambridge University Press, 1983), 152–94, which treats the period as a struggle over community, whereby the anti-Jacobins defined traditional community norms and punished the Jacobins for violating those standards. This interpretation does not consider the importance and politicization of faction fighting that occurred before the Terror or the struggle over who would control local institutions.

I

Structures and Events

It would be difficult to find a *pays* in France with more vulgar manners, more dissension, more hatred, [or] more jealousy. I will go further still and say, more bad faith, pride, [and] haughtiness without merit and without talent.... There are few towns in France as dirty as Aubagne.... Its inhabitants live in the cafés, tobacco shops, and gambling houses.
  – Dr. Bernardin Ramel, a native of Aubagne, as cited in L. Barthélemy,
    Histoire d'Aubagne: Chef-lieu de baronnie, depuis son origine jusqu'en 1789

On Sunday, 7 January 1787, around nine o'clock in the evening, a dozen or so men were celebrating King's Day.[1] The group was formal, what contemporaries called a *chambrée*, a male association that met occasionally for drink and chat. The men had rented the meeting room overlooking the Grand' Rue in Aubagne. The celebration was important because there were guests present who were not normally invited. As the men danced and smoked around the fire, another group outside began pelting rocks through the windows. They broke a half dozen panes and the window frame itself. Then they ran off. A quarter of an hour later, they returned and began singing a well-known song but transformed the lyrics into "mocking and bloody threats."

Nothing more came of the incident. Apparently, authorities or the plaintiffs decided not to pursue the assailants, who will always remain unknown. Still, this apparent case of minor vandalism and harassment has exceptional significance. Some of the men who signed the complaint had

---

[1] The story has been reconstructed from a small sheaf of untitled documents in ADBR, 6B 6056.

futures as anti-Jacobins. One of them, the master mason, as he styled himself, Joseph Guillermy, was a leading member of the gang: he murdered well over a dozen Jacobins in 1795 both in Aubagne and in Marseille. Another, Jean-Baptiste Jougan, a gardener, was among those who murdered the Julliens, whose deaths opened our story. Other celebrants were involved in more purely political anti-Jacobin activity from the beginning of the Revolution and continuing into the anti-Jacobin takeover in July 1793. One was Antoine Coste, who joined the vigorously anti-Jacobin municipal council of May 1795. Another especially prominent plaintiff was the notary Georges Cartier, who was reasonably suspected of using his position as *commissaire du directoire exécutif* in 1796–7 to protect the gang after its first killing spree was over. None of those present at the King's Day celebration was a future Jacobin.

The King's Day disturbance opens a window into the social patterns in the town before the Revolution. Those who attended obviously liked one another well enough and the friendships were strong enough to transform themselves into political allegiances later. Although the *chambrée* was not a direct forerunner of the gang, because many celebrants stayed out of the quarrels of the Revolution, the social composition of its members and guests illustrates a pattern of association that was common in other walks of life. This *chambrée* largely excluded the men from the agricultural sector, and it drew its membership from within the town walls and from a mix of bourgeois and artisans, particularly from the food and drink trades (seven of the seventeen plaintiffs were in these occupations). As it happens, this parallels the composition of the gang very closely. The occupations of the attendees and the futures of some of them raise other important questions: What is the significance of the sociology of the factions in revolutionary Aubagne? To what extent did the factions have antecedents in the Old Regime? Did the King's Day incident foreshadow a much bloodier future? To what extent did the sociology of the faction reflect divisions in the town?

The Social Structure of Aubagne

Despite its small size, Aubagne was typical of the hundreds of agro-towns of Provence.[2] These were large agglomerations in which every social class inhabited a heavily concentrated urban center. Peasants inhabited this

---

[2] Maurice Agulhon, "La notion de village en Basse-Provence vers la fin de Ancien Régime," in *Actes du 90ᵉ Congrès national des Sociétés savantes, Nice 1965* (Paris: Bibliothèque Nationale, 1966), 277–301.

urban center, too, and went out each morning to tend their fields. The rural area, called the *terroir*, was home to many peasants as well. There were a few hamlets in the *terroir* and a great many *bastides*, or country houses. These were secondary residences for the local bourgeoisie or for the more prosperous farmers.

The differences with the rural and urban geography of northern France were remarkable. Here, rural society was organized around fairly small villages that sold their surplus at nearby market towns. Networks of such small towns channeled their produce to larger towns or cities. Such villages were fairly homogeneous, while small-scale manufacturing and the services were concentrated in market or administrative centers. In Provence, by contrast, the agro-town combined all of the functions that were dispersed further north. Aubagne was a typical Provençal town, except it was too close to Marseille and Aix-en-Provence to have much in the way of administrative infrastructure. It did possess an important seigneurial court belonging to the bishop of Marseille that remained vigorous until the end of the Old Regime.

Economically and socially, however, it fit the criteria for an agro-town. It was an important market center for the agricultural products grown in Aubagne and in the region – grains, good-quality wine, and olives mostly – and it also drew small dealers from smaller centers nearby like La Penne, Auriol, and Roquevaire. Fruits like cherries, peaches, and pears and garden crops like onions and garlic also contributed to the local economy.[3] A number of impressive mountains and rocky areas, more than a quarter of the total surface, made part of the town impossible for regular cropping. The rest was useless dry brush. Tax experts in the early nineteenth century considered the cultivatable land very fertile and well tended. The river Hauvanne, which ran parallel to the Marseille–Toulon highway for a part of its course, had been diverted for centuries to irrigate the cultivatable land. The river also powered two flour mills that the municipality itself owned. A handful of olive presses and a few tanneries were closely related to the town's agricultural vocation. A number of small potteries gave the place some notoriety, and its location on the road between Marseille and Toulon gave rise to a thriving set of inns and taverns.

An examination of land use explains much about the local economy. Just 10 percent of the cropland was arable. This followed the simple biennial rotation that was common almost everywhere in the Midi. Only the

---

[3] The remarks in the rest of this paragraph and all of the next are derived from ADBR, P4/26, *Expertises communales*, various dates from 1809 to 1820.

most fertile of the arable land was cropped continuously, with vegetables following wheat every other year. On land of lower quality, wheat or rye alternated with fallow. The overwhelming proportion of the land was dedicated to viticulture, some 86 percent. Meadows and tiny pastures accounted for the rest. The animal population would necessarily have been small, not enough to provide sufficient manure, which instead consisted of straw and crushed seashells that farmers bought at the market in Marseille. Given the nature of Old Regime viticulture as well, complicated capital equipment was rare, limited to carts for transport and the simple scratch plows of the region.

For all that it was situated at the center of a region of commercial agriculture and at the hub of major transportation routes, Aubagne was not a dynamic place. From 1730 until the Revolution, the population rose by less than 20 percent, to 7,069 souls. By contrast, Marseille grew by about a third over a shorter period, while the kingdom as a whole grew by 40 percent after the death of Louis XIV.[4] The occupational structure thus had probably not changed very much for many generations before the Revolution broke out. Somewhat over 60 percent of the households in 1790 lived directly from agriculture; slightly over 25 percent of the households made a living from building, clothing, food and drink, and transport; and about 10 percent were in the clerical service sector, were minor officials, or were retired. This latter group included the local bourgeoisie that the Jacobins hated so much, men whose fortunes in the end were modest, nothing like the colossal shipping fortunes of Marseille or the breathtaking opulence of the *parlementaires* or lawyers in Aix-en-Provence.

Aubagne's was a solidly patriarchal population. Men headed over four-fifths of the households with very little variation by occupational group. Similarly, nearly 75 percent of the heads of households were married while a widow headed just 15 percent of the households. Households varied considerably in size, depending upon the occupation of the household's head. With the exception of those in the transport sector, married artisans' households were smaller than those in agriculture. The median size of artisan households was four people; of peasants, five. Where peasants

---

[4] AC Aubagne, unclassified, "Etat de la population de la commune d'Aubagne pendant les années 1729–1790," n.d. [1823?]. This may have been based on an extrapolation from the number of births. Another count from the census of 1794 gives 7,230 people (ibid., *registre des délibérations*, f. 186v, 5 Fructidor An II – 22 August 1794). The population of Arles actually fell between 1760 and 1789 (Fabio Sampoli, "Politics and Society in Revolutionary Arles: Chiffonistes and Monnaidiers" [Ph.D., Yale University, 1982], 35).

owned their own property then, these larger families would have created pressures to divide the holding or to encourage children to move. Where peasants rented, moving was the only option for some of the children.

Matching the names of fathers in the birth records of the 1780s with the names of taxpayers of the *contribution mobilière* of 1792 shows the population to have been amazingly mobile. Just 35 percent of the fathers in the prerevolutionary decade were present as taxpayers in 1792. Moreover, this mobility varied enormously by occupational group. Just 17 percent of those in agricultural occupations, fewer than one in five, persisted throughout the decade. This must have reflected the highly seasonal demands of the viticultural economy, which required a lot of labor during the spring for plowing and fertilizing and again in the late summer for picking. With the understandable exception of the transport trades, persistence among those in the building, clothing, and food and drink trades was much higher, around 60 percent. Among the services and the bourgeoisie, the rate was over 90 percent. The nature of the viticultural economy militated against many people establishing themselves.

In 1790, about two-thirds of the households in Aubagne lived in the town proper, and of these, someone in a rural occupation headed about half of them. The town intra muros, then, had a very large peasant population, a phenomenon that was much more rare further north. People lived very close to one another – the older parts of the town that survive comprise two- and three-story buildings that abut one another on typically narrow streets. The old town is built on a very steep hill that peaks on a flat square on which the parish church stands. The chapel of one of the confraternities faces it across the square.

Proximity did not produce homogeneity or a fluid intercourse between groups. Wealth, for example, was a huge divider, and no doubt this explains many of the other social divisions within the town. The median payment in *contribution mobilière* in 1792 for peasants and artisans in Aubagne was about 4.5 livres; for professionals and the bourgeoisie, it was about 11.5 livres.[5] Thus, the top drawer possessed over two and a half times as much wealth as did working people. Moreover, while the professionals and the bourgeoisie constituted about 20 percent of the taxpayers, they paid somewhat less than half the taxes. In addition, the amount the very wealthy possessed was even greater than this. The

---

[5] AC Aubagne, unclassified, "Imposition mobilière de 1791 [*sic*]." There were 1,327 male taxpayers in 1792 and 1,322 male heads of household in 1790, so the tax is certainly an accurate representation of the distribution of wealth in the town.

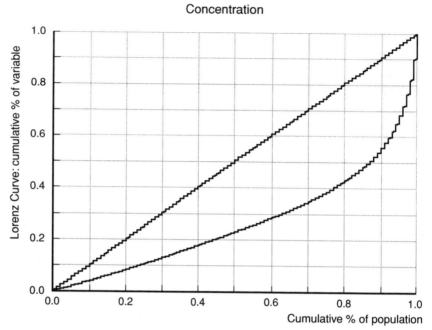

FIGURE I.I. Lorenz curve, Aubagne 1792.

top 10 percent of taxpayers accounted for 43 percent of the taxes. In social terms, the professionals and the rentier bourgeoisie comprised 80 percent of this group. Its median payment was seven times that of all other taxpayers. Such disparities in wealth are certainly very great, but similarly skewed distributions occurred in other towns.[6]

---

[6] Fabio Sampoli, "Chiffonistes and Monnaidiers," 58–62. The Gini index for Aubagne is 0.4752, indicating a midpoint between perfect inequality (1) and perfect equality (0). By way of comparison, this is not very different from the United States in 2000 but is considerably more unequal than contemporary France, Canada, and the United Kingdom. For other Mediterranean communities, see J. Davis, *People of the Mediterranean: An Essay in Comparative Social Anthropology* (London: Routledge & Kegan Paul, 1977), 88. The Gini index for Salon-de-Provence based on the 1788 capitation role (AM, Salon, unclassified) is 0.4878. I wish to thank Mme Françoise Pelé, *archiviste municipale*, for providing me with a copy of her Excel file of this document. These calculations are possible thanks to the online software at http://www.wessa.net/co.wasp. For other towns, see Pierre Deyon, *Amiens, capitale provinciale* (Paris: Mouton & Co., 1967), 244–5. Pierre Goubert, *Beauvais et le Beauvaisis de 1600 à 1730, Démographie et sociétés*, 3 (Paris: S. E. V., E. N., 1960), 261. Following the same method as T. J. A. Le Goff (*Vannes and Its Region: A Study of Town and Country in Eighteenth-Century France* [Oxford: Clarendon Press, 1981], 39) produces a pyramid of wealth similar to that of Vannes.

The nearly complete commercialization of agriculture in Aubagne was another major difference with the agriculture of the northern plains. The classic texts of agrarian history in Old Regime France stress the issue of ownership, and all of them conclude that many peasants, if not a majority, had too little land on which to survive. As subsistence farmers, the amount of land they had, not the market, determined how well they could survive. In Aubagne, almost all peasants were both cultivators and consumers, and so market prices for wine and grain were more important than the amount of land. Although it is not possible to calculate a poverty line and with it an estimate of what percentage of cultivators fell below that line, it is possible to show that peasants in Aubagne were perhaps more fortunate than were many of their counterparts elsewhere.[7]

Aubagne was in the midst of a small island in Provence where peasants enjoyed a greater share of the landed revenues than any other group (Table 1.8). Moreover, the disparity between their numbers among landowners and the share of revenue was not as great as it was elsewhere. That may be cold comfort, of course; because the median value was relatively low, the value of that land and therefore its revenue-generating capacity was that much less.[8]

The most fortunate group was the local bourgeoisie. Although there was a handful of outside owners, mostly resident in Marseille, most of this land was held by residents of Aubagne. Moreover, the grip of the nobility was quite limited. With the abolition of noble titles in 1790, the tax roll does not distinguish them, but it is possible to isolate them. The three families of former nobles, the Seigneurets, the Martels, the Albertas, comprised just seven separate landowners (out of 1,460) and accounted for just 2 percent of the revenues received by owners whose occupations are known – far less if all owners' revenues had been included.

---

7 In northern France, the Parisian Basin, and in Brittany, for example, the amount of land (not landed revenues as represented in Table 1.8) peasants owned generally varied between 20 and 40 percent (see Gérard Béaur, *Histoire agraire de la France au XVIIe siècle: Inerties et changements dans les campagnes françaises entre 1715 et 1815*, vol. 139, *Regards sur l'histoire: Histoire moderne* [Paris: Sedes, 2000], 26).

8 Michel Vovelle, "Structures agraires en Provence à la fin de l'Ancien Régime," in *De la cave au grenier: un itinéraire en Provence au XVIIIe siècle: de l'histoire sociale à l'histoire des mentalités* (Quebec: S. Fleury, 1980), 135–62. In nearby Auriol, Roquevaire, and Allauch, the peasant share could rise to 75 percent. All three are bourgs where the bourgeoisie was not as prominent. Among the elites, the Church and nobility owned considerably more elsewhere than in Aubagne; the bourgeoisie, significantly less (René Baehrel, *Une croissance: la Basse-Provence rurale de la fin du seizième siècle à 1789: essai d'économie historique statistique*, Rééd, ed., *Démographie et sociétés*, 6 [Paris: Éditions de l'École des Hautes Études en Sciences Sociales, 1988], 397–401).

The church, too, was very much a minority landowner. The survey lumps all former church land into just three categories and labels it as belonging to the nation. This is too crude and there are ways of rectifying this, but for the moment the survey is accurate enough in suggesting the relative unimportance of the Church as a landowner in Aubagne.

If the former privileged orders were fairly inconspicuous as landowners, the local bourgeoisie was inordinately prominent. The bourgeoisie had triple the landed revenue that their numbers would justify, and the average revenues were nearly two and a half times greater than those of the peasants or of any of the other subcategories, for that matter. This was a bourgeoisie more or less evenly divided among wholesalers, trained professionals, and rentiers. Many of them were probably retired, judging from when many of them were married. About one in ten of the bourgeoisie were women, most of them widows, which again suggests that landed income was a way of supporting the elderly. But for bourgeois women, this was a relatively unimportant source of support. The median value of their property was 100 livres less than that of bourgeois men. No doubt the death of their husbands had forced many women to distribute part of the estate to their children by the time the survey was taken.

The landholding of the bourgeoisie was prominent but not dominant. A breakdown of the top quartile of landowners' revenues by occupation shows that all classes had representatives at the top (Table 1.9).

There was a small class of important peasant landowners in Aubagne. Although they could not compete with the bourgeoisie in terms of the share of the landed revenues it controlled, it did have revenues that lifted it far above the generality of peasants and other small landowners. There was also a small category of artisans who also belonged in the upper quartile of landowners. Although they were a minority, their existence showed that the elite of the landed hierarchy was a diverse group. Nor was their ownership somewhat accidental, in the sense that they owned garden plots or came in to land through the accident of inheritance or marriage. This would have been the case for their counterparts at the bottom end of the scale, but at the top landownership was an important extension of business for the better-off carters, mule drivers, bakers, butchers, potters, and innkeepers.

The landowning structure thus distributed revenues among broad groupings of local society. Although the bourgeoisie clearly dominated, it did not monopolize. Land may have been spread out among rich and poor, as it was everywhere in the Old Regime, but it did not polarize a narrow homogenous elite against everyone else.

An analysis of wealth derived from the *contribution mobilière* high-lights the importance of the diverse elite and the prominent place of the bourgeoisie within it. This was a complex tax that aimed to capture revenue from signs of wealth like horses and domestic servants. It also taxed rents, including those of buildings (Table 1.10).

The inclusion of rent, even agricultural rent, into the calculation means that the *contribution mobilière* offered a representative image of the distribution of wealth in a community like Aubagne. The analysis underlines the conclusion about the discrepancy between numbers of peasants and the proportion of wealth they enjoyed. Peasants were the most deprived group in Aubagne. A great deal of the relative poverty was in agricultural pursuits, and in Aubagne this was in the *terroir*. The mean tax there was half that of the town proper. This section also had the reputation in the Revolution as the most loyally Jacobin. Furthermore, artisans, whether they lived in the *terroir* or not, were as badly off as the peasants. In other words, working people, most of whom worked with their hands, constituted about 80 percent of the population but had just over half the wealth.

Women among the working people were not particularly worse off than the men. Their mean and median tax payments were scarcely different. One finds them, of course, in traditionally female trades – laundry, sewing, and so on – but they headed up other businesses in their own right, too. This was especially true in the agricultural sector, where there were some female tenants and owner-occupiers. The difference with female employment was that while women entered a variety of callings, they were still fairly few of them earning a living in their own name. Among the working population, women headed just 13 percent of the enterprises.

The real discrepancies between men's and women's incomes showed up among the bourgeoisie. Male professionals and rentiers had incomes whose averages were again half as high as those of women and medians that were an astonishing 72 percent higher. Once again, marital status probably accounts for most of these discrepancies. Many of the women in this category were widows whose fortunes had probably already been partially distributed to their heirs upon their husbands' deaths.

But the menfolk were very well off. Men or women, the bourgeoisie as a group paid nearly three times what their numbers might suggest, and the median value of the assessment was three and a half times that of working people. So the rich were very comfortably rich, as they usually are, but more important, once outside the agricultural sector, the elite were dramatically less diverse. In the top quartile, the bourgeoisie paid nearly 70 percent of the tax, and in the fifty most heavily taxed category, all but five were in the bourgeoisie. No fewer than twenty-five of those were labeled simply bourgeois, which suggests they were retired or inactive rentiers; nine were priests, some also retired; and the rest were in the legal professions or were wholesalers, sea captains, or high government officials. In other words, the higher up in the tax table, the more homogeneous the elite became.

The typical member of the local elite, then, lived off invested income or derived a living from offering various kinds of professional services. There are no account books that would permit a detailed study of their economic activity, but it is possible to stitch some of it together because so many of them became Federalists or had their names slapped on the émigré lists, and so had their property confiscated. These allow a snapshot of the structure of wealth of a comfortable bourgeois in a small town in Provence at the end of the Old Regime.

Take, for instance, the property of Emmanuel Lieutard, barrister, last mayor of Old Regime Aubagne, and a member of the *comité général des sections* that led the anti-Jacobin Federalist revolt in the summer of 1793.[9] He owned a country house, or *bastide*, surrounded by vines and fruit trees, a small meadow with a workshop of some sort nearby, and three houses in town, two on the Place de la Liberté and another on the Grand' Rue. The 1791 tax roll assessed this at 145 livres revenue, although, according to the municipality in 1794, it generated just over 1,100 livres.

Then there is Jean-Baptiste-Aubagne-Michel Martinot, a notary whose whole family was deeply involved in anti-Jacobin activity throughout the decade. His brother, Pierre, was the former chief parish priest, retired just before the Revolution but who still had enough energy left to become president of the *comité général* in 1793 and even more to be deeply suspected in the planning of the activities of the murder gang. Jean-Baptiste himself was also prominent in the Old Regime as a municipal officer and, after the Revolution broke out, in defending the old municipality against the Jacobin upsurge in 1791–2. He was also, of course, a prominent Federalist whose property was later confiscated after the Jacobins returned

---

[9] This and the next two examples come from ADBR, 1Q 80, "Liste des biens des émigrés français situés dans le département des Bouches-du-Rhône...Cinquante-septième liste...Commune d'Aubagne," n.d. [An III]. Also see ibid., 1Q 531, p. 76, for further information on Lions, and p. 90 on Lieutaud.

to power. And an impressive portfolio it was. He owned two *bastides* on the outskirts of town with their accompanying arable land, vineyards, fruit trees, and meadows. He also owned four houses in Aubagne itself. The two outlying farms alone were estimated at over 40,000 livres.

Impressive as such bourgeois properties were, they did not permit their owners to live in overwhelming luxury. Barthélemy Lions, for example, wholesale merchant and also member of the *comité général*, owned an irrigated meadow in the *terroir* and three buildings in town, his own one-story house, an inn, and a tannery. He shared his house with his grown son and three boarders, but there were no servants living in it. He did a fair amount of entertaining, as there were twelve chairs in the dining room, but otherwise his furniture was old and worn. Still, he had a taste for the finer things. There were a half dozen impressive mirrors, a small library of books, and a few paintings in gilt-edged frames. But it was a modest existence all the same because the entire contents of the house sold for just 3,700 livres.[10]

The peasants who worked the land not only were divided hierarchically by wealth but also had access to the land in different ways. A substantial proportion owned the land, while the rest rented. To judge from a sample of leases in the archives, rented land could be held between one and six years on a sharecropping basis, or for a fixed rent, or for a combination of both.[11] Unlike the typically large farms of the North, tenants here cultivated small holdings, themselves sometimes divided into even smaller plots. Also, unlike the large farms in the Paris basin, tenants here did not stay a long time, one or two leases being the norm.

The vast majority of peasants in Aubagne were viticulturalists. Wine is a notoriously volatile crop. The sharecropping accounts show that the range of a crop's value could vary immensely from one year to the next. The crop of 1795, for example, was double that of most years. This volatility could put some people in trouble and force them to borrow. It is not possible to know the extent of peasant indebtedness, but it was probably fairly high. One sample suggests that the common feature of debt was to borrow a large sum and pay back only the interest at 5 percent.[12] Even repaying the interest alone could be a burden. Most repayments ranged between 20 and 40 livres, and because the wage for

---

[10] ADBR, 1Q 672, pièces 99–106, October 1793.
[11] Based on a reading of several dozen leases in ADBR, 14 E 531.
[12] Based on an examination of thirty-three receipts taken from the year 1786, letters A through G, in ibid., 411 E 110.

an agricultural laborer was about 1 livre a day, such obligations would have been difficult to meet.

Debt had a political resonance during the Revolution. Some prominent anti-Jacobins were moneylenders – the Christins, the Dondes, the Cucunis, Mathieu Rousserie, and others – but only on a handful of occasions. Other individuals who stayed out of politics had more impressive portfolios of debtors. Jacques Barthélemy, for instance, lent impressive sums to a dozen people, all on the eve of the Revolution, a reflection, perhaps, of the crisis in viticulture in 1788–9.[13] Yet not all credit involved the urban elite lending to the poor. Many peasants lent to other peasants in what amounted to a very decentralized market. Even so, Jacobins were aware of the political aspect of debt. On one occasion, they proposed a moratorium on collections and rather naively suggested that wealthy capitalists in Marseille could repay the debts as an act of compassion and solidarity.[14] Nothing came of this.

Factions

If the social structure predicted political loyalties on a one-to-one basis, we might expect that wealth and land ownership would determine choices in the Revolution. The fit, however, is not perfect. Political loyalties themselves were more or less intense, and therefore the mix of social variables that affected commitments during the Revolution varied too. The social variables that are available – wealth, literacy, residence, and occupation – also varied in their importance depending upon the degree of political commitment being measured. Paradoxically, at the level of the most committed, between the murder gang and the terrorists, the social variables mattered the least. This opens the way to another approach to the sociology of faction, the importance of informal associations.

Contemporaries often commented on the divisions in the town. They also made assumptions about who was likely to belong in what category. Such representations of themselves and one another can be characterized in many ways, as a language of class or at least of social difference, as a language of insider versus outsider, or as a language of order versus democracy. Jacobins thought of themselves as representing the people, the poor, and the oppressed. Their enemies were the bourgeois,

---

[13] Ibid., 1Q 532, "Etat général des créanciers des émigrés du District de Marseille," n.d.
[14] William Scott. *Terror and Repression in Revolutionary Marseilles* (New York: Barnes & Noble Books, 1973), 55–6.

a term they never defined with any precision because everyone knew who they were. Presumably, they meant the town elite. The elite thought of themselves as men of order, as custodians of sound municipal institutions, and as defenders of the rule of law against ruffians and murderers. After 1791, they no longer claimed to be responsible defenders of the old municipal order with its complex rules of co-optation and its biased regime of taxes and fees. Instead, they embraced much of the Revolution as the Constituent Assembly defined it, but they were fierce enemies of destructive Jacobin utopias.[15] Their description of themselves as conservatives suggests that the Jacobins were right in describing them as the bourgeois.

Such descriptions and epithets were abbreviated codes that compressed a more complex reality. Each side represented itself and its opponents accurately, albeit cryptically. Thus Jacobins on the whole did represent working people and the relatively poor, but more than that, they drew a lot of support from the peasantry, especially from those who lived outside the town walls; from the illiterate; and from the poor. They were less successful in appealing to the artisans, some of whom actually became notorious anti-Jacobins and even murderers during the White Terror (see the appendix, Table 1.1; Table 1.7a). The anti-Jacobins were indeed wealthy, literate bourgeois and urban dwellers, although they drew some popular support as well (Table 1.2). In other words, differences in wealth, cultural level, occupation, and residence underlay many political loyalties.

A more refined analysis, however, shows that the factors behind these generalizations varied in importance depending upon the degree of political commitment being measured. Three subgroups – adherents, municipal officers or leaders, and finally, the truly passionate – all illustrate different perspectives on the nature of Jacobins and their opponents. A direct comparison of the characteristics of the adherents, those who attended the anti-Jacobin meeting known as the Olive Festival in February 1792, with the signatories of the pro-Jacobin petition of that same month demonstrates the importance of tax payment, occupation, and residence in determining political loyalties (Table 1.4e). Yet when these three factors are measured together, the analysis underlines the overwhelming importance of the divide between the peasantry and everyone else. This model washes

---

[15] See AN F[1b] II Bouches-du-Rhône 11, "Proclamation. Cartié, commissaire du directoire exécutif auprès de l'administration municipale du canton d'Aubagne à ses Concitoyens," n.d. [1797?].

out residence as a defining characteristic between the two groups. It also shows the importance of the peasant base to the Jacobins. The division between the peasant base and everyone else emerges dramatically, and while wealth counts, it mattered a good deal less in distinguishing the two groups.

This conclusion poses a new problem: what bound the peasants together in a political alliance that excluded some of the town's poor? Put another way, about a third of those who attended the Olive Festival shared characteristics in common with the Jacobins. Anti-Jacobinism appealed to men who resembled Jacobins, at least as far as occupation and wealth are concerned. The model identifies seven extreme cases or outliers that should have been Jacobin. They were all peasants of modest means – which were the characteristics of many Jacobins – but a disproportionate number (five of seven) of them lived intra muros. The broader group of twenty-six that the model identifies as anomalies were mostly artisans (eighteen), fairly poor (mean tax of 4.3 livres), and overwhelmingly resident within the town (twenty-three). Among the artisans, only one lived in the *terroir*. Residence then appears to matter in defining some anti-Jacobins whose other characteristics might have put them in another political category. Perhaps there is a factor that lies outside the model that accounts for these apparent anomalies. One clue is that thirteen of the seventeen urban artisans lived in Section 2, the Black Penitents section, as it was known, the section that voted heavily anti-Jacobin in the elections of February 1792.

The second subgroup, the leaders or municipal officers, complements these observations (Table 1.6a–d). Serving as a municipal officer was another level of commitment, because unlike the participants in the Olive Festival or the signers of the petition of 1792, service was continuous and visible. These were the leaders of their parties, men who had the confidence of their rank and file. Leaders and followers shared many characteristics, but each set of leaders differed significantly from the others. The high proportion of peasants among the terrorist municipal officers shows that the terrorist phase of the Revolution witnessed genuine peasant power. Their opponents originated at the opposite end of the occupational spectrum. Seventy percent of the anti-Jacobin municipal officers of the summer of 1793 came from the town's bourgeoisie and professions. Wealth also divided the two sets of leaders, much more than it did the followers. Anti-Jacobin councillors were four times wealthier than their terrorist successors. Literacy also separated the municipal officers. Almost all (thirty-five of thirty-seven) anti-Jacobin municipal officers could sign their names, while for the Jacobins, fewer than two-thirds could. The final characteristic that distinguished leaders and followers was residence in one of the town's sections. The Jacobin strength in the *terroir* was especially prominent.

When all of these factors are taken together, however, only the tax payment of the municipal officers remains statistically significant (Table 1.6e). The Jacobins drew their leadership from the poorer sector of the town, men who were also peasants and many of whom lived in the *terroir*. The calculations confirm the conclusion that Jacobinism was a genuinely popular movement. As we shall see in the narrative, Jacobinism did not come to Aubagne from the outside or from the top down. Its appeal was indigenous and deeply rooted.

Another measure of commitment, this time of the willingness to inflict harm on the opposing faction, comes from a comparison of the characteristics of those indicted as gang members in 1801 and of the members of the terrorist *comité de surveillance* in 1794. Not all gang members were murderers, but they did condone and even celebrate the killers. The members of the *comité de surveillance* denounced fellow Aubaniens for crimes that could lead to a death sentence before the Marseille Revolutionary Tribunal. An analysis of these men is an analysis of the most violent men of each faction.

They actually resembled one another a great deal. Neither was an elite group. Instead, the usual markers of occupation, wealth, residence, and literacy all show how little difference there was between each group. Both gang and *comité de surveillance* members drew their support from ordinary working people of modest means. Differences in residence mattered a little, with gang members concentrated within the town walls. Each side was more literate than the town as a whole, 100 percent in the case of the *comité de surveillance* and close to three-fourths in the case of the gang, a reflection perhaps of the greater ability of artisans who lived within the town walls to sign their names.

These four test variables are all outcroppings of the very large label of class. People with certain characteristics of occupation, wealth, education, and residence chose to support opposing political options. Jacobinism and anti-Jacobinism found roots within different parts of the community. Yet these divisions had complex components that went beyond considerations of occupation and wealth. The anomalies are especially interesting. While there were hardly any elite Jacobins, the anti-Jacobins drew on some popular support. This would show up in the elections of 1792, in the social composition of the rank and file, and finally in the gang.

Social structure certainly mattered, but a socially determined model of faction is too simple. The analysis so far has shown that groups of individuals with definable characteristics opted for opposing factions. If these groups had always hated each other, then the polarizations of the Revolution ought to show up in the social patterns of the Old Regime. If prerevolutionary social relations were more fluid, then we need to explain how the events of 1789 and after produced the factions. The assumption that the factions expressed a timeless hatred reduces the role of the Revolution to a catalyst that hastened an already-endemic conflict. An argument that the Revolution had a more creative role would allow for diverse social patterns in the Old Regime but would also try to show how the Revolution transformed them. Political conflict would have more autonomy to shape events and decisions. The argument will be that politics after 1789 mattered both in how it reconstructed access to power and how it made preexisting alignments lethal. The purpose of the rest of this chapter is to assess the importance of the social in determining the factional outcome.

Associations and Friendships

Bourgeois versus peasant, rich versus poor, town versus *terroir*, literate versus illiterate – these were all major social distinctions in Aubagne that were paralleled in the social composition of the Jacobins and anti-Jacobins. But this does not mean that latent conflicts simply exploded during the Revolution. Social relations before the Revolution were quite fluid.

One sign of this was in godparenting patterns among men. Godparenting was a voluntary relationship that the church developed to encourage bonds outside regular families and thus to reduce conflict. In Catholic Europe, the relationship was one of friendship among adults and of patronage and protection for the child.[16] For the parents, the ideal was to seek out godparents of higher status. For the godfathers, it was an

---

[16] For a twentieth-century discussion, see Davis, *People of the Mediterranean*, 223–4; John Bossy, "Godparenthood: The Fortunes of a Social Institution in Early Modern Christianity," in *Religion and Society in Early Modern Europe, 1500–1800*, ed. Kaspar von Greyerz (London and Boston: German Historical Institute; Allen & Unwin, 1984), 194–201.

occasion to offer protection and patronage. Despite the very sharp distinctions between rich and poor, this ideal was frequently attained in Aubagne.

If the cleavages of the 1790s had antecedents, a high degree of solidarity among occupation and wealth levels among men might be expected. Yet this was not the case. No correlation existed between occupation and tax payments of fathers and godfathers. Thus the relations of fictive kinship did not reproduce the social hierarchies of the town. Instead, these voluntary relationships showed an openness among groups, whether occupation, wealth, or literacy are the measures. The largest group of fathers, the men of the peasantry, chose godfathers outside the rural sector in just under half the cases. A peasant father chose a bourgeois or professional godfather 15 percent of the time. Economically, fathers were able to choose godfathers in a superior quartile of taxpayers. Fathers in the lowest quartile chose godfathers in a superior quartile over three-quarters of the time. Fathers in the top quartile chose men in their own quartile 42 percent of the time and only rarely (15 percent) in the lowest. Literacy also showed the openness of choice. Illiterate fathers chose literate godfathers 40 percent of the time.

In other words, far from reflecting the sharp stratification one might expect from an examination of the distribution of wealth, fictive kinship or friendship and esteem crossed social divisions. Nonetheless, the search for patterns of relationships reveals that some connections did predate the Revolution. Formal relationships between two sets of militants – the terrorist *comité de surveillance* and the anti-Jacobin gang – did not exist. They did not marry into one another's families, they did not stand as godfathers for one another's children, and they did not witness one another's marriage ceremonies. But these groups did form relationships within their separate spheres. Brothers and brothers-in-law did serve in terrorist institutions together. On the anti-Jacobin side, a witness and the groom emerged twenty years later as comrades on the Federalist side. Mathieu Rousserie, the café owner who became a killer, was related to several anti-Jacobins and to other members of the murder gang through godparenting and his in-laws.

One can only speculate on what the hidden factor was that structured these relations, but one possibility was the penitent societies. These were lay brotherhoods whose purpose was to decorate and maintain their chapels, offer mutual aid, promote charity, participate in processions on feast days, visit ailing brothers and assist them in prayer, and see their departed brothers off to the next world with appropriate pomp

and dignity from the chapel to the cemetery.[17] The penitent societies
were supposed to transcend the social inequalities of lay society. Their
costumes symbolized common bonds because each brother wore an identical ankle-length gown and covered his head with a large pointed hood
with openings only for his eyes. This ideal of a common Christian brotherhood reflected a genuine reality. Notables and working people mixed
easily in the common devotions. These societies were never particularly
large, and if they exceeded more than one hundred or so members, the
men often formed another society. If that happened, the different societies
were known for their colors– white, black, blue, and so on.

The archives of Aubagne's societies have disappeared, but it is possible
to know a little about them.[18] There were three of them. The oldest, the
Black Penitents, dated from the sixteenth century. It patronized the Gray
Penitents, whose color recalled the traditional funeral shroud of the poor.
It borrowed members from the Black Penitents, who served a five-year
term of arranging decent burials for the indigent. The Black Penitents also
patronized some *chambrées*, the all-male, sometimes devotional societies.
It may well be that the *chambrée* that was celebrating King's Day in 1787
was such an offshoot. The third society, the White, formed after a schism
within the older society in the early seventeenth century. All three societies
enlarged or rebuilt their chapels, hired resident priests to say masses for
the dead, preserved precious relics, and spent or borrowed impressive
sums of money on tableaux depicting the apostles, souls in purgatory, or
the martyrdom of saints. Much of their rivalry consisted in showing off
how splendid their embellishments could be, and once a year at the end
of August, they undertook choral singing contests along the Grand' Rue.

No lists of members have survived, but the signatures appended to various building contracts show that each confraternity displayed the same
social mixing among the brothers as existed elsewhere. Yet the societies

---

[17] These generalizations are based on Maurice Agulhon, *Pénitents et francs-maçons de
l'ancienne Provence* (Paris: Fayard, 1968), 86–112. Marie-Hélène Froeschlé-Chopard,
*La religion populaire en Provence orientale au XVIIIe siècle, Bibliothèque Beauchesne.
Religions, société, politique,* 7 (Paris: Beauchesne, 1980), 143–220. Michel Vovelle, *Piété
baroque et déchristianisation en Provence au XVIIIe siècle; les attitudes devant la mort
d'après les clauses des testaments* (Paris: Plon, 1973), 202–14. During the Revolution,
Régis Bertrand, "'Sommeil' ou 'Clandestinite'? Les Pénitents de Marseille entre Louis
XVI et Louis XVIII," *Provence historique* 39, no. 156 (1989), 185–95.

[18] Except for the archive reference, details in the next four paragraphs are taken from
Barthélemy, *Histoire d'Aubagne,* ii, 122–51. See also César Couret, *Histoire d'Aubagne,
divisée en trois époques principales, contenant la description des antiquités de Saint-Jean
de Garguier, et des notices sur les illustrations du pays* (Aubagne, 1860), 29–35.

in Aubagne were by no means little havens of equality outside daily social hierarchies. They differed from one another because the reputations of the societies attracted different sorts of people. In effect, the Black Penitents were known as the society of the notables, and for a long time the White Penitents struggled financially. The Black Penitents were in Section 2, the section that was home to most of the artisans who attended the anti-Jacobin Olive Festival; to seven out of ten anti-Jacobin municipal officers in 1793; and to a majority of those indicted in the murder gang. Although the evidence is circumstantial, the penitent societies may well have structured political loyalties in ways that went beyond more traditional ones of class.

A petition about forty men submitted in August 1795 illustrates the overlap between the Black Penitents and the gang.[19] They demanded the return of a painting of Saint John the Baptist that once hung in the chapel of the Black Penitents. The signatories contain the names of some remarkable people; Mathieu Rousserie, later accused of murdering a dozen people at the start of the White Terror; Pierre Martinot, retired priest who inspected the ear of one of the Julliens at the same time in Rousserie's café; and other accused gang members, including Chisostome Marin, François Sicard *dit* René, and Paul Rey. A handful of other signatories were also present at the King's Day celebrations eight years before, while others participated in other kinds of anti-Jacobin activity, like the campaign to retain Antoine Jourdan as justice of the peace in 1791 or in the Federalist institutions of the summer of 1793. If the signatories reflect the members of the Black Penitents, this was indeed the confraternity of notables. A handful had been municipal officers in the Old Regime. Of those who can be identified on the tax roll of 1792, only one was in the agricultural sector, nearly 60 percent were bourgeois or professionals, while the rest were artisans, mostly in the food and drink trades. They were also very rich, with the median payment in *contribution mobilière* of 16 livres, about four times the town average. But there were men of modest means in the group as well, as about one-third paid less than eight livres, including some of gang members. The Black Penitents were an intra muros institution that excluded practically all of the future Jacobin constituency. No known Jacobin signed the petition. Here then was an institution where anti-Jacobin alliances could be incubated, just as the White Penitents probably incubated Jacobin ones.

[19] ADBR, 24F 155, "Les habitants de la Commune d'Aubagne Aux administrateurs du district de marseille," 1 Fructidor An III – 18 August 1795.

It would make sense that the Penitents did not exist in a vacuum and that the brothers took additional steps to cement their ties. Reinforcing relationships through godparenting would be logical. Without a list of members, this is impossible to know, however. Business relations among the brothers would make sense also, and some of these suggest very long-standing family relationships with a particular confraternity. For instance, in the early eighteenth century, the officers of the Black Penitents signed a contract with Marc-Antoine Rémuzat to inspect some masonry work. His great grandson, André, son of another Marc-Antoine, also a prosperous mason, was a member of the Federalist neighborhood watch committee in 1793. André's father had attended the King's Day celebration of 1787. In 1739, the officers hired another mason, Joseph Guillermy, to do some major repairs and improvements. In 1790, the municipality hired his grandson, another attendee at the King's Day celebration, to build the town's first *autel de la patrie*.[20] This was Joseph Guillermy, one of the gang's most vicious killers.

Other continuities between the Black Penitents and anti-Jacobin politics are less certain but probable because of the rarity of the particular surnames in the town's population. These show up in both the brotherhood's contracts and the lists of anti-Jacobins. Thus Mille, Seigneuret, Beausset, de Paris, Martel, and others recur in both lists, which suggests even hereditary associations with the Penitents that later translated into political commitments during the Revolution. Such commitments could be practically lock-step. The last chaplain of the Black Penitents before the Convention abolished these associations at the end of 1792 was Etienne Deprat, a descendent of many members of the society. He became a member of the Federalist neighborhood committee a few months later.

The murder gang was not the continuation of the confraternity. But the penitent society established a form of association and a habit of trust among its members that carried over into other activities. Although the gang and the penitents were very different, both reflected a diverse membership, both were concentrated in one part of the town, and both were intra muros.

Penitent societies could have structured local politics in other ways as well. In Aubagne, they appear to have affected the outcome of the municipal elections of 1791 and early 1792, as we shall see. Because the social structure of the urban sections did not differ, the varied reputations

---

[20] AC Aubagne, *registre des délibérations*, 93, deliberation of 10 July 1790. Barthélemy, *Histoire d'Aubagne*, 132.

of the White and Black Penitents must have attracted different kinds of voters. Abstentions worked in such a way as to exaggerate outcomes in favor of one of the two factions. A similar relation between penitents and politics existed elsewhere. At Sisteron, for example, one of the penitent societies was militantly anti-Jacobin.[21] At Salon-de-Provence during its vicious struggles in February 1793, anti-Jacobins roamed the streets shouting, "Vive les noirs! We're on top now, we will triumph." Their password was also *noir* and anyone who did not know it risked being "assassinated."[22]

All individuals in Aubagne at the end of the Old Regime had many ways of identifying themselves and of arranging their relations with their fellow Aubaniens. Each of the markers that made them distinct also signified a relationship with other people. Thus, people could identify themselves in terms of their family relations; their occupation; their wealth; their educational level; and as Catholics, through godparenting and membership in a confraternity. These relationships were common throughout many, if not all, of the small towns of the period. No doubt rivalries and even strong dislikes existed, but there is no sign of endemic feuding or anything unusual in the social structure that might stimulate it. The inequalities, the massive mobility, and the vulnerabilities of the poor all had counterparts elsewhere.

The Economy and Taxation

Certain features did make parts of Provence potentially explosive, however. Not the concentrated population of towns like Aubagne, not the close proximity of neighbors intra muros, not the democratic sociability. Instead, the local economy was extraordinarily vulnerable to the wider market. Almost everyone in the rural sector depended totally on selling wine to pay for bread because so much land was dedicated to viticulture. Yet the terms of trade of these two commodities was shifting away from viticulturalist consumers in the later years of the Old Regime.[23] The cost of food relative to wine was rising (Figure 1.2). Viticulturalist communities like Aubagne's would have found food relatively more expensive. Of course, such pressures had occurred many times in the past. Yet the

---

[21] Vovelle, *Piété baroque et déchristianisation en Provence*, 211n1.

[22] ADBR, L 2045, *Les commissaires du département des Bouches-du-Rhône à leurs frères et amis de la société des antipolitiques d'Aix*, 18 [?] February 1793.

[23] Ibid., 4P 26, "Contribution foncière. Relevé du Prix des Grains et autres Denrées ... " [1807]. Other prices in Baehrel, *Basse-Provence rurale*, 554–6.

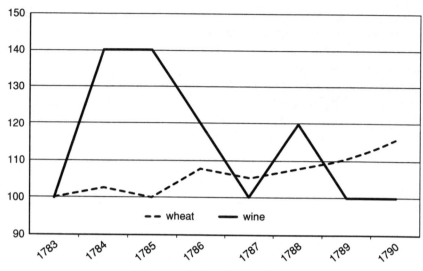

FIGURE I.2. Wheat and Wine Price Indexes, 1783–1790.

political convulsion of 1788–9 changed the basis of how such a classical subsistence crisis played out, as Georges Lefebvre pointed out long ago. If viticulturalists entered the revolutionary era under pressure, one hope for alleviation lay in a reform of the municipal tax structure. Local taxes throughout Provence targeted consumers of flour and other foodstuffs, and in Aubagne, many of these consumers were peasants. The first years of the Revolution created a political opening where ordinary folk could imagine that shifting the tax burden would offer them better. Greater fiscal equity appealed to people who were more vulnerable than their counterparts in grain-producing communities. Demands from northern communities during the Revolution – breaking up the commons, legal limitations on the cumulation of farms, sale of national property in small lots, controls on the grain trade and on prices – would have done little for small-time viticulturalists. Shifting fiscal burdens and creating democratic political institutions would.

2

The Olive Festival

The story begins in the late winter of 1791–2 with a festival. This was the *fête des olliviers*, the Olive Festival, a traditional Provençal and Mediterranean folkloric gathering that celebrated the flowering of the olive trees and more generally the coming of spring after the usual short winter.[1] It is a remarkable fact that almost all those who attended the *fête des olliviers* in Aubagne that year were associated with the murderers three years later, while those who tried to prevent it, the municipality, the Jacobin club, and others, were prominent among the victims. Indeed, the most spectacular victim of the Year III (1795) was Jean-Baptiste Domergue, the mayor of Aubagne three years before. He went to great lengths to disperse the fête. Conversely, one of the victims of the hangings in September 1792, eight months after the fête, was attacked in part because he had attended the fête.

Of course, a festival commemorating the flowering of olive trees is an unremarkable event in normal times. What made this one a revealing moment in local social and political relations was the context. For the context revealed the extent of the splits and the depth of the factionalization in the town well before the lynchings and well before the murders began.

The Olive Festival took place on Sunday, 12 February 1792. Attendance was by invitation only. The festivities were to take place on the outskirts of town, at the château of Belloi, the summer residence of the

[1] L. Barthélemy, *Histoire d'Aubagne: chef-lieu de baronnie, depuis son origine jusqu'en 1789* (Marseille: Laffitte, 1972), ii, 275.

bishop of Marseille. It was also the place, so oral tradition has it anyway, where Domergue's body was found once the murders began during the Year III. The tradition is based on a confusion, but given Domergue's role in the forcible suppression of the festival, the story is one of those that ought to be true.

The Olive Festival then was a marker in local history, one that contemporaries used to define political loyalties. Why did it matter so much? Suppressing the Olive Festival was necessary for the Jacobins to retain their recently acquired control of the municipal council. The elections that occurred in the few months before the Festival were very bitter because the stakes were so high. To understand that, it is necessary to re-create the town's history. The structure of power in the Old Regime and how the Revolution and local revolutionaries challenged it is the key to understanding the importance of the Olive Festival.

Whoever held municipal power was a vital issue. Why this was so was a function of how the town financed itself in the Old Regime, how the tax burden was distributed, and by extension how the town regulated the most important food-processing and distribution networks. It was probably always unpopular. The Constituent Assembly's reform of taxation, the partial suppression of the seigneurial regime, and the restructuring of municipal government opened the way for popular discontents to express themselves. New institutions allowed those who felt the old system had disadvantaged them to imagine a new form of local governance.

Feudalism and Taxation

Aubagne presided over a rich array of quasi-feudal rights in the Old Regime. Most important were the rights of banality, that is, the requirement that all those within the town's jurisdiction have their grain ground and their loaves baked at the local mills and ovens. The banality was an indemnity for constructing and maintaining expensive capital projects, and as such, the consumers of the equipment paid a premium over and above what they might have paid in a free market. For wheat ground in the mill, the tax was 20 sols per quintal, half that for grains like rye. The town had sold its ovens in the seventeenth century, along with its banal rights. The sale had occurred to settle the town's debts, and so the contract contained a clause permitting the town to revoke the sale along with compensation for the owner. The farmers who leased the ovens from the private owners collected a small per capita tax on every person older than four years of age within the town's jurisdiction until the ovens were finally closed down in 1825.[2]

The town's regulation of local economic life went considerably beyond the services of mills and ovens. The number of bakers was fixed by law. The town set the price of bread on the basis of the market price of grain. This allowed the town to hold down the price of bread somewhat in times of shortage, at the bakers' expense, of course. The town collected a modest tax on grain and flour, called the *piquet*. It also regulated the supply and price of meat. It signed an agreement with a supplier who then distributed the animals to the butchers who slaughtered them and prepared the meat. The butchers then collected a tax on the meat by weight from consumers, six pennies to the pound for pork, or 25 sols per quintal for fish, for example. The town also farmed out its right to collect fees on weighing or measuring nuts, almonds, figs, oil, and wine. Taxes and fees like these on food and wine were deeply unpopular throughout Provence. Revolts against them were almost routine.[3]

The feudal lord of Aubagne was the bishop of Marseille. Lordship affected the town principally through the seigneurial court. This was not as abusive as one might think, probably because the court also offered many other judicial services to the townspeople. In any case, the municipality was gradually acquiring some of the bishop's rights, presumably because they had ceased to be lucrative to him. The town had acquired the banal mills and the market rights as far back as the sixteenth century. In 1724, it obtained all rights to police from the officers of the court, and

[2] Ibid., i, 373–93. On the *banalités* in general, see Michel Derlange, *Les communautés d'habitants en Provence au dernier siècle de l'Ancien Régime* (Toulouse: Association des publications de l'Université Toulouse–Le Mirail: Eché, 1987), 108–15.

[3] Terms of the leases in ADBR, 135E BB 35, ff. 222–30, 23 March 1785. On the disturbances, see Louis Barthélemy, *Une émeute à Aubagne contre impôt des farines au XVIIe siècle* (Marseille: 1880), BM Marseille 1570. Jean Nicolas, *La rébellion française: mouvements populaires et conscience sociale (1661–1789)*, L'univers historique (Paris: Seuil, 2002), 250. Suzanne Pillorget, "Une crise de colère des paysans d'Arles: les émeutes frumentaires des 2 et 3 janvier 1752," in *Actes du 92e Congrès national des société savantes, Strasbourg-Colmar 1967; Section d'histoire moderne* (Paris, 1970), 383–91. René Pillorget, *Les mouvements insurrectionnels de Provence entre 1596 et 1715* (Paris: A. Pedone, 1975), 171–2, 900–5. René Baehrel, *Une croissance: la Basse-Provence rurale de la fin du seizième siècle à 1789: essai d'économie historique statistique*, ed. Rééd, *Démographie et sociétés*, 6 (Paris: Éditions de l'EHESS, 1988), 317–27. Michel Vovelle, "Récit fidèle de la révolte d'Arles, arrivé le 2 janvier 1752," in *Mouvements populaires et conscience sociale: XVIe–XIXe siècles: actes du colloque de Paris, 24–26 mai 1984*, ed. Jean Nicolas (Paris: Maloine, 1985), 490–500.

in 1736, it assumed responsibility for road maintenance. In return the
bishop renounced his right to collect tolls.[4]

Aubagne also collected taxes both its own government assessed and the
direct taxes the royal government assessed. More precisely, it collected an
octroi, a tax on goods entering through the town walls, and it collected
the taille, *vingtième*, and capitation for the Crown.[5]

Fiscality was the major source of popular grievance in the early years
of the Revolution. An examination of the town's budget in the Old
Regime explains why this was so. The budget of 1780 is a good example
(Appendix, Table 2.1).[6]

The most arresting feature of the town's budget is that those who were
subject to royal taxes did not always pay them directly. Townspeople
owed nearly 47,000 livres in royal and provincial taxes but raised only
36,000 livres directly. The town's other revenues made up this shortfall.
These revenues came from the domain, that is, the rents on mills, milling
fees, taxes on the sales of pigs and fish plus the *piquet*. The domain
account paid for 6,100 livres in capitation, or head tax, plus another
4,000 livres in miscellaneous direct taxes. In other words, approximately
10,000 livres of royal taxes were not levied on intended taxpayers but
on users of municipal services. This practice was a major advantage to
landowners or the well off in general. They paid the *taille*, the principal
royal tax, but because of this burden shifting, they paid it at a reduced
rate. An accounting practice made this even more advantageous. The
sum to be collected in *taille* was calculated only after other revenues were
factored in. Thus, an advantageous set of leases from the domain would
reduce the amount collected in taille. In fact this tilting in favor of the
payers of the taille must have been occurring throughout the century,
because in the nation as a whole, rents rose much more quickly than
taxes did.

These accounting devices had real consequences. For example, the
royal capitation was supposed to be a tax on apparent wealth, not a tax
on consumers of municipal services. Even when circumstances in 1790
forced the redaction of a genuine tax roll, the first in half a century, the rich
managed to evade a great deal of the tax. The town council set the maximum to be paid at 20 livres, no matter how wealthy the taxpayer was.

---

[4] Barthélemy, *Histoire d'Aubagne*, i, 262–4.
[5] Raoul Busquet, *Histoire des institutions de la Provence de 1482 à 1790* (Marseille: Barlatier, 1920), 277–86. Lease for the taille and capitation in ADBR, 135E BB 35, ff. 230–1, 11 April 1785.
[6] Ibid., BB 27, ff. 66–71, *registre des délibérations*, 30 April 1780.

Of course, the wealthier one was, the greater the bonus this maneuver represented.

Although Provence was a *pays de taille réelle*, aristocratic exemptions created few burdens for roturier taxpayers in Aubagne because there was so little aristocratic land. Instead, the town's well-off families, a far bigger group than the aristocracy, had a fiscal cushion and were able to shift their burdens to some extent to consumers. These people paid a premium for the banalities, fees, and the *piquet*. Moreover, these consumers would have included viticulturalists, in other words, most of the peasantry. Thus, rich landowners did not pay the capitation except insofar as they were also consumers. In brief, the fiscal arrangements of the town created a potential alliance between relatively poor peasants in the *terroir* and the peasants who lived in the town proper, on the one hand, and urban working people, on the other. As it turned out, this town-country alliance was a vital element in the Jacobins' support.

The Contest for Power

The fiscal system explains the importance of municipal power. Aubagne limited access to municipal office in unusual ways. There were no property qualifications to hold office but one did have to have been born in Aubagne or to have married an Aubanienne. This provision excluded a large number of men (women, of course, had no political rights) because of the very large turnover of labor. To judge from the marriage registers, very few of these migrants settled permanently in the town since the vast majority of grooms in the 1780s were already natives.

The exclusion of migrants probably did not have much effect on political life. The factionalism of the 1790s was not between outsiders and insiders. While Jacobins certainly spoke the language of hostility to wealth and privilege, they were not outsiders. Both Jacobins and anti-Jacobins were overwhelmingly natives.

The council numbered sixty men, too large a number to form an oligarchy, despite the restrictions on membership.[7] Besides the birthplace and marriage provision, the men had to be Catholics and chosen from "the most qualified." Fifteen members were to rotate off every year, which meant that a councillor served a term of four years. At the end of December each year, the councillors participated in a complex system of co-optation to renew their ranks. No doubt the system was designed

---

7 ADBR, 135E BB, 24, *registre des délibérations*, for the most recent set of regulations.

to prevent the council from falling into the hands of a clique. It also had the potential to recruit ordinary people because there was no wealth requirement. But the council was neither a clique nor representative of all social layers within the community. The turnover on the council was very great. The rules on replacement made 120 men eligible for selection to the council in the years between 1781 and 1788. If those selected in 1781 had been selected again in 1785 after their first term was up, then fifteen men would have repeated; in the next year, another fifteen; and so on. In all, there could have been up to sixty repeaters. In fact there were about a dozen. That is, about one in five councillors served more than one term, a rather low rate of incumbency by modern standards. But if a large number of men could take their turn in municipal governance, not all men had an equal chance. The rich were exceptionally well represented. The median payment of fifty-seven councillors on the 1791 *contribution mobilière* was 16 livres, nearly quadruple the median payment of the population as a whole. Furthermore, of those whose occupations are known, roughly 60 percent came from the commercial, professional, and rentier bourgeoisie. The next largest category was agricultural at 25 percent, but these individuals were an unrepresentative minority of the people of the *terroir*. Their median tax payment was quadruple that of the agricultural sector as a whole.

Town governance, and therefore the ability to fix the town's budget, was in the hands of the rich, a group that excluded the vast majority of peasants, artisans, and shopkeepers. This elite group certainly did well out of the Old Regime fiscal arrangements, but they were prepared to bend before the overwhelming national demand for fiscal reform in 1789. This became clear as the councillors and the town's occupational groups drafted their *cahiers de doléances* for the Estates General. The corporations chose men who were more representative of the community than the Old Regime council had been, but they still deferred to the elite. Because artisans' corporations were much more numerous than the professional ones, more artisans participated in the town's electoral assembly in March 1789.[8] The median tax payment of those who can be retrieved was significantly lower than that of the town council (9.3 livres as opposed to about 16 livres), and the dispersal was very great (standard deviation 15.3 livres); only five of the twenty-five delegates had been members of the council, but it had always been a fairly open body anyway. Although it was composed of many new faces, the town

[8] AC Aubagne, *registre des déliberations*, 107, session of 29 March 1789.

assembly that chose electors for the meeting at Aix to draft the general cahier of Provence chose the urban elite all the same. One delegate was a noble, another was the town's seigneurial judge, and all six of them were members of prominent and wealthy families. The province's general cahier they helped to draft was not a conservative document. It demanded equal taxation and representation for the Third Estate, as the town had been demanding since the end of 1788. Town notables also demanded that the town be represented in the provincial Estates, because of its population and its heavy tax burden.[9]

The town's cahier advocated a serious reform of finances. It demanded that the banalities be redeemed and that all taxes, like the *piquet*, that raised the price of food be abolished. It demanded that the privileged orders' land be subject to tax. The overall level of the land taxes would therefore drop but the cahier despaired of what arrangement would replace the present system. One scenario anticipated the final reform the revolutionaries adopted: a territorial land tax paid in cash with no exemptions combined with a *capitation* on wealth. The cahier emphasized the desire to open up commerce, especially in wine, to wider markets. Thus it complained about the tax farmers' virtually unlimited rights of search, even of women's clothes; their right to ambush those transporting goods; their vexatious inspections at their bureau on the road to Marseille, and so on. They demanded the abolition of taxes on the resale of wine, and the end of preferences given to wines from Catalonia and Languedoc in the Marseille market.

Municipal governance should also be reformed drastically. Instead of the complex system of co-optation, the cahier demanded that the town council be elected by all taxpayers.[10] Fiscal equality, poor relief, economic development, weakening of taxes on consumption and commerce,

---

9 Ibid., *registre des déliberations*, 22, session of 31 December 1788, also session of 21 January 1789 (p. 42), demanding a reform of the provincial estates that was truly "representative of the Provençal nation." Also session of 29 March (p. 107). J.-B.-J. Brémond, *A nosseigneurs des états pour la communauté d'Aubagne* (Aix: Chez J. B. Mouret fils, 1788). NYPL *Z-10313 no. 4. Lieutard, *Mémoire pour la communauté d'Aubagne* (Aix: Imprimerie de la Veuve d'André Adibert, 1789) NYPL *KVR 6200. For the province as a whole, see Monique Cubells, *Les horizons de la liberté: naissance de la Révolution en Provence (1787–1789)* (Aix: Edisud, 1987), 130–46.

10 AP, vi, 249–51, "Cahier de doléances de la communauté de la ville d'Aubagne." But this version has no relation to the one in the *registre des déliberations* (87–107) in the AC. Even the title is different: "Doléances remontrances et reclamations de la ville d'Aubagne, sénéchaussée d'Aix-en-Provence." The editors of the *AP* appear to have loosely summarized the original. Relying on this version alone leads to some quite misleading conclusions.

governance by men of property on a broad suffrage – the cahier was a liberal document. It signifies that the men who drafted it, none of whom ever became Jacobins and many of whom were later anti-Jacobins, were not counter- or antirevolutionary.

Nonetheless, many ordinary folk distrusted those who were drafting the final cahier.[11] For days before that general meeting, peasants carrying cudgels milled about the public squares and streets. Some threatened to burn the town down, destroy the grain storage bins and the notaries' offices, sack the houses of the rich, make the bourgeois pay up, and refuse to pay their debts and seigneurial obligations. In this emotional atmosphere, the delegates of the corporations and the inhabitants of the town met on Sunday, 29 March 1789, to draft the cahier and elect delegates to the general assembly at Aix. Almost immediately, a drummer led peasants armed with clubs into the meeting hall. Their spokesman, Dominique Pichou, from a solid family of cultivators in the *terroir*, unleashed a violent verbal attack on how the town was run. He demanded the suppression of the tithe, the *piquet*, and baking fees; he said he no longer recognized the seigneur, the bishop of Marseille, because everybody was equal now; that the only authority he recognized was that of the King; that he no longer feared M. Ramel, the mayor; and that he would rip out the liver of the son of the second consul or vice mayor of the town. The demonstrators forced the councillors to lower the price of bread, sign an agreement on paper headed by a fleur-de-lis, and to announce it through the town crier.[12]

The verbal violence of this angry tirade with its chilling threats and its loathing of the old elite obviously point forward. But the language also derived from a long tradition of rural revolt. In earlier times, whenever quarrels among the elites weakened the state, ordinary people had imagined a better future stripped of the vexations of ordinary life. The key was to restore a simpler society with no intermediaries between an uncomplicated community of equals and the king, the source of earthly justice. The irate denunciations of the privileged, seigneurs, the bourgeois, and the

---

[11] AM Marseille, 25II 2, "Aubagne, 1789: Troubles, émotions populaires."

[12] AC Aubagne, *registre des délibérations*, 111–12, session of 1 April 1789. Protests about the *piquet* and high prices were common throughout Provence in the spring of 1789. See Cubells, *Horizons de la liberté*, 94–6. For Aix-en-Provence where the *piquet* and bread prices provoked a riot on 25 March 1789, see *Copie du procès-verbal de l'émeute arrivée à Aix le 25 mars 1789, adressée en original à messeigneurs Neker, de Villedeuil et de Beauvau (27 mars)*, [1789] ADBR, 100E 41.

leading families; the refusal of indirect taxes and seigneurial and ecclesiastical imposts, all of which were illegitimate usurpations; the denunciations of usury and the refusal to pay loans; and the threats to maim people and destroy property – all these derived from this idealized community. All had been heard before.[13] Like many Old Regime rebellions, too, this one in Aubagne was an armed petition. Unlike the Old Regime, however, the Revolution's restructuring of access to power allowed such ancient ideals to recombine as a violent democratic ideology.

Pichou's trajectory into radicalism and terrorism would make him exceptionally prominent. While the future of those who marched into the meeting hall with him would not be so outstanding, the witnesses against the demonstration contain some striking individuals: Mathieu Rousserie, innkeeper-killer; Martinot, notary–gang paymaster; Antoine Sivan, whose tavern would be a favorite with anti-Jacobins; and, most spectacularly of all, Joseph Jourdan, *huissier royal* in 1789, one of the victims of the lynchings in Aubagne in September 1792.

Significantly, crowds tried to intimidate authorities into abandoning an inquiry into the incident. On 15 April, a band of about two hundred youths from Marseille, mostly dockworkers, armed with drawn sabers and accompanied by a dozen horsemen and peasants from nearby Le Penne, invaded the town. Their purpose was to persuade judicial authorities to drop the inquiry. Pleas gave way to threats as the youth, "overexcited and uninhibited with wine," disrupted proceedings in the bishop's summer residence. The judges then made their way to the town square, where an agitated populace demanded a release of the prisoners and an end to the proceedings. Amid the negotiating with the judges, the crowd destroyed the tax office that collected the *piquet*. The judges agreed to postpone their activities. Someone in the crowd then proclaimed a general amnesty "in the name of the King." Another group, a handful of dockers from Marseille, along with "the most seditious women of Aubagne," demanded the release of the prisoners "in the most brutal tones." Overwhelmed with "overheated people without education drunk with wine," the judges watched stupefied as the people tried to get the town crier to proclaim the amnesty. The town council thought of mobilizing the bourgeois to protect the judges, but too late. After much carousing in the cafés

---

[13] Yves Marie Bercé, *Revolt and Revolution in Early Modern Europe: An Essay on the History of Political Violence* (Manchester, UK: Manchester University Press, 1987), 6–14, 24–33.

and the taverns the rest of the night, the Marseillais stumbled home the next morning.[14]

As a foretaste of future practices, the events at Aubagne were all-important. It was the first of dozens of interventions from Marseille into local politics throughout the region. Even before it became a Jacobin doctrine, the sense of solidarity with beleaguered patriots everywhere was already in place. Moreover, the youth of Marseille were in fact the embryonic National Guard, which formed at about this time. Their commander, Lieutaud, now celebrated as a patriot but soon to be loathed as one of many turncoats, led the Aubagne expedition. Other continuities existed as well. One of the prisoners the crowd wanted released was Félix Aufran who became a leader of the anti-*piquet* forces in Aubagne over the next two years. Finally, the crowd demonstrated an unprecedented daring. Petitioning, even demonstrating, toward authority was not new, but by proclaiming an amnesty, even in the name of the King, the crowd was anticipating a sovereign authority to administer justice, an authority they would later claim more directly.

More generally, the events in Aubagne in March and April 1789 point to a variant on interpretations of crowd action during this period. Elsewhere, crowds represented the broad community and claimed an implicit right to impose general norms and to force authority to do its duty.[15] This model applies in the Midi but not always. In Aubagne and throughout the region, the community itself was bitterly divided. The witnesses against the armed demonstration, the recourse to the bourgeois against those demanding an amnesty from the judge, and the intervention of the Marseillais to support one faction, all show how divided the community was, even at this early stage. No consensus was possible when the interests of justice and order were in such opposition.

The notables on the town council in their turn embraced the national revolution with delirious enthusiasm. They endorsed unequivocally the reforms of the Night of the Fourth of August and with them the renunciation of the privileges of Provence and its special institutions. They endorsed the province's deputies' renunciation of their "particular rights

---

[14] AN Ba 10, *Procès-verbal du 16 avril 1789.* AC Aubagne, *registre des délibérations,* 162–4, "Arrêté de la cour des comptes, aides et finances de Provence du 29ᵉ may 1789." Monique Cubells, "Marseille au printemps de 1789: ville de dissidence," *Annales du Midi* 1 (1986), 78–9.

[15] Colin Lucas, "The Crowd and Politics," *The Transformation of the Political Culture, 1789–1848,* vol. 3, *The French Revolution and the Creation of Modern Political Culture,* ed. K. M. Baker et al. (Paris: Pergamon Press, 1988), 259–85.

that contradict the system of equality and uniformity that is going to be the mark of the French constitution."[16] Although no one could have been certain what these principles would be in practice, some consequences were clear from the beginning. The town had already lost the seigneurial court. Although the banality rights remained until their owners received compensation, their days appeared to be numbered. The elimination of particular rights also spelled the end of the provincial Estates. Suppression of provincial rights also meant standardized taxation and therefore an end to fiscal privilege in all its forms, not only for the Church and the aristocracy but for the Third Estate as well. Moreover, it was the Old Regime town council that wrote these enthusiastic addresses endorsing the Revolution.

Mobilizing Opposition

Aside from the disturbances over the *piquet*, the town passed through the tumultuous year with few disturbances and certainly with no municipal revolution that overthrew local oligarchies elsewhere. Indeed, the fear of brigands that swept through Aubagne, as it did in so many other places in the summer of 1789, reinforced local solidarities and with them social hierarchies.[17] This showed itself in the organization of the National Guard. Formed at the end of August, always short of weapons, haphazardly put together, its leading officers were nonetheless drawn from the town's elite. Four of the eight commanders were nobles, and the rest originated in leading families like the Martinots, Sivans, and Moussards. Many of them had helped draft the town's cahier.[18] When these officers made political commitments later, all of them became anti-Jacobins. Thus, the elite families could accommodate the Revolution of the Third Estate but resisted the Jacobin surge.

The elites found it more difficult to accommodate demands closer to home. The unhappiness over the *piquet* continued to simmer until a group of concerned active citizens decided to petition for its reform. Active citizens had the right to vote under the new electoral law. This meant that they paid at least three days labor in taxes, so the petitioners had some property in the community. At nine o'clock in the morning on

---

[16] AC Aubagne, *registre des déliberations*, 193–4, session of 6 September 1789.

[17] See Timothy Tackett, "La Grande Peur et le complot aristocratique sous la Révolution française," *AhRf* 335 (2004), 1–17.

[18] AC Aubagne, *registre des déliberations*, 189–90, session of 27 August 1789.

20 June 1790, they met in the chapel of the White Penitents to finalize a petition they had been working on for some time. They spoke of being "cut with sobs from chests exhausted by a kind of famine that was more cruel than famine itself." Working people were "reduced to the most frightening misery" because of the *piquet* tax. In the nature of things, the poor were far more dependent on bread for nourishment than the rich, so the tax was more of burden on them. The petitioners claimed that the poor paid three and a half times more per head through the *piquet*, a tax on consumption of basic necessities, than they would if there had been a simple per capita tax. The banality of the ovens added more to the burdens because residents of the *terroir* and bakers were quite capable of baking their own bread. Other taxes and fees, like the octroi and the weigh station, were equally onerous.

Finally, there was a hint of things to come in the language of hostility toward the elite. The petitioners expected the councillors to be paternalistic and left hanging the consequence of their failure to live up to their obligations. They also said that those who called in the *maréchaussée* from Marseille and the commissioners from the Parlement to repress and prosecute the demonstration of 15 April 1789 against the *piquet* should pay the expenses of the repression themselves. Such men were "avid for blood," excessively hostile to mere "transports of anger" and "shivers of fear."[19] Those arrested were innocent of any crime; disturbing the municipality's deliberations did not merit such a heavy-handed riposte. This continued the hostility toward the bourgeois elite that boiled up in March 1789.

Consequently, the petitioners demanded the abolition of the *piquet* and the banality of ovens, as well as the abolition of exit taxes; fees for weights and measures; sales taxes on the sale and resale of wine; and finally, the abolition of all taxes on locally produced wine. The National Guard should be organized; greater publicity was required for council meetings, especially those where finances were on the agenda; and finally, elections should be held on Sundays to ensure greater turnout of the active citizens.[20]

[19] This language was not exaggerated, as five people had been hanged and fourteen sentenced to the galleys for their participation in the antifiscal riots nearby in 1789. See Cubells, *Horizons de la liberté*, 114.

[20] AC Aubagne, "Elections, Adresse & Pétition faites à Messieurs Les Officiers Municipaux de la Ville d'Aubagne, par un certain nombre de Citoyens actifs de la Communauté de ladite Ville," n.d. [20 June 1790].

These active citizens were demanding a complete overhaul of municipal taxation. The demand for the abolition of all forms of indirect taxation and fees on foodstuffs would have shifted the burden of taxation much more to property holders and away from consumers or consumers of municipal services. The Constituent Assembly would eventually impose a system like this, one that abolished all but the most minor fees and indirect taxes, including most municipal ones. The revolutionary system of taxation depended heavily on direct taxes on property owners and to a lesser extent on other sorts of producers, but in 1790, such a system was still being debated in Paris. The council of Aubagne and the new Department of the Bouches-du-Rhône rejected the petition because it would anticipate the Constituent Assembly's reforms and because the owners of banalities would have to be indemnified for their losses.[21]

The town council was not rejecting all tax reform, although it was certainly backing off the wider demands for reform that the cahier made in 1789. The difference between the town and the active citizens' petition was over the scale of the reform. The town took a narrow view, rejecting abolition of fees and the clever accounting devices that shifted the burden of direct taxes and arguing for redemption, not abolition, of the banality of the ovens. Even before the Revolution, the town had launched several lawsuits about this, including an appeal to the Royal Council in Versailles, seeking ways of reversing the sale to a private family in 1644. Although they always claimed their leadership was popular, their narrow interest as landowners was in play, too. Reabsorbing the ovens into the town's domain would keep direct taxes down, a device the notables already had achieved with the banality of the mills.[22] These efforts continued into the Revolution. As patriot influence on the council grew after 1790, so did the enthusiasm for outright abolition. Other councillors and the Department were urging redemption, something that some argued was not going to happen soon.

The council had no trouble rejecting the active citizens' demands for a broad reform. They insisted that the *piquet* was an essential contribution to the town's finances that it paid for the capitation as well as local services like paving streets, repairing fountains, and so on.[23] They also

---

[21] Ibid., "Arrêté du Directoire du département des Bouches-du-Rhône du 14 janvier 1791."

[22] The dossier on the subject of redemption of the banality of ovens before the Revolution is very large. See the various consultations and minutes in ADBR, 135E DD 10, for efforts in 1779.

[23] AC Aubagne, *registre des délibérations*, 84–6, session of 23 June 1790.

argued that the fees on weights and measures were essential and that the banality had to remain until its redemption. The cahier and the petition of the active citizens had demanded that all this be abolished. The council had thus set itself against a significant sector of public opinion. It argued that the financial health of the commune was essential, but the petitioners countered that it was a matter of life itself.

Six petitions submitted between June 1790 and August 1791 kept activity in the town high. The first, the June 1790 petition of active citizens, attracted twenty-two signers. Gury claimed another 166 adherents who could not sign, very likely peasants living in the *terroir*. The second, in favor of the master baker Antoine Taurel's defiance of the banality of ovens, gathered fifty-four signatures. The third protested against the banality, against one of the companies of the National Guard, against the recent elections of the justice of the peace, and against the activity of three men who later became active anti-Jacobins. The fourth was a petition against the town's octroi, or tariff.[24] The fifth, the result of a mass meeting in the *terroir* at the White Penitents' chapel, rehearsed the various options available, from redeeming the banality alone for the small sum of 1,200 livres or taking back the ovens, too. Finally, the sixth petition made the point that the banality hurt the poor the most. Moreover, because the municipality was deprived of that revenue, it had been necessary to establish the *piquet* earlier in the century.[25] All the petitions showed a detailed knowledge of the history of the ovens, and all of them assumed the links between local taxation and feudal rights. In other parts of the country, antifeudal, antitax issues and subsistence issues tended to be separate. In the nature of things here, it was impossible to sever them.

The petition drives also formed popular leaders. All six petitions attracted men who would have a career as prominent Jacobins: Domergue, the first Jacobin mayor and a murder victim; Joseph Guillen, a future member of the terrorist *comité de surveillance*; Honoré Jourdan, a member of the terrorist municipality; Taurel, himself a municipal officer;

[24] Ibid., 184–5, session of 13 October 1790. Ibid., 2D 150, *registre des délibérations*, 174, déclaration faite par Gaspard Arnaud et [Jean-Louis] Baudisson, 26 February 1791. Ibid., 179–81, session of 27 February 1791. Ibid., *registre des délibérations*, 10 April 1790.

[25] AN D XIV 2, "Extrait de la Délibération du Conseil général de la Commune et de tous les chefs de famille assemblés à La chapelle Des penitents blancs," 10 July 1791. Ibid., "Citoyens actifs le la ville d'Aubagne A Messieurs le maire et officiers municipaux de la ville d'aubagne," 21 August 1791. A copy claims 157 signatures met in the Cordeliers; therefore, it is likely a petition from the club.

Jean-Jacques Paumond, a member of the terrorist municipality, later murdered in the prison massacre at Marseille in June 1795; and so on. In addition, petitions were rallying supporters around the fiscal issue. The continuous agitation these men promoted attracted more and more supporters until the riot of August 1792 abolished the banality of ovens from below.

Elections

The disputes over the *piquet* and the banalities mobilized many ordinary people beyond the corps of future Jacobins. This showed in the elections to the council in November 1790. Four council seats were open. Future Jacobins took all four. The winners included the baker Taurel; Domergue; and the mayor who would preside over the Terror, Jean-Baptiste Camoin. The future Jacobins also elected a few to the position of notable, the most important being Dominique Pichou, the fiery peasant protester of 1789 and a future soldier in the battalions that marched to overthrow the monarchy in August 1792.

The anti-*piquet* forces knew they had achieved a great victory. One of the newly elected councillors, Félix Aufran, spoke of his dedication to "divine equality." Aufran, of course, had been arrested for his role in the antifiscal riot of 29 March 1789 in Aubagne when the town was drafting its *cahier de doléances*. Now vindicated, he denounced "these miserable instigators who by their enormous arrogance [grand orgeuil porté à l'extreme] have always been [our] enemies.... They spurn patriotism and civic virtue."[26] Clearly the memory of 1789 burned brightly.

The election of the justice of the peace in January 1791 revealed the cleavages within the town. After several days of voting, authorities declared Antoine Jourdan, the former judge of Aubagne's seigneurial court, the winner by 187 votes to 88 for his opponent, the anti-*piquet* candidate Jean-Baptiste Camoin. But the election was divisive. Jourdan got 134 of his votes in the Black Penitents section and just 53 in the more populous White. Camoin's breakdown was a mirror image, a mere six in the Black and eighty-two in the White. The town had divided along neighborhood lines and not for the last time. Moreover, the anti-*piquet* forces soon complained about voting irregularities, claiming that underage men or passive citizens had voted, and that the vote was the result of a

---

[26] AC Aubagne, *registre des délibérations*, 140, session of 8 December 1790.

cabal.[27] Complaining about procedural violations was a device to get the result overturned, but higher authority sustained Jourdan's election.[28]

With the frequent meetings and petitions, it was logical for the anti-*piquet* forces to form a club. On 13 March 1791, a petition from one hundred active citizens demanded authorization to form the Society of Friends of the Constitution and Patriotic Club. It would meet in the Chapel du Louve in the *terroir*, which the active citizens had used several times for their petition meetings. Camoin, having recovered from his defeat in the elections for the justice of the peace, argued the meeting should be held in the chapel because the petitioners were "almost all men of the countryside." A slight majority of the councillors (10–7) voted to require the Club to meet in the town.[29] The Club soon settled in to the refectory of the former Cordeliers Monastery. One hundred fifty members attended one of the first meetings. The first two secretaries were Noel Castelin, a future member of the terrorist *comité de surveillance*, and Nicolas Gury, a victim of the murder gang. The Club quickly affiliated itself with the Club at Marseille. Later still it changed its name to Society of Friends of the Constitution under the title of the Fraternal Anti-*Politiques* Brothers, to conform to the usage of clubs nearby; and it claimed six hundred members.[30] This was probably not an exaggeration. It was equivalent to about half the active citizens in the town.

The formation of the Club was a major event in the town's political development. Most Jacobin clubs were middle-class creations that then had to reach out for a constituency. In Provence at any rate, bigger clubs like that of Marseille sent out "Republican missionaries" to found sister clubs in small towns and villages.[31] The experience of Aubagne points

---

[27] Ibid., 2D 150. ADBR, L 364, Camoin, Freze, Berenger, and Castelin to District of Marseille, 14 February 1791. The authors, all soon to be prominent Jacobins, wrote on behalf of the White Penitents Section.

[28] AC Aubagne, *registre des déliberations*, 190–1, session of 1 March 1791.

[29] Ibid., 193–4, session of 13 March 1791. ADBR, 135E BB 42, f. 69, municipality to District of Marseille, 24 February 1791.

[30] Ibid., L 1061, "Extrait du premier registre des déliberations du club...d'Aubagne," 21 March 1791. Ibid., L 277, club to Electoral Assembly of Bouches-du-Rhône, n.d. [September 1791].

[31] Edmond Poupé, "Les Papiers de la Société populaire de Saint-Zacharie," *Bulletin de la Société d'études scientifiques et archéologiques de la ville de Draguignan* (1905), 3–18, founded by the Marseille Club. Jacques Guilhaumou, *Marseille républicaine (1791–1793)* (Paris: Presses de la Fondation nationale des sciences politiques, 1992), 47–76. Michael L. Kennedy, *The Jacobin Club of Marseilles, 1790–1794* (Ithaca, N.Y.: Cornell University Press, 1973). There was considerable support from artisans in the Club at

to a third model. Here the club came into existence after nearly two years of incessant agitation over specific local issues. Moreover, it did not have to solicit popular support so much as provide a venue for it. The Club was an expression of widespread support of working people, especially those in the *terroir*. Popular support for radical positions in the Revolution is usually explained by invoking high bread prices that made folks open to the propaganda of middle-class extremists. Aubagne and much of Provence clearly followed a different trajectory. The galvanizing force in this case was hostility to municipal taxation and regulation of the food trades. Eventually this posed the broader question of governance. Because Aubagne's type of governance was common to many small towns and villages in Provence, and because the issue of the *piquet* was very widespread in 1789, the Aubagne model might well explain why there were so many clubs in the region: they were an expression of struggles that had begun earlier and that were still unresolved. From their foundation, clubs like these were more than discussion groups; they were instruments of political struggle.

The Club also looked forward. Its foundation permitted a more continuous agitation and better organization. The various affiliations and especially the affiliation with the Club in Marseille bound the fate of smaller clubs like Aubagne's to a political dynamo. These histories were now inextricable. More than ever, they could join in the vast national conversations among the clubs. No doubt Aubagne's, like the other clubs, spent a great deal of its meeting time reading the national press out loud to one another or discussing the printed resolutions and addresses of other clubs. It joined the conversation early. Like hundreds of other clubs, its members celebrated the news of the recovery of the King from his illness in March 1791 by petitioning for a Te Deum Mass.[32] It later denounced the émigrés whom the Jacobins thought were plotting against the nation. Some were, but the club's solution was to demand the confiscation of the property of all émigrés without a judicial hearing. No doubt the club acquired this idea from the dozens of other clubs that were demanding the same thing. All the same, it was a violation of the Declaration of the

---

Arles from the beginning (Sampoli, "Politics and Society in Revolutionary Arles," 171–2) and in the *Club des Anti-politiques* at Aix-en-Provence (Félix Ponteil, "La société populaire des Anti-politiques d'Aix-en-Provence, d'après des documents inédits (1790–1795)," *Revue historique de la Révolution française*, 13 (1918), 30–3.

[32] AC Aubagne, *registre des déliberations*, 213, session of 29 March 1791.

Rights of Man's clauses about protection of property and due process rights.[33]

Moreover, the depth of popular support and the organizational strength of the regional club network made the efforts of their enemies futile for the next four years. Jacobinism was so entrenched because its adherents believed they were the community, not just a local one, but a vast national network of like-minded brothers. The Club at Aubagne articulated this vision of the clubbists' responsibilities to this wider community. It would be common currency over the next few years. They swore, "The F[raternal] anti-*politiques* B[rothers] of Aubagne are ready to march anywhere the needs of the *patrie* summon them, to fly to the assistance of their brothers and exterminate all the enemies of the Declaration of the Rights of Man."[34]

The belief in the existence of a community of patriots was fundamental to Jacobinism in this region. It was the rationale for the dozens of civic missions from 1791 to 1793, and even the most magnificent mission of all, to Paris in July 1792 to overthrow the monarchy. As the club movement developed, however, another community emerged in opposition, one that also had a popular following. The Jacobins affected to believe this other community was based on a narrow self-interested clique concerned, as the Old Regime council had been, only with its privileges. This was a dangerously simple analysis.

Meanwhile the tax burden continued to roil local politics. The mayor, Carbonel, proposed the immediate replacement of the *piquet* with a head tax on all property holders while everyone awaited the phasing in of the new fiscal reforms. The council refused this because it was too complicated, was open to abuse, and would double taxes on property holders.[35] Nonetheless, Carbonel continued his activities to seek relief. He was trying to arrange the redemption of the banality of the ovens. This was an immensely popular position. The Club had submitted a petition in support of it. The common people ardently and passionately endorsed it. Excitement was so great that some feared any delay would provoke disturbances. "All Aubagne," Carbonel declared at a council meeting, "is rising up, driven by an ardent and boisterous spirit which self-interest, caprice,

---

[33] AN C 124², "Adresse de la Société des Amis de la Constitution d'Aubagne... séante aux pénitents gris," 1 July 1791. I am grateful to Timothy Tackett for this reference.

[34] ADBR, L 277, third letter of club to Electoral Assembly of Bouches-du-Rhône, n.d. [September 1791].

[35] AC Aubagne, *registre des délibérations*, 215, session of 27 March 1791.

and vengeance sustain.... Only interest and religion keep men at peace while the general fermentation might suggest otherwise.... Patriotism alone bolsters local authorities in the painful exercise of their duty."[36] Indeed, the council feared serious violence. In early May, the procurator of the commune denounced the circulation of a placard in patois "containing horrors against some citizens."[37]

So the stakes were high in the November 1791 local elections. The experience of the previous two years showed there were too few votes on the council to reform the *piquet* and the banalities. Reformers had done very well in November 1790, and they could hope to do even better this time thanks to the organizing abilities of the Club. The mayoralty, four council seats, and ten positions as notables were open. The Jacobins swept the elections. Domergue won the mayoralty, easily defeating Pierre Martinot, the retired curé and representative of the pro-*piquet* forces (Carbonel did not run and Louis-Dominique Berenger, the procureur, resigned just before the elections). The enthusiasm for Domergue was enormous. His supporters ignored the District's nullification of elections and the order for new ones. The District had ceded to the protests of the pro-*piquet* faction when it alleged procedural violations. No matter. Mayor Carbonel resigned citing fatigue. Several other Jacobin councillors including Camoin and Aufran also resigned, citing overwork but probably in protest. The next day, 13 December, a boisterous crowd, "a riot," some said, tried to force the installation of Domergue in "the name of the people." They tried to persuade the curé, Templier, to sound the church bells to summon the citizenry. When he refused, they did it themselves. When asked who authorized them, the crowd replied that it was the wish of the entire people. Domergue's investiture, then, was an example of the demands of popular sovereignty overriding the formal law, just as the popular grant of amnesty had been in 1789. Amid this altercation, "an immense crowd of inhabitants of every social station, most of whom were armed," along with some Marseille National Guardsmen, fetched Domergue from his house. As the church bells were pealing, a trumpeter led the crowd to the town hall. Many of them included country people from the *terroir* who brought their weapons along to celebrate. They forced the municipal councillors to proclaim Domergue and his friends. The new mayor and councillors then appeared on the balcony of the town

---

[36] Ibid., ff. 6–6v, session of 13 May 1791.
[37] Ibid., 232, session of May 7, 1791.

hall, where they took the civic oath to the delirious approval of the crowd and then repaired to the parish church to hear a Te Deum.[38]

But the crowd was not quite anonymous. Language that makes the crowd seem anonymous recurs often in this period. It usually obscures individual actions and gives the crowd a formlessness that is difficult to penetrate. Depicting the crowd as amorphous and unpredictable was a way for administrators to distance themselves from the action, to portray themselves as helpless, and to dissipate responsibility. In this case, however, the Club and some of the actors revealed their roles. According to the Club, the resignation of Carbonel and the Jacobin councillors threw the people into such consternation and despair that the Club had to act. "We would be lacking in our duty," they informed the Department, "if we did not inform you of the investiture that we did to-day, for the good of the *patrie* and for nothing else.... A great number of patriots wearing an olive branch in their hats, are going to the feet of the sacred tabernacles to give thanks to the immortals because of this worthy installation."[39]

The Club also had a long reach. As chair of the White Penitents electoral assembly, Domergue had summoned the National Guard from Marseille, ostensibly to keep order, possibly as a way of restraining the unreliable elements of the local Guard. Far from doing that, however, the Marseillais stood aside and let the installation occur. Moreover, the day after the popular installation, another petition from well over 150 illiterates implored the Department and District to recognize Domergue. The language was as brazen as that of the Club in its invocation of the primordial legitimacy of popular action. The decree quashing the elections was not in the public interest, they said. The failure of the current town council to have the new tax rolls ready (which defined the right to vote) "made the good people tired and exasperated." The people are "dedicated to the Law. No power, no administration has any right to suspend its execution. [The people] has given itself magistrates of its choice who support the Constitution." The petitioners implored the District to confirm "this election and this installation so much desired and

---

[38] AC Aubagne, *registre des délibérations*, ff. 45–45v, letter from Mr. Templier to municipality, n.d. Procès- verbal du 13 décembre 1791 and in the bundle entitled "Elections," letter of municipal officers to District, 13 December 1791. Copy in ADBR, 135E BB 42, ff. 75–7 and L 1044. Ibid., L 292, "Extrait du procès verbal de la municipalité d'Aubagne, 13 décembre 1791." Ibid., L 266, *Procès-verbal* of Michel and Daniel, 29 December 1791.

[39] AC Aubagne, "Elections," Les Amis de la Constitution Antipolitiques D'aubagne to Department of Bouches-du-Rhône, 13 December 1791.

applauded."[40] Although the contradiction between requesting that authority endorse the installation on the one hand and the demand that authority accept the crowd's action on the other weakened the argument, the thrust was clear. Authority had to stand aside when the people spoke. For the Club, as for the undifferentiated crowd, popular consecration overrode the irregularity of Domergue's accession to office. Moreover, Club and crowd overlapped. Club members also signed the petition of the illiterate, as did Domergue and the members of the acclaimed municipality. Popular acclaim was the ultimate legitimacy, a reason to celebrate.

A recurring theme of the period had clearly emerged: when popular sovereignty and the law were in conflict, only the wishes of the people were legitimate.

While the crowd respected some forms of acclamation and celebration, it ignored strict legality. Nonetheless, the elections would be run again. The Department and the District both agreed with several petitions that passive citizens had voted. So had men who failed to submit proof that they had paid their taxes.[41] So there was a second vote. On 6 January 1792, Domergue won again, this time over Louis Mille, the pro-*piquet* candidate (Domergue's body would be buried on Mille's land in 1795).

The passionate dispute over the legality of the elections revealed much about the cleavages in the town. Each side was aware that this was a dispute between social groups living in different neighborhoods. At the time of the electoral assembly of the Department in September 1791, Nicolas Gury, the secretary of the Club and a teacher, copied out a letter from the Brothers recommending Jean-Baptiste Camoin for a position, as "a most zealous patriot and the one our aristocrats fear the most." But the enemy was not the handful of real aristocrats in the town. Instead, "the people of Aubagne are still enchained by the bourgeois, who in all times, have tyrannized them," claimed a petition alleging skulduggery on the part of the Black Penitents Section against the White.[42] The bourgeois wanted to stall their actual voting well into the night and into the next morning in the hopes that the cultivators would get discouraged and go home. The Black Penitents were largely "composed of bourgeois, men

---

[40] Ibid., petition of 14 December 1791.

[41] ADBR, L 955, avis du district de Marseille, 26 November 1791 (draft, no pagination), revision on ff. 94v–107, 1 December 1791. AC Aubagne, "Elections," decree of District of Marseille, 1 December 1791; of the Department, 11, 26 December 1791. Also in ADBR, L 955, 26 December 1791.

[42] ADBR, L 277, second letter of club to Electoral Assembly of Bouches-du-Rhône, n.d. [September 1791].

of law, and *des gens de pratique* of Aubagne, accustomed to dominating the people . . . in order to hide the many depredations and to continue the horde of abuses that are favorable to them." They denounce the "grossness and ignorance of the country people" while they represent themselves as enlightened.[43] On the other hand, those who successfully protested the first election saw their opponents as lawless and themselves as decent. The most glaring example the protesters cited of lax standards was none other than Gury himself, who paid no tax, "neither in Aubagne, nor anywhere in the world." The "agents of despotism and anarchy" intimidated the "honest citizens," "peaceable citizens, men of property [*gens de bien*]." They also ignored the formal requirements of the law and claimed that "all those who knew how to express their thoughts was an active citizen."[44]

An analysis of the election results confirms the reality of this language of social hostility. Moreover, between the first election in November 1791 and the second in January 1792, this polarization became more intense. Turnout shot up, but it favored the anti-Jacobins. In November, only 217 active citizens voted for mayor, but in January 1792, 432 did. Nonetheless, Domergue picked up very little of this new interest. He got only 18 more votes in January, when the combined total of his opponents increased from a derisory 10 to a very impressive 215. New voters were obviously hostile to the Jacobin mayor. But there could be a different set of voters if the election continued over more than one day. This would explain why the Jacobins did so well for positions on the council. They took all four of them because after the first round for councillor, the voters in the Black Penitents section went home, while the Jacobin voters in the White Penitents stayed on. The next day, 9 January, both sides returned in force for the elections for the procureur (450 voters) and the results were as close as the mayoralty election. Barthélemy-Charles Boeuf defeated his opponent by just 22 votes. This result must have been satisfying, however. The loser was the former procureur, Louis Berenger, a vociferous opponent of any reform of the *piquet*. Two days later in the elections for the town notables, the turnout had dropped to only 268 voters.

---

43 Ibid., "Les Citoyens actifs soussignés & les illettrés dénommés ci-après de la Commune d'Aubagne . . . À Messieurs les administrateurs du département des Bouches-du-Rhône," 5 December 1791.

44 Ibid., "Extrait d'une pétition des citoyens actifs," 1 December 1791. The petition with signatures is deeper down this bundle. At the time the petition was submitted, the statement about Gury was probably correct; a few months later, he was assessed 5 livres for *contribution mobilière*.

Anti-Jacobin voters again stayed away and the Jacobins clearly ran a slate. All of their candidates won with totals varying between just 213 and 223.

In short, the Jacobins did much better in the January rerun, which they opposed, than they had in November. Nonetheless, their electoral strength had its limits. They could get no more than 230 votes, and a high turnout put their majorities at risk. Their actual support among the citizenry was no doubt greater than their voting strength, however. To be qualified to vote, one had to produce a receipt that one had paid one's taxes. This must have depressed the Jacobin turnout because of the poverty in the *terroir*. Moreover, the Jacobins were much stronger in the White Penitents Section than in the Black. Domergue won the White section with 70 percent of the vote but got just 33 percent in the Black. This same discrepancy recurred in the elections for the procureur and most of the councillors. The town had divided on neighborhood lines, as it had during the elections for the justice of the peace in February 1791. Although a social dimension underlay the geographic, it was no longer entirely one of working people versus the elite. The anti-Jacobin vote was too large. Social conflict was attracting more people and was becoming more complex.

Breaking Up the Olive Festival

By January 1792, an increasingly large group of opponents were challenging the Jacobin ascendancy. These opponents began circulating a new round of petitions to have the elections canceled a second time. Along with the former allegations that the unqualified had voted, petitioners claimed that their voters, especially those in the Black Penitents, had been intimidated. Some reported that armed men were patrolling near the polling places.

The anti-Jacobins were organizing. On 17 January, they met at the *bastide*, or farm of Rousserie *fils*, the café owner, a well-known sponsor of games of chance on his premises. The meeting attracted 160 people, "bourgeois and artisans," who no doubt discussed town politics for three hours. Two bellicose drummers led them back to town in combative spirits. They shouted, "Vive l'aristocracie, vivent les aristocrats!" Once at the town hall, they hissed and shouted more slogans.[45]

---

[45] Ibid., *registre des délibérations*, f. 50v, "Denonciation...de faits anti-constitutionels," 17 January 1792.

The next day, around midnight, loud knocking on the door of the house of Sieur Bruno Aubagne Jourdan awoke one of the neighbors. A neighboring woman tiptoed cautiously into the street because she was suspicious. She pressed her nose against the glass and peered into a room lit only by a candle in a paper goblet. The light made eerie shadows on their faces. Squeezed around a table were not only Aubagne Jourdan, the former municipal officer, but also his son, as well as Honoré Lion *fils*, Antoine Jourdan des Coquières, and the son of the barrister Martinot. All of these men were either members themselves of the last municipal council of the Old Regime or members of the town's wealthiest and most prominent families. She reported a chilling exchange. Aubagne Jourdan asked where things were. They replied that everything was ready; that they could not wait until they came on them; that it was necessary to fire first [*qu'il falait faire feu dessus*]; that if they didn't watch out, they would put their feet on their throat.[46] Who "they" were in this exchange was unclear.

This meeting was obviously a plot. Those who celebrated on the streets on 17 January shouting proaristocratic slogans continued to meet at the café Rousserie. They also paraded through the streets wearing masks. Consequently, on the evening of 11 February, the council issued a proclamation forbidding "masks, wearing women's clothes, illicit assemblies, any outdoor fête such as a dance to the sound of a drum, . . . bonfires, or other things intending to assemble the people."[47] The agitators took this as a provocation. That same evening, when the town crier proclaimed the order on illicit assemblies, a crowd around the café Rousserie razzed him. Then someone set bonfires in over a dozen barrels laid out in the street. Patriots responded by organizing a huge crowd "of every estate and all sexes" who danced the farandole, the high-stepping Provençal reel led by drummers and torchbearers. They also sang the revolutionary song "Ça ira." A counterdemonstration of more than two hundred people armed with swords and drawn sabers also danced through the streets. A mysterious tall man wearing an illuminated barrel on his head led this crowd. Another leader was François Sicard *dit* le Renet, a peasant who later joined the murder gang.

The Jacobin Club and the municipality, often the same people, thought these demonstrations presaged something worse: "it is vital to restore

---

[46] ADBR, L 292 and AC Aubagne, *registre des délibérations*, f. 51, session of 18 January 1792.

[47] Ibid., f. 53v, session of 11 February 1792.

public order," they claimed.[48] Clearly the extent of anti-Jacobin feeling in the town was great. As the elections showed, the opposition had also become a popular movement. This is why they had to suppress the Olive Festival.

The day after the various parades and bonfires, 12 February, the tumult began again. This time the drummers led the crowd to the Château Belloi, situated on an outcropping overlooking the town. Some said four hundred people from Aubagne, Marseille, and several nearby villages were invited by the bourgeois. Festivities would begin at the inn of Antoine Sivan with a dance in which the dancers would be armed with swords, a traditional feature of the celebration. Three former battalions of the National Guard, anti-Jacobins all of them, also marched to the château. Those streaming to the château were obviously not a narrow elite. Instead, they were misleading "a great part of the people into order to inflate their party." Because the new National Guard was not ready, the municipality decided to call on citizen-patriots for support as well as 150 guardsmen from Marseille who were on maneuvers nearby that morning.[49]

The anti-Jacobins at the château were in high spirits because ever since the early morning, they had been celebrating the news that the Department had annulled the elections. The luncheon and the dancing were in full swing, too, when at one o'clock in the afternoon Domergue, a few municipal officers, the Marseillais, and the Aubagne volunteers arrived at the closed gates of the château. A hail of stones flew over the walls at them. Some hothead even fired a couple of shots that fortunately hurt no one. At the same time, about fifteen dancers armed with sword sticks and followed by a few drummers advanced on the patriots while about two hundred men armed with drawn swords tried to surround the patriots from each side of the avenue leading to the château. For some reason, this maneuver did not work, and the patriots advanced to the terrace of the château and eventually into the interior apartments. Then, according to Domergue, the anti-Jacobins tried to discredit the municipality and the "good citizens." They began to wreck the château – "the invitees had broken and crushed tables, chairs, window panes, glassware, crockery, tore down the tapestries and other furniture."[50] This, of course, stretches

---

[48] ibid., f. 54, meeting of Sunday morning, 12 February 1792.

[49] The department found this too much of a coincidence to be believed, but no evidence of collusion between the Jacobins of Marseille and those of Aubagne ever turned up (see the untitled summary of correspondence in ADBR, L 292).

[50] AC Aubagne, *registre des délibérations*, f. 56, meeting of 12 February 1792. There is a rather vague report in *Journal de Marseille*, issue of Saturday, 18 February 1792. B.N.

credulity rather far. No matter, the festivities at the château of Belloi were broken up, and the invitees scattered.

Jacobins were able to take advantage of their military ascendancy over the town to entrench themselves further politically. A few hours after the *fête des olliviers* was broken up, the municipality ordered everyone to store their weapons at home. When the invitees of the Château Belloi persisted in hanging about on the Rue Mirabeau (formerly the Grand' Rue) in defiance of a municipal curfew, the council decided to install two garrisons of the Marseillais and "the citizens most friendly to the Constitution" at either end of the street. Based in the Hôtel Bras d'Or and in the Hôtel Lion d'Or on the Toulon road, they were to patrol the streets, break up gatherings, and in case of refusal or "marked resistance, to use the ultimate rigor."[51] By eleven o'clock at night, the little groups in the street had scattered to various rural *bastides*. More guardsmen from Marseille, six hundred of them no less, including some artillery, arrived later to secure the victory. They would stay for the next three weeks. Their mission was to keep order, to sustain the Jacobin municipality.

The repression and intimidation continued. The municipality now decreed the disarming of the entire population. The Marseillais and the "good citizens" were authorized to confiscate any weapons they found in house searches. On Domergue's orders, a group of peasants from the *terroir* arrested a couple of invitees at the Château Belloi ostensibly for their own protection. This was a hint of the vigilantism to come. Moreover, as if these violations of constitutional norms were not enough, the municipality undertook a venomous campaign against the signers of the petition that had provoked the department to order the new elections. The petition was a tissue of lies and falsehoods, containing "the most atrocious calumnies," according to the town procurator Charles Boeuf, and, he hinted, the enemies of the municipality had suborned the signatures. There were thirty-six signatures on the petition, and slowly but surely, the Jacobins were able to force about fifteen individuals to disavow their adhesion. Some people even swore before the council when Domergue summoned them that they had never signed the petition at all.

The dispute over the January elections was resolved but not in a manner that legitimized the Jacobin victory. The anti-Jacobins' second round of

---

8° L^{cII} 635 (11). Further details in René de Chauvigny, *Le cardinal de Belloy et l'église de Marseille de 1789 à 1802* (Avignon: 1930), 106–8.

[51] AC Aubagne, *registre des délibérations*, f. 57, meeting of 12 February 1792.

petitions was at first unsuccessful. On 3 February the District of Marseille endorsed the elections. The arguments of the petitioners were unacceptable. "There would be the greatest danger," said the District, "in providing the minority of sections with the means of assembling as active citizens, to protest against all elections and thus destroy the work of the majority."[52] In other words, process was largely irrelevant to the result. It was the same argument the Club and the crowd in Aubagne had used in the demonstrations in favor of Domergue's installation in December.

The petitioners appealed this stunning decision immediately to the Department at Aix-en-Provence. On 9 February, the Department quashed the decree of the District and ordered new elections at the end of the month.[53] But this was a very short-lived victory. On 26 February, the District settled the matter with an extraordinarily high-handed decree. The Department had ordered the newly elected municipal officers to be replaced by their predecessors or, where that was not possible, to appoint trustees. None of the former municipal officers was willing to do this, however, so the District simply appointed the just sacked Jacobin municipal officers and notables as trustees![54] After this, the Department failed to intervene to control the District. The expedition of the National Guards of Marseille and other towns to intimidate the Department in Aix-en-Provence is the likely explanation. The intervention in Aubagne was part of a much wider surge of revolutionary enthusiasm designed to support the brothers in outlying Clubs. It solidified the Club's victory in the municipal elections not by a legal resolution but by force.

Nor was this the only occasion that the District of Marseille intervened to guarantee the Jacobin ascendancy in Aubagne. Right after the suppression of the Olive Festival, the invitees submitted a long complaint about the dispersal of their meeting and the pillaging of the château. The District rejected it totally. "The only guilty ones are those who by their uncivic language, provoked insurrection, bloodletting, and pillaging while resisting the legal authority of the municipality," they said. The municipality of Aubagne and the National Guard of Marseille deserved praise for their actions in restoring tranquillity.[55]

---

[52] ADBR, L 955, 179–80, *arrêté du directoire*, 3 February 1792.

[53] Ibid., 247–51, *arrêté* of 28 February 1792.

[54] Ibid., 251–3. Copy in ibid., L 266.

[55] Ibid., L 955, 247–51, *arrêté* of 28 February 1792, copy in ibid., L 292. This is a handy copy as well of all the correspondence surrounding the affair, some of which is apparently lost.

Reflections

The dependence of democracy in Aubagne on the legal support of the District and on physical coercion from Marseille is thus clear enough. Even within the town, the Jacobins' rhetoric did not adequately describe the clash of factions. According to them, they represented the vast majority of the population struggling against a narrow-minded and greedy cabal of the old elite. This old elite had been living for far too long on the abuses of the tax system, and the arrival of true representation would result in a fairer sharing of the burdens of public service. There is a great deal of truth in this. Up until the cycle of disputed elections in 1791–2, Jacobins did voice the frustrations of a very large number of people against a municipal council that clung vainly to the system of fees and indirect taxes on food and other agricultural produce. The municipal Law of October 1789 that replaced co-optation with elections and that empowered most male taxpayers to vote or stand for office undermined this elite's ability to maintain the abusive system.

Yet the Jacobin rhetoric did not fully describe their opponents. The disputed elections, and especially those of February 1792, showed the existence of an opposition that was much larger than the rhetoric suggested. This opposition comprised more than just the old elite. Although the social composition of the anti-Jacobins was not yet clear, the elections showed that the town split sharply along neighborhood lines. The agitation of 1790 and 1791 also showed that the Jacobins' natural home was in the *terroir*, outside the town gates. The social divisions and the social basis of political loyalties in the town were more complicated than the language of politics suggested.

On the other hand, the clash of factions should have ended in 1792. Contrary to all expectations, the new tax system that the Constituent Assembly designed was very close to the Jacobins' most excited dreams. The Assembly reduced the importance of indirect taxes enormously, and as far as municipal taxation was concerned, indirect taxes ceased to exist. While banalities and fees remained in legal limbo, it is unlikely they were collected. Government then would depend much more than before on direct taxes, in this case the *contribution foncière* and the *contribution mobilière*, which replaced the *taille réelle* and the *capitation*. The town's rich paid more under this reformed system. Municipal taxes were now much more fair. One might have expected local politics to settle down.

Why then did the clash of factions continue? Once the new fiscal system was in place, no one on the anti-Jacobin side ever made a public defense of the old. Instead, they abandoned the defense of the traditional municipality and repositioned themselves as champions of order. This, of course, was also a defense of property and position. Their continued resistance, sometimes clandestine, sometimes in the open, justified the Jacobins' high-handedness or even their violations of the law.

The Jacobins also raised their sights. Their remarkable success encouraged them to imagine a more ambitious outcome to their agitations. Knowledge that they were partners in similar struggles with other Jacobins must have been enormously energizing. Moreover, a careful reading of their petitions, especially that of June 1790, shows an embedded idea that the bourgeoisie was expendable. The councillors of the old municipality had not lived up to their obligation to be charitable. Instead, they had lived off the sweat of the suffering poor; and in their use of repression against a mere flight of anger in 1789, they had demonstrated how ruthless they were prepared to be in defense of their privileges. In other words, social justice would never be secure until those who benefited from exploitation were punished, or even eliminated. The bitter language in the petition prefigured the politics of 1792 and beyond into the Terror. It led to the attempt to eliminate the bourgeoisie altogether.

In this effort, the Jacobins of Aubagne were no different from the brothers elsewhere. Thanks to this continuing support from the outside, the story of a small town in Provence became more and more spectacular.

3

Aubagne's Universe

Marseille, Aix, and Arles, 1789–1792

The crisis of February 1792 in Aubagne showed how important the alliance with the brothers in Marseille was. In turn, the incidents surrounding the Olive Festival show that Marseille was passionately interested in promoting the fortunes of Jacobins in its hinterland. From then on, the destinies of the small town were a function of the history of the neighboring metropolis. To understand what happened in Aubagne, one must understand how Marseille came to be a Jacobin powerhouse.

An examination of the wider universe in which radical politics in Aubagne operated also demonstrates a number of features of democratic politics that would otherwise be impossible to recover. The broad context therefore helps us to understand Aubagne itself. Democratic politics in this region was far more than the familiar round of voting, club meetings, pamphlets, petitions, and the press. Such things were Jacobin politics in the lower key. At the highest key, democratic politics required a constant mobilization, a ceaseless movement of marches, and expeditions of extraordinarily high energy. This was the expression of sovereignty in its purest form: direct, dazzling, violent, and often cruel.

Glimmers of Liberty: Marseille

The source of popular politics in Marseille and the other urban centers of what became the Department of the Bouches-du-Rhône was the same as that in Aubagne: municipal taxes. By the time the Estates General began meeting in Versailles in May 1789, tax privileges for the Provençal nobility were no longer an issue.[1] A majority in meetings of the Second Estate had accepted equal taxation, but matters of seigneurial privilege and municipal taxation remained. Because taxes were collected through the municipalities, the issue of governance arose in Marseille as it had in Aubagne. The struggles were so turbulent that forms of governance in 1789 varied with bewildering speed. The traditional council had to enlarge itself, only to be replaced by another called the Council of Three Orders. This body in turn gave way to different restorations of the old council. None of these lasted more than a few months until the implementation of the municipal law in February 1790. One issue emerged much earlier than it did in Aubagne: control of the armed forces. In Marseille, this involved patriots attempting to drive royal troops out of the city. Within the civilian population, two armed forces vied for ascendancy: the young citizens, a force of six thousand that supported the patriots; and the *garde bourgeoise*, a more official group with its own blue uniform that supported the antipatriots on the town council. The royal commander of the city; the Parlement in Aix-en-Provence, and most controversial of all, the prevotal court that judged with no appeal and in secret, under the comte de Bournissac – all these vainly tired to impose order on the turbulent city.

All the regular institutions of government had lost control of the city by the spring of 1789, while the improvised ones were not yet strong enough to replace them. Joyous celebrations and terrifying violence occurred frequently between March 1789 and May 1790. Sometimes the two were impossible to distinguish. The celebration around the arrival of the comte de Mirabeau to shore up his local base from 16 to 19 March 1789 led to the first riot. His reception was delirious because earlier in the Estates of Provence, he had denounced oppressive taxation, especially on foodstuffs, the scandal of hunger, and the constitutional arrangements of the Estates. In Marseille, people threw down fronds in front of his carriage during his visit and set bonfires in barrels on the street to celebrate his arrival. During his first visit to the Comédie, the audience forced him to take a place in the center gallery while young men down below stood on one another's shoulders to paste a banner before him. An actress read a poem to him. As he left, a military band accompanied him back to the Hôtel des Ambassadeurs where he was staying on the Rue Beauvau. Blazing torches

---

[1] Étienne Chompré, *Discours prononcé dans l'assemblée des communes de Marseille, le 20 mars 1789, par É. Ch., citoyen de ladite ville* (s.l.: [1789]) BM Marseille, Collection Léon, iv bis. Raoul Busquet, *Histoire de Marseille*, 4th ed. (Paris: R. Laffont, 1945).

lit the way. Children ran through the streets singing his praises. Three or four hundred young men and three hundred carriages accompanied him on his return to Aix. The people saw in Mirabeau "a savior and a father," a disgruntled municipality reported, because he had led them to expect a reduction in the price of basic necessities.[2]

Excitement remained high after Mirabeau's departure. Orators denounced the *piquet*, the farmers of other food taxes, and high prices. The assemblies that drafted the cahiers and demonstrations on the street reiterated these denunciations. Rioters on 23–4 March pillaged the house of one of the tax farmers. Many of them carried pistols and knives. Crowds of up to twenty thousand threatened merchants' warehouses along the quays. Although authorities blamed foreign sailors for the troubles, the fact they also reduced bread prices by half suggests that they also knew the sources of trouble were closer to home.[3]

These disturbances led to the formation of the militia of young citizens, to the Council of the Three Orders' replacing the municipal council, to the arrest of some of the rioters, to a royal amnesty, to the official manipulations of the price of bread and meat, to the abolition of the entry fees on all food entering the city, and to more serious repression. The comte de Caraman the commander of the province, entered the city at midnight on 20 May, guided by torchlight, and was welcomed with an ironic victory arch erected near the Porte d'Aix bearing the inscription, "Conqueror of Marseille."[4] He suppressed the Council of Three Orders, disbanded the militia of young citizens, and replaced it with a civic militia that was dominated by the local nobility.

This arrangement did not last either. News of Necker's fall in Versailles put the city on a permanent war footing, ready for any eventuality, including a foreign invasion. Amazing rumors rallied former rivals.

[2] AM Marseille BB 290, ff. 31v–32v, letter to Gallois de la Tour, Intendant of Provence, 20 March 1789.

[3] Louis Stouff, "Les revendications économiques et sociales de la population Marseillaise dans les cahiers de 1789," *Revue d'histoire économique et sociale* 32, no. 3 (1954), 264. Monique Cubells, "Marseille au printemps de 1789: ville de dissidence," *Annales du Midi*, no. 1 (1986), 67–70, and *Les horizons de la liberté: naissance de la Révolution en Provence (1787–1789)* (Aix: Edisud, 1987), 94–5, 170–8. AM Marseille BB 290, ff. 36–36v, municipality to Monseigneurs de Caraman et de la Tour, 24 March 1789. *Déclaration de la Jeunesse-Citoyenne de Marseille, composant la Garde bourgeoise* ([Marseille]: n.p., 1789). BM Marseille Xd 2938. AN H 1274, Gallois de la Tour to Necker, 24 March 1789.

[4] *Lettre intéressante sur l'arrivée des troupes du Roi à Marseille, le 20 mai 1789* ([Aix]: 1789) BM Marseille Xd 2990.

Stories of the murder of Mirabeau; of the arrest of forty deputies of the Third Estate; of Paris on fire; of a horrible massacre in the capital swept the region.⁵ But the closing of ranks was temporary. On 29 July, the people of Marseille marched to Aix-en-Provence and released sixty-nine peasants, men and women of all ages. They were in prison because of the subsistence and antitax riots of the spring. Separate groups left Marseille between nine o'clock at night and four the next morning. There was a band with trumpets and drums, people carried even old harquebuses, and some pinned white, blue, and red ribbons to their hats. Once the marchers had released the prisoners, the people of Aix prepared a fraternal meal at open-air tables. A triumphal cortege of former prisoners, liberators and 300–400 youth from Aix accompanied them back to Marseille, where thousands cheered their arrival, including apparently even monks, nuns, Greeks, and Jews. Everyone wore the new patriotic ribbon. Soldiers put flowers in the barrels of their muskets; people wept openly. The justification for this extraordinary event was simple: high prices and speculation had made the people desperate, and the real criminals were the selfish rich.⁶ This was the follow-up to the expeditions that accompanied Mirabeau from Marseille to Aix in March and to Aubagne in April to support the patriot cause.

Another riot on 19 August led to the shooting death of one of the officers of the patriot guard. This originated in a rivalry between the newly formed Guard of aristocrats and the recently dissolved young citizens' Guard that had formed earlier in the spring. A pro-patriot crowd was pelting the aristocratic Guard with stones in the Place de la Tourette abutting Fort Saint-Jean. Some of the young guard intervened to prevent the aristocratic guard from dispersing the crowd. Someone, no one ever knew who, fired a shot that killed a young officer named Garcin. The crowd then drove the aristocratic militia from the square, chased them down, and tore off the uniforms of some of them. Accompanied by four torchbearers, they paraded the officer's body on a ladder to the house of one of the antipatriot municipal officers. Later they sacked the house, threw furniture and linens out the windows, and set them aflame. These disorders

---

⁵ Blanc-Gilli, *Discours prononcé dans le Conseil des Trois-Ordres Réunis, au Conseil Municipal ordinaire de la Ville de Marseille, le 18 juillet 1789 et publié à la demande qui en a été faite* (1789). BM Marseille Xd 2959.

⁶ Mathieu Blanc-Gilli, *Le triomphe de l'Humanité. Récit de l'expédition du Peuple de Marseille à Aix pour délivrer les Prisonniers de différens pays de la Provence, accusés de séditieux* (n.p.: 1789). BM Marseille 5041. Anonymous, *L'Heureuse journée ou le triomphe des braves marsaillais* (n.p.: [1789]). AM Toulon L 60.

led to the arrest of twenty-seven men, including the future Jacobin leaders, Trophime Rebecquy and Omer Granet.[7] The allegation was that they,
along with other future Jacobins like Brémond, the Reynauds, and Mossy
the younger, had made incendiary speeches and motions from the tables
at the café Français that incited the crowd.[8]

These arrests became a public relations disaster for the government. It
assigned the case to a prevotal court under the comte de Bournissac, a
court that judged even capital cases without appeal and whose verdicts
were to be carried out immediately. The court's enemies, like Mirabeau
in the National Assembly, also denounced its frightening secrecy, its
arbitrariness, its confining of the accused under inhuman conditions. Its
defenders denied all this. They claimed that the accused had genuine
legal protections, that only three accused had been moved to the island
prison of Château d'If at the mouth of the harbor at their request. They
could fish there and receive friends who sailed out to greet them.[9] The
details mattered little. The dispute was a contest of wills over judicial,
and ultimately royal authority over the city.

Authority lost the debate, thanks to Mirabeau. On 26 January 1790, he
delivered a passionate speech to the National Assembly. He alleged that
Bournissac had already judged the affair in his mind, that many would be
going to the scaffold, that the government's motive was not punishment
for rioting but political repression. The accused were defenders of the
parti populaire, in the dock for denouncing abuses the previous spring
and for being involved in the liberation of the prisoners in Aix. They
were not responsible for any violence or arson; outsiders, brigands, taking

---

[7] Anonymous, *Siège de la tourrete ou les evenemens des 23 Mars et 19 Août 1789* (Lau-
sanne: 1789). BM Marseille Xd 2934. *Quès-A-Co? ou Histoire des troubles et révolutions
modernes de Marseille, 1789* (Paris: Cailleau, 1789). BM Marseille Xd 2958. *Quatrième
supplément au Journal de Provence, Du Samedi 19 Août 1789* in AN DXXIX 54. C.
Lourde, *Histoire de la Révolution à Marseille et en Provence: de 1789 au Consulat*,
3 vols. (Marseille: Laffitte, 1974), i, 100–12. Busquet, *Histoire de Marseille*, 325–6. Laurent Lautard, *Esquisses historiques: Marseille depuis 1789 jusqu'en 1815; par un vieux
Marseillais*, 2 vols. (Marseille: Impr. de M. Olive, 1844), i, 54–6. Un Citoyen [Antoine
Brémond Julien], *Lettre a messieurs les représentans de la cite au Conseil municipal de
Marseille.*

[8] AN DXXIX 53 d. 160, fragment of interrogation of Joseph Savourin, n.d.

[9] *AP*, x, 257–8, 427–8, speeches of Mirabeau and the abbé Maury, sessions of 26 November
and 8 December 1789. The court had been established earlier in May 1789 with jurisdiction over riot and disturbance. See BM Marseille, Collection Léon, vii, 360–70. See
also Toussaint Pascal, *Mémoire présenté à l'Assemblée Nationale par les Sieurs Toussaint
Pascal, François-Omer Granet, & François-Trophime Rebecquy, détenus au Donjon du
Chateau-d'If* (Marseille: De l'Imprimerie de Jean Mossy, 1789), BM Marseille Xd 2957.

advantage of a chaotic situation, had done these things and the citizens had chased them away. A wave of arbitrary arrests, often in the middle of the night, interrupting the most tragic family moments (he cited a man being arrested as his wife was dying), illegal arrests, violation of decrees of the National Assembly, and capricious procedures completed the picture. Mirabeau meant to develop an image in his listeners' minds of a city in fear, subject to Bournissac's personal vengeance. If he is allowed to succeed, he said in his peroration, the city will be enslaved. Far in the future, old men will show their children the scaffolds on which men died for demanding liberty. Dramatic as the speech was, Mirabeau proposed a moderate solution: that the case be tried before the regular royal courts of Marseille.[10] The Assembly adopted this position on 12 March.[11]

Meanwhile, the patriots won the municipal elections of 12 February. The electorate delivered a major rebuke to Bournissac and the prevotal court because those with the largest majorities either were accused or were in prison. This was a victory won without many votes from the very poor either, as the old tax rolls still defined the right of active citizenship. Patriot support must have derived from a combination of the poor who cheered them on and from the relatively small number of active citizens. The election sparked a large celebration as well. The forts fired their cannon; an artist quickly painted a large tableau of Liberty presiding over the new municipal officers that would hang in the town hall; and the crowd fêted the new municipal officers as they paraded through the city with "cries of joy and benediction." This popular acclaim also celebrated the community, for the patriots' victory belonged to everyone. It also expunged the divisive past. "All the Citizens melded together," the *Annales Patriotiques* reported, "now only formed a single family. Joy and peace shone in everyone's eyes, in everyone's heart."[12] The ceremony marked the end of a period of strife and the beginning of another of wholeness and serenity. Left unsaid was the inference that the enemies were outsiders like Bournissac or Mirabeau's brigands. Such rhetoric simplified a more complex reality, but it did provide a handy reference on how to understand opposition if the community splintered again.

Bournissac resigned himself to the result of the election, observing that most of the winners were "notoriously turbulent men." He went on to

---

[10] *AP*, xi, 332–49, session of 26 January 1790.

[11] Ibid., xii, 140, session of 12 March 1790. The prisoners were released on 1 April and placed under house arrest while proceedings continued because the long imprisonment had damaged their health (*Annales patriotiques de Marseille* 9, [n.d.], 128).

[12] Ibid., 9, [n.d., after 17 February 1790].

report that the excitement was so great that his life was now in danger. All members of the tribunal were now at risk "from the men of blood to which Marseille has just been subject."[13]

Sovereign Justice

Another challenge from an outsider again provoked a massive response.[14] On the evening of 20 March, the marquis d'Ambert, colonel of the Royal Marine regiment, refused to identify himself to the guard at the Porte d'Aix as he entered the city. Worse, he seized a guard by the collar and violently insulted the new council and the National Guard. He also challenged the National Guard to fight with his men. No one dismissed this as the intemperate language of a cartoon aristocrat who was clearly spoiling for a fight. Instead, the next morning, a Sunday, as word raced through the streets and cafés, a huge crowd appeared before the town hall demanding justice. Soon the whole city was in an uproar. Thousands of guardsmen from the village of Allauch and from as far away as Toulon roamed the streets. An officer of the Royal Marine, Bernadotte, the future marshal of Napoléon, promised that the corps would not intervene to save their colonel, so at least a clash with the soldiers would not occur. For some reason, d'Ambert showed up at the town hall at midmorning. Authorities barely restrained the furious crowd. As he took refuge, the people "demanded justice loudly and threatened to carry it out themselves." Some threatened to behead him. The stand off continued into the next day. The council laid down barrels filled with earth around the town hall with the openings of the hall defended with cannon. More cannon in the vestibule of the building provided a second line of defense. More than

---

[13] AN DXXIX 53 d. 160, letter to *garde des sceaux*, 6 February 1790.

[14] The story is taken from *Annales patriotiques de Marseille* 9, [n.d.], 115–19. *Anecdotes curieuses. Détail historique de l'affaire de M. ci-devant Marquis d'Ambert, Colonel du Régiment de Royal-la-Marine. Extrait du Journal Patriotique Sortie triomphante des Victimes innocentes de l'Aristocratie* (Marseille: De l'Imprimerie de Jean Mossy, Père & Fils, 1790), BM Marseille Xd 3043. Also the report of the *comité des rapports* in AP, xii, 378–9, session of 27 March 1790, reprinted in Jh. F. M Goupilleau, *Satisfaction honorable et complète pour les Patriotes marseillais. Rapport fait...*, par Me Goupillot... de l'Assemblée Nationale, sur l'affaire du ci-devant Marquis d'Ambert, Colonel du Régiment Royal-la-Marine* (Marseille: Mossy, 1790), BM Marseille Xd 3171. Also Lourde, *Histoire de la Révolution à Marseille*, 227–42, and Georges Guibal, *Mirabeau et la Provence* (Paris: A. Fontemoing, 1901), 218–31. AN D XXIX 54 d. 162, "Information prise par nous Jean-François Lieutaud, lieutenant général de police et officier municipal...," 23 March 1790.

three hundred men remained on guard until the crowd dissipated some time later.

The *Annales patriotiques de Marseille* took this incident as a sign of the crowd's restraint and the good sense of the municipal administration. In fact, it was an omen. Moreover, the crowd's threats to impose justice on its own reflected a desire to punish, not to defend itself. The d'Ambert Affair did not pose a physical threat so much as a moral outrage to them. And this outrage could raise thousands of protesters from far away and from within the city. Once protesters departed from their routines, once they swarmed, the possibility of violence accompanied them. As it happened, the outcome failed to satisfy the crowd. Authorities released d'Ambert. The city's Districts (or wards) were outraged. As he was released from his two-week ordeal, a sizable escort took him to the Porte de Rome to protect him from furious national guardsmen who left their posts to threaten him.[15]

Only potential threats drove the liberation of the 'Bastilles of Marseille, the three forts, on 30 April–1 May. The seizure was not spontaneous. A few days before the dramatic events, the Club had enlisted the city's Districts in a proposal that patrolling the forts be shared by the army and the National Guard.[16] The municipality later claimed the forts had to be seized to forestall a plot that ministers in Paris were masterminding to recapture the city. After the defeat of Bournissac's repression and the forced withdrawal of royal troops, ministers would use the forts as a new base. The municipality cited as evidence the accumulation of provisions in the forts and the training of cannon filled with grapeshot on the docks and at the town hall rather than on possible foreign enemies. The commanders refused any explanation for this ominous behavior, so the city risked becoming "the tragic spectacle of ministerial vengeance."[17] Patriots added another dimension involving shady dispatches from Nice

15 Aihaud, *Dénonciation du lieutenant-général-Criminel de Marseille à l'Assemblée Nationale. Extrait de la Délibération du District de la Loge N° 18, transféré au Palais* (Marseille: Chez Jean Mossy, Père & Fils, 1790), BM Marseille 3039. *Précis de ce qui s'est passé à Marseille relativement à l'affaire de M. le marquis d'Ambert*, ibid., Xd 3023. Jean Mossy, *Délibérations du District N° 4 aux Carmes Déchaussés, des 7 & 9 Avril 1790; auxquelles ont adhéré tous les Districts qui se sont trouvés assemblés lors de sa députation Délibération du 9 Avril 1790* (Marseille: Chez Jean Mossy, Père & Fils, 1790), ibid., Xd 3094.
16 AN F⁷ 3659¹, Beausset to Marquis de Miran, 28 April 1790.
17 AM Marseille, BB 291, ff. 159v–161, letters to Saint-Priest and to deputies of National Assembly, 1 May and 3 May 1790. Ibid., ff. 162v–163, same to Mirabeau, 5 May 1790. Quote from ibid., f. 169, same to deputies, 18 May 1790.

(foreign territory at the time) and the maneuvering of foreign navies. The forts could assist such a foreign invasion or prevent food shipments from entering the harbor.[18] In addition, a fraternal outdoor meal of National Guardsmen from Marseille, Allauch, and Aix on the Allées de Meilhan preceded this daring adventure. Perhaps the heady toasts, the high spirits, the satisfying meal, the joyous farandoles weaving in and out of the colorful banners, the crowds cheering from the windows and rooftops – perhaps all this encouraged the seizure. At any rate, at three in the morning, a small volunteer force of fifty men took Fort Notre-Dame de la Garde overlooking the city with a ruse. They claimed to the fort's commander that the attacking force numbered two thousand. Believing himself greatly outnumbered, he surrendered. The attackers claimed to be acting for the nation. Someone then ran up a flag just after sunrise. The wife of one of the volunteers was scanning the hill from her top window looking for the signal. She ran to inform the municipality. Some councillors, a few of them recently out of prison themselves, took possession of the fort.

The commanders of the other two forts realized what had happened and took defensive measures. They ordered drawbridges pulled up, openings barricaded, and cannon pointed out of the portholes. Hearing this, huge crowds, delegations, national guardsmen from all the thirty-two districts, and a vast mass of twenty thousand peasants from the surrounding villages, descended on the town hall demanding action. A compromise with the commander of Fort Saint-Nicolas at the southern end of the harbor mouth permitted the guard to share duty with the soldiers. Soon after, the commander agreed to release three thousand weapons to arm the National Guard.

The seizure of Fort Saint-Jean at the northern end of the harbor, on 1 May, ended with massacre. Patriot municipal officers negotiated the surrender of the fort, but while they were transferring weapons to the National Guard, an officer, Major de Beausset, ordered his men to

---

[18] Address of Brémond-Jullien at the bar of the National Assembly, in *L'Observateur marseillais. Journal patriotique*, 13 June 1790, 65–6. Reprinted in *AP*, xv, 721, session of 29 May 1790. See the general narrative in S. Vialla, *Marseille Révolutionnaire: L'armée-Nation (1789–1793)* (Paris: 1910), 71–80, and Paul Gaffarel, "La prise des bastilles marseillais," *Rf* 72 (1919), 314–25. Paul Gaffarel, *Histoire de Marseille sous la Révolution* (Marseille: Comité du Vieux Marseille, 1932–7), 42–3, a version that differs from that of the newspaper. For the importance of feasting as affirming community, see Catherine M. Bell, *Ritual: Perspectives and Dimensions* (New York: Oxford University Press, 1997), 123–6.

raise the drawbridge. The soldiers refused and crowds of people and National Guardsmen poured into the fort. They believed that the order to raise the drawbridge was a prelude to massacring all the patriots inside. Other rumors immediately flew about the city that the crowds had found cannon inside the fort ready to fire on demonstrators, filled with lead balls and grapeshot. Others said someone found a lit match near some powder barrels. As in the taking of the Bastille in Paris in July 1789, the crowd now believed de Beausset had been preparing to betray them. The National Guard had to rescue him and tried to escort him to safety at the town hall, several hundred yards along the quay. But Beausset escaped and took refuge in a wigmaker's shop. The crowd was now furious, convinced the Guard had let him escape and that he would elude punishment just as d'Ambert had. They seized him, beat him, and hauled him through the mud. Like de Launay in Paris, someone cut off his head. An exalted crowd, including some soldiers from the Vexin regiment and some women, paraded it on the end of a pike in triumph throughout the city. Someone attached other body parts to the tail of a horse, which then dragged the remains through the city. This was a great moment for the murderers, and the *Courrier de Marseille* excused it. Alluding to the failure to mete out justice to d'Ambert, the editors wrote, "These are the unfortunate consequences of the cowardly condescension of the Courts: the People will exact vengeance itself, when it loses hope the Laws will avenge them." Despite the murder of one of their officers, this was a liberation for the soldiers in the fort. They embraced the guardsmen as brothers, as if they too had escaped from slavery.[19]

Once again, a mass mobilization of the population produced violence. This time the consummation was the humiliation of an ill-tempered and arrogant man; the degradation of his body by dragging it in the mud; the jubilant display of the trophy; the discarding of the corpse by burying the

---

[19] *Courrier de Marseille*, 5 May 1790, 26–38, for the entire story; see p. 38 for the quote. *Marseille sauvée ou les trois Journées à jamais mémorables. Extrait du Courrier de Marseille*, N° 4. (Marseille: De l'Imprimerie de F. Brebion, 1790), BM Marseille Xd 3021. Also *AP*, xv, 495–9, session of 12 May 1790, which differs in important details with the newspaper account. Lourde's source appears to have been the newspaper account (Lourde, *Histoire de la Révolution à Marseille*, 249–65). See also Lautard, *Marseille depuis 1789 jusqu'en 1815*, i, 79–82. Rolf Reichardt, "Prise et démolition des 'Bastilles Marseillaises' événement symbole révolutionnaire," in *Marseille en révolution*, ed. C. Badet (Marseille: 1989), 53–62. Finally, Gaffarel, "La Prise des bastilles marseillaises," 314–25. AN F⁷ 3659¹, Comte de Saint-Priest to Président de Assemblée Nationale, 11 May 1790. AM Marseille, BB 291, f. 159, letter to Saint-Priest, 1 May 1790.

parts in two different cemeteries without a funeral ceremony; and finally, the assertion of the moral rightness of popular justice. Like the editors of the Jacobin newspaper, the municipal officers excused the atrocity as an "accident," inflicted on "this last guilty one" and "rebel." For them, the crowd had no agency. "The Sieur de Beausset," they wrote, "already condemned by public opinion, surrendered himself boldly [*s'est livré lui-même*] to the resentments of the people who were indignant at his excesses.... Providence seems to have abandoned him to its inevitable vengeance. He perished miserably in the crowd that overwhelmed him."[20] Somehow his murder just occurred. No one needed punishment because, by this reasoning, no one was responsible. Such perspectives allowed authorities to avoid investigation and punishment. Later the municipal officers charged that dwelling on de Bausset's murder was a deliberate diversion to blacken the glorious and justifiable seizure of the forts.[21]

When radicals formed the Jacobin Club on 11 April, several features of the Revolution in Marseille were already evident.[22] Unlike many other places where radicals remained in the second rank until the crisis of 1792, passionate democrats were prominent in Marseille from the beginning. The establishment of the prevotal court following the disturbances of 19 August 1789 provided them with a perfect opportunity. Apart from the three arrested who were in prison at the Château d'If, Pascal, Granet, and Rebecquy, the court's summary powers outraged many others: Charles Barbaroux, the young barrister and future Girondin leader in the Convention; Antoine Brémond-Jullien, barrister, tireless pamphleteer, and future town councillor; Etienne Chompré, tutor of young women and future official of the Marseille revolutionary tribunal; Chompré's attorney, Etienne Seytres, a barrister disbarred for defamation and a future Club firebrand; Mourraille, future Jacobin mayor; Mathieu Blanc-Gilli, future deputy to the Legislative Assembly; and so on. Several of these men later slipped into obscurity, or worse, deviated from the correct line, but until the crisis

[20] Ibid., f. 161v, letter to deputies of the National Assembly, 3 May 1790; also cited in Guibal, *Mirabeau et la Provence*, 250. See also their letter to the President of the Paris Club in AN F⁷ 3659¹, 5 May 1790.

[21] Etienne Martin, *Adresse du Conseil-Général de la Commune de Marseille, à l'Assemblée Nationale, sur la démolition des Forts, & portant une nouvelle dénonciation du Sr. de St-Priest* (Marseille: De l'Imprimerie de J. Mossy, Père & Fils, 1790), BM Marseille Xd 3075. See also Auguste Mossy, *Adresse au Peuple Marseillais par M. Auguste Mossy, notable* (Marseille: Mossy, 1790), 4 (BM Marseille Xd 3061), where de Beausset is pronounced guilty.

[22] On the founding, see Michael L. Kennedy, *The Jacobin Club of Marseilles, 1790–1794* (Ithaca, N.Y.: Cornell University Press, 1973), 30–1.

of 1792 forced some agonizing choices, many others remained committed to an enthusiastic struggle against enemies of all kinds. Several, whether they broke with the Club or not, would eventually die for these beliefs.

Distrust of the central government, but not, of course, of the King himself, was consequently very great. Even before the disturbances of 19 August, local leaders tried to keep royal troops out of the city. When the comte de Caraman entered Marseille after the disturbances in March and April 1789, he had to agree to leave his soldiers outside the city. The 19 August affair gave the government the pretext to flood Marseille with troops, about four thousand of them. This occupation instantly became another grievance for the radicals. The newly formed National Guard was a weak counterweight. Too many aspired to be officers, and the disputes over whether the municipal council should appoint the officers or whether the citizenry should elect them directly delayed the organization. Only the decree of 12 June 1790 that required the election of officers finally settled the issue.

This explains the importance of the control of the forts. Putting them under municipal control forestalled a counterrevolution. This would be one of the early examples of clashes between patriots and the military throughout the country over the subsequent next two years. Locally, the tension over the place of the military would lead to violent clashes in Aix-en-Provence, Marseille, Toulon, and Arles.

The seizure and attempted demolition of the forts was also instructive of a style of democratic practice. The seizures were the result of mass action. No doubt the protests of the municipality that they were a cork on a sea of popular hostility to the military exaggerates their passivity. Still, they did not initiate these actions either. This was especially clear in the attempted demolition of Fort Saint-Nicolas. Crowds simply showed up after the occupation with bars, hammers, and other tools and began taking it apart. Only after the demolition had been under way for a few days was the municipality able to stop it.

Spontaneous action found its apologists. Sometimes this was innocuous. At the local federation at Le Beausset in the new department of the Var, for example, delegates of municipalities, clubs, and militias swore mutual aid against all enemies. This laid the groundwork for the dozens of future expeditions to aid nearby oppressed patriots, and with it the idea of the spontaneous rising against enemies everywhere. Another example would be the attitude of authorities to plainly illegal actions or even to atrocities. They frequently tolerated actions like these if they sympathized with the results. The key that this had happened often lies in the construction of the documents they left in the archives. They represent the crowd as anonymous and faceless but at the same time as having complete control. They depict themselves as under great threat from the crowd and so they are helpless before it.

The struggle against the prevotal court and the military lasted eight months, from August 1789 to May 1790. The weight of that authority produced a theory, as yet not fully formed, of a democratic legitimacy that was extraordinarily radical. It is tempting to interpret this extremism as a desire for regional autonomy, but this would be misleading. None of the pronouncements from the radicals criticized the distribution of authority between the central government and the localities. Their critique was not Federalist, to use a later term. Instead, sovereignty belonged to the people, who could exercise it anytime. When that happened, all institutions had to bend. Thus, in early December 1789, Chompré was arrested for having criticized the military commander, the comte de Caraman, "who he argued was entirely subordinate to the authority of the people."[23] Another witness elaborated, saying Chompré had said that Caraman was not even "free... to choose the place where he wanted to have supper."[24] Evidently another participant had claimed, "No one could order the people and that the people ought to command everyone; that this was their right." The vesting of total authority in the people legitimized insurrection. Another participant spoke of stimulating the fishwives of Marseille to rise up, and that with the right foulmouthed speech [*discours poissard*], an army of women ought to revolt. Chompré again linked the absence of legitimacy with the desirability of revolt. Someone quoted a letter of his in which he said that, in March 1789, "the people of Marseille ought to have gone en masse to Aix [and to have] hanged all the judges of the Parlement from the trees on the promenades, that they were scum." Thus, from the beginning, popular justice was an expression of direct democracy.

Unlike other places in the region, including Aubagne, opposition in Marseille appears to have wilted. Dissident elements in the National Guard tried to close down the club forcibly in August 1790, but when that failed, their leader had to flee to Paris in disguise to avoid lynching. Others languished in prison for over a year. Meanwhile, the patriots

---

[23] Lourde, *Histoire de la Révolution à Marseille*, i, 134.

[24] *AP*, xi, 310, speech of the abbé Maury of 23 January 1790, citing depositions from the Bournissac inquiry. All other examples in this paragraph derive from this source and page.

and the Club continued their electoral successes. Thus, in May 1790, voters elected a complete slate of Jacobins as alternate deputies to the Constituent Assembly. Similarly, electors across the department chose Jacobins as administrators for the Department of Bouches-du-Rhône in September 1791. Four of the ten were members of the Club in Marseille, while a fifth was J.-B. Camoin, leader of the anti-*piquet* forces in Aubagne. The affiliation of the others is unknown.[25] Jacobins won the elections to the new Legislative Assembly in October 1791. All of the delegates from Marseille had been deeply committed in the struggle against the prevotal court, and two of them, Omer Granet and Mathieu Blanc-Gilli, had been imprisoned for their role in the affair of 19 August 1789. Martin, the Jacobin mayor, also became a deputy. Pierre Mourraille, a noted mathematician and unswerving radical despite his advanced years, replaced him.

The Swarm to Arles

The patriots of Marseille now had an exceptionably strong base from which to mount operations toward the rest of the region. Although there were expeditions to support patriots in Nîmes, Avignon, and Aix-en-Provence, the most spectacular and enduring were those to Arles.[26] Like Aubagne and Marseille, Arles had split into factions as early as 1789 over the same issues: municipal taxation and town governance. Like Aubagne, too, the ascendancy of one faction over another was precarious. Patriots, known locally as Monnaidiers, founded their Club early in 1791 to consolidate their good showing in the local elections.

Yet with the backing of the King and the Constituent Assembly, their opponents, the Chiffone, managed to take over both the club and the municipality. On 12 September, the mayor of Arles, Antonelle, "foaming with rage," as a hostile chronicler put it, persuaded the Electoral Assembly of the Bouches-du-Rhône, meeting in Aix to choose the deputies to the new Legislative Assembly, to act. It endorsed his plan to have all the clubs in the department raise four thousand men to march on Arles. Officers of the National Guard in Marseille, Apt, Pertuis, and Aix-en-Provence responded to the call immediately. "All the patriots must be ready to rise," Antonelle wrote, "and be ready to march

---

[25] ADBR, L 277, Procès-verbal, assemblée électorale, 18–19 September 1791.

[26] Unless otherwise indicted, the description of events in Arles comes from Sampoli, "Politics and Society in Revolutionary Arles: Chiffonistes and Monnaidiers," 143–255, and Pierre Serna, *Antonelle: aristocrate révolutionnaire, 1747–1817* (Paris: Editions du Félin, 1997).

[on Arles].... There, a monstrous league defies the nation... mistreats patriots and loudly cries for the counter-revolution."[27] In Antonelle's mind, the monstrous league represented far more than mere political opposition. The Chiffone takeover had historical significance. It shattered an era of fraternity, patriotism, and happiness. The consequence was "a mental aberration... that soon became demented, a perfect delirium, and this deplorable folly... [led to] a spirit of hatred against patriotism and persecution of patriots... a veritable fury."[28] To restore serenity after such chaos and fear, the Chiffonistes had to be expelled.

The news that Louis XVI had accepted the new Constitution and the royal declaration of 18 September persuaded everyone to draw back from Antonelle's appeal.[29] Nevertheless, as the guardsmen were marching home, the incident showed again an aspect of democratic politics. An appeal to rise against enemies brought a massive mobilization. Nor did this appeal have to originate with an official body. It could work through the clubs or any body that had a patina of democratic legitimacy. The Electoral Assembly had no business ordering militias into action, nor did it have any right to order the arrest of two Chiffone sympathizers. Chompré justified these measures when he informed the Department that the Assembly would remain in session to ensure that authorities took the necessary measures against Arles. In other words, holding administrators accountable overrode deference to their authority. Obedience was conditional.[30]

So long as the Chiffone was in power in Arles, however, nothing was settled. Patriots throughout the region, therefore, undertook a two-pronged campaign to unseat them. The first was directed at the Department; the other was to persuade the new Legislative Assembly to reverse

[27] BM Arles MS 812, "Mémoire historique et chronologique des troubles d'Arles..." 1791. Ibid., MS 632, Veran, "Journal historique de la Révolution dans Arles." Also quoted in *AP*, 640.

[28] Pierre-Antoine Antonelle, *Observations sur le compte rendu au Roi, par M. Debourge, l'un des commissaires civils envoyés à Arles, en exécution du décret du 23 septembre 1791* (Paris: Impr. de la Société Typographique, 1792), vii–viii. BM Arles MS 656 n° 3.

[29] *Proclamation du roi du 18 septembre 1791* (Marseille: Mossy, 1791). BM Marseille 5807.

[30] Much of the story can be followed in Louis Blancard, Raoul Busquet, and J. B. Riboulet, *Inventaire des archives départementales postérieures à 1789... Bouches-du-Rhône. Documents de la période révolutionnaire, série L*, 3 vols. (Marseille: Impr. de Barlatier et Bathelet, 1889–1923), i, 45–52; in Lourde, *Histoire de la Révolution à Marseille*, ii, 298–312; and in Gaffarel, *Histoire de Marseille sous la Révolution*: 65–6, 80–5.

the decisions of its predecessor against the Monnaidiers. Both campaigns succeeded magnificently.

The Club and the municipality of Marseille denounced the Department for its alleged softness toward the Chiffonistes. Because the Department refused to become anyone's docile instrument, the Marseillais determined to replace it. Early on a rainy Sunday morning, 26 February 1792, a force of National Guardsmen from Marseille and elsewhere, perhaps three thousand in all, dragging with them a half dozen artillery pieces, invaded the departmental *chef-lieu*, Aix-en-Provence. Their leader, said Lautard in his typically waspish fashion, was a wigmaker, "a general worthy of these soldiers."[31] Patriots overwhelmed the Swiss d'Ernest regiment. To prevent bloodshed, authorities agreed to confine the soldiers to their barracks and eventually to expel them from the city. They had to surrender their weapons. As a result, most of the departmental administrators fled. A spokesman for the disorderly mass of armed citizens, a man who "roared like a lion," demanded that the departmental administration move to Marseille. Referring to the "insurrection" in Arles and invoking the necessity of defense against the "horrible projects" of the aristocrats, he justified the demand as an act of citizenship. "True citizens," he said, "ought not to wait to be ordered to defend liberty when it is threatened from every direction. Consequently, you ought not to hesitate to fulfill our demand."[32] For whatever reason, the demonstrators appear to have lost sight of their goal of transferring the administration until they finally carried it out the following August. Nonetheless, the club movement in the Bouches-du-Rhône now effectively dominated the administration.[33]

The Club and National Guard also dominated the department militarily. The possibility of Arles being defended from Aix or Avignon was now effectively nil. Once again, the assault on Aix reflected many features

---

[31] Lautard, *Marseille depuis 1789 jusqu'en 1815*, i, 120. S. Vialla, *Marseille Révolutionnaire: L'armée-Nation (1789–1793)* (Paris: 1910), 221–8.

[32] *AP*, xxix, p. 407, session of 6 March 1792, Administrators of Department of Bouches-du-Rhône to Legislative Assembly, 29 February 1792. AM Aix-en-Provence, LL, 76 ff. 82v–89v, "Procès-verbal des Evénemens des 26 et 27 février 1792," 1 March 1792.

[33] Blancard et al., *Documents de la période révolutionnaire*, series L, i, 86–9; plus *Procès-verbal de la municipalité d'Aix*, 1 March 1792 in *AP*, xxix, 408–12. Kennedy, *Jacobin Club of Marseilles*, 100–1. See also AM Marseille, 4D 2, ff. 34–35v., three letters to Granet, Blanc-Gilly, and to deputation of the Bouches-du-Rhône, 26–28 February 1792, where they mention that 1,700 men had left Marseille before four in the morning on 25 February, joined in Aix by thousands of others from all over the Department. They heard nothing in advance and were powerless to prevent them leaving. Lourde, *Histoire de la Révolution à Marseille*, ii, 412–21.

of extreme democratic politics during the period. One of these was the swarm of patriots from almost everywhere. The Marseillais were also able to overpower the city because they had support from within. As they approached, a crowd prevented municipal authorities from closing the town gates. Further, the National Guard of Aix intervened at several points in the three-day occupation on the side of the invaders. This collusion undercut the authorities' ability to act. Nor was the invasion simply a Marseille-only event. Late in the afternoon of the first day, four hundred men arrived from Aubagne as well as from villages along the way like Roquevaire and Auriol. On the second day, unarmed guardsmen from Arles turned up. These arrivals could have been spontaneous, but the sequence also suggests some coordination among the clubs.

As frequently happened whenever a swarm occurred, someone attempted a lynching. The Marseillais claimed to recognize a recruiter for secret counterrevolutionary armies in Arles, and the crowd attempted to hang the poor wretch from a lamppost. A guardsman had to cut him down after they had hoisted him two feet off the ground with the rope around his neck. The crowd finally acceded to the municipality's pleas to spare him, but this was not the end. The town had to put a couple of refractory priests into safe custody in the town hall. Significantly, it also had to keep a watchful eye on the prisons, especially at night.

Finally, the authorities' description of the event had a particular cast. Throughout their report, they never named anyone in the crowd or among the commanders of their own National Guard, although they must have known some. The Marseillais were particularly faceless and authorities frequently described them vaguely as "outsiders [*étrangers*]." The crowd, however, did recognize the people they wanted to lynch, including an unfortunate Italian mason who supported the antipatriots in Marseille nearly three years before. The administrators' failure to name insurgents must have been deliberate, even complicitous. Administrators, of course, were in a difficult position. They had to explain why they lost control of the situation, and they were particularly convincing that the outsiders and their local collaborators were impossible to resist. The local National Guard had largely gone over to the side of the invaders, and the Swiss had disarmed the sentinels in front of the town hall. After sunset, the Swiss and the Marseillais threatened to fire on each other with their artillery from either end of the Cours Mirabeau. An artillery duel in the dark posed an unimaginable danger to everyone, including ordinary citizens in the cross fire, so the municipality was able to persuade the Swiss to retire to their barracks. But authorities sometimes failed to act, too. They left the d'Ernest regiment to its own devices after the Marseillais threatened to blast them out of their barracks with their cannon. In effect, officials were willing to abandon the Swiss because, they explained, some very unsavory characters in earlier town faction struggles lined up to defend them on the promenades as the Marseillais arrived. Punishing the radicals for the invasion would play into these people's hands. Thus, the Swiss were allowed to march out of town while crowds and national guards seized their weapons for themselves.

The second front against Arles was the Legislative Assembly itself in Paris. There the tactic was to depict the Chiffonistes as insurgents against the Constitution. They represented Arles itself as a new point in the counterrevolutionaries' master battle plan. The city council of Marseille even sent one of its members, the talented lawyer Charles Barbaroux, to Paris to lobby the case.[34] Everyone claimed to see the same telltale signs that had preceded the infamous rally of anti-Jacobin National Guards at the Camps de Jalès and the attempted pro-Catholic takeover of Nîmes in mid-1790. "The loutish and ignorant fanatics of the [Department of the] Gard... are flowing into Arles by the hundreds," a speaker in the Assembly reported.[35] The Club at Aix-en-Provence outlined the stakes for the patriots. Unless Arles ceased to be a rallying point for counterrevolutionary conspirators from Nîmes and elsewhere, the entire Rhône-Rhine axis would be exposed to foreign attack beginning with a Spanish expedition against poorly defended Aigues-Mortes at the mouth of the Rhône.[36] A preemptive move on Arles would be justified. The Marseillais could take

---

[34] See, for example, Loys and Barbaroux to council of Marseille, 21 February 1792, in J. Pétion et al., *Mémoires inédits de Pétion et mémoires de Buzot & de Barbaroux, accompagnés de notes inédites de Buzot, et de nombreux documents inédits sur Barbaroux, Buzot, Brissot, etc.* (Paris: H. Plon, 1866), 404–6. Charles Barbaroux, *Lettre écrite à M. le président de l'assemblée nationale, par les députés extraordinaires de la commune de Marseille et des patriotes monaidiers d'Arles, sur les commissaires civils envoyés par le roi dans cette dernière ville (17 mars)* (n.p.: [1792]). BM Marseille 5809. And his *Quelques-uns des mensonges du commissaire Debourge, dans ses observations sur l'affaire d'Arles, dévoilés par Barbaroux, Bourget et Esménard... précédés d'une lettre de, A. Antonelle* (Paris: Impr. du Patriote français, 1792). BM Marseille 5665.

[35] Lourde, *Histoire de la Révolution à Marseille*, i, 642. See also *AP*, xxxix, 614–6, *Adresse des amis de la Constitution de Nîmes*, 26 February 1792. And BM Arles MS 657, no. 6, *Copie de la lettre écrite par Mr. L'Accusateur public de Nîmes, Département du Gard, à celui des Bouches-du-Rhône, le 20 janvier 1792*; ibid., n° 11, *Arrêté du Conseil du Département des Bouches-du-Rhône, extraordinairement assemblé du 15 Mars 1792, l'an 4e de la Liberté* (Aix-en-Provence: Pierre-Joseph Calmen, 1792). Also ADBR, L 290, Department of Gard to Mayor and council of Marseille, 6 March 1792 (copy).

[36] Ibid., L 2045, "Adresse des amis de la Constitution d'Aix... à Assemblée nationale," 16 January 1792.

the city and disarm the antipatriots. At the same time they could purge
the local administration and the Department for permitting the canker to
develop this far. Indeed, the collusion reached right up to the "executive
power," which constantly adopted antipatriot policies.[37]

The invasion of Aix suddenly intersected with this campaign for action
against the Chiffoniste municipality. The Chiffonistes panicked at the
news from Aix. For them, the Marseillais were a disorderly mob, their
spontaneity a sign of danger, the flight of the Department on that Sunday morning a sure signal that all authority was collapsing. Stories flew
through the region that the Marseillais intended to liberate the patriots
imprisoned in Avignon – the very ones responsible for the murders of La
Glacière in the Palais des Papes. From there, they would move on to Arles
to wreak vengeance on behalf of their Monnaidier brothers.

Action was now imperative. Rumors flew about that the Chiffone was
taking Monnaidiers as hostages against an attack from patriot National
Guards. Others said the hostages would be suspended from their ankles
from the ramparts should the Marseillais attack, so they would be mattresses for their cannonballs. Others said their heads should be used as
paving stones.[38]

News like this persuaded an already-sympathetic Assembly in Paris to
side with the Monnaidiers. The deputies brushed aside the claims that
Arles was only defending itself as a ruse. The Department in Aix and the
Assembly in Paris thus took the offensive. On 15 March, the Department
ordered each municipality to have a tenth of their National Guard units
ready to march anytime. On 13 March, the Assembly went even further.
They ordered all prisoners in Arles released. They also ordered the formation of a large force of mainly National Guards based in Marseille, Arles,

---

[37] Charles Barbaroux, *Les attentats des administrateurs de la ville d'Arles, du directoire
du département des Bouches-du-Rhône et des commissaires civils, constatés d'aprés les
piéces déposées au comité de surveillance* (Paris: Impr. de la société typographique, 1792),
esp. pp. 28–33. BM Arles MS 656; BM Marseille Xd 2380. Barbaroux, *Quelques-uns
des mensonges du commissaire Debourge.* Jean-François-Xavier Ménard, *Opinion de
M. F.-X. Ménard . . . sur la situation de la ville d'Arles, et sur les troubles qui agitent les
départements méridionaux, prononcée à l'Assemblée nationale, le 12 mars 1792* (Paris:
Impr. nationale, 1792), BM Marseille 5667. Lagrange, *Compte rendu à l'Assemblée
nationale sur la conspiration des chiffonnistes de la ville d'Arles, par Lagrange, membre
du directoire du district de cette ville, et Pascal, Dame et Bourjeaud, officiers municipaux*
(Paris: Impr. de Guérin, 1792). BM Avignon 48566.

[38] AM Arles D2, 171–3, council session of 1 March 1792. BM Arles MSS 633, Veran
journal, 1792, near entry of 1 March.

Montpellier, Beaucaire, and Nîmes to root out counterrevolutionary forces in Arles, Avignon, and Carpentras.[39] Nevertheless, the Department lost control of the situation to its own commissioners, Bertin and Rebecquy, who independently requisitioned guardsmen. At least 1,200 Marseillais with artillery arrived in Aix on 22 March to the evident consternation of the Department. In fact, the largest swarm of national guardsmen so far was just beginning. Around six hundred from Aubagne were moving through nearby Penne, and another imposing force from Marseille was making its way to Tarascon. Volunteers from Aix appeared before the Department demanding permission to share the glories and the danger with their brothers from Marseille. The town of Roussillon in the Vaucluse complained that it could not support the volunteers pouring through.

Patriots claimed the Department was soft on counterrevolutionaries, but in reality, its officials were split. A small patriot majority had always been present, and after the invasion of Aix, it dominated. Thus, the official voice of the Bouches-du-Rhône could be as radical as any club. In December, for example, they denounced the small city of Carpentras near Avignon for leading the resistance to French sovereignty over the Comtat Venaissin. "Any power, any authority ceases when the *patrie*, when the people are in danger," they told the Legislative Assembly. "The people have been threatened, and still is. Patient during misfortunes, they are implacable in their vengeance, when anyone threatens their liberty, when anyone tries to force them to resubmit to the yoke of slavery which they have so generously broken. Until now, we have restrained their hatred against a [counterrevolutionary] town . . . but we cannot always master their resentments."[40] Authority then had to cede to the people in action. Resistance to the popular will was not only impossible; it was illegitimate. Moreover, circumstances justified the municipality of Marseille taking the lead. As they explained to the officials of the Department of the Gard, the sovereign nation knew of the multiple treasons. The nation summoned her defenders, especially her most fervent ones, the Marseillais.[41] Even the much-denounced Department encouraged a mass rising in defense of liberty. "Citizens," they proclaimed, "it is all too

---

[39] *AP*, xxxix, 636–7, session of 13 March 1792. Blancard et al., *Documents de la période révolutionnaire, série L*, i, 83–4. See also B[arbaroux] to "Messieurs," 13 March 1792 in *Mémoires inédits de Pétion*, 417–20.

[40] Cited in Lourde, *Histoire de la Révolution à Marseille*, ii, 131.

[41] Ibid., 321–2.

true that the enemies of the Revolution want to stoke the fire of civil war in the Midi of France. Rise up! Time is pressing, the crisis is drawing near. . . . Citizens, you took up arms to become free! We invite you to use them against the malevolent individuals who spread desolation and fear all around us. Your administrators call out for your support. Aide us with your zeal and courage and the triumph of the Constitution is assured."[42]

By the time the Department rallied to the idea of a mass mobilization, Arles was already under patriot control. It had wilted at the first sight of the advance guard of the Marseillais and their followers on 25 March. But this was no ordinary military expedition. As the Marseillais left Tarascon, hundreds of ordinary women, children, and old folks flocked along with the citizen-soldiers. The stream of people swelled as refugees from Arles in nearby villages ran to join, and when the crowd approached the city, others emerged from within to join them, tears streaming down their faces.[43] The Chiffonistes escaped to the nearly impenetrable wetlands of the Camargue just to the south to avoid reprisals. The decisive event for them was the change of ministry in Paris on 10 March. The Chiffonistes rightly interpreted the appointment of Jacobin ministers as a huge setback. It meant that the help they had been attempting to secure from regular troops in Avignon and Toulon would not materialize. Vast numbers of national guardsmen from the Hérault, Gard, Drôme, the future Vaucluse, and the Bouches-du-Rhône would overwhelm them if they resisted.

Yet the transition back to Monnaidier power was not at all peaceful. The Vauxhall and the Rotonde, both literary clubs for the well-off, as well as the hall where the Chiffonistes met, were razed. The commissioners Bertin and Rebecquy had to warn their men that "forced contributions" were illegal. Despite the warnings, the patriots destroyed some town properties, a few rural *bastides*, and a flour mill. Some of their leaders incited them to far worse. Pâris, a doctor and a future President of the Department, shouted that, innocent or guilty, the Chiffonistes ought to be hanged. In fact, some were beheaded. A crowd decapitated one unfortunate because he did not know a password and threw the parts into the Rhône. Several dismembered corpses were seen floating a few miles down river. Three other bodies were found decapitated near the Porte de la Cavalerie on the banks of the river.[44]

[42] Reprinted in Blancard et al., *Documents de la période révolutionnaire, série, L, i,* 99. Date is 8 April 1792.

[43] "Extrait d'une lettre d'Arles avec grand detail de l'armée Marseilloise . . . Du 29 Mars 1792," in BM Marseille, Collection Léon, xviii, 118.

[44] BM Arles MS 633, Veran journal, entries near April 1792.

For the delirious patriots, the point was not the pillage or the murders but the restoration of an idealized civic harmony, the balance that Antonelle claimed had been overturned when the Chiffonistes deluged the Club with their members. The restored Jacobins announced, "At last, calm reigns over our city, along with patriotism that was banished from it for such a long time. We give a magnanimous example of the moderation and mercy in victory that our liberators urge upon us. All our fellow citizens, misled by the factious . . . abjure their error and shower the Marseillais with benedictions." Our enemies, they continued, spread rumors of atrocities, but such outrages are the work of outsiders.[45] In other words, after the delirium and the discord, the community was whole again, its naive dupes forgiven and absorbed back into the fold, the enemy once again portrayed as divisive outsider. The process of restoring a serene community, however violent, could not therefore be criminal. Everyone would repeat this casting of recent history as disruption, expulsion, and repair frequently in the next few years. Both Jacobins and anti-Jacobins would write their history this way.

Aubagne was a part of these marches and countermarches of the National Guard. After Domergue and the Jacobins settled into control of the municipality, the Marseille National Guard stayed on to oversee the reorganization of Aubagne's Guard.[46] Many of the notables who commanded the Guard in 1789 had resigned over the following two years. While some of the companies remained in the hands of the anti-Jacobins, the municipality felt confident enough in the remainder to send them on local expeditions. Many of them participated in the final march on Arles in March 1792. They also showed the same penchant for spontaneous behavior that other guards had shown when the people were in arms. Around thirty of them descended on the farm of Mas Neuf in Mouriès-les-Baux near Tarascon, took all the bedrooms for themselves, ate the chickens and rabbits, and robbed some clothes. They threatened to burn or demolish other farmhouses. Camoin, the commander, tried to impose a levy on the entire village of 12,000 livres, some of it to be delivered in small bills. On their way home from Arles in April, many of them, perhaps several hundred, decided to sack the château in the village of Velaux, northwest of Marseille. Not only that, but some also tried to destroy the château while others carted away to Aubagne household goods belonging

---

[45] BM Arles 656, n° 10, address to "Frères et amis," 5 [?] April 1792.
[46] AM, Marseille, 2H 33, Domergue to MM le maire et officiers municipaux de Marseille, 18 February 1792.

to the owners. Their motive is unclear but the château was owned by the
Albertas family, who also owned some property in Aubagne and who
were major landowners in nearby Gémenos.[47]

The battalions of other towns and villages also participated in such
direct action. The swarms were responsible for many forced contributions, assaults on municipal officers and unpopular priests, threats of
hangings, confiscation of farm animals, and disarming the bourgeois.
Authorities did their best to control these actions. The National Guard
of Aix arrested seventy-one Aubaniens, who cooled their heels for a few
weeks in jail. But as in earlier episodes of crowd action, like the popular hangings in Marseille and Aix in 1790, authorities sometimes had a
hard time condemning the swarms in principle. The Department warned
against those who took advantage of the "credulity of the people," "to
mislead opinion through exaggerated ideas of patriotism and Liberty."[48]
Earlier commentators posed the problem of direct democracy very clearly.
If the people pretended to dictate to authorities they had elected, or if they
set unreasonable demands, public order would be overturned; all rights
would become uncertain. "No more public tranquility, no security for
anyone, the most formidable tyranny, the tyranny of all, destroys Liberty,
leaving no other hope for the best Citizens than to see anarchy replaced
by a one man despotism."[49] This was the beginning of the debate over
the legitimacy and the utility of direct sovereignty – it would be a theme
for the rest of the period.

Reflections

The march of Aubagne's National Guard on Arles and its attack on the
château of Velaux showed how far local politics had evolved over the
previous three years. From a protest on taxation and fees, the movement
was now a much broader campaign against enemies near and far. In
effect, the experience of the Revolution itself had radicalized local opinion. Antifiscalism died as an issue in local politics once the reforms of the

---

[47] AC Aubagne, Police – différentes correspondances, small folder on the Velaux affair.
AN F⁷ 3659², Procès-verbal, municipalité de Velaux, 5 April 1792. Ibid., deposition of
Jacques Daussande, 4 April 1792. "Extrait des registres des délibérations du conseil de
la ville et Commune de Salon," 5 April 1792. ADBR, L 3059, dossier of Coste, Berenger,
etc., April 1792, arrested for stealing bed linens at Mouriès.
[48] Ibid., address of 8 April 1792. Also in AM Marseille, 13D 28.
[49] AN F⁷ 3659², "Proclamation des commissaires civils envoyés par le Roi dans le Département des Bouches-du-Rhône," 12 April 1791.

Constituent Assembly became reality at the end of 1791. The new fiscal system drastically reversed the mix of direct and indirect taxes of the Old Regime. Municipalities would no longer finance their needs through indirect taxes and fees, but from modest surtaxes, or *centimes additionnels*, tacked on to direct taxes. Although the municipal banalities remained, people ignored them. Taxes and fees on food, therefore, disappeared. The heavy reliance on direct taxes did not affect landowners very much, as the totals for the taille and the *contribution foncière* were about the same. The new taxes did remove the caps on the wealthy so that the new system introduced real fiscal justice. It also more than doubled the number of taxpayers, but the addition of newcomers to the *contribution mobilière*, which replaced the capitation, evoked no protests. Possibly, people who had paid no direct tax before could find some compensation in the disappearance of the indirect levies that they no longer paid. The minimum payment for the *contribution mobilière* was also around 3 livres, just enough to qualify the taxpayer as an active citizen. As the experience of the Old Regime had shown, exclusion from governance could be costly. The right to vote could be a worthwhile investment.

Taxation and governance were inseparable. Yet the Jacobin victory of 1792 did not ensure popular governance. This insecure victory explains why the struggle continued, but it does not explain why local and regional politics became more and more violent. As fiscal issues receded, and as the power of the local and regional Jacobin network revealed itself, the brothers began to revive parts of the peasant program that had been in abeyance since the disturbances in Aubagne in March 1789. This would be a society with the enemy eliminated altogether, with, in effect, no need for struggle because the enemy was no longer. With each defeat of the hated opponent, with every magnificent expedition, with every speech that swore undying dedication to liberty, the scope of what was possible enlarged.

The shape of this utopia was modest: as their brothers like Antonelle sketched it, the ideal was a tranquil community of honest working people. But the dysfunctional, aberrant polity their unscrupulous enemies defended stood in the way of realizing this goal. The methods needed to eliminate this polity and this enemy had to be perforce aggressive and violent. Even existing revolutionary institutions would have to give way to the awesome power of the sovereign in action. The lynchings of 1792 would show another far more shocking example of extremist politics.

4

Murders in Provence

Some people got away with murder in Aubagne in 1792. And so the town took another step toward the massacres of the Thermidorian period and toward the *grande affaire*. The most spectacular murder of the revolutionary era in Aubagne took place on 18 September 1792. Shortly after one in the morning, a frenzied crowd, "composed of citizens of each sex and every age," hanged Joseph Jourdan a former *officier ministériel*, an official of the court who collected fines, in the public square.

The crisis had begun six hours before when the town council got word that Jourdan was "running the greatest risk [and] that there was the greatest fermentation against him." Public opinion was "accusing him of the crime of counter-revolution." Five municipal officers wearing their sashes of office ran to the Bourg du Mouton post where Jourdan was standing guard and escorted him into protective custody at the town hall. The crowd followed them and quickly invested the town hall. While the councillors demanded calm, people shouted one denunciation after another. "From time to time, frightful cries both from inside and outside troubled the town hall and forewarned a rage, a fury, and an impatience that was almost impossible to contain," as the usually laconic council minutes put it. The crowd insisted that a proper, legal written denunciation be drawn up, and the councillors, only too happy to stall for time until fatigue overcame the people, went along. Amid the tumult, straining to hear above the din, anxious faces now lit with candlelight, the councillors scribbled out the complaints against Jourdan. No one could denounce a crime but the anger against him was bitter and longstanding. The delaying tactics worked for only so long, and some began to demand further action. The arrangement was to permit Jourdan to leave so they could take him to theJustice of the Peace. He would then swear out a formal complaint, but, unfortunately, the National Guard lost control. With his wife and son screaming and struggling to hold on to him, some in the mob seized him. The councillors claimed they were powerless to stop the mob from dragging him "down the staircase and outside the town hall like a torrent rolls a rock broken off a mountain." No one paid any attention to the municipal officers who chased after the crowd to try to remind them of their civic duty to respect the rule of law. During the entire ghastly business, the mob sang the revolutionary song "Ça ira."[1]

At first glance the lynching at Aubagne appears to fit the model Pierre Caron outlined in his classic work on the September Massacres in Paris.[2] According to Caron, these occurred because the crowd was preempting the émigrés' and other counterrevolutionaries' plots to fight their way out of the prisons and to slaughter patriots. This in turn was a function of the external threat, the advancing Prussian army. Yet for the Midi and for Aubagne, there was no single triggering event such as the fall of Verdun that adds such explanatory power to Caron's narrative. In the first place, Jourdan had a past. He had been among those denouncing the crowd that attempted to disrupt the electoral meeting of March 1789. One of those he denounced was Dominique Pichou, now a prominent clubbist. Secondly, the region witnessed lynchings before France declared war in April 1792, and the rhythm of the lynchings does not track the fortunes of the war on the faraway northern frontiers. Fear of foreign intervention was a constant in the Midi, even before war was declared. Rumors of a Piedmontese invasion, an intervention from the Spanish navy, or complaints about inadequate defenses had been common since 1789. Fear of conspiracy also appeared from the very beginning. Yet neither by itself produced lynchings. In the absence of a triggering event like the fall of Verdun, we must look elsewhere to explain the timing of the massacres of the summer of 1792. In effect, the answer lies in the increasing intensity of democratic politics and in the patriots' raising of their ambitions. The powerful dislodging of traditional political structures and the fact that the successor regime was not yet settled opened a space to imagine a much

---

[1] There is an extensive documentation about Jourdan's murder. Aside from the sources named below, most of the story has been reconstructed from AC Aubagne, *registre des délibérations*, f. 107 meeting of 17 September 1792; A.N., F⁷ 3659³, municipal officers of Aubagne to "Messieurs les administrateurs du district de Marseille," 18 September 1792, 2:00 a.m. (copy). Another copy in BM Aubagne, bundle entitled "Police différentes correspondances, 1790 – An III."

[2] Pierre Caron, *Les massacres de septembre* (Paris: Maison du livre français, 1935).

more utopian outcome: the physical elimination of enemies. A catharsis in violence would produce a harmonious and tranquil community.[3]

Murder and Retaliation

Lynching was a common phenomenon in the Southeast from a very early date. After the murder of M. de Beausset in Marseille in May 1790, the crowd massacred the barrister Pascalis and two others in Aix-en-Provence on 14 December 1790.[4]

These lynchings were far from a sudden spasm. Pascalis had outraged patriot opinion with a notorious speech at the last ever meeting of the Parlement on 27 September that regretted the suppression of Provençal liberties. In his peroration, he proclaimed that he wanted "to live and die as a citizen of Provence, a good and loyal subject of the Count of Provence, King of France."[5] According to the Department, this speech was full of "unconstitutional, seditious and incendiary maxims."[6] The speech incensed public opinion and the rival clubs. The municipality ordered all manuscript copies seized from local printers. But the patriots wanted more. The Jacobins, or *anti-politiques*, attributed the municipality's failure to prosecute as collusion with the enemy.[7] Such a perception, that authority was failing to do its duty, would eventually justify vigilantism.

---

[3] Persuasive as Caron still is, the phenomenon of lynching in the Revolution is undergoing some revision: see, for example, Claudy Valin, *Autopsie d'un massacre: journées des 21 et 22 mars 1793* (Saint-Jean-d'Angély: Editions Bordessoules, 1992), where the emphasis is on retaliation and rage. For Paris, stimulating and argumentative: Frédéric Bluche, *Septembre 1792, logiques d'un massacre* (Paris: R. Laffont, 1986). Antoine de Baecque, "Le sang des héros. Figures du corps dans l'imaginaire politique de la Révolution française," *Revue d'histoire moderne et contemporaine* 34 (1987), 553–86 and especially his *The Body Politic: Corporeal Metaphor in Revolutionary France, 1770–1800* (Stanford, Calif.: Stanford University Press, 1997), where the emphasis is on the imaginary of violence.

[4] *Grand détail des évènements arrivés à Aix, au sujet d'une contre-révolution, dont les principaux auteurs, qui étoient l'Avocat Pascalis, le ci-devant Marquis de la Roquette, et le Chevalier Guiraman ont été pendus par le bourreau et leurs têtes tranchées, par Blanc-Gilli*, (Marseille: Brébion, 1790). NYPL 0347074, BM Marseille 5603, and ADBR, 100E 41. Anon., *Aristocrates pendus à Aix*, (Marseille: J. Massy, [1790]), 2. BM Marseille 5602.

[5] AN D XXIXbis 13, N° 142, pce 19, "Discours prononcé au Parlement par Mr Pascalis le 27 7bre 1790."

[6] AC Aix-en-Provence, LL 74, f. 9v., deliberation of 27 September 1790.

[7] Félix Ponteil, "La société populaire des Anti-politiques d'Aix-en-Provence, d'après des documents inédits, (1790–1795)," *Revue historique de la Révolution française*, 13 (1918), 39–43.

The attack on Pascalis and his associates involved a preemptive attack on an ethereal conspiracy in addition to reprisal for unpopular opinions. As later investigations showed, dubious characters had made approaches to ordinary people. In one attempt, a woman who appeared to be a governess claimed that the Democrats in Aix "don't want the Pope, and that they want to annihilate Religion. . . . That a bloody war is being prepared that will soon erupt."[8] Others said recruiters had asked them to join a society of mutual aid for artisans or for the poor. Others spoke of mysterious meetings in upper rooms, of strangers in blue or white coats, of coaches speeding by with curtains drawn.[9]

Two days before the murders, a violent confrontation between patriots and partisans of a new royalist club had broken out at one of the cafés along the promenades. The antipatriots, with the support of some officers of the Lyonnais regiment, rushed out of the café, shooting and waving their sabers while patriots returned fire from the cover of the plane trees and fountains. Authorities tried to appease the crowd by ordering the regiment out of town. The crowd fanned out into the countryside and seized Pascalis and the chevalier de La Roquette from their residences. The municipality took them into protective custody and requested reinforcements from the National Guard of Marseille. In fact, the Marseillais joined in the massacres. The crowd howled for the deaths of Pascalis and La Roquette as their escorts took them to prison. Already a patriot leader of the anti-*politiques* in Aix, the abbé Jean-Joseph Rive had advocated the politics of street justice. "Any man, whoever he is," he had written, "ought to have his head sacrificed on the street lamp, if one day he becomes an enemy of the *patrie*."[10] That night, the club leaders staved off cries of "A la lanterne! A la lanterne!" from its own members and from the contingent of Marseillais. Despite the efforts of the municipality and the military, the crowd surrounded the prison at eight in the morning on the fourteenth December demanding Pascalis, "He's guilty, he ought to die." They hanged Pascalis and La Roquette from a lamppost along the promenades. The Marseillais carried his head aloft on a pike during their triumphal march home, and the crowd finished the day by retrieving

[8] *Procédure prise par le tribunal du district d'Aix sur les plaintes rendues par Mr l'Accusateur Public, querellant en sédition, voies de fait & Contre-Révolution d'après les évènements arrivés dans ladite Ville le 12 Décembre 1790, suivie du Mémoire justificatif de Mrs les Officiers du régiment de Lyonnois* (Aix: Mouret, 1791), 129. BM Marseille 5608/1.

[9] Ibid., 131.

[10] Cited in Georges Guibal, *Mirabeau et la Provence* (Paris: A. Fontemoing, 1901), 410.

another "conspirator" from his *bastide*, bringing him to Aix under escort of his local National Guard and hanging him as well. No one prosecuted the perpetrators.

Vengeance, not fear of aristocratic plots or foreign intervention, motivated the Massacre of La Glacière in Avignon. On 16–17 October 1791, around sixty people were slaughtered in retaliation for the murder of a patriot in the Cordeliers Chapel. This was a premeditated reprisal that continued systematically for several hours. The attackers hauled victims from prison cells or abducted them from their homes, and took them to the Palais des Papes. The assailants then stripped them of jewelry and valuables. Soon after, they bludgeoned them to death with iron bars or gun barrels, or stabbed or hacked them with sabers, knives, and bayonets. They dragged them down massive stone stairs of the palace by their feet or hair. They tossed one after another into a deep latrine near the icehouse and covered the bodies, some still alive, with lime. Despite a huge wave of indignation that swept the country, the Legislative Assembly in Paris pardoned the perpetrators because they were patriots. One of them, the appropriately named Jourdan *dit* Coupe-Tête, terrorized the region for years until he was executed for corruption and embezzlement during the Terror.[11]

Vengeance also explained much of the violence in the civil war in the Comtat. In January 1792, for instance, a mob murdered the general who vainly tried to defend the papal forces in Cavaillon against an attack from patriots from Avignon. The killers believed that someone had lured them into the town while the victim prepared an ambush from hidden cannon. The crowd stripped the general's clothing, pierced his body with bayonets, and dragged the corpse through the streets.[12]

In February 1792, in Marseille, the mob strung up a woman, well known as a flower seller along the promenades. Her habit of taunting

[11] René Moulinas, *Histoire de la révolution d'Avignon* (Aubanel, 1986), 200–6, and especially his riveting *Les massacres de la Glacière: Enquête sur un crime impuni, Avignon 16–17 octobre 1791* (Aix-en-Provence: Edisud, 2003), *passim*. See also *Procès-verbal de l'insurrection arrivée à Avignon le 16 octobre 1791, durant laquelle M. Lescuier a été indignement assassiné, dans l'Eglise des Cordeliers, sur les marches du maître-autel. Dressé en présence de deux cidevant Députés à l'Assemblée Nationale Constituante, et de plusieurs Citoyens-Soldats de différens Départemens du Royaume* (n.p.: n.d.). BM Avignon Ms. 2540/8. *Relation des évènemens arrivés à Avignon le 16 octobre 1791, et jours suivans, publiée par les Notables, Administrateurs provisoires de la Commune de cette Ville* (n.p.: n.d.). BM Avignon Ms. 2540/10.

[12] C. Lourde, *Histoire de la Révolution à Marseille et en Provence: de 1789 au Consulat*, 3 vols. (Marseille: Laffitte, 1974), ii, 138–9.

patriots particularly outraged other female passersby. After one exceptionally noisy dispute, authorities took her into protective custody in the town hall. The crowd invaded the council meeting room, where, despite the pleadings and threats of authorities, they broke open the door of her cell and dragged her into the street. While the city's procurator, Seytres, hollered "Force à la loi!" from the balcony, the mob hanged her three separate times from a lamppost.[13]

The murders of the general and the flower seller were done in the heat of the moment. The mobs had a long memory as well. In January 1793, self-appointed judges in Aix-en-Provence concocted a trial of citizen Verdet, former president of the Department of the Bouches-du-Rhône. They hanged him near the *Fontaine d'eau chaude* on the present-day Cours Mirabeau. The executioners were not defending themselves but getting revenge. Verdet's "crime" had occurred much earlier, in February 1792 during the invasion of Aix. Some said he had called out the aristocratic Ernest regiment to defend the town hall from the people. In fact, he had run afoul of the Club who denounced him as an enemy.[14]

Except for the Verdet murder, these lynchings occurred before war broke out, so no one was in actual danger or responding to imminent threats. The mix of motives varied with each incident. Sometimes, fears of war and of aristocratic conspiracy were prominent; sometimes they were absent. Vengeance and reprisal against visible enemies were always present, motives that had a lot to do with establishing dominance in local politics. Moreover, the crowd never acted in a vacuum apart from authority. No one was ever punished for these incidents because authorities were broadly sympathetic to the crowd's goals, if not always their means. Thus, according to one commentator, the three hangings at Aix in December 1790 showed that the "people was blindly jealous of its new-found liberty and inexorable towards those who dared even to imagine subverting it."[15] After the same incidents, Blanc-Gilli, an official of the Department and future deputy to the Legislative Assembly, claimed that the events themselves proved "the existence of an infernal conspiracy whose aim

---

[13] AM Marseille, 4D 2, ff. 35–35v, maire et officiers municipaux to les députés du département des Bouches-du-Rhône, 28 February 1792. Further analysis in L. E. Talamante, "*Les Marseillaises*: Women and Political Change during the French Revolution, 1789–1794" (Ph.D., University of California, Los Angeles, 2003), 1–13.

[14] *Mémoire historique de l'assassinat du citoyen Verdet / (Signé : Pasturel, Verdet)*, (Aix: Vve Adibert, l'an second de la République française). BM Marseille 5615. ADBR, L 287, "Dénonciation contre Verdet," n.d., [December 1792?].

[15] *AP*, xxi, 550–1.

was to massacre we administrators, then the Patriotic Circle [the Club], and generally all the good citizens who have shown themselves to be the friends of the Revolution that has regenerated us."[16]

Summer of 1792

Throughout the spring and summer of 1792, the entire Rhône Valley witnessed a huge wave of antiseigneurial and antiaristocratic uprisings. Amid fears of an aristocratic plot, battalions of the National Guard, behind their own tricolor flags and marching to the music of their bands, set about demolishing the châteaux of suspected conspirators brick by brick. In the Bouches-du-Rhône, the troubles began at the end of March, mostly in the north and northwest of the Department, in the Districts of Arles and Tarascon. Militants vandalized the houses of the rich or of former seigneurs, burned archives and notarial papers, attacked municipal officers, looted wine cellars, raided forests, and so on.[17] In Barbentane, near Tarascon, and possibly elsewhere, peasants attacked the houses of the bourgeois and the former nobility. Unlike similar risings in 1789, the attackers included insubordinate members of the National Guard. Some claimed fiery members of the Club incited the uprisings.[18]

The hangings at Aubagne were part of a much wider blaze of vigilante justice. The incidents did not spread in ink-like fashion the way the Great Fear of 1789 did, with the news traveling sequentially and rapidly in well- defined paths. In 1792, knowledge of killings nearby undoubtedly had some influence, as did the knowledge that authorities would not punish them. General circumstances common to the entire region mattered,

---

[16] *Lettre de M. De Mirabeau, à M. Le Président du Cercle patriotique de Marseille . . . Lettre de M. Blanc-Gilly* (Marseille: Impr F. Brébion, 1791). BM Marseille collection Léon, xxvi, p. 47.

[17] Michel Vovelle, "Les troubles sociaux en Provence de 1750 à 1792," *De la cave au grenier: un itinéraire en Provence au XVIIIe siècle, de l'histoire sociale à l'histoire des mentalités*, (Quebec: Les Presses Comeditex, 1980), 221–62. Martine Lapied, *Le Comtat et la Révolution française: naissance des options collectives* (Aix-en-Provence: Université de Provence, 1996), 132–40. BM Arles, MS 657, pce 28, *Arrêté de l'administration de département des Bouches-du-Rhône sur les excès, pillages & dévastations, du 16 juin 1792* (Aix: Pierre-Joseph Calmen, 1792). ADBR, L 125, 22–6, 66, two letters of department to deputy Baille, 14 April and 4 May 1792, where the attack on the château of Velaux is specifically mentioned. See also Edmond Poupé, "La Démolition du château de Flayosc, 3 mai 1792," *Bulletin de la Société d'études scientifiques et archéologiques de la ville de Draguignan* 22 (1898–9), 34–57.

[18] ADBR, L 1533, letters of municipal officers of Barbentane to "messieurs [district?], 25 and 27 April 1792.

too. One of these was undoubtedly the anxiety over the alleged unwillingness of the government to protect the region against an invasion from the Piedmontese or the Spanish.[19] Except for incidents like the lynchings at Marseille, applying Caron's model of a fear of domestic plotters working with foreign enemies leads to unsatisfactory results. Crowds did not always kill because the victims were fifth columnists. Rather, the murders reflected the continuing struggle of factions within communities. Aubagne was a prime example.

Summer in Aubagne

Soon after the suppression of the Olive Festival, opposition returned. Antoine Sivan reopened his tavern without permission. "From the beginning of the Revolution [Sivan] has openly favored and protected these nocturnal assemblies under his roof," the council complained. Fears of sinister goings-on appeared soon after. At the end of May, some women, "whose virtue is very doubtful," dragged some other women and "children of the two sexes" into a "frenzied" demonstration against the "good citizens." With a drum suspended from her neck, the leader took her followers to the town hall, after which they dispersed. The council thought the menace serious enough that it called out the National Guard battalion from the *terroir*.[20] Two weeks later, a handful of young men set a large bonfire on the Rue Mirabeau (formerly the Grand' Rue). They also waved sabers under the noses of the municipal officers. All this was ominous because secret meetings, parades through the streets, and bonfires had preceded the Olive Festival.

Yet the anti-Jacobins felt threatened, too. In early May, "the people" erected a streetlamp in front of the houses of the Widow Jourdan and the innkeeper Sivan. At least two other lampposts were erected later. Illuminating the suspicious comings and goings at these houses was necessary, the council argued. In any case, lighting helped passersby dodge stones falling from the arches, and because they were on the main highway, they lit up the houses where people satisfied "their frenzied passion for gambling."[21] Anti-Jacobins took this as a threat to hang them. So, most

---

[19] *Observations de la commune de Marseille sur l'état actuel du département des Bouches-du-Rhône présentés à l'Assemblée nationale par Barbaroux et Loys, députés extraordinaires de cette commune* (Paris: Imprimerie de la Société typographique, aux Jacobins Saint-Honoré, 1792). BM Arles MSS 656, pce 13.

[20] ADBR, L 997, 23, letter of 30 May 1792.

[21] AC Aubagne, *registre des délibérations*, f. 78, session of 3 May 1792.

of the same young men who had set the bonfire cut the mock gallows down. This provoked a large crowd in response who shouted, "We want the lamps! We want the lamps!" The council maintained the ropes were too feeble to hang anyone, so the lamps stayed.

The bonfire and the attempt to tear down the lampposts incited a general search for evidence of counterrevolutionary plots. A crowd including some National Guardsmen burst into the house of Dr. Moussard and triumphantly carried off a suspicious letter from Antoine Jourdan, the former justice of the peace. Domergue himself led the search for more compromising material in the small hours at Sivan's. At dawn, the same troop went to another recipient of suspect letters, Sieur Tourneau. When they demanded that he open the door, his wife appeared at the window, where they showered her with curses. No one got in all the same.[22]

The anti-Jacobins protested in revealing language. "The proprietors [of Aubagne]," they claimed, "have been under the yoke of the most frightful tyranny for several months: a party composed of the poorest taxpayers has taken over the administration." They complained of threats the municipal officers, particularly Camoin and Domergue, had made at the time of the Olive Festival; of forced contributions for the various expeditions of the National Guard; hostage taking to extort contributions; and most spectacularly of all, alleged that "armed peasants" seized a pious woman from her bed, dragged her to the improvised lamppost, and put the rope around her neck.[23] Despite these inflammatory charges, the District of Marseille's investigation sided with the crowd and with the Jacobin municipality. The report glossed over the lampposts and reported that the town was calm. For the anti-Jacobins, therefore, the lesson was the failure of the local and higher administrations to protect them from threats. The lamppost incidents even suggested that the municipality would not protect them from illegal searches of their homes or threats to their lives.

Yet for the patriots, the enemy at home was just part of the many-headed hydra. They had always thought of themselves as part of a broad movement deeply connected to regional and national events. Just as the marches to Aix and Arles showed their response to the regional, so too the march to Paris showed their link with the national. The purpose was to remove the center of the conspiracy, the perjurer, Louis XVI whose vetoes protected the counterrevolutionary enemy. A half dozen of the

[22] Ibid., ff. 85–8, sessions of 15–18 June, 1792. There is another report, obviously quoting the petition, in ADBR, L 943, 101, department to District of Marseille, 18 June 1792.

[23] Ibid., L 292, "A messieurs Les administrateurs du département des Bouches-du-Rhône," n.d. [June 1792?].

most dedicated members of the club and National Guard set off to join the Marseillais on their famous march to Paris on 2 July. These included Dominique Pichou, the radical municipal officer, and Jean-François Etienne, the National Guard officer who had threatened the Moussards a short time before. The council opened a voluntary subscription to defray their costs – the anti-Jacobins would have described this as a forced contribution – while the club recruited especially in the *terroir* and vetted the volunteers' revolutionary credentials, just as the club in Marseille did with its volunteers.[24]

The club also set about organizing a petition to the Legislative Assembly demanding the overthrow of the monarchy. Such an institution was a relic of the Gothic past, they said. In any case, the King's brothers, the "sanguinary aristocrats," and the King himself were aiding the nation's enemies. They were preparing treason to oppress the "greatest and most beautiful people of Europe, [to return them] to the most cruel and shameful servitude."[25] The Club invested huge efforts in gathering the three hundred signatures.

Summer in Marseille

Such petitions were common in the summer of 1792, and Aubagne's petition followed the lead of the Club and authorities in Marseille. While authorities and the Club announced the formation of the famous Marseille battalion to Paris and protested against the King's vetoes,[26] patriots began spontaneously to take matters into their own hands.

Unruly elements staged a theatrical lynching in Marseille of Lafayette that played with his nickname "Hero of Two Worlds" and the constant depiction of him on a white horse. Lafayette, of course, had ruined his reputation in radical circles long before for his role in the Massacre of

---

[24] AC Aubagne, *registre des déliberations*, f. 88, session of 1 July 1792. ADBR, L 1974, "Les membres du comité extérieur de la société des anti-politiques d'Aubagne" to "comité extérieur du club de Marseille," 24 June 1792. J. Pollio and A. Marcel, *Le Bataillon du 10 Août: recherches pour servir à l'histoire de la Révolution française* (Paris, 1881), 93–136.

[25] AN D XL 7, doss. 12, pce 21, "Adresse de la société des amis de la Constitution, sous le titre des frères anti-politiques, séante aux ci-devant Cordeliers de la ville d'Aubagne..." 12 August 1792.

[26] *Adresse d'un grand nombre de citoyens actifs de la commune de Marseille, lue à l'Assemblée nationale, dans la séance du 19 juin 1792* ([Paris]: De l'Imprimerie nationale [1792]) in AN C 152. *Adresse du conseil général de la commune de Marseille, à l'Assemblée nationale* (Marseille: Impr. A. Mossy, [27 juin] 1792). BM Marseille collection Léon, xxxii, 23–9. *Adresse des marseillais aux hommes libres des 83 départements*, ibid., 257–60. Also in *JdM*, 12 July 1792.

the Champ de Mars in Paris in July 1791. On 11 July 1792, a crowd strung up an effigy of Lafayette on one of the promenades in Marseille. Around three in the morning, when all was quiet, officials removed and burned it. On the night of the 14 July, Bastille Day, after much stirring oratory and renewals of oaths during the day, patriotic feasting in the evening, and farandole in which women and children participated still later, someone hanged another effigy of Lafayette, this time with a slogan pinned to it: "This is what happens to traitors." The next afternoon, a justice of the peace took the thing to the Palais de Justice, where the people recaptured the "Zero of Two Worlds," attached it to the tail of a white donkey (donkeys symbolized fools who had violated community norms and therefore deserved humiliation and even death in many places in Europe – the white was a specific allusion to Lafayette's white horse), dragged it around to the sewer outlets in town, and finally tossed it into a sewer pit when the joke got tiresome.[27] But this was obviously a serious and not-too-funny joke. The rehearsal quality for the real hangings to come is clear: the direct exercise of popular justice, the vain attempt of authority to thwart its course, the attack on prisons, and the hanging and its aftermath. This incident also prefigured another feature of the lynchings: the demonstration of bitter disgust and mortification of a corpse through ceremonial.

The Legislative Assembly's declaration of *la patrie en danger* (11 July) arrived in Marseille no later than 17 July. It provoked a massive mobilization. The municipal council declared itself in permanent session, established a secret committee with unspecified powers, and issued an impassioned proclamation to the citizenry. The moment for understanding and compromise had passed. "The exterior and interior enemies [of the friends of liberty] have armed against us every slave they could find. Emboldened by the indulgence of the loyalty of the French, they do not fear the indignation of the people. But the whole of France has arisen. Let the aristocracy tremble, let the moderates hide. The moment for victory or death has arrived."[28]

The enemy was desperately close, as it turned out. Amid the excitement, a crazy rumor, so typical of the foreign-domestic plot phobia of the revolutionary decade, began to circulate.[29] Some said that troops,

[27] Ibid., 20 July 1792.
[28] AM Marseille, 1D 3, ff. 13v–16. Poster in BM Marseille, collection Léon, xxxii, p. 23, and in AM Marseille 13D 31.
[29] *JdM*, 26 July 1792, for the most detailed description of the rumors.

dressed in the green livery of the King's brother, the comte d'Artois, the white and yellow uniforms of the Hapsburgs decorated with the Bourbon fleur-de-lis, and, in case anyone missed the point, wearing buttons with "I serve" written in German on them, would soon seize the artillery in the forts at the mouth of the harbor and slaughter the sentinels. The conspirators would spare anyone who knew the secret password; then they would slaughter the patriots. The password was fiendishly macabre: the letters *MG*, which meant "massacre général." Once they had taken the city, the plotters intended to set fire to everything and butcher all the patriots as they emerged from their homes. After this, they would exterminate all the local administrators on the altar of the *patrie*.

Like all such conspiracies, patriots nicked this one just in time.[30] On Saturday, 21 July, someone announced the plot was going to unfold with a farandole, the pretext for large crowds to gather and to begin the slaughter of patriots. The patriot crowd seized one ringleader, a Sieur Boyer, a merchant clothier, from prison where he had been put in protective custody because onlookers had cried, "A la lanterne! A la lanterne!" Two earlier attempts on the prison had failed, but in the early evening, a large crowd demanding that "justice be done" made authorities begin official interrogations before a justice of the peace. The crowd interrupted the proceedings the next morning, seized the victim, and beat him to death on the streets. The crowd then suspended the corpse from a lamppost on the Rue de la Prison.

The same day, authorities seized two other conspirators, both fencing masters, but had to release them to a crowd that invaded the town hall. Incredibly, the crowd turned them over to the city jailers. But the next morning, someone discovered a pile of buttons embossed with large white fleurs-de-lis on a yellow background by the seashore. This confirmed the rumors of an imminent invasion. Despite the authorities' and the guards' best efforts, the crowd seized them from prison, beat them to death, and hanged their bodies from the lampposts. Later the same day, they hanged

---

[30] AN F⁷ 3659³, "Extrait sommaire des 4 procès-verbaux dressés par la municipalité de Marseille sur les événements des 21, 22 et 23 juillet dernier." Also "Extrait du Greffe de la Municipalité de cette Ville de Marseille," 22 July 1792. René de Chauvigny, *Le cardinal de Belloy et l'église de Marseille de 1789 à 1802* (Avignon, 1930), 119–25. Pierre Espeut, "Un faux complot à Marseille. Massacres des royalistes Olivier, Boyer, Beaucaire, Belan et des religieux Minimes Nuirate et Taxy, les 21, 22, 23 juillet 1792," *Provincia* 19 (1939), 59–92. *AP*, xlvii, 550. Caron, *Les massacres de septembre*, 367, 367n1. Lourde, *Histoire de la Révolution à Marseille et en Provence*, iii, 64–8. Laurent Lautard, *Esquisses historiques. Marseille depuis 1789 jusqu'en 1815; par un vieux Marseillais* (Marseille: Impr. de M. Olive, 1844), i, 137–46, 148–52.

a wigmaker whose intemperate language at the wrong time cost him his life. Once again, the crowd had turned him over to authorities only to beat him to death later while he was being escorted from one prison to another. The incensed crowd then hanged him from a lamppost. It was the second lynching that year – the first was the flower seller – that was based not on fear of conspiracy but on revenge.

Early the next morning, 23 July, they beat two monks to death, after springing them from custody in the Hôtel de Ville itself. Once again, authority was powerless despite endless appeals for calm, including a moving speech from the constitutional bishop. Women stripped the monks of their clothing and dragged the corpses through the streets. Finally, they hanged the bodies from the lampposts, and then later dragged and dumped them in one of the more prosperous quarters of the city.

As in the lynchings at Aubagne the following September and at Aix-en-Provence in December 1790, the documentation emphasizes an opposition between authority and crowd. This was the intent of the authors but it is not always justified. Although authorities used all the moral suasion they could, they shared certain features of the crowd mentality. Fantastic as the Hapsburg émigré rumors were, everyone believed a variant of them, not just the gullible populace. Thus, a general assembly composed of the municipal officers, notables, officers of the National Guard, and delegates of the Club met at the Hôtel de Ville to deliberate over the crisis. The mayor, Mourraille, informed them that "the deliverance of the *patrie en danger* demands the reunion of our wisdom and our forces. The enemy is attacking us from within and is threatening us from without. The bomb was set to explode within our walls, Providence exposed it and soon we will know all the points of the explosion."[31] If officials and the crowd shared a similar idea that political danger was a function of subterranean plots, the crowd did not set itself in opposition to legal authority. Rather, they supplemented, encouraged, or forced official positions. When that was inadequate, they took justice into their own hands. For example, the town council of Marseille explained that the crowd executed Boyer because they feared he would get off the way the marquis d'Ambert had two years before, despite his haughty insults to the National Guard. Moreover, recourse to popular justice was necessary, the council

---

[31] AM Marseille, 1D 3, f. 19, *registre des délibérations*, meeting of 23 July 1792. See also address from Department to Legislative Assembly, session of 7 August 1792, in *AP*, xlvii, 550. Finally, see "Avis important de la municipalité de Marseille," 24 July 1792, warning people to have no faith in lists of conspirators that were circulating but at the same time referring to the plot that had just been spiked (*Journal de Marseille*, 28 July 1792).

implausibly claimed, because the law was silent on what to do about traitors "who have so often abused [the people's] trust." The people had long regarded the two priests as "sworn enemies of the *chose publique.*" Everyone knew they had long been in contact with enemies in Rome and throughout Italy. In other words, authorities considered the lynchings ill advised, perhaps even deplorable, but not criminal.

The lynchings were a restorative. After the cycle was over, "Marseille appeared to be inhabited only by members of a single family, [whose members] spoke only a single language, the language of liberty." The guards fired off cannon. People planted liberty trees everywhere, with slogans like "Live Free or Die!" pinned on them. The planting on the Place de la Bourse was a scene of great celebration as merchants pledged their fortunes to *la patrie.* The constitutional bishop blessed it with the American consul in attendance. The official cortege wound its way to the *autel de la patrie* at the end of the Canebière, where everyone renewed their civic oaths. Spontaneous farandoles "where women of every class" mixed with the men, snaked through the streets. The municipality had to ban such joyous dancing to get people to go back to work. Further dancing continued into the night all the same.[32] The six killings in less than three days were thus a kind of catharsis, relief that the plot had been spiked, a celebration of a restored unity, an eruption of patriotic ecstasy.

If patriotic harmony was restored, the population still needed direction. The municipality pleaded for public confidence and support; reminded people that the city's commercial reputation depended upon orderly government within the city; and tried to focus attention on the major internal enemy, the King. The foreign powers were as menacing as ever. With the nation's attention riveted on the northern frontiers, the invasion routes through the Alps were wide open. Consequently, a combined ad hoc group of elected authorities decided to raise a volunteer force of six thousand men.[33] Like many other authorities throughout the country,

---

[32] Ibid., 4D 2, ff. 85v–89v, letter to Mr Granet, Député du département des Bouches du Rhône à l'assemblée Nationale à Paris, 31 July and 1 August 1792. BM Marseille, Ms 1419, ff. 18–19, lettre du 24 juillet 1792. AM Marseille 13D 31, avis de la municipalité, 21 and 24 July 1792 BM Marseille, collection Léon, vol. 32, p. 33, "Arrêté de l'assemblée générale" of 26 July, forbidding the farandole because "des personnes mal intentionnées" could lead the people astray, in ibid., p. 38. See also *Journal de Marseille,* 2 August 1792. See the letter of the US Consul on these events in National Archives and Records Administration, College Park, MD, Microfilm roll T-220, Cathalan to Jefferson, 1 August 1792.

[33] *Adresse des autorités administrative, municipale et judiciaires de Marseille, assistées des chefs de l'armée, et de M. l'évêque métropolitain; délibérée dans une assemblée extraordinaire, tenue à la Maison commune, le 23 juillet, l'an quatrième de la Liberté à*

those in the Bouches-du-Rhône decided to ignore the King's veto on the deportation of refractory priests because of "the danger to the *patrie* and the first of laws which is the safety of the people."[34] At the same time, authorities ordered the city's sections or wards into permanent session and mandated they make a census of all inhabitants and their weapons.

Summer in Provence

After the declaration of *la patrie en danger*, lynchings exploded through-out the region. At Toulon between 28 and 31 July, frenzied mobs killed about a dozen people, including a handful of administrators. These out-rages also followed a general congress of clubs at Toulon in which members denounced Lafayette and accused department administrators of being soft on counterrevolutionaries. Other lynchings occurred at Brig-nolles, Evenos, again at Toulon, and Cuers. The combined authorities of the Var tried to stave off further killings by establishing a special tribunal for the guilty, like their colleagues did in the Bouches-du-Rhône at about the same time. But they did so in vain. The cycle continued with killings at La Roquebrussanne, Beausset, Draguignan, Antibes, once again at Toulon, and finally at Roquebrunne. Overall, crowds killed nearly twenty people in August and September in the Var. They hauled some from con-vents where they had taken refuge or dragged them from hospital beds.[35]

The news that crowds and national guardsman, including those from Marseille and Aubagne, had overthrown the monarchy on 10 August provoked a new round of lynching. On 16 August, administrators in Arles proclaiming the overthrow of Louis XVI had just entered the Place Saint-Esprit when they heard that "a citizen had been killed and that his body was being dragged through the nearby streets."[36] Later, the mob killed two men, both of them dockworkers. They beat them to death,

l'Assemblée nationale (Marseille: de l'Imprimerie de Jean Mossy [1792]). BM Marseille. Collection Léon, xxxii, 386–92.

[34] Ibid., 347.

[35] E. Coulet, "Le massacres des administrateurs du Var (juillet 1792)." Paper presented at the *Actes du quatre-vingt-neuvième Congrès des sociétés savantes, Lyon, 1964* (Paris: 1964), 419–42. Gaffarel, *Histoire de Marseille sous la Révolution*, 368, 373, 387–8. Mal-colm Crook, *Toulon in War and Revolution: From the Ancien Régime to the Restoration, 1750–1820* (Manchester: Manchester University Press, 1991), 115–6. Edmond Poupé, "Le Département du Var, 1790 – An VIII," *Bulletin de la Société d'études scientifiques et archéologiques de Draguignan*, vol. 40, Mémoires 38 (1934–5), 177–8, 185–6.

[36] AM Arles, D2, *registre des délibérations*, f. 312, session of 16 August 1792. They posted a guard over the corpse until the Justice of the Peace (JP) could arrive. They were quicker removing the corpse of the other "citizen" killed at three in the afternoon. See also Fabio Sampoli, "Politics and Society in Revolutionary Arles: Chiffonistes and Monnaidiers" (Ph.D., Yale University, 1982), 269, 280.

stripped them of their clothing, and dragged them naked through the streets of the town.[37] One of those killed two days later was already dead when he was hanged from a lamppost.

When the so-called *comité des sabres* that organized the killings in Arles in August and September 1792 could not find two men it was looking for, members paraded their wives and daughters on the backs of donkeys. Men carrying lit torches hauled one woman out of her bed late at night. The assailants stripped the women half naked, pulled one of them off a donkey, forced her to her knees, and made her abjure the Chiffonistes and Christ Himself. Jeering crowds sexually molested other women. They beat and whipped some so badly that they died a few days later. This parade on donkeys was a traditional practice signifying humiliation, but the nudity and molestation were horrifying innovations.[38]

Later in September, the mob in Arles cut the throat of Aymard Pesse, aged sixty, a *homme de loi*. He had been "a counter-revolutionary, one of the leaders of the Chiffone party and whom the people have delivered to their fury." Shortly after, there were two other killings. The mob seized a mason from an outlying village, brought him to Arles and killed him. Then they killed a gendarme along the road from Tarascon, where they had seized him. They paraded his head into town on the end of a pike.[39]

Events at Pertuis showed the bitter struggle of factions. A mob dragged about six or seven people through the streets and then slaughtered them. The victims included some women and a municipal officer. They also pillaged the houses of about thirty people. They attempted to retrieve the mayor from prison, where he had taken refuge for his own safety. His allies barely saved him from hanging. The mob included soldiers of the National Guard and some municipal officers. The mayor's enemies

37 BM Arles, MS 812, *Mémoire historique et chronologique des troubles d'Arles depuis le mois de juillet 1789 jusqu'à 1798*, no pagination.
38 Ibid., MS 667, n° 4, *Il est temps de parler ou mémoire pour la commune d'Arles* (20 Germinal An III – 9 April 1795), 17–18. Ibid., MS 812, *Mémoire historique et chronologique des troubles d'Arles*, September 1792. Fabio Sampoli, "A Popular Traditional Punishment in a Revolutionary Context: The *Promenade Des Anes* in Arles," *Proceedings of the Annual Meeting of the Western Society for French History* 8 (1980), 205–19. *Déclaration des sentimens des vrais républicains de la commune d'Arles.* (Arles: [G. Mesnier], 1795), 3. BM Arles A 9388.
39 AN BB[18] 174, Extrait des registres du greffe du tribunal du district d'Arles, 28 September 1792. According to *Arrêtés de l'administration du Directoire du district d'Arles, qui, en exécution des lois des 20 Floréal et 4 Messidor an troisième, dénonce aux tribunaux les assassinats, vols, dilapidations, concussions, commis dans la commune d'Arles, sous la tyrannie* (Arles: de l'Impr. de G. Mesnier fils, 1795 – An IV), 6–7 (in BM Marseille 5673 or BM Arles MS 667). Ten people were massacred in September alone in Arles. This is certainly an exaggeration but is useful as an indication of the memory of events.

included the local club. The brethren invoked the sacred principle of
resistance to oppression against an authority that assisted "the destruction
of all the friends of Liberty" who "although invisible, protected us from
the blows." Although the causes of this incident are obscure, factions were
competing for the allegiance of the peasants. According to two patriots,
"these monsters" of the rival faction aimed at getting them, they who
"enlighten these peasants, [they who] make the advantages of our holy
Constitution known to them and who preach to them continually the
importance of supporting it."[40]

Two cases of vigilante justice occurred in Avignon, one in mid-August
and the other in November. In the first case, the poor wretch, an Italian
accused of stabbing a grenadier, had to be hanged a second time when
the rope broke on the first attempt. In the second, the mob murdered at
night and threw the two corpses into the Rhône.[41]

Also in mid-August, a group of patriots kidnapped enemies being
escorted to prison at Carpentras and shot them. For the Jacobins, the
incident was not particularly deplorable. "If something can calm the
painful sentiments that inspired a bloody execution," they observed, "it
is the knowledge of the character of the wicked people who have been
killed [*immolés*]."[42]

Again in mid-August, a crowd at La Ciotat, a stone's throw from Aubagne, "seized one Ladeveze, who was sacrificed to its just vengeance."[43]
This was the result of a longstanding struggle of factions in the town.

Throughout August and September, crowds murdered twelve or thirteen more people in about a half dozen incidents in Marseille alone. One
of them occurred at the very doors of the Club on the Rue Thubaneau.[44]

Finally, just a few days before Jourdan's murder, a crowd in the village
of Auriol, also right next door to Aubagne, hanged two individuals on the
Place des Capucines in plain sight of two commissioners of the department. Although the details are obscure, the commissioners were in the

[40] ADBR, L 125, 178, Department to commissaires du département à Pertuis, 17 June
1792, 8:00 a.m. Ibid., L 2045, comité de correspondance to frères et amis d'Aix, 18 July
1792. AN F⁷ 3659³, Copie de la lettre écrite au Ministère de la Justice par le commissaire
du roi, près le tribunal du district d'Apt, 18 July 1792, and Commissaire du roi auprès
du tribunal correctionnel des Bouches-du-Rhône to Ministère de la Justice, 26 July 1792.
ADBR, L 2075, Billard and Bayou to frères et amis, 30 June 1792.

[41] Moulinas, *Histoire de la révolution d'Avignon*, 250.

[42] ADBR, L 2045, comité de correspondance to frères et amis [club of Aix-en-Provence],
11 August 1792.

[43] *JdM*, 21 August 1792.

[44] Paul Gaffarel, *Histoire de Marseille sous la Révolution* (Marseille: Comité du Vieux-
Marseille, 1932–7), 101–6, special edition in AM Marseille BIB 6395–6.

village to support the Club against a faction on the municipal council. A battalion of the National Guard of Marseille helped the crowd. The bodies hung from the trees in the square until the next morning when a priest and two choirboys carrying lit torches buried the two unfortunates.[45]

Hangings in Aubagne

The murders in Aubagne, then, were part of a much broader wave of vigilante justice that erupted throughout the region. As it had elsewhere, the declaration of *la patrie en danger* spurred defensive responses and opened the way to people taking matters into their own hands. When they heard the news, the council at Aubagne declared himself in permanent session. For the following five months around the clock, at least one councillor was present in the town hall to order whatever precautions were necessary. Domergue suggested that the council requisition two men of each company of the rural National Guard to protect the council. Following the lead of Marseille, the council also decided to form a secret surveillance committee whose purpose was "to oversee the political situation scrupulously" and to receive denunciations. The club formed a parallel committee, the Committee of Prudence, that kept the municipality up to the mark. It even made arrests and kept in close contact with its counterpart in Marseille. Finally, the council issued the thrilling proclamation "Aux Aubaginiens [*sic*]:"

The external and internal enemies, seconded by a perfidious power [an obvious reference to Louis XVI], have armed all the slaves they can against us . . . [but] let the aristocracy tremble, let the moderates hide themselves, the moment has come for victory or for death. Liberty is a virgin daughter of the divinity to whom we can offer only a pure incense. . . .

Whoever dares, in word or deed, manifest sentiments of slavery can only be regarded as a traitor and will be punished as such by the legitimate authorities.[46]

---

45 Georges Guibal, *Le mouvement fédéraliste en Provence en 1793* (Paris: Plon-Nourrit, 1908), 7–8. Gaffarel, *Histoire de Marseille sous la Révolution*, 106n1. J.-J.-L. Barges, *Documents sur l'histoire de l'église d'Auriol, et de son clergé pendant la Révolution française de 1789 à 1804* (Paris: Goupy et Jourdan, 1888), 80–1, where the author's source is one of the choirboys. AC Auriol, *registre des délibérations*, session of 18 September 1792, citing an *arrêté* of the Department of 15 September. See also ADBR, 5Mi 262, *état civil*, Auriol, entry of 13 September 1792.

46 The steps and the manifesto are outlined in the council minutes of 18 July in AC Aubagne, *registre des délibérations*, ff. 89–89v. This followed the municipality of Marseille's establishment of a *comité secret de surveillance* because of a "saint devoir de veiller scrupuleusement sur la situation politique de la Cité" (AM, Marseille 13D 31,

The crisis encouraged participation in surveillance of enemies, but denunciation did not work in such a way as to reflect citizens exposing a tiny cabal of conspirators. Instead, they reflected general fears and made the faction struggle more acute.[47] Usually, the actors were prominent activists who would go on to participate in the Terror or in the *bande d'Aubagne*.

Some denunciations that the secret committee gathered were peculiar, as most rumors are. They do show how the public quickly demonized certain classes of people. Thus, one of the first denunciations came from the Grayrard sisters, who noticed a giant tent strung out along the mountain peak close to the château of Joulhian.[48] Others said that armed men also visited the château and that somehow the curé of Cuges was involved. The rumors reflected only baseless fears as it turned out. The women had misinterpreted the sunlight reflecting on the varnished roof tiles of the château. Ridiculous as the story turned out to be, it did show a common feature of the revolutionary period and the war: the belief that the local aristocracy and the clergy were up to something suspicious, perhaps even aiding the foreign enemy.

No one ever tracked down the next denunciation, the story of ghostly armies marching at night, hundreds of men and horses, apparently. Later gossip had it that many local émigrés were holed up at various *bastides* around Cassis, La Ciotat, and Aubagne. Some said that many citizens from Cassis had already been bribed with handfuls of *louis d'or* to serve as guides to the émigrés in the mountains.

Stories about secret armies gathering in the remotest areas unknown to anyone had a long life. Thus, one of the Sivan brothers – the very ones who denounced Jourdan – was named as a witness to a conversation in which a pair of market gardeners at the end of July had claimed, "How with six thousand men, and without anyone knowing [*sans que cela se sache*], could the coup fail like that and fail to get caught like this and like that [*il falloit s'y prendre comme ceci, comme cela*]?"

Other denunciations reported threats against the municipality. Some women at the washhouse claimed the municipal officers were scoundrels

---

Le conseil général de la Commune de Marseille, en état de Surveillance permanente, aux Marseillais, 17 July 1792). The municipality of Aubagne was copying not only the institution of a secret committee but also the very text of this proclamation.

[47] Another approach, relating denunciations to revolutionary ideology, is Colin Lucas, "The Theory and Practice of Denunciation in the French Revolution," *Journal of Modern History,* 68 (1996), 768–85.

[48] The denunciation register is in a bundle of papers in AC Aubagne titled "Police différentes correspondances, 1790 – An III."

and rascals. A fish merchant claimed the councillors were felons "and in a couple of days we will cut everything off." Sieur Venuse, a shoemaker from Aubagne, apparently said, "If only there were two hundred men like me, we'll see." Such threats were more than bluster and those uttering the disgust at the municipality were not as anonymous as might first appear. Three years later, the fish merchant and Venuse had become members of the murder gang; the man who reported on secret armies became one of their victims.

Specific denunciations reveal still more about the ongoing factional struggle. Thus Demoiselle Marie Beaumont denounced the cloth merchant, Louis Anselme Olive. She saw him with an unknown priest of around fifty years of age , hat pulled over his eyes and wearing dusty sandals, trying to get out of town by avoiding the guard posts on the main roads. As it happened, Olive had attended the *fête des olliviers*. He became a member of the anti-Jacobin *comité de surveillance* and then emigrated. Marie Beaumont herself was the wife of Louis Poutet, future member of the terrorist *comité de surveillance* and later victim of the *bande d'Aubagne*.

Other denunciations revealed some crucial relationships among the murder victims. A Jacobin militant, Joseph Sivan accused a Sieur Cazalet of saying that when the émigrés arrived, "they would hang all the clubbists. Joseph Jourdan, Guillermy the mason, and Pierre Gautier *dit* Figuières, talked of nothing but the business of the émigrés and they desired their arrival." Cazalet was the business manager of Pons Arnaud, the first lynching victim in Aubagne, and clearly a friend of Joseph Jourdan, the second victim. Guillermy would be humiliated during the hanging ceremony to come and move on to become one of the leading killers. Gautier had been instrumental in the bonfires of a few months before and would be the principal killer of Nicolas Gury, the former secretary of the Club, in 1795.[49] In short, the denunciations revealed the factions; they did not pit citizens against conspirators, as the revolutionary theory of denunciation assumed.

As it had elsewhere, the news of the fall of the monarchy incited the most extravagant action. From their new camp in Paris, Dominique Pichou and J.-B. Camoin, both municipal officers, leading Jacobins, and future terrorists, wrote an "atrocious and incendiary" letter to the club in Aubagne "to urge them to disarm and plunder [*faire main basse*] the bourgeois of the town." Another municipal officer admitted they wrote the letter to "incite all the members [of the club] to fall on the bourgeois and

---

[49] Ibid., "Procès-verbal de la municipalité d'Aubagne, relatif au Sr Jourdan."

the other honest men of the town and hang them, break them, and crush them," while claiming to the clubbists "that this is the Parisian law."[50]

Not having the actual letter from Paris is unfortunate, but other towns witnessed similar incitement to direct action. At Manosque in the Basses-Alpes, for example, on 4 August, a crowd of two hundred people hanged the chaplain of the local prison, an infirm and nearly blind monk in his eighties, from a tree. The next day, they hanged three more priests they had hauled out of the prison.[51] Some said the club at Marseille incited these outrages. The mayor claimed the Marseillais had written a letter to the brothers in Manosque that said, "The *patrie* is in danger, the time for great blows has come. Marseille has given the example, Toulon has followed, Paris is shaking. Providence has delivered three rascals to you, strike!"[52] The "great blows" must have been the lynchings in Marseille and Toulon at the end of July. In any case, about ten days later, the Marseille club's patriotic missionary, François Isoard, arrived and menaced the antipatriots with more vengeance to come. He said he would call on ten thousand Marseillais to retaliate "for the calumnies of the aristocrats... that there would be no quarter, that either they would take his life, or he theirs."[53] Such wild talk panicked many in the town so much the municipality took Isoard and his companions into protective custody. This only provoked an expedition, another swarm, of five hundred national guardsmen from Aix-en-Provence, Pertuis, and smaller towns. They levied a heavy contribution on Manosque, an indemnity according to them for their expenses, a forced contribution or punishment according to others. For the outsiders, however, such interventions were essential to fulfilling their promise to aid oppressed patriots everywhere.

The notion that the moment had arrived to seize their liberty occurred at Aubagne as well. In a few weeks, the crowds attacked ecclesiastical institutions, particularly the Ursuline nuns and the summer residence of the bishops of Marseille; captured the baking ovens; and most spectacularly of all, hanged two political enemies, Pons Arnaud and Joseph Jourdan.

The incidents began with a renewal of the struggle against the town's baking ovens and this time, crowds were determined to settle the issue for

[50] ADBR, L 3556, *procès-verbal* against Etienne Suzan, 22 July 1793. Dominique Pichou was one of the alleged signatories.
[51] H. Brun, "Manosque révolutionnaire," *Annales des Basses-Alpes. Revue Trimestriel de la société scientifique et littéraire des Basses-Alpes* 15 (1911), 31–3.
[52] Cited in Jacques Guilhaumou, *Marseille républicaine (1791–1793)* (Paris: Presses de la Fondation nationale des sciences politiques, 1992), 109.
[53] ADBR, L 2045, municipality of Manosque to [?], 20 August 1792. Copy in AC Aix-en-Provence, LL 250.

themselves. At seven in the morning on 24 August, two young men beating drums headed a parade of women armed with pikes. They sang the "beloved 'Ça ira.'" A large crowd of other women and children "of the two sexes" followed. The demonstrators captured the four baking ovens. The women drove the two town criers before their menacing pikes. They protested the high fees for fuel and baking in the ovens. Although the National Guard soon arrived in force, no one wanted a violent confrontation. Authorities appeased the crowd by letting events take their course. The women forced the town criers to announce "on behalf of the people and the *citoyennes patriotes guerrières*" that baking fees and the price of charcoal would be cut in half.

Later that day, the Ursuline nuns asked for the protection of the municipality when an "immense multitude" broke into the convent in the early afternoon and began smashing furniture. The crowd also demanded that the nuns leave immediately. After a meeting with the town councillors in the refectory, the terrified nuns agreed to leave, provided they could take their belongings. The town councillors eventually persuaded the crowd to disperse, but not before some uttered bloodcurdling threats against some municipal officers, threats that included hanging them from the public lampposts.[54]

While the crowd was sacking the Ursulines nunnery, another "immense people of every age and every sex" broke into the château of Belloi, the site of the *fête des olliviers*, and began smashing furniture there as well. Children set fire to the broken pieces and someone else set fire to the Grand Bastide, a farmhouse that belonged to the château. Later that night, according to the council, those "suspected of sentiments contrary to the Revolution, lost their minds, because this immortal Revolution was going so well and, in an excess of folly, they threw their furniture out of their windows" into the street. Of course, it is very unlikely that the victims destroyed their own furniture. No matter, all along the Rue Mirabeau and the Toulon road, children again set fire to the furnishings. These must be the events the historical memoirs drafted later in the decade referred to as the systematic vandalism of the houses of the antipatriots. The memoirs even assert that the crowd burned eight to ten houses as well, although the municipality's report says nothing about this.[55] At any rate, the council warned parents that their children were in danger from

[54] AC Aubagne, "Extrait d'une déclaration faite par le citoyen Joseph Arnaud, ex-officier municipal d'Aubagne," 31 March 1793.
[55] AN F¹ᶜIII, Bouches-du-Rhône 6, "Notice historique sur la commune d'Aubagne," n.d. [An IX].

falling pieces of tables, beds, and wardrobes. They also warned that the parents would be responsible for any fires that spread to the rest of the town and demanded that parents take their offspring home. The rest of the night was apparently calm, and a doubled National Guard patrol maintained order while the councillors stayed up all night alert to any eventuality.

Early the next morning on 25 July, a crowd sacked and torched another *bastide*, La Demande. They threw the debris from the fire into the well or into the river Huveaune. The same thing happened to the *bastide* of Mon Plaisir, which belonged to M. Ramel, the last mayor of the Old Regime. They vandalized other isolated houses and set fire to their inhabitants' furniture. The National Guard officer reported that "they could no longer be masters of the people who are in an uncontrollable fury."[56] Because force would no longer work, someone thought a distraction might. So the council had some citizens begin a farandole. It was so successful that more and more people joined, and soon it filled the entire town. By two in the afternoon all danger was over. That evening, the farandole began again, amid cries of "Vive la Nation!" and "Ça ira; ça va." As night fell, everyone went home.

These riots did not come out of nowhere, nor were they a sudden convulsion of anger. Instead they had a context that stretched back to the Old Regime. The Jacobin council sided with the rioters and justified the action in ways that showed they, too, knew the legal history of the ovens. The council characterized the privatization in 1644 as a fraud, not a sale. They recalled a suit in the Cour des Aides in Aix-en-Provence trying to subject the ovens to the *taille*. This would have reduced the landowners' tax burden, but the town lost. The system remained in place "by the aristocratic force of despotism." The council also recalled the referral of the case to the king's Conseil d'Etat (the "Council of the Tyrant," as they expressed it) where, like many Old Regime lawsuits, it languished. They councillors went beyond the legalese of the legal briefs to express vividly what the Old Regime fiscality of foodstuffs meant to the poor. The failure of the courts to redress meant the bakers were still obliged to bring their uncooked dough to the ovens; the country people who were allowed to bake their own bread at home nonetheless had to pay a tax "like the *piquet*" tax on flour, a tax levied "even on nursing infants."

---

[56] AC Aubagne, *registre des délibérations*, ff. 97v–98, deliberation of 24 August 1792. Department approves actions of the municipality and urges that goods removed from the monastery be sent to Marseille as soon as possible (ADBR, L 982, 28–9, letter to Aubagne, 24 August 1792).

Fraud, of course, was inevitable, but local courts assessed fines and fees so haphazardly that they risked ruining the victims.

The municipal council was totally sympathetic to the crowd's action. After all, reforming the banalities had been one of the grievances that prompted the formation of the Club of anti-*politiques* in the spring of 1791. Abolishing the taxes and fees on food was the core issue of Jacobin support. With the insurrection of 24 August 1792, the council wrote, "The citizens of the country side have recognized their rights, they have resisted oppression and the just refusal of the payment of an iniquitous right has exempted them from it until now. Today, the entire people have made a holy insurrection, they have reclaimed the property reserved for them by their ancestors...and have rendered justice itself." The capture of the ovens thus represented the culmination of the struggle against the fiscal exactions on foodstuffs that had begun in 1789.

This intervention tugged the council's emotions. But it also recognized that the only way to reduce the "effervescence" of the people was to seize the ovens.[57] The crowd's capture of the ovens was thus a restoration of justice. The Jacobin council was merely recognizing that fact, because the despotism of the Old Regime courts was inherently a denial of justice. But the strategy had also changed since the petitions of the active citizens in 1790 and 1791. With the people sovereign, capable of imposing their own justice, appeals to authority for redress were no longer necessary. The story of the banality of the ovens is also a story of the development of a particular kind of popular democracy.

The struggle over the ovens was a platform from which to define factions, a precipitate of that factionalism. Fiscality had been the motor of mobilization and defining of political positions, but once that happened, fiscality receded in importance. Other issues would take its place, including one's position on murders, political violence, and popular sovereignty in general.

The two victims knew each other as well as the owner of the ovens. They all socialized at Sivan's inn, a well-known rendezvous for anti-Jacobins, where they read subversive newspapers. The innkeeper's son,

---

[57] AC Aubagne, *registre des délibérations*, ff. 99v–100, session of 27 August 1792. Needless to say, this went far beyond the Law of 15 August 1792 that reduced the rights of former feudal owners. In 1825, the Tribunal de Première Instance in Marseille condemned the commune to compensate the Félix family for revenues lost between 1791 and 1795 because of the seizure of the ovens but ordered the family to repay the commune for any banalities collected after their abolition in 1790 (ibid., bundle entitled "Fours," "Extrait des registres du greffe..." 18 August 1825).

Probace Sivan, accused Jourdan of having wished for the arrival of the émigrés earlier that July. The rumors of an émigré-sponsored slaughter in Marseille had evidently spread to Aubagne.

On 1 September, the crowd lynched Louis Arnaud de Pons *dit* Cory. Serious allegations had been circulating throughout the town for some time. On the morning he died, the people arrested Arnaud and his tenant farmer, Jean-Louis Jourdan, and turned them over to the National Guard, who then imprisoned them for their own safety. The municipality did not take this incident seriously enough. They realized that the "people [were] very irritated" and that their "fury was becoming more and more formidable." So they put the men in protective custody. They also acquiesced to the crowd's demand that they record denunciations. They took only a handful, however, before breaking off to attend a memorial service in the parish church for those killed on the frontiers and in the assault on the Tuileries in Paris on 10 August. On their return from the memorial service, the councillors spent the rest of the afternoon observing "the very great fermentation" of the people. They retired for supper at the Lion d'Or when the popular mood appeared to have settled down. Around eight in the evening, Arnaud's two sons burst in, tears streaming down their faces. They reported that a crowd composed of "coquins et citoyens" had surrounded the prison and was going to kill their father. The councillors rushed back to the town hall to retrieve their sashes of office, but on their way out of the tavern, they heard "a large populace that was singing 'Ça ira.' We supposed the evil deed was done and in effect, they told us right then that all had been consummated." Almost immediately, the crowd began to dance the farandole in celebration "on the corpse of the said Arnaud." One celebrant, Rey *dit* Bourrasque, who was later a victim of the murder gang, was waving his sword wildly at several passersby. The next morning, Arnaud's body was still suspended from a lamppost on the Rue Mirabeau. Arnaud's family was so distraught that they could not take charge of the body. The councillors had to arrange for the curé and the Gray Penitent society to take responsibility for burying it. Normally, this society arranged a decent burial for the indigent, not solid landowners. By nine-thirty in the morning, Arnaud was laid to rest.[58]

---

[58] Ibid., *registre des délibérations*, ff. 101–2, deliberations of 1 and 2 September. Interestingly, this killing is not included in Caron's list. ADBR, L 999, municipality to district, 2 September 1792, and ibid., L 3129, deposition of Joseph Coste, before the general committee of the sections of Aubagne, 15 August 1793, for the farandole story.

If there was an inquiry into Arnaud's murder, nothing has survived. Arnaud himself was a merchant draper and landowner, of modest wealth. He may also have been related to the anti-Jacobin Monier family on his wife's side and through them to some of the more important anti-Jacobin families, but by the time of his death that relationship was rather distant. So if there was a social dimension to the killing, nothing remains in the archives. Nevertheless, some clues do survive. They relate to the factionalism of the town and targeted the victim as a political enemy. Thus, Jean-Jacques Michel, an ironmonger, reported that he heard from a shepherd that Arnaud had said that "someone should erect a gallows every thirty feet to hang all those who had been at Velaux" and that "the dead olive trees on his property ought to be used to hang the peasants." A few individuals, including Joseph Jullien and one of his sons, repeated a story that Arnaud had been very angry with one of his own sons for buying a National Guard uniform in Marseille without permission. They claimed that the son had cut the uniform into pieces to appease his father. The son, Emmanuel, no doubt to his eternal regret, confirmed the story.[59] A few hours later, Arnaud was murdered. Three years later, so were the Julliens.

Jourdan too was a political enemy. The first to denounce Jourdan on the night of the murder was Probace Sivan *fils*, the son of the inn-keeper and, unlike his father, a prominent Jacobin. According to young Sivan, Jourdan read *L'Ami du roi* in his father's tavern as soon as the post arrived; he and his friends expected the émigrés to arrive the previous July; and they "celebrated the counter-revolution with joy and pleasure."[60] Sivan's brother Joseph quoted Jourdan's friend, Cazalet, as saying that "when the émigrés come in, they will hang all the members of the club ... [that] the clubbists and the peasants ... [were] all brigands." Moreover, the Sivans' stepmother, whom Probace described as the "scourge of his father's house," told him every time she saw him with "the peasants or the artisans, to have nothing to do with them, that they were brigands."

Jourdan was not a popular man and his job as a collector of fines was by definition unpleasant. As early as January 1791, someone assaulted

---

[59] AC Aubagne, "Police différentes correspondances, 1790 – An III," denunciation register.

[60] A.N., F⁷ 3659³, Procès verbal de la municipalité d'Aubagne, relatif au Sr Jourdan, 17 September, 1792. Copy in ADBR, L 3064, titled "Extrait du verbal de Consigne, de mise sous la sauve-garde du Sr Joseph Jourdan officier ministeriel à Aubagne et des dénonciations faites contre lui." What is probably the original is in AC Aubagne, bundle titled "Police différentes correspondances, 1790 – An III."

him while he was on duty.[61] The *fête des olliviers* also revealed Jourdan's opinions as an antipatriot. On the day the National Guard of Aubagne and Marseille broke up the festival, Pierre Etienne, a poor rural worker, found himself on the avenue leading to the château de Belloi. There he ran into Jourdan, who grabbed him by the stomach, of all things, and threw him up against a wall, nearly maiming him. "All this is your fault," Jourdan supposedly said, "rotten bugger of the club." Charles Boeuf, the windy procurator of the commune, also claimed Jourdan was "one of the chief invitees and subscribers to the list of the Olive Festival and of the disobedience to the law and to the orders of the municipality that has occasioned so much trouble and so much disorder in this commune."

These were vague denunciations. Those who made them certainly wanted to settle scores for old wrongs. They also meant to harm Jourdan because they made these denunciations the night of Jourdan's captivity, in an extremely volatile situation. They must have known, however, that reading newspapers and chewing opponents out for their political opinions or issuing unjust fines long before were not crimes in a legal sense. Instead, the context matters. Representatives of the crowd made the denunciations, when the people were dictating to officialdom. Such complaints reflected the lethal polarization between the clubbists and the anti-Jacobins. More than that, a theory of revolutionary justice underlay these complaints.[62]

The Anthropology of Vigilante Justice

The lynchings were a reflection and a consequence of an already deeply divided town. For contemporaries, the purpose of each incident was to warn the other side.[63] The mock lampposts, the bonfires that earlier had signaled trouble, the various threats, and so on, were all admonitions designed to intimidate.

---

[61] ADBR, L 482, Berenger to "Monsieur," 2 January 1791.

[62] Ibid., L 3110, "Dénonciation faite au comité de surveillance du [sic] cette commune d'Aubagne, faite par le citoyen Jean-Pierre Jourdan dit Tarenne...," who denounces two of Jourdan's brothers who accused him of participating in the hanging. They accosted him on the Grand' rue in June 1793, beat him with a walking stick all over his body, and shouted, "Give me your knives, your sword, and your pistol, we'll kill you with it [sic]."

[63] For what follows, I have learned much from Brian Singer, "Violence and the French Revolution: Forms of Ingestion/Forms of Expulsion," in *The French Revolution and the Birth of Modernity*, ed. Ferenc Fehér (Berkeley: University of California Press, 1990), 150–73.

The denunciations fit into this context. They must have been intimidating to the targets of the denunciation, but they also painted that person as distinct, an outsider, someone decent society avoided. Although the words and deeds of the ostracized person were not illegal, the public knowledge that they had occurred signaled that they were dangerous and thus that person could be cast out of regular society.

The lynchings usually occurred in full view and so were a demonstration of how far one side was prepared to go to intimidate. This was deliberate because an essential part of the action required the crowd to haul the unfortunate victim from prison or from protective custody. The crowd was therefore stronger than legal authority. The executions also took place at public intersections, in Marseille, at the Place du Palais, at the door of the Club in the center of town, on the Canebière, in the boulevards in Aix-en-Provence, at the corner of a café near the Place de l'Horloge in Avignon, and on the Rue Mirabeau in Aubagne.

Rituals over the disposal and burial of the body symbolized the ultimate humiliation of the victim, even in death. In many cases, Jourdan's being one of them, the municipal officers were as quick as possible about cutting down and interring the victims. They were clearly shocked at the spectacle, as they were with Arnaud's, where they considered it scandalous the corpse had been hanging all night, no doubt with gawking spectators nearby.[64]

Sometimes, though, the municipal officers failed to interrupt the process. Then the crowd's intent played out. Exemplary punishment became an excruciating spectacle. One example would be the unfortunate Etienne Rouzier of Salon. On the night of 9–10 March 1793, a band of killers removed Rouzier from his home just outside one of the town gates. They hanged him from a tree, shot him, and finished him off with swords. They then put eyeglasses on the nose of the corpse, and adjusted the body as if it were reading a piece of paper nailed to the tree from which they had hanged him.[65] This must have been an inside joke of sorts whose ultimate meaning is now lost. The intent to get revenge and humiliate remains clear, however.

In Marseille, the two monks were hanged in one place after another three different times in three different places, in front of cafés that

---

[64] ADBR, L 959, 21, letter of 2 September 1792.

[65] Ibid., L 3044, *acte d'accusation*, 7 Floréal An III – 26 April 1795, in both mss. and printed versions. Without going deeply into the local history of Salon, it is hard to know much about Rouzier. The capitation role of 1788 lists an "Estienne Rouzier, bourgeois" paying a very modest 3/10/-livres (AM Salon, uncataloged).

aristocrats haunted, and in front of churches and convents, the better to warn of the fate for those who plotted against the people. In Toulon, in July, one administrator was beheaded and then suspended upside down, a sign, no doubt to the horrified onlookers, of contempt and revulsion.[66]

Lynching was the ultimate vigilantism, the ultimate expulsion from the community, but it did not end there. Violently ripping off clothing, before or after the mob killed, occurred frequently. Because clothing helped define an individual, enforced nudity was a stripping of identity, another humiliation, another way of marginalizing someone. Display and mortification of the body was a continuation of the excising.

The contrast with a patriotic death was remarkable. For example, during the celebrations of the first Bastille Day at Gémenos, a village just a few kilometers from Aubagne, a distraught national guardsman from Toulon stabbed the former seigneur and President of the Cour des Comptes, M. d'Albertas, to death. The National Guard fell on the lone killer, stripped him of his uniform and threw him naked into the local prison. Less than a month later, the Parlement of Provence sentenced the murderer to be broken on the wheel, the last such sentence it ever gave.[67]

Patriots reacted emotionally to the murder. Expressions of vengeance, demands for a formal degrading ceremony for the parricide who had dishonored the uniform, and emphasis on the murderer's betrayal of a solemn occasion were all common. Eulogists emphasized M. d'Albertas's respectable age, his role as exemplary father, and his charity to the poor. The funeral ceremony attracted national guardsmen from Toulon, Marseille, and Aubagne. The White Penitents of Aubagne also participated.

A patriot's obituary recalled the deceased's services to the community and the features of a good life. The victims of lynchings and their families

---

[66] Espeut, "Un faux complot à Marseille," 88. Coulet, "Les massacres des administrateurs du Var," 433.

[67] *Relation de l'horrible assassinat commis sur la personne de Mr d'Albertas père, au milieu du festin civique de la Garde Nationale de Gemenos, le 14 Juillet 1790, par le nommé Anicet Martel, du lieu d'Auriol* (Aix: Calmen, 1790). BM Marseille Xd3454. Also in ibid., Collection Léon, xxiv, 429–65. This last version also contains the death sentence. See also Lourde, *Histoire de la Révolution à Marseille et en Provence*, i, 285–6. Martel was avenging the death of his father whom d'Albertas had imprisoned by lettre de cachet. The crowd in Toulon took Martel's side during his execution and when he escaped, vainly tried to assist his escape (AM Toulon, L 330, *procès-verbal du 3 août 1790*). See also the eulogy for the young man killed during the Tourette scuffle in Marseille in August 1789: Etienne Chompré, *Aux Manes de notre compatriote Gautier*, ([1789]), BM Marseille Collection Léon, xii, 17–20, where the emphasis is on glorious immortality and sacrifice.

received no such treatment. Even the families of the victims appear to have accepted that the body of their loved one had been definitively excluded from the community. Thus, in Aubagne, Arnaud's sons did not receive their father's body but allowed the Gray Penitents to make final arrangements. The Widow Jourdan accepted the municipality's urgent request to bury her husband.[68] In Aix, the barrister Pascalis was hanged on 14 December 1790 and buried the same day, and so rapidly that the clergy did not include the usual details about the names of his parents.[69] In Arles, nurses at the hospital, not families, buried the victims of the killings of 16 August. Most of the victims in Marseille were buried the day of their death, often by order of the justice of the peace, not the more normal day after. One, Christophe Belan, the garrulous wigmaker, was discovered "in the fortifications of the Porte d'Aubagne" and buried the day he was found. Regular funeral ceremonies must have been impossible in these circumstances.[70]

The Theory of Vigilantism

The ceremonial of these lynchings was inseparable from theories of popular justice. Some of these ideas originated in Old Regime notions that the sovereign dispensed justice. If the people were sovereign, they could dispense justice. This would explain Jacobin authorities' hesitation to punish popular initiatives. Justice in the Old Regime was also supposed to be public and exemplary, a demonstration of the awesome power of the sovereign. So was popular justice in the Revolution. The Old Regime origins of lynching as inflicting exemplary punishment are obvious. Some of the rituals surrounding the corpse also had Old Regime origins. Dragging bodies of the already dead and hanging them on a gallows and then throwing the corpse on a refuse heap was a traditional practice when the crime was particularly heinous. Mutilation of the corpse, dragging it face down through the streets, hanging it upside down from the gallows,

---

[68] AC Aubagne, 201E 1620, *registre des décès*, 18 September 1792. The register notes the "request" to his wife that he be buried that day.

[69] Etat-civil, Aix-en-Provence, Sainte-Madeleine, 14 December 1790.

[70] Etat-civil, Marseille, La Trinité, 22 July 1792. Ibid., Notre-Dame des Accoules, 21 and 22 July 1792. Espeut, "Un faux complot à Marseille," 72–3. On the family's role in traditional burying practices, see Edward Muir, *Ritual in Early Modern Europe*, 2nd ed., New Approaches to European History (Cambridge: Cambridge University Press, 2005), 48–9.

parading body parts about in triumph, were all part of a European repertoire of popular justice.[71]

Old Regime court practices and the popular justice of the Revolution
diverged as well. Popular revolutionary justice was radical both in its
forms and in its goals. The failure to seek restitution or apology; the
absence of mercy; the failure to provide a confessor; a single punishment; the sovereign's direct assumption of justice; and above all, the near
absence of procedure all distinguish the two. Even Babeuf's and many
others' assertions about the lynchings in Paris in 1789 – that the people
learned how to be brutal from a brutal royal system – overplay the desire
of a gradually liberalizing royal justice to inflict punishment through torture and physical pain. Ordinary people retained much older notions of
pain and humiliation.[72]

In any case, the combination of royal justice with revolutionary practice produced a thoroughly radical result. Yet reconstructing the theory
of popular revolutionary justice is also hard because most of the sources
condemn its most spectacular feature, vigilantism. But they rarely condemned it outright.[73] Paradoxically, they frequently recognized the value
of popular initiative. One of the best examples, one that does not condemn, is the report in the Jacobin *Journal des Départements méridionaux*
on the six lynchings in Marseille the previous July. When the people heard
of the arrest of one of the plotters, "tired of seeing traitors unpunished,
they wished to administer justice themselves." The people were "justly
infuriated," "satisfied their rage against this infamous conspirator," and
because two of the plotters were "already condemned [by the confes-
sion of another plotter, it appears], nothing could restrain them."[74] The
municipality's version was very similar. An "infernal plot was unfolding
at Marseille," they wrote, "[but] our brave ones [*nos braves*, perhaps
the National Guard] . . . seized the leader of the wicked, and the people

---

[71] Julius R. Ruff, *Violence in Early Modern Europe, 1500–1800*, vol. 22, *New Approaches to European History* (Cambridge: Cambridge University Press, 2001), 195, 203. William Beik, *Urban Protest in Seventeenth-Century France: The Culture of Retribution* (Cambridge: Cambridge University Press, 1997), 64–5. Richard Mowery Andrews, *Law, Magistracy, and Crime in Old Regime Paris, 1735–1789* (Cambridge: Cambridge University Press, 1992), 383.

[72] Ibid., 283.

[73] An exception : *Discours prononcé par le Citoyen Perrin l'aîné, Maire de la Commune d'Aix, sur l'Autel de la Patrie, le 28 Octobre 1792, l'an 1er de la République, pour la présentation du serment de maintenir & défende les personnes et le propriétés* (Aix: Impr. David, 1792), in ADBR, 100 E 41.

[74] *JdM*, 26 July 1792.

in fury, stuck him themselves with the sword of the law.... Thus, the impunity of crime engenders the arms to combat it which magistrates ought to have foreseen."[75] The newspaper had an identical reaction to the murders in Toulon. The people, "tired of the perfidy of several administrators, and of the sanguinary plots of several wicked people, administered justice on nine of them [*s'est fait justice de 9 d'entre'eux*]."[76] In these accounts, popular justice was an alternative to formal justice, not its perversion, legitimate when the formal system failed, a device to satiate justifiable anger against wrongdoers. In any case, the Department of the Bouches-du-Rhône also pointed out the value of a preemptive strike against the enemy.[77]

After no less than five separate lynchings in Aix-en-Provence in early 1793, shocked officials explained that the people believed that criminal justice was too slow in its procedures and too easy in its punishments. Further, "the people being sovereign, it had the right to exercise justice itself and to punish those it believed were guilty."[78]

Many Jacobins were ambivalent about popular justice, of course. They usually condemned popular justice in the present and praised it in the past. The Club at Marseille could locate a "good" justice in 1789 but claimed that in the present, the Nation needed only to contain its enemies.[79] The Club also warned against those who "cover a guilty selfishness, ancient animosities, long-standing hatreds with the veil of the revolution.... [Beware those who would] claim proscriptions, pillage, arson, exactions and all these criminal contributions... as a virtue, as an act of patriotism."[80]

Recognizing the right of insurrection while being prepared to overlook excesses was a classic formulation during the Revolution. Those guilty

---

75 *Lettre de la municipalité de Marseille à M. Pétion, maire de Paris*, n.d., in ibid., 16 August 1792.

76 Ibid., 31 July 1792.

77 AN F⁷ 3659³, letter to Minister of Interior, 20 November 1792.

78 ADBR, L 285, Municipality of Aix to representatives of the people, 6 March 1792 [sic].

79 *Adresse des amis de la liberté et de légalité de Marseille aux citoyens du département des Bouches-du-Rhône du 20 octobre 1792* (Avignon: Imprimerie Sabin Tournai, 1792). BM Marseille Xd3217. Another address, same title, dated 26 October 1792 in ADBR, L 2076. A very clear example of this distinction in *Discours prononcé à la séance des Amis de la Liberté et de l'Egalité de Toulon, le 29 octobre, l'an premier... par Jean-Louis Bonhomme aîné, un de ses membres* (Avignon : S. Tournal, 1792). BM Avignon, Atl. 314/134.

80 *Adresse de la Société des Amis de la Liberté et de l'Egalité de Marseille, à toutes les Sociétés affiliées du Département*, (Signée : Chompré, président, etc.), (Marseille: Rochebrun & Mazet, 1793 [1792]) BM Marseille 5332.

of excess were misled, dupes of their own innocence. Thus, no malicious intent existed, and so no powerful reason to prosecute.[81] The administrators of the Bouches-du-Rhône explained, "Men misled, no doubt by the enemies of the Republic are carried away by excesses that are subversive of the social order, by vandalism, arson, [and] pillage."[82]

The distinction between the past and the present was inherently unstable, however. Raking up the past, as the "Republicans of Marseille" pointed out, could only damage the patriots' cause.[83] Anyway, Jacobins also assumed that victims were guilty. Although they deplored violence, the revolutionary elite shared the presumption that having rendered rough justice, the body politic was now whole and safe. Just days after the killings in August, for example, the club and municipality of Arles justified popular action not on the ground of past oppression or popular ignorance but on the grounds of necessary, salutary justice:

The danger to the *patrie* and great crimes have provoked great reprisals. The people have risen, it has shown its enemies how formidable it is, if it wishes to use all its means. Yet when the terrible device of its power has made its enemies tremble, when it has dissipated them, as the wind blows the dust before it, when it has made some victims as an example and for public vengeance, it can from now on only show itself magnanimous and forgiving; then everything ought to return to order. This happy moment has come, Citizens.[84]

Several months later, this club and the municipality invited all those who had fled the city to return on the grounds there was no longer any danger.[85] The guilty had been punished; the body politic restored to wellness.

There may have been similar discussions like this in Aubagne, but no evidence has survived. There were repercussions, however. At the end of September, a trio of commissioners from the club at Marseille went to Aubagne, where they "enlightened the people of this town on its true

[81] On the issue of intent as a powerful extenuating or aggravating circumstance in French legal culture see, Andrews, *Law, Magistracy, and Crime in Old Regime Paris,* 285–9.

[82] *Adresse des administrateurs du département des Bouches-du-Rhône,* 9 October 1792 (Marseille: J. Massy, 1792).

[83] Petition of 15 February 1793 in *AP,* lix, 118, session of 23 February 1793. As Minister of Justice, Danton used a similar argument that to pursue the case of the events in Toulon in July; namely, that it would be too divisive (Coulet, "Les massacres des administrateurs du Var," 441).

[84] BM Arles, MS 639, *Proclamation des administrateurs provisoires de la commune d'Arles,* 20 August 1792 (Arles: G. Mesnier fils, 1792).

[85] Ibid., *Adresse de la Société des amis de la liberté et de l'égalité de la ville d'Arles, du 9 octobre 1792, l'an premier de la République française.*

duties; they obtained a promise from them that they would never again deviate from those duties and they [the commissioners] obtained their sincere repentance."[86] Yet policy was nowhere near as straightforward as this might suggest. The executive officer of the District of Marseille, who could have ordered a formal judicial enquiry into Jourdan's death, brought all proceedings to a halt. In the end, as appalling as the means were, Jourdan was guilty and so nothing more needed to be done. Thus, "the tragic end of the unfortunate Jourdan," he wrote. "His imprudence could have brought on his end but the public vengeance inflicted on him ought to content itself with a single victim. The death of a guilty person is a public calamity even when it is necessary for society."[87]

The municipality, too, was inclined to defer to the popular will. In its last word on the subject, the municipality claimed that despite its best efforts, "the popular torrent overwhelmed everything [*le torrent populaire a tout entrainé*]." It noted that the lamentations of Jourdan's wife and son had pierced their hearts but concluded, "Hélas! Qui peut résister au peuple français en fureur?"[88]

A long nine months later, the councillors would have their answer.

---

[86] Report in *JdM*, 27 September 1792. See also the issue of 29 September.

[87] AN F⁷ 3659³, letter of 18 September 1792 (copy). Not a word, it should be noted, about Pons Arnaud.

[88] Municipality to District of Marseille, 18 September 1792 in a bundle at the AC Aubagne titled "Police, différentes correspondances."

5

Vigilantism and Federalism

The improvised lampposts remained standing in Aubagne until the late spring of 1793, when the anti-Jacobins finally tore them down. Many welcomed the event as deliverance. In a sense, therefore, the massive intimidation of enemies was successful, at least for a time. An early history of the town treats the events of August and September 1792 as the beginnings of the Terror in Aubagne, about a year before many historians say it began in the country as a whole.[1] If that was so, the Terror – terror of a different sort than the classic one, to be sure – in Aubagne was not a reflexive series of actions designed to save the country from foreign invasion and domestic counterrevolution. Instead, it was the Jacobins' response to dealing with their local enemies. Such a violent response was bound to lead sooner or later to a counterresponse, but for the moment, the Jacobins were secure.

Jacobin Governance: Aubagne

One of the reasons for the security was that many anti-Jacobins fled the town. How many fled is unknown, but there is one list that suggests that at a number of the leading anti-Jacobins took refuge in the safer neighborhoods of Marseille. The notary Georges Cartier, for example, one of the prominent leaders in trying to get the Jacobin electoral victories of 1792 overturned, was denied a *certificat de civisme*, a written affidavit of civic virtue, because he was "unworthy." Apparently, he had held

[1] AN F¹ᶜIII, Bouches-du-Rhône 6, "Notice historique sur la commune d'Aubagne," n.d. [An IX].

assemblies of "suspect citizens" in his home. Shortly after, he closed up his offices and moved to Marseille. The municipality promptly presumed him an émigré and placed seals on the doors.[2]

Not all prominent anti-Jacobins fled, of course, either because they could not afford to or because they were prepared to take the risk. We know they were present because they vouched for individuals who applied for *certificats de civisme* or certificates of residence that protected the holder from the application of the émigré laws.[3] By all appearances, they were quite subdued. Aside from the obvious warnings the violence of the previous year had demonstrated, opponents had been disarmed. Following a decree of the Electoral Assembly of the Bouches-du-Rhône, which went well beyond its mandate of choosing members of the new National Convention, the town ordered the disarming of all those hostile to the new order. Their guns were to remain secure in the town hall until the *patrie* was no longer in danger, that is, until victory had been won.[4] Consequently, anti-Jacobin activity vanished.

Jacobins remained alert to any possibility of opposition, however. On 25 February, Domergue presented a petition on behalf of the Club demanding that the council establish a "secret and particular committee," composed of members from the council itself. Its purpose was "as much for surveillance as for receiving denunciations related to the Revolution [and for] the safety and prosperity of the Republic." The efforts of this committee of the council were to be coordinated with the *comité de surveillance* of the Club. Interestingly, one of the four members of this committee soon became part of the anti-Jacobin council, which suggests that the local politicians could still cooperate in small ways.[5]

The establishment of the secret committee shows that fear of clandestine opposition continued. The council was prepared to go further still. On 9 April, the mayor, Camoin, announced that there was an "underground fermentation" in the commune that aimed at "disorganizing everything." It was necessary to defeat the local counterrevolution by any means available. But he feared outsiders, too, because he persuaded the council to nominate two commissioners to visit the post office to verify all incoming

[2] AC Aubagne, *registre des déliberations*, f. 140v, session of 9 February 1793. See also, ADBR, L 1002, f. 55, municipality of Aubagne to District, 17 February 1793.

[3] Examples AC Aubagne, *registre des déliberations*, f. 154, session of 27 March 1793, f. 157, session of 17 April, 1793.

[4] Ibid., f. 112, session of 14 October, 1792.

[5] Ibid., f. 145, session of 25 February 1793. On the other hand, the basis of cooperation may have evaporated too, as the individual in question, Sabin Brémond, did not sign any of the denunciations.

letters and to seize "suspect" newspapers.[6] The results of intercepting the post the previous year had been interesting but meager. This time, the secret committee discovered no dangerous material.

Nonetheless, tensions remained high. One denunciation was very interesting. In late April 1793, Joseph Jullien and his son were at work in the fields when around lunchtime they saw a woman unknown to them coming down the road with what appeared to be provisions in her apron and a basket on her head. This appeared suspicious to them so they followed her. She led them down a path off the main road to Gémenos to the *bastide* belonging to the Barthélemy brothers. The Julliens took cover among the spring growth. Shortly after, they saw another female farmhand arrive on a donkey carrying flasks full of wine. An hour later, the former prior Michel and another man arrived. The Julliens concluded from this that several persons were hiding at the *bastide*.[7]

Whether there were and what became of this denunciation is unknown, but its significance lies elsewhere. The Julliens had retailed the story about Arnaud, the hanging victim, having forced his son to shred his National Guard uniform. Father and son were right to have been leery of the Barthélemys. Their *bastide* was not very far from where the Julliens were murdered in the Year III. And one of the accused killers was none other than one of the Barthélemy brothers, the owners of the shady *bastide*, in this case Lambert *dit* La Machine. Once again, suspicion and revenge had long-standing and venomous roots in Aubagne.

Eavesdropping led to another denunciation. In early May, Nicolas Gury, the town's recording secretary and archivist, was passing by the National Guard post at Bourg la Mouton, when he saw the maidservant of the émigré Louis Mille. She was carrying a rolled-up napkin containing what appeared to be provisions. She approached the lieutenant on duty, the notary Jean-Baptiste Martinot, and appeared to start to pass a message to him. All Gury heard was the phrase, "on behalf of," when Martinot silenced her and told her to meet him later at his house. Gury knew nothing more, but he concluded that "given the counterrevolutionary movements that are manifesting themselves; that Louis Mille, one of the first [of them] who showed themselves in this commune, must be at his *bastide*, in order to join with the 'infernal-revolutionary gang.'"[8]

---

[6] Ibid., f. 156, session of 9 April 1793.

[7] Ibid., unclassified, denunciation register, dossier titled "Police, differentes correspondances, 1790 – An III."

[8] Ibid., denunciation of 8 May 1793.

The incident shows once again how well the antagonists knew one another well before the *bande d'Aubagne* began operations. In this case, Martinot was a leading anti-Jacobin and was involved in the gang. Louis Mille, besides being present at the *fête des olliviers*, allowed his *bastide* to be used to dump corpses once the *bande* started up. Gury himself was buried there in 1795.

The secret committee spent more time on the sad case of Rose Chataud, widow of Étienne Raud, than on any other. Rose Chataud was in her late forties or early fifties and near indigent. Loneliness, hunger, and ostracism had driven her half mad. For some time, she had taken to the streets late at night, roaming about, begging for food. Once she threw a huge rock at the heavy door of the hospital. It made such a sound that the mother superior sent the beadle and another servant to investigate and get rid of her. Other people lied and made false promises to get her to go away. She prayed in stables or in the main church at the chapel of Saint Anthony, where she made a spectacle of herself, tugged at her clothes, and did inappropriate things. If her landlord locked her in her room to keep her from going out at night, she shouted out the window at passersby that she was a prisoner or she sang. One young man, a baker, said that because his trade required him to get up early, he always heard her commotions.[9]

There was no direct implication for the town's politics in the story of poor Rose Chataud. It does show a tendency that would be quite marked later on, of townspeople using extraordinary institutions to resolve an ordinary problem. Furthermore, although Rose was apparently left alone after this, it also shows how alert the town councillors were to any disturbance and their willingness to record it for future reference. But it also shows how quiescent street life was just before the Jacobins were forced out, as all the secret committee was able to turn up were complaints of noise at night and overheard conversations.

The other problem of Jacobin governance was the subsistence issue. This was a problem that plagued the entire country in late 1792 until the harvest came in the following summer. Whether the grain harvest of 1792 was genuinely bad is hard to know, but there were serious problems in the Midi with the two major cash crops, wine and olives. Excessive rain and flooding had done serious damage in the spring of 1792, and unnatural cold the following autumn had damaged the olive trees that had survived the extraordinarily severe winter of 1788-9.

---

[9] Ibid., denunciations of 30 April, 1793. ADBR, 201E 1596, marriage of 29 June 1768.

The Revolution's currency, the assignat, lost value from the beginning. Prices soared, particularly the price of food, people hoarded cash, grain dealers avoided public markets, and wages failed to keep up.

The subsistence issue drove a sharp wedge between rural producers and urban consumers in the North, and one might have expected it to divide Aubagne *ville* from its *terroir*, and thus undermine the Jacobin constituency. But events did not play out this way. Aubagne imported the shortfall of grain and regulated the price of outside supplies. Local grain producers had already exhausted their supplies when the town began arranging imports so regulation had a minor effect on them. If any constituency was hurt by the subsistence crisis of 1793, it was those in the food trades, especially the bakers, innkeepers, cabaret owners, and so on. And this group had never been conspicuous Jacobin supporters.

On the whole, the subsistence issue did not begin to catch the council's attention until the late winter, in February 1793. On 18 February, Camoin, the mayor, noted that this was an exceptionally bad "arrière saison," the time when the town had to live between harvests. The council also had to replace a lot of grain it had earlier borrowed from Marseille. Besides, the treasury was bare, and so it was impossible to lay in stocks against future shortages. On top of that, the war meant that there were many more travelers, volunteers, and soldiers passing through, all of whom put more pressure on supplies. Behind all these sensible reasons, there lay the "secret hoarding and lack of circulation" of grain. Whatever the reason, it was essential to deal with this situation for the good of humanity "but additionally to prevent the misfortune that could occur if a shortage of grain should occur." Consequently, the council voted to acquire grain in Marseille, which would then be sold at the public market of Aubagne, "to be distributed to the citizens and the bakers, according to their needs. This will be recorded and permits issued by the municipality and the guardian of the market who will both keep a record of transactions, in order to keep an eye on the malevolent who might horde supplies until the next harvest."[10]

The council persuaded a few rich citizens to put up the money to buy stocks in the market in Marseille, while Camoin himself negotiated the necessary exit permits from his colleagues.[11] This appeared to have solved the problem, but a while later, the subsistence question returned. Apparently, pilfering meant that grain destined specifically for the poor

---

[10] AC Aubagne, *registre des délibérations*, f. 142v, session of 18 February 1793.
[11] Ibid., f. 145, session of 26 February 1793; f. 158–8v, session of 29 April 1793.

had disappeared and that grain merchants and the rich cheated. They had agents buy for them to evade limitations on large purchases, farmers sold off the market to private individuals, and somehow the rich managed to buy at below market price for themselves. The poorest thus had to buy "at an exorbitant price." The council voted to make sure that the poor were supplied. They decided to inspect the stocks of any citizen "suspect of having provisions of wheat"; to verify who had more than they needed, and to transport this grain to the local market. These people would be compensated on the basis of their original cost plus a 5 percent profit.[12] Shortages had now driven prices up by over 40 percent between the end of February and the end of May.

None of the Jacobins' policies was very radical. On subsistence policy, the Jacobins acted well within the script of Old Regime administrators, with their exhortations to aid the poor, in their fears of disturbance and riot, in their scrounging from other jurisdictions, and in their reliance on private support. The one potentially radical idea, that grain prices be pegged to wages, got no support.[13] Otherwise, the council improvised as the crisis deepened. They subsidized mule drivers to persuade them to keep transporting wood to the municipal ovens; voted to link bread prices to those in Marseille, presumably to prevent anyone from playing one market off against another; bought outside grain once again and voted to set the bread price from that acquisition below the grain price set by local petty merchants; and so on. Their biggest prize was providential. At the end of May, the city of Marseille released a very large amount of grain that local privateers had captured.[14]

In Aubagne at any rate, subsistence policy was not the stepping-stone to more radical social innovation, let alone the confiscation that came a year later. Indeed, the Jacobins paid no attention to the Law of 4 May 1793, sometimes known as the First Maximum. This permitted departments to fix a ceiling on grain prices on the basis of a predetermined scale. There is no indication at all that Aubagne did this or that it bought grain in Marseille on the basis of controlled prices. After all, Provence had always been heavily dependent on foreign imports, and controls on import prices would simply have diverted grain ships elsewhere. Furthermore, a highly diversified agricultural economy that had developed cash crops on

---

[12] Ibid., f. 159v–60, session of 29 April 1793. On the big picture, see Judith A. Miller, *Mastering the Market: The State and the Grain Trade in Northern France, 1700–1860* (Cambridge: Cambridge University Press, 1999), *passim*.

[13] AC Aubagne, *registre des délibérations*, f. 162v, session of 15 May 1793.

[14] Ibid., f. 165v, session of 24 May 1793; ff. 165–7, sessions of 26 May, 1 June 1793.

everything from wine and olives to fruit and garlic would not be aided by legal controls that were developed with the northern cereal economy in mind. Consequently, everyone ignored the law.

The mundane details of governance and piloting the town through the subsistence problems of the first half of 1793 had never been a strong point for the Jacobins. Political passions were, and these were now, easily provoked. Thus, at the end of November 1792, those who had marched to Paris to overthrow the monarchy returned. The town does not appear to have been entirely ready to meet the overwhelming number of visitors, for along with the six local volunteers came the Phalange Marseillaise, perhaps some hundred-odd men, many of whom arrived with high expectations for a lavish welcome that did not materialize.[15]

The town failed to plan for the usual fraternal banquet of copious food, music, dancing, and patriotic speeches. The guests had plenty of opportunity to express their unhappiness. In effect, the arrival of so many soldiers allowed bar owners to double the price of wine, which produced complaints not only from locals but also from the Phalange. A week after their arrival, they surrounded the town hall to denounce the "tyrannical stubbornness of the citizens of Aubagne." Some hotheads even threatened a hanging or two. The council minutes noted the descriptions of the ruffians who made these threats. One of them had the distinguishing feature of every thug of the period: smallpox scars. The council caved in. Even though it was illegal, they imposed price controls on wine because, they said, the price rises were the result of the "greed of a certain number of miserly citizens and the malice of hoarders and monopolists," of a coalition of "enemies of the people, of the Republic, and by fanatics." Needless to say, price controls reduced the supply to nothing, so when the victorious Marseillais were scheduled to move on, some nearly refused to go until they had made an example.[16]

The town's commitment to a vigorous republicanism remained despite such setbacks. There was the establishment of the secret committee to receive denunciations, the vigilance against any manifestation of dangerous religious sentiment, the censoring of the post, and the refusal of *certificats de civisme*. Just after news arrived in Marseille that the war

---

[15] Ibid., f. 128, session of 18 November 1793.
[16] Ibid., f. 123v–24, sessions of 21–29 November 1792. ADBR, L 48, 155, session of 28 November 1792 and ibid., L 126, 127, Camoin to *citoyen général* St.-Hilaire, 29 November 1792. Both say back pay was the issue.

on the northern frontiers was taking a bad turn, authorities there established a "revolutionary committee" to be "composed of 12 citizens to watch over, judge without appeal, and have punished the enemies of the Republic."[17] A few days later in Aubagne, a "central committee" (the secret committee or a new one formed in imitation of the "revolutionary committee" in Marseille?) demanded that authorities in Marseille hand over eight suspect individuals who had fled, most of whom were well-known opponents who lent their homes for clandestine plotting or for organizing the *fête des olliviers*. The purpose of demanding their return was "to teach them to learn to dance the Carmagnole."[18]

Jacobin Governance: Marseille

That rebellion was a long time coming. In Aubagne, the overthrow of the Jacobin municipality came from the outside. The shock value of the hangings, and the continuing repression combined with a reasonable management of the subsistence issue, subdued the Jacobins' enemies. Marseille's intervention in local politics once again was the result of an anti-Jacobin coup.

That coup is known in the literature as Federalism. Although the term is inescapable, it is unfortunate. Jacobins invented it and the so-called Federalists never used it, at least not in Aubagne or Marseille. Where the term connotes a willingness to act independently of Parisian initiatives or inspiration, it is useful, but to the extent that it implies the desire for a federal system of government or nostalgia for the provincial liberties of the Old Regime, it is positively misleading or even wrong. Riffaterre, the great historian of Federalism in Lyon, preferred the term *anti-Jacobin*, and while this is better, the anti-Jacobins had a more positive vision of government than this would suggest. Like Jacobinism itself, Federalism evolved from an anti-Jacobin, prodemocratic, law-and-order movement to a haphazard authoritarianism and, perhaps even in places, royalism of one type or another. In Aubagne, Federalism represented the victory of those who attended the *fête des olliviers*.

[17] Ibid., L 48, 174, session of 16 March 1793. Despite the similarity in name, this was not the same kind of institution as the *comités de surveillance* established by the Law of 21 March 1793. The Marseille body was unelected and had extensive judicial powers.
[18] Ibid., L 1974, *Comité central d'Aubagne to Citoyens frères républicains de Marseille*, March 19, 1793.

Marseille intervened many times in politics in Aubagne but never with more unfortunate results than during the Federalist episode and its aftermath.[19] That intervention was a consequence of fierce struggles within the port city that had begun toward the end of 1792. The basic issue was the dominance and unscrupulousness of the Club. The clubbists in turn were opposed by the Sections, originally thirty-two neighborhood electoral assemblies, which continued to meet after the voting concluded. The sectional rebellion was a slow-motion coup against the institutions of Jacobin dominance that terminated with the closure of the Club. The first blow was the establishment of the Popular Tribunal on 1 October 1792. Although everyone welcomed it as a device to channel the vigilante instinct, it became an institutional counter to the Criminal Tribunal of the Department, understandably perceived as a Jacobin stronghold. The second was the impeachment on corruption charges of the mayor and other officials early in 1793, a move the Jacobins supported because they saw them as insufficiently militant. While there were many activities that the Club and the Sections supported, like forced loans from the rich and the establishment of the new Revolutionary Tribunal, the Sections gradually attracted those who feared the Club's high-handed tactics were a threat to their personal safety or to their property.

National politics also intruded on the local scene and made a delicate situation all the more venomous. Gradually the Sections threw their support to the so-called Girondins in the National Convention, while the Club supported the Montagnards. This split in national politics had begun over a disagreement of the timing of a preventive war on Austria in the spring of 1792 with the journalist and deputy Brissot arguing for immediate action and Robespierre arguing that France was ill prepared for a war at that moment. The Girondin-Montagnard split widened over the morality of the September Massacres in Paris, with the Girondins convinced that their opponents had tried to use the occasion to have them murdered, while the Montagnards defended them as necessary in the circumstances. The chasm opened impossibly with the King's Trial in December 1792 and January 1793. Montagnards argued that the people had already found the King guilty. To decree anything but death was to repudiate the insurrection that overthrew the monarchy on 10 August.

[19] Paul R. Hanson, *The Jacobin Republic under Fire: The Federalist Revolt in the French Revolution* (University Park: Pennsylvania State University Press, 2003), 81–92, 154–60, is a handy narrative. It underplays the violence of local politics, however. See also Jacques Guilhaumou, "Les fédéralismes marseillais en 1793," in *Marseille en révolution*, ed. C. Badet (Marseille, 1989), 105–13.

Few Girondins doubted the King was guilty or that he deserved death, but perhaps to flaunt their democratic credentials, they argued that a referendum should decide the King's fate. The Montagnards argued in reply that a referendum would be so divisive that it could provoke a civil war. The Convention narrowly defeated the *appel au peuple*, as it was called, but the Jacobin press vilified the *appelants* mercilessly after this. On 31 May–2 June 1793, the Paris National Guard surrounded the Convention and forced the deputies to expel the *appelants*.

Local bodies took sides in the struggle in the Convention very early. The Department of the Bouches-du-Rhône, for example, emotionally denounced all mercy for the King. "Even to question," they said, "whether Louis the Last ought to be judged is treason; to dare to argue that he cannot be judged is to be a traitor to the *patrie*.... [Judge] this great guilty one who is already condemned by the people, you [the Convention] are its faithful organ."[20] The General Council of the Commune of Marseille complained about the endless delays, not in bringing on the trial, but in executing the "execrable monster."[21]

The Club in Marseille condemned moderation: "Ah! when a revolution is made, moderationism is like cowardice when a battle is beginning."[22] A mass petition of the "People of Marseille" stated that Louis should be condemned as if he were an illegal combatant in a war rather than be accorded a presumption of innocence. The *appel au peuple*, therefore, was treason.[23]

In other words, all the major institutions of Marseille took a solidly anti-Girondin line, a ruthless and pitiless politics of regicide, all of it couched in the most uncompromising language. So did Aubagne. Clubs and official bodies throughout the region endorsed a "salutary fermentation," against a dangerous and stultifying "moderationism." The King's trial had revealed a moderate faction in the Convention, one that included some members of the Bouches-du-Rhône delegation, like the former Jacobin sensation Charles Barbaroux. The voting of men like Barbaroux

[20] *Addresse de departement des Bouches-du-Rhône à la Convention nationale*, 29 December 1792, in BM Avignon, MS 2524, n° 121.

[21] *Adresse du Conseil général de la Commune de Marseille à la Convention Nationale* (Marseille: Rochebrun, Mazet, [21 December] 1792), in BM Marseille 5324.

[22] "Lettre de la société populaire de Marseille à la députation des Bouches-du-Rhône, rédigée par Leclerc fils" in *Courrier d'Avignon*, 4, 31 December 1792.

[23] "Adresse du peuple Marseillais à la Convention nationale," n.d., in *Rapport d'Alexandre Ricord, fils & Mainvielle, députés extraordinaires des Bouches-du-Rhône auprès de la Convention nationale* (Paris: Galletti, 1793), 17–22 in BM Marseille, 5825.

provoked bitter denunciations and accusations of betrayal. But the Club went further. In mid-March 1793, it submitted another giant petition demanding in vain that the *appelants* resign from the Convention. The *appelants* were traitors, cowards, perfidious, in league with the foreign enemy, unfaithful representatives, and unworthy delegates of a free people. At this point, too, the petition claimed to speak not only for the Club but also for all twenty-four urban sections as well as the administration and affiliated clubs, including, no doubt, that of Aubagne. Everyone purported to support the faithful deputies, the regicide Montagnards, the "sainte Montagne." But the Club had a solution if the unfaithful deputies refused to resign. It demanded that the Paris Jacobins, the Cordeliers Club, and the Paris Sections purge the Convention by force and punish the traitors. For good measure, the ministers and the prevaricating generals had to go, too.[24]

The crisis of the spring of 1793 was far worse than the one the country had faced the year before. With the Convention's declaration of war on Great Britain and Spain, the war was much closer to the South. There were reports from time to time of enemy warships at the very mouth of the harbor in Marseille, a test, no doubt, of the artillery in the forts at the end of the docks. There was a constant nervousness about the readiness of the fleet at Toulon and suspicions of the civilian authorities watching over the arsenal and the fleet.

In the second week of March, counterrevolutionary risings in fourteen departments of the West broke out. At almost the same time, the French position in the Low Countries began to crumble from Austrian attacks, a crisis that eventually led to treason from General Dumouriez. The Club and the Jacobin authorities in Marseille responded to the crisis on the frontiers and the outbreak of civil war in the Vendée with an extraordinary energy. "Unite, patriots!" the Department exclaimed, "watch over the perjurers! Vigilant sentinels, be at your posts! Our enemies have traitors who serve them; the *patrie* is in the greatest danger. Those indifferent to the peril that threatens us must be exterminated.... Let the wrath of the people threaten all those who do not want to fight, let all

---

[24] *Copie de l'adresse des citoyens de Marseille à la Convention Nationale, en date du 17 mars 1793...* (Paris: Impr. patriotique et républicaine, 1793). BM Marseille 5329, which also prints the club's own address. The fuller version in the *AP*, lx, 420–4, reprints the deliberations of the sections as well, but not the club, so both sources must be consulted. Three sections called for the physical expulsion of the *appelants*, another demanded they be executed, still another seemed to suggest that the Convention itself would not be legitimate so long as the *appelants* were present.

the traitors and the prevaricators fear the vengeance of the sole, the true, the Eternal Sovereign!"[25]

The practical application of these vigorous sentiments showed the huge difference between how the Convention and the Marseillais approached the crisis. The Convention imposed conscription, established a Revolutionary Tribunal to deal with treason in high places, authorized summary justice to punish armed rebellion, and so on. In Marseille, authorities were much more concerned with organizing a preemptive strike against the internal enemy. As an institution representative of much official opinion, the Trois Corps was well placed to take a lead. This was an unusual body of the Department, District, and Commune of Marseille. Sometimes it even invited the Club and Sections to join in its deliberations. Two days after the Department's dramatic warning about the internal enemy aiding the foreigner, the Trois Corps decided to replace the Popular Tribunal with a "revolutionary committee" composed of twelve citizens. Unlike the Popular Tribunal, which was supposed to channel the vigilante instinct, this new body would "watch over, repress, judge without appeal, and punish the enemies of the Republic." This was another kind of revolutionary tribunal, despite the name, more proactive and, above all, different because the new judges were militant Jacobins, men who were appointed, not elected. Some were members of the all important Central Committee of the Club, like François Isoard.[26] If there was a consensus on a new kind of revolutionary tribunal, everyone also accepted the idea of a Committee on Forced Contributions, or *comité de secours*, euphemisms for a war tax on the rich. The Sections would soon demand that they be subject to democratic, that is, Sectional control. In other words, the Sections, soon to be the basis of anti-Jacobinism, endorsed exceptional institutions. Anti-Jacobins were not antirevolutionaries.

The split between Sections and Club developed over the narrower issue of how to define and deal with internal enemies. For the Sections, there had to be an institutional process; the Jacobins had other ideas. At a secret meeting of the Club's Central Committee, Isoard and others presented the ultimate plan, the great gratifying purge of every enemy at a stroke. At dawn on the morning the plan was to unfold, the town criers would

[25] *Proclamation de l'administration du département des Bouches-du-Rhône, du 14 mars 1793, l'an second de la République française. Aux Armes citoyens, aux armes,* BM Arles MS 640.

[26] ADBR, L 48, 178–9, deliberation of 16 March 1793. See also Paul-Albert Robert, *La Justice des sections marseillaises. Le tribunal populaire 1792–1793* (Paris: A. Rousseau, 1913), 67–70.

announce a curfew. Then businesses would be closed, people forbidden to peer out their shuttered windows, and the city gates shut. Forty battalions of the National Guard would secure the city and man the ramparts. Artillery companies would guard the heights above the promenades, as well as the broad and strategic avenue, the Canebière. In addition to disarming all suspects, 700–800 of the worst of the worst would be herded into the church of Saint-Homobon.[27] A guillotine would be on display on the Place Saint-Jean held at the ready for the new revolutionary tribunal. Isoard, a member of the Club's Central Committee and of the new revolutionary tribunal, predicted that there would be requiem Masses on the morning of the event.

Some municipal officers and some members of the Club feared all this was a prelude to a huge massacre of internal enemies. Nor was it reassuring that one extremist told an official that he expected the execution of only 150–60 people, as if this diminished the outrage. Moderates in the Club and municipality hastily forestalled the frightening project. They managed to limit the action to a disarming of suspects only. This began at five in the morning on 19 March.[28] Still, extremists resented being thwarted like this and blamed the softheadedness of the mayor, Mourraille, and the procurator, Seytres, for heading them off. Soon they were blaming them both for "moderationism" and for tyranny and vexations.[29] In any case, the Jacobins' overreach may have induced the political class to draw back. After 19 March, nothing more was heard of a new tribunal, nor of a war tax on the rich. The municipality soon authorized those who had been disarmed to retrieve their weapons.[30]

---

[27] The church and adjoining convent were eventually replaced by a vaudeville theater known as the Alcazar, which is now the site of the splendid Bibliothèque municipale. It was also a stone's throw from the site of the Jacobin club of Marseille.

[28] *Copie de la déposition faite par le citoyen Etienne Seytres au Comité Central des Sections & au Tribunal populaire d'accusation* (Marseille: Jouve, [mai 1793]), BM Marseille, 5348. Another copy in ADBR, L 3037. Ibid., *Jugement rendu par le tribunal criminel du département des Bouches-du-Rhône, qui condamne à la peine de mort Louis-François Dominique Isoard... du 2 vendémiaire de l'an quatrième Républicain*, especially his letter to the Jacobins at Digne (pp. 9–10) that confirms Seytres's account. And ibid. (and in ibid., L 1044), *Mourraille à ses concitoyens* (Marseille, 1793) also confirms Seytres. See also Lautard, *Esquisses historiques. Marseille depuis 1789 jusqu'en 1815*, i, 191–2.

[29] Jacques Guilhaumou, *Marseille républicaine (1791–1793)* (Paris: Presses de la Fondation nationale des sciences politiques, 1992), 179.

[30] *Résumé des procès-verbaux des délibérations des sections de la commune de Marseille, un exposé général de leurs Travaux, depuis leur Permanence* (Marseille: Jouve, 1793, l'an deuxième de la République Française), 9–10. BM Marseille 1882. This document says

In retrospect, the disarming of 19 March launched the break between Jacobins and their future opponents. In effect, the extremists in the Club had broken the uneasy consensus that the revolutionaries had achieved by drawing a veil over past events. Throughout the autumn and winter of 1792–3, no matter how they coped with the lynchings, all agreed that the outrages were in the past and that popular complaints would go through the Popular Tribunal from then on. If they genuinely were in the past, there was no need to disturb the veil. The Central Committee of the Club broke an implicit covenant. The anti-Jacobins were not prepared to tolerate continuing popular vigilantism.

Massacres outside Marseille also helped break the consensus. The massacres of 1793 were not particularly different from those of 1792. The responsibility of the clubs is more evident, but this may be an artifact of the documentation. Otherwise, the desire for revenge, the continuation of factional struggles and the justifications showed that no break had occurred. The difference was that some members of the elite concluded that if the Popular Tribunal could not deflect popular justice, perhaps it was time to take more repressive measures.

Aix-en-Provence may have been the most violent city in the entire region. Some of the earliest hangings in the region had occurred in December 1790. Over a period of six weeks beginning in January 1793, five more massacres occurred as mobs seized defenseless prisoners from the poorly guarded jail. They hanged about ten or twelve individuals from lampposts on the boulevards, from trees near the Rotonde, or in nearby meadows. Frequently, the prisoners sensed what was happening and began to weep for their lives, but the killers told them they were only being transferred to Marseille. Once near the Rotonde, the killers pretended to interrogate victims by asking about some minor crime. An accomplice then snuck up behind the victim, slipped a rope around his neck and the group hoisted him from the lamppost. Often, the killers claimed to be acting on behalf of the Club. Sometimes the killers had to wait a long time for revenge. Referring to the hanging in January 1793 of Verdet, the former president of the Department, one of the killers said he deserved it for having put himself at the head of the Swiss regiment that defended Aix against

---

the two exceptional bodies were established on 26 March, but this must be a misprint. On the rearming, see pp. 55–6. On the conditions around the disarming, see ADBR, L 1949, "Extrait des registres des délibérations de la septième section républicaine de Marseille," 16 May 1793.

the National Guard incursion eleven months before. "We had to make examples because they are aristocrats," one of the killers exclaimed.[31]

The last popular execution in March 1793 was an exception to this pattern. Despite a National Guard escort and despite the fact that it was two in the afternoon, women seized a prisoner, a recently arrested bottle-stop maker, and hanged him. They had accused him of rape and of communicating venereal disease to his victims. As his escort rounded into the Rue de l'Official from the Rue de la Boutique Rouge, the women showered the grenadiers with stones, some prisoners escaped, and the guardsmen ran after them. In the confusion, "a considerable multitude of women captured one prisoner, strung a cord around his neck and hanged him from a lamppost before the shop of citizen Villemus." None of the officials present, nor any of the guardsmen, recognized any of the women.[32]

The hangings at Salon-de-Provence became a notorious example of Jacobin misrule. Like Aubagne, factions in Salon fell out over elections. The non-Jacobin municipality elected in December 1792 feared that extremists would murder their supporters and their wives and children, and that they would call in fanatics from Marseille to restore "order."[33] Sure enough, the Department sent in national guardsmen from surrounding villages under the supervision of commissioners drawn from the Club in Marseille. As they did in Auriol a few months before, they imposed heavy taxes on "the rich" to support the occupation. The town resisted and expelled the outsiders but this only provoked a second invasion on 20 February of 750 regular troops. The invaders imposed a curfew, disarmed everyone, and paraded through the town swinging ropes, saying, "Voilà notre pouvoir exécutif!" In a now-familiar mise-en-scène, those arrested were removed from prison and three were murdered, apparently by the national guardsmen from nearby. How many were chopped up with swords and how many hanged is unclear, although in one case, the victim could not be hanged because his feet were still touching the ground, so he was shot twice with a pistol. One killer let one prisoner

---

[31] See among many depositions in Ibid., L 3043, that of Joseph Courbon, p. 30 of the printed record, and of Jean-Baptiste Estif (p. 24), both dated 18 April 1793.

[32] Georges Guibal, *Le mouvement fédéraliste en Provence en 1793* (Paris: Plon-Nourrit et cie, 1908), 37–8. *Courrier d'Avignon*, 8, 9 September 1792. M. Roux-Alpheran *Les rues d'Aix, ou, Recherches historiques sur l'ancienne capitale de la Provence* (Montpellier: Presses du Languedoc, 1985), i, 663–4; ii, 67–9. ADBR, L 288, "Copie de la lettre écrite aux citoyens commissaires de la Convention nationale à Toulon par la municipalité d'Aix, le 6 mars 1793 ... " Ibid., *Procès-verbal* of *cit* Arnaud, 6 March 1793.

[33] Ibid., L 2014, "Extrait de la délibération du conseil tenu en séance publique dans la maison commune, présent plus de quatre cents personnes," 13 December 1792.

escape because he was too old to be an aristocrat, although that did not prevent the Club's commissioners from trying to track him down. Another person from a nearby village was buried alive. The now Jacobin municipality feigned complete ignorance of who committed these outrages. Some said that the new mayor claimed – true or not – that the victims had hanged themselves.[34]

The killers had implicit support, at the very least. Later investigators blamed the commissioners of the Department, most of the Jacobin municipal officers, and the justice of the peace, who not only failed to follow through but also used arrest warrants as a way to extort money. Some said they met in a room known as the "chambre rouge" at a local inn, to plan their exploits and feast on game and wine they had stolen.[35]

The Sections

With the Jacobin extremists planning a vast settling of accounts and with violence ubiquitous throughout the Department, it was reasonable to ask where this was going to end, whether the slaughter was moving to another level. A debate that had begun among Jacobin administrators and clubbists and that had shown many ambiguities, confusions, hesitations, and ambivalences was now beginning its resolution. After the narrow escape on 19 March and with the lynchings in Aix and Salon before them, anti-Jacobins viewed their opponents as bloodthirsty monsters who would stop at nothing to satisfy their cupidity and base appetites. After the failure of the disarming episode on 19 March, let alone their vaster but thwarted ambitions, Jacobins suspected that the condemnation of

---

[34] Marc Codaccioni, "Les Troubles révolutionnaires à Salon," DES, Faculté de Droit d'Aix (1962), 57–65. *Les Habitans de la Commune de Salon, département des Bouches-du-Rhône, réunis en société populaire au comité de sûreté générale de la Convention nationale* (Salon, 1 ventôse, An III), *passim*, in library of AM, Salon. ADBR, L 3037, *Jugement rendu par le tribunal criminel du département des Bouches-du-Rhône, qui condamne à la peine de mort Louis-François Dominique Isoard... du 2 vendémiaire de l'an quatrième Républicain.* The most detailed account is Guilhaumou, *Marseille républicaine*, 137–59, and his "Mouvements populaires et commissaires jacobins. L'exemple de Jacobin François Isoard (printemps 1792–printemps 1793)," in *Mouvements populaires et conscience sociale: XVIe–XIXe siècles: actes du colloque de Paris, 24–26 mai 1984*, ed. Jean Nicolas (Paris: Maloine, 1985), 552–4.

[35] ADBR, L 3319, *procès-verbal* [*Tribunal du district de Salon*], 16 Floréal An III – 5 May 1795. For hangings in Les Baux, see ibid., L 1533, "Les commissaires de conseil général de la commune des baux en permanance" to [department ?], 8 March 1793. Department of Bouches-du-Rhône to Convention, n.d., in *AP*, lxiii, 496, session of 28 April 1793.

violence in politics was a ruse for something far worse, unnamed but sinister.

Temporary alliances were still possible. The Sections supported the Club in its campaign against the mayor, Mourraille, and the procurator, Seytres. For the Club, this was payback for their role on 19 March; for the Sections, it was to weaken the Jacobin hold on the municipality. No one could say this, so they denounced Mouraille on 12 April for high living and illegal tactics during his reelection campaign. The Sections denounced Seytres for peculation, diversion of funds, favoritism in the allocation of jobs, and so on.[36]

Both the Club and the Sections looked to the representatives on mission from the Convention, Bayle and Boisset, for a lead. Although they were normally pro-Jacobin, they ordered the arrest of Mouraille and Seytres. From the Jacobin point of view, however, they blundered in ordering that the trial be held before the Popular Tribunal, whose judges were elected by the Sections. The Club would have preferred the Criminal Tribunal, whose judges were reliable stalwarts. More troubling still was the arrest of the dockworker Jean Savon. Some said that at the theater, Savon bellowed against scenes he disliked. Whenever the audience shouted at him to shut up, he threatened to hang them. Such outbursts must have upstaged the actors. For the Sections, Savon incarnated every aspect of Jacobin excess. As an officer in the National Guard the previous September, he had arrested suspects with great zeal, a zeal that some suspected continued into vigilantism. The Sections described him as a "monster that Marseille [has] long lamented having given birth.... This wicked person, soiled with murders ... still had the means to satisfy his insatiable cupidity while forcing the peaceable citizen whose hearth he disrupted, to pay for his life through monetary extortion whose rate he arbitrarily and irrevocably fixed."[37]

Finally, the imprisonment of the Orléans branch of the royal family in Marseille in late April, including the sleazy opportunist and regicide Philippe Egalité, was deeply suspicious. In this case, the representatives' contradictory statements about the reasons for the choice of Marseille as

---

[36] *Résumé des procès-verbaux des délibérations des sections de la commune de Marseille,* 9–16. BM Marseille 1882.

[37] Ibid., 18. AM Marseille, 13D 40, *Aux commissaires nationaux. Extrait des registre des déliberations de la septième section de la ville de Marseille,* 25 April 1793. ADBR, L 1943, "Extrait des registres des déliberations de la section treize," 15 April 1793.

the site of the imprisonment only fueled suspicions of an ulterior motive. Perhaps, someone was plotting to restore the monarchy and put Egalité on the throne.[38]

Suspicions of an ulterior motive and the desire to nudge the trials forward helped redefine the Popular Tribunal. Its original role was to be the passive recipient of denunciations. Now it became a device to erode the Jacobin base. Section 23 concluded that the imprisonment of the Orléans family was bound to attract hordes of suspicious outsiders. To forestall their plots, the section proposed that each section form a *comité de surveillance* with the citywide Central Committee of Surveillance to coordinate their efforts. This soon became the General Committee of Thirty-Two Sections, whose purpose expanded to the collection of evidence against Savon, the preparation of written proofs for submission to the Popular Tribunal, and the reception of denunciations about abuse of power. Because formal bodies like these now collected denunciations rather than the citizenry as a whole, the Popular Tribunal became much more of a political instrument of the Sections.[39]

The Club was scandalized at the more assertive role of the Popular Tribunal and the Sections in the trials of Mouraille, Seytres, and Savon. They asserted that this put the Revolution as a whole on trial, that new men were infiltrating the Sections, often cloaking their nefarious designs with the language of patriotism.[40] The Sections responded with a lusty denial of aristocratic infiltration. They justified their intolerance for intriguers, not by calling attention to newcomers but by saying that times had changed. While keeping the veil over recent events was desirable, they said, it was intolerable to give free reign to "perverse men [to] dispose of the existence and fortune of the Citizens. . . . [T]hey borrow the language

---

[38] *Résumé des procès-verbaux des délibérations des sections de la commune de Marseille,* 41–4.

[39] ADBR, L 1950, "Extrait *Parte in quà* des délibérations de la 23me Section," 29 April 1793. Ibid., L 1955, undated, untitled draft. Also règlement of 13 May 1793 and letter to Section 7, 23 May 1793. Ibid., L 1949, letter to the Sections, n.d. Also, "Extrait *parte in quà* des registre des délibérations de la section n° 3, séance du 27 avril 1793."

[40] On this issue of new men, see William Scott, *Terror and Repression in Revolutionary Marseilles* (New York: Barnes & Noble Books, 1973), 77–81, who argues against the assertion the Sections were taken over by new comers. Actually, there were newcomers in that the social composition of the sections changed significantly as the influence of the club was contested. During the spring of 1793, the dominance of artisans gave way to that of clerks, salaried workers, and younger (and older) men. See Michel Vovelle, "Le Sans-culotte marseillais," *Histoire et mesure* 1, no. 1 (1986), 93.

of patriotism the better to seduce; . . . to make us servile."[41] The Club had said the same thing a few months before.

The representatives' mishandling of the agonizing political crisis in Aix was more serious still, another step along with 19 March and the arrests in driving the wedge between Jacobins and Sections in Marseille. In effect, the Egalité section in Aix had begun issuing arrest warrants for leading clubbists there, accusing them of involvement in the multiple hangings in the city. Yet the Club had a powerful ally. The Department supported the Club's demand to close all the Sections in Aix, the disarming of sympathizers of the sections' cause, and the arrest of others.[42] When the representatives supported these measures, the sections in Marseille proclaimed their anger and soon forced the Sections in Aix to reopen.[43]

Hotheads on the Department council responded with trying to provoke an insurrection against Marseille, an insurrection that more than anything else caused the Federalist rebellion. The President of the Department, Dr. Pâris from Arles, and several leading Jacobins, tried to raise an army from the entire Midi against the Sections of Marseille. They formed the grandiose-sounding Central Committee for the Salvation of the Midi. With headquarters at Salon, still governed by the unscrupulous extremists installed the previous February, they put out an appeal to local clubs to help them raise 150,000 troops. Thus, a new expedition would liberate Marseille from the "merchants, capitalists and rich" who had seized the city. Should the Sections succeed, they predicted, the patriots would be executed and Marseille would declare its independence from France. Even now, patriots were vexed, blood was flowing in the street, and the counterrevolution was raising its ugly head. "The Saviors of the Midi are ready, if necessary, to march on Marseille, fall on the Sections . . . and deliver the oppressed patriots," they exclaimed on 29 April. Once again, as in the disarming episode the previous March, the truly exalted imagined a mighty smashing of the enemy in a single blow. It never happened, of course, despite moral support from Jacobin

---

[41] *Résumé des procès-verbaux des délibérations des sections de la commune de Marseille*, 33. Also ADBR, L 1972, "Exposé du 29–01-93 à mai 1793. Convention."

[42] This Jacobin aggressiveness was widespread. On 9 April, the municipality of Arles arrested forty-three Chiffonistes, or anti-Jacobins (Sampoli, "Politics and Society in Revolutionary Arles," 283). Also in Marseille, tensions were very great at the end of April. There was a rumor that a list was circulating containing the names of 150 people who would soon be executed. See ADBR, L 3127, "Extrait des registres des délibérations de la Section no 14, dite L'Oratoire," 22 April 1793.

[43] Guibal, *Le mouvement fédéraliste en Provence*, 56–65.

municipalities like Aubagne's. Even the normally pro-Jacobin municipality of Marseille balked. The threat from the Salon Central Committee evaporated when their opponents on the Department council summoned the committee to disperse or face the consequences.[44]

Still, the affair did not end there. The attempt to raise an army against Marseille accelerated the sections' major reassessment of the polity within the city. Specifically, it led to a complete break with the representatives, to the closure of the Club, and to overt defiance of the Convention.

The Sections were appalled at the representatives' support for the closure of the Sections in Aix. They were also suspicious that the representatives were supporting the Central Committee in Salon. Consequently, they began to intercept their correspondence. Late one night, armed men invaded their apartment looking for papers. They broke the lock on a strongbox that contained valuable letters. The representatives took this as their cue to flee to Montélimar with, they said later, their lives in peril. Several Jacobin leaders fled too, claiming to other towns that Marseille had raised the standard of the counterrevolution and that people were openly sporting the *cocarde blanche* in the streets.[45] Once safe in Montélimar, Bayle and Boisset abolished the Popular Tribunal and suppressed the Central Committee of the Sections that was gathering evidence for it.[46]

This decree further outraged the Sections. They declared themselves in a legal state of resistance to oppression. The representatives had declared themselves "Heads and protectors of a party that bases its shameful hopes on extending anarchy and license," they said. "If resistance to oppression

---

44 *Résumé des procès-verbaux des délibérations des sections de la commune de Marseille*, 57–8. Codaccioni, "Les Troubles révolutionnaires à Salon," 70–2. "Arrêté de l'administration du District de Marseille du 10 mai 1793, l'an second de la République," in BM Arles, MS 640, pce 9. Guibal, *Le mouvement fédéraliste en Provence en 1793*, 92–5. C. Lourde, *Histoire de la Révolution à Marseille et en Provence: de 1789 au Consulat* (Marseille: Laffitte, 1974), iii, 223–6. ADBR, L 2075, "Copie de la lettre écrite par la Correspondance de Pelissanne ... " n.d. Ibid., 100E 42, *Arrêté de l'administration du Département des Bouches-du-Rhône Du 14 Mai 1793, ... Relatif au Rassemblement qui s'est formé, à Salon; sous le nom de comité Central.* Ibid., L 1002, f. 117, municipality of Aubagne to District, 13 May 1793.

45 *Compte-rendu à la Convention Nationale, par Moyse Bayle et Boisset, représentans du peuple envoyés dans les départements de la Drôme et des Bouches-du-Rhône, pour le Recrutement des trois cent mille hommes* (Paris: Impr. nationale, 1793), BM Marseille 5819, reprinted along with their decree of 2 May in *AP*, lxv, 594–5, session of 12 May 1793.

46 *Arrêté des représentants du peuple français délégués près les départements de la Drôme et des Bouches-du-Rhône*, 2 May 1793 in AP, lxiv, 595, session of 12 May 1793.

is one of the first rights consecrated as a base of any free government, there
has never been a more just and more urgent application of it than against
this decree." Even the unwieldy Trois Corps supported this defiance.[47]
Naturally, the Popular Tribunal stayed.

Then, the man who single-handedly epitomized wanton massacre
throughout the Midi, bearing no doubt some resemblance to how the
cartoons at the time depicted him – squat, bug-eyed, curled moustache,
ample girth stuffed with pistols and a saber – showed up to swagger in
the street: Jourdan Coupe-Tête, with a band of armed sidekicks, strangers,
and others up to no good who suddenly appeared out of nowhere. No
one mistook the arrivals for a coincidence, and everyone wondered why
Bayle and Boisset consorted with this criminal. As he was the man whom
opinion held personally responsible for the massacre of La Glacière in
Avignon in October 1791, this was a warning louder than words of what
the extremists intended. Not surprisingly, Jourdan was quickly packed
off to Fort Saint-Jean. His henchmen scattered.[48]

Continuing their sterling record of crisis management, Bayle and Boisset on 14 May charged that the inhabitants of Marseille were in a dishonorable stupor, unsuspecting tools of the foreign tyrants. "Republicans,"
they exhorted, "you delivered yourselves from the priests, princes, and
kings, do not fear the despotism of these men whose morals are depraved
by luxury, for whom selfishness is a god, and equality a torment."[49] The
Sections brazenly dismissed the deputies and their appeal to social division. They pointed out that the Convention had ended their mandate on
30 April, and nothing they ordered after that date, especially their slander
of Marseille, had any legal validity.[50]

Once they returned to Paris, the representatives retrospectively dis-
cerned an Orleanist plot of their own. Forestalling this conspiracy, they

---

[47] *Extrait des Registres des délibérations de la vingtquatrième section de la Commune de
Marseille, Séante au Bon-Pasteur...* (Marseille : Jouve, 1793), BM Marseille 5343.

[48] *Résumé des procès-verbaux des délibérations des sections de la commune de Marseille,*
59.

[49] Cited in Paul Gaffarel, *Histoire de Marseille sous la Révolution* (Marseille: Comité du
Vieux-Marseille, 1932–7), 138, special edition in AM, Marseille BIB 6395–6.

[50] *Arrêté de l'administration du département des Bouches-du-Rhône, du 19 mai 1793, l'an
2ᵈ de la République française, Portant rappel des six mille hommes levés en dernier
lieu, et protestation expresse de ne plus obtempérer au aucuns Arrêtés, Proclamations
& Ordres venant de la part des Citoyens Moyse Bayle & Boisset, Commissaires de
la Convention nationale, rappelés auprès d'elle par la loi du 30 Avril dernier,* in BM
Arles, MS 640, n° 10. See Aulard, *RACSP,* iii, 533–5 for the text of the decree. See also
Courrier d'Avignon, 540, 29 May 1793.

now claimed, required the closure of the Sections and the arrests in Aix. The arrival of the Orléans family also explained the sudden turn of Marseille opinion against them, as suborned newssheets set to work to dupe the people.[51] The quality of information given to the Convention never rose above this deplorable and misleading level their own representatives had just delivered. Consequently, as so often in the Revolution, an ally to whom one had sworn loyalty to the grave was suddenly an enemy unmasked. Marseille, once so solid in its defense of the Revolution, in its heroism on 10 August, in its lusty demands for the immediate death of Louis the Last, and in its full-bore denunciations of the *appelants* – all positions supported by the Montagnard majority in Paris – had frivolously succumbed, as so many others had, to the seductions of a self-seeking minority of the rich. It was a dangerously simple, not to say simpleminded, assessment.

Whether anyone had declared the counterrevolution, or who was secretly advancing the Orleanist plot, or whether the entire collectivity suddenly had become soft-witted dupes, these were imaginative allegations. The more practical issue was the fate of the Popular Tribunal. Authorities initially obeyed the representatives' decree of 2 May that the tribunal cease operations but as soon as the extremists in Salon issued their call to arms, the Sections reinstated it. The city was illuminated in celebration. Furthermore, arrest warrants were issued for the commissioners thought responsible for the massacres in Salon in February and March. This included the ubiquitous Isoard, the central figure in the disarming episode in March, as well as the Jacobin mayor of Salon, David. Many Jacobins were thus imprisoned in Fort Saint-Jean while still others fled the city. On 15 May, the Popular Tribunal condemned to death Jean Savon, his brother and a comrade, for abuse of power, violation of property rights, excesses, and arbitrary acts. Unlike the terrorist tribunals to come, the accused did have legal representation and could call witnesses in their own defense. But the Popular Tribunal was also revolutionary because there was no appeal. The accused went to their deaths the next day.[52] On 22–3 May, the tribunal exonerated Mourraille and Seytres.

Also on 22 May, the Department, without, one suspects, the fire-eating Jacobins, decreed the establishment of Sections in every commune that

---

[51] See their letter to Committee of Public Safety of 28 April 1793 in Aulard, *RACSP*, iii, 518–20, where there is no mention of an Orleanist conspiracy. See also Guibal, *Le mouvement fédéraliste en Provence*, 68–72.

[52] ADBR, L 3100, printed judgements of 15 and 21 May 1793. Robert, *Tribunal populaire*, 90–7.

would meet continuously. This recalled the mobilizations of 1792, and for the same reason: without an aroused people, the republic would be lost. They were to denounce those who wished for a restoration of the Old Regime, and anyone who endorsed any other power destructive of the "sovereignty of the people," or the unity of the republic.[53] As in so many other areas, the doctrine of an aroused people transcended factional lines.

Unlike Lyon, where an insurrection against the town hall brought Jacobinism to a bloody end on 29 May, in Marseille the Sections filled the power vacuum their pressure created. The Jacobins fled or retreated. Also, unlike Lyon, the Sections' capture of local institutions did not involve an insurrection and a purge. At the municipal and district levels at least, personnel did not change. Instead, the elected officials tilted more and more to the Sections, exasperated as they were with the Club. The final straw was the challenge from the Central Committee in Salon. The town council of Marseille denounced the plots of interior enemies, intriguers, and agitators.[54] Later, on 27 May, they demanded that Marat be executed, "this being vomited from the depths of Hell, [whose goal] is to transform France into a vast cemetery."[55]

In early May, the Jacobins also lost influence over the District. The administrators trumpeted their peaceful effort to "unmask intrigue and reduce it to the weakness and the nullity it deserves," a triumph of the "force of true principles" over the "supporters of crime, [and punishing] the wretched by the simple triumph of virtue."[56]

But the triumph of virtue in Marseille was unstable. If local institutions were bending before the heavy winds from the Sections, they would also show the ability to resist later that summer.

Meanwhile, the Convention failed to sustain Boisset's and Bayle's decree of 2 May abolishing the Popular Tribunal. Instead, they merely

---

[53] Louis Blancard, Raoul Busquet, and J. B. Riboulet, *Inventaire des archives départementales postérieures à 1789...Bouches-du-Rhône. Documents de la période révolutionnaire, série L*, 3 vols. (Marseille: Impr. de Barlatier et Bathelet, 1889–1923), iii, 170–1.

[54] *Proclamation de la municipalité de Marseille*, 1 May 1793, in *AP*, lxiv, 199, session of 6 May 1793. Also in *Courrier d'Avignon*, 462, 1 May 1793.

[55] ADBR, L 1969, *Adresse de la municipalité de Marseille à la Convention nationale*, 27 May 1793. Of the sixteen councillors who signed this petition, eleven signed the regicide petition of January 1793 (see note 24); twelve signed that of 17 March against the *appelants* (*AP*, lx, 422).

[56] *Arrêté de l'administration du district de Marseille du 10 mai 1793, l'an second de la République*, BM Arles MS 640, n° 9.

suspended it until representatives of the Sections could be heard at the bar of the Convention.[57] This opened a split between the General Committee and the judges. The General Committee claimed that "suspension" did not mean cessation of cases currently before the court or within its jurisdiction. They ordered the judges to continue their work. In any case, a cessation would mean the "loss of all the fruit of this popular institution . . . and suspect persons would escape the vigilance and the severity of the laws."[58] The judges were more scrupulous and resigned when they heard of the suspension decree from the Convention. This was unacceptable to the Sections that reinstated the tribunal on 6 June.[59] When some of the judges of the old Popular Tribunal refused to join, the sections replaced them. When the municipality declined to attend the inauguration ceremonies on 10 June, the sections purged it too.[60]

After the collapse of the anti-Marseille insurrection at Salon, orators at section meetings questioned whether the Club had any positive contribution to make to civic life. Some alleged that it was a source of attacks on property and that members at its meetings planned carnage and pillage.[61] These debates led to a final decision to close the Club altogether. On 3 June at seven in the evening, the sections locked up the Club, inventoried weapons, removed three cartloads of furniture, took fifteen flags local privateers had captured to the Temple of Liberty, and transported the flag of the *fédérés* of 10 August to the town hall. Many club members surrendered their cards. Anti-Jacobin celebrants stuck the cards on the

[57] ADBR, L 3100, *Décret de la Convention nationale du 12 mai 1793 . . . Qui suspend l'exécution d'un Arrêté pris [le 2 mai] par les Commissaires de la Convention dans les départements des Bouches-du-Rhône et de la Drôme, et qui suspend également le Tribunal Populaire établi à Marseille.* See also Aulard, *RACSP*, iv, 129–30, summary of debate of 12 May 1793, and *AP*, lxv, 598, session of 12 May 1793.

[58] ADBR, L 3100, undated handwritten proclamation, undated [17 May]. Also, Gohier, Minister of Justice to [?] Paris, 28 May 1793, enjoining the sections to obey the Law of 12 May. By the time this would have reached Marseille, the tribunal would have been reinstated.

[59] *AP*, lxvi, 556, session of 16 June 1793, ADBR, L 3100, deliberation of the *Comité générale des 32 sections*, 6 June 1793. Robert, *Tribunal populaire*, 113–21.

[60] *Courrier d'Avignon*, n° 147, 11 June 1793. This issue also reports dissidence from the majority from three sections, important enough that artillery companies of the National Guard had to be alerted. The next issue reports the sections removing the municipal officers on 12 June and replacing them with nominees of the sections, as well as the sections securing the arsenal and forts – a coup, in other words. (Ibid., n° 148, 14 June 1793).

[61] Guilhaumou, *Marseille républicaine*, 190–3. But at least one section (Grands Augustins) supported the club and praised its role in the city, all while supporting the Popular Tribunal (ADBR, L 1941, *registre des délibérations*, 30 April, 7 May 1793).

end of pikes and paraded through the now illuminated city. Apparently, news of the violence at Lyon had persuaded the clubbists to cave in.[62]

The cleavage between Sections and the Club produced a realignment of national and local politics. This ensured that the sections would support the Girondins following their expulsion from the Convention on 31 May–2 June. In effect, the break between the *appelants* and the sections that occurred with the King's trial was healed after mid-May. After Boisset and Bayle fled Marseille, and after the arrest or flight of the Jacobin leaders following the antisection rising in Salon, the fight moved to Paris. Isoard fled to the bosom of the mother society, where he informed his comrades of the dangers for the patriots in Marseille. Yet when Boisset and Bayle claimed to the Convention that Marseille was in a state of counterrevolution, Barbaroux, the leading *appelant*, defended the city, saying that a place where the poor could not steal from the rich could vex only the anarchists. Led by Section 13, Grands Carmes, all but five of the twenty-four urban Sections of Marseille apologized for having called him "perfidious" for his vote for the *appel au peuple*.[63]

National and local politics intersected directly with the delegation from the sections to the Convention, which arrived in late May. After several anxious days waiting to address the deputies, they blamed the representatives on mission for the suppression of the Popular Tribunal and the Sections' Central Committee. They demanded that the Convention maintain the tribunal because it "merited, by the wisdom of its measures and the integrity of its judgements, all our confidence."[64] The reception from the Montagnards in the Convention and in the radical press was extremely hostile. They feared an attack. During the weekend the Girondins were expelled, Barbaroux urged the delegation to scatter for their own safety. Armed sansculottes surrounded the hotels of the delegates – "men with mustaches still stained with the blood of the citizens they murdered on

---

[62] *Courrier d'Avignon*, 560, 6 June 1793. *Ibid.*, n° 144, 8 June 1793 (this last is a very rare publication from the General Committee explaining the reasons for the closure of the club, dated 4 June 1793. It is not in the BNF or the BM Marseille.) See also AP, lxvi, 705, letter of 13 June from department read in session of 19 June 1793.

[63] *Courrier d'Avignon*, n° 120. ADBR, L 1968, *La Section 13 à Barbaroux* (Marseille: Impr. Rochebrun & Mazet, 1793). The five sections were 8, 9, 10, 14, and 20.

[64] *Adresse des trente-deux sections composant la commune de Marseille à la Convention nationale* (Paris: n.p.), BM Marseille 5334, reprinted in AP, lxv, 316, session of 25 May 1793. See also ADBR, L 3127, *Les députés de la Section 8 à ses commettants*, 26 May 1793, reporting on their warm reception from the Convention, dismissing the catcalls of the Marats and Dantons.

2–3 September [1792]." Four delegates were arrested, while others tried
to escape but were turned back at the Porte de Charenton. Others escaped
anyway and made their way on foot to Fontainbleau, there getting a coach
to Lyon.[65]

Once they heard of the fate of their delegates and of the insurrection
of 31 May–2 June in Paris that expelled the Girondins, a General Assembly of the Sections, the General Committee, and the Trois Corps held an
all-night emergency meeting on 7–8 June. No one was allowed to leave.
Among other things, they decided to establish a committee to regulate the
price of foodstuffs, request voluntary contributions to subsidize the price
of food, requisition four battalions of the National Guard for permanent
duty, propose each department raise a small army of five hundred men,
establish a commission of 170 members to protect the Convention that
would move to Bourges, and establish a special court "to judge all crimes
against national security."[66] About four days later, the sixty-four members of the new municipality, two for each section, accompanied by the
Trois Corps, took an oath on the alter of the *patrie* not to recognize the
Convention. The next day, in the presence of representatives from Lyon,
Nîmes, Beaucaire, and Montpellier, there was a memorial service for
those killed in Lyon on 29 May. The General Committee issued a manifesto declaring Marseille in the legal state of resistance to oppression.
They would be marching to liberate Paris from the anarchists.[67]

Meanwhile, different voices in Paris were condemning the sections in
Marseille. The militant *Journal de la Montagne* of Paris announced, "All
the rich, all the big capitalists, too cowardly to take up arms, . . . have
taken over the Sections and dominate them with their insolence. In these
false Sections where the voice of the people is stifled, they vomit horrors
against the Mountain, against the Jacobins of Paris, [and] against all
the societies which profess the principles of pure republicanism."[68] In
the Convention, Jean-Bon-Saint-André, usually thought to be a rather
colorless future member of the Committee of Public Safety, invited the

---

[65] Ibid., L 1968, "Rapport fait aux trente-deux Sections de la Ville de Marseille et de son
territoire, par leurs Com^res députés à la Convention Nationale," 7 July 1793. See p. 24
for the quote. Also ibid., "Avis aux bons citoyens par le Comité-Général des trente-deux
Sections," mid-June 1793.

[66] *Courrier d'Avignon*, 9 June 1793.

[67] ADBR, L 1995, "Extrait des registres des délibérations de la Section 24, séante dans
l'église du Bon-Pasteur," 11 June 1793. Also *Courrier d'Avignon*, n° 152, 18 June 1793.
Quotation cited in Gaffarel, *Histoire de Marseille sous la Revolution*, 143.

[68] *Courrier d'Avignon*, n° 1, 1 June 1793.

citizens of Marseille to form vigilante groups to hunt down the judges and turn them over as outlaws; while Legendre, a regicide with a particularly grisly fascination with body parts, proposed that surrounding towns and villages invade the city to support oppressed patriots.[69] Knowingly or not, proposals like these revived the strategy of the Salvation Committee of Salon, a formula for chaos and civil war.

Moreover, the Convention settled the issue of the Popular Tribunal early. The deputies accepted Collot d'Herbois's proposal that the Popular Tribunal's cases be transferred to the Criminal Tribunal of the Var.[70] In effect, the tribunal's suspension would be permanent. A few weeks later, the Convention criminalized anyone who worked with the tribunal. On 19 June, the deputies decreed anyone associated with the Popular Tribunal as "so many assassins, in a state of rebellion against the decrees of the Convention." They were therefore outlaws subject to immediate execution by judgement of any court, upon simple verification of their identity. Anyone who cooperated with the court, even as a witness, merited the death penalty.[71]

Reflections

By early June, even members of the faraway Convention could perceive the differences between the Club and the sections in Marseille. These differences were on a narrow range, as many violent disputes often are. Both sides endorsed a vigorous republicanism, an uncompromising hostility to royalism, a thorough application of the émigré laws, and the logic of an extensive war on foreign despots on land and sea, with the necessary sacrifices of men and money. Both sides also accepted the logic of exceptional institutions and, in some cases, the suspension of due process rights. For all their undoubtedly sincere commitment to the rule of law, the sections endorsed the Popular Tribunal, whose existence was extralegal. Its powers as a final court of appeal also made it revolutionary. For

---

[69] *AP*, lxvi, 704–5.

[70] Ibid., 92, 130–1. The department formally prohibited the gendarmerie from transferring the prisoners. Poster of *arrêté* of 18 June 1793 in BM Arles, MS 640, n° 16. See also Marat's letter to the president of the Convention in *Journal de la Montagne* 7, 8 June 1793. The deputy Leonard Bourdon at the Jacobin club declared Marseille in a state of counterrevolution (Ibid., 7, 9 June 1793).

[71] *AP*, lxvi, 704–5, session of 19 June 1793. See also the report in *Journal de la Montagne* 19, 20 June 1793. Some patriots from Marseille had earlier appeared before the bar of the Convention and denounced the "judicial assassins" who "every day immolate the patriots of 10 August" (Ibid., 653, session of 17 June 1793).

the sections, however, it was an essential defense of lives and property against popular vigilantism and Jacobin predations. Not only that, in March, they also accepted a revolutionary tribunal and a committee on forced contributions, provided that these were not simple instruments of the despotism of the clubs. Their solution to the risk of exceptional institutions was democratic control, but they laid aside any reference to the National Convention as an authority or an arbiter.

Above all, it never occurred to them to surrender the history and symbols of local republicanism. The glories of Marseille's struggle for liberty in the distant past and in the early years of the Revolution, the struggle against counterrevolution in Arles and the Comtat, the march to Paris in the summer of 1792, and the valor of the *fédérés* on 10 August – all this was a recent history that legitimized their present, and they would not permit a Jacobin cabal to usurp it. The removal of the battle flag of the *fédérés* from the Club after its closure to the true center of civic life was thus a rectification of an appalling error.

The clubbists often ignored the Convention too with their disarming of suspects, proposed revolutionary tribunals, and war taxes. But they rallied in time for this to be disregarded. On either side, the issue was never fundamentally loyalty to the Convention, which was too far off, almost always misinformed, and frequently irrelevant. Instead, the dispute was over local issues in which the clubbists were willing to risk a "salutary fermentation" and to plead even on the eve of their defeat with their fellow citizens, "Children of the same *patrie*, let us be generous enough to throw a veil over the crimes and mistakes of our brothers and rip it open only to enlighten those who must judge them."[72] For the *sectionnaires*, language like this was disingenuous, as the Club itself had broken the consensus in March that vigilantism was in the past. Moreover, the Club no longer supported the idea that the Popular Tribunal would substitute for vigilantism because extremists in the Club were proposing another round of massacres or had even encouraged them at Salon. Besides, no one on the side of the Club had ever proposed a prosecution of such egregious actions, and by demanding the suppression of the Popular Tribunal, they were preventing it. On the other hand, the *sectionnaires* were not willing to risk a "salutary fermentation" because some things were so appalling that the veil covering them had to be lifted.

[72] *Les républicains du Club de Marseille, à leurs frères de toutes les Sociétés et Sections de la République, Salut. (25 mai 1793)* (Marseille: n.p., [1793]), BM Marseille, 1884 and Xd1760. Also ADBR, 156E, AC Roquevaire 214.

Even more extraordinary was language regretting the passing of the Club's monopoly on political debate and the allegation that the *sectionnaires* adopted the discourse of patriotism to isolate the true friends of the people. "Watch as our enemies cry out first against the violation of laws, against popular disturbances," one Jacobin warned, "the better to prevent the people from stirring itself to holy insurrections, and [the better] to assure the impunity of their crimes."[73] For Jacobins, the language of law had thus become a language of seduction, a ruse masking a shadowy criminality.

The debate ultimately was about the recent past, about what had happened in 1792, about whether the hangings at Aubagne, Marseille, Aix-en-Provence, Salon, Auriol, La Ciotat, and Arles had to be passed over; whether the lawlessness during the expeditions like the one to Velaux on the part of the Legion of Aubagne had to be tolerated, its perpetrators never called to account; whether the violence unleashed at Arles and Salon was best forgotten. In trying to distinguish the acceptable from the unacceptable, each side developed principles, with the sections standing for notions of democratic accountability while the clubs throughout the region demanded a more practical politics of unrelenting war against all enemies. The sections certainly produced persuasive arguments. They lost during the struggles of the summer of 1793, however, only to see these ideas and principles revived after the Terror, in far less promising circumstances.[74]

---

[73] ADBR, L 3037, [François Isoard], *Discours prononcé par un membre de la Société Républicaine de Marseille* (1793), 3.

[74] The sections had also developed a political theory of sectional sovereignty by the spring of 1793 (see Jacques Guilhaumou, "Fédéralisme jacobin et fédéralisme sectionnaire à Marseille en 1793 (Analyse de discours)," *Province historique* 36, no. 148 (1987), 193–203.

6

Federalism

From the beginning of the insurrection against the Convention, the Federalists acted like revolutionaries. As a result, they drew on parts of the repertory the Jacobins had also developed. The most dramatic part of the rebellion, the attempted march on Paris, was identical to any one of the marches of the Jacobins, including the march to overthrow the monarchy the previous year. The expression of solidarity with brothers elsewhere, the arrogation of sovereignty to themselves, the recourse to exceptional measures, and the justification of repressive measures by appeal to public safety were common to the Jacobins and anti-Jacobins. This made the anti-Jacobins revolutionaries in their methods. Replacement of the Convention by another body that would meet in Bourges was also revolutionary. They also never ceased to invoke the great days of the local revolution, especially the overthrow of the monarchy. But as experience would show, the doctrine of mass arousal and popular sovereignty also led them down a path that had proved so dangerous for the Jacobins: exemplary justice and exceptional measures of repression, including vigilante justice.

Federalism in Aubagne

Federalism in Aubagne reflected the struggle of factions, each one dependent on its outside counterparts for support. No faction in Aubagne could set itself against the predominant tendency in Marseille. Thus, the municipality had to accede to the Department's order on 22 May to open the

Sections.[1] As in Marseille, the Jacobins did not feel strong enough to call on their considerable support in the town for support. Nicholas Gury, sometime secretary to the anti-*politiques,* attempted to call on support from the brothers in Toulon, but the newly formed Sections responded by requesting an expedition from Marseille of three hundred men.[2] This scotched Gury's project.

Then, on 3 June at three in the afternoon, the anti-Jacobins held a meeting at the hall of the hospital of Aubagne where the sections formed a *comité de surveillance* of thirty members who in turn chose a *comité général* of twelve members. All of them were elected unanimously. Those present then took an oath that was nearly identical to the standard republican oath "to maintain with all our power, liberty, equality, the one and indivisible Republic and to remain at our post rather than permit any violation of it." They then added another part to their oath, "to guard an inviolable secret over any matter that is assigned to us." Anti-Jacobin government was to be no more transparent than that of its enemies.

For all intents and purposes, the *comité général* took over the running of the town by the second week of June, and it installed a town council to its liking on 24 June. The new councillors began with an oath, prescribed by the department, not to recognize any acts of the convention in Paris after 31 May, until its liberty had been restored.[3] The next fatal step was to authorize a loan to finance the nineteen volunteers from the town to join the Marseillais army that was preparing to march on Paris to restore liberty to the Convention.

The club was closed right away, the speaker's rostrum was broken up into pieces, and the parts were burned in ceremonial fires around the town; there was a celebratory bonfire in the middle of the Grand'rue, the town was illuminated and a Te Deum chanted in the parish church, just as there always had been for great public events. The crowd, it was said, cried out over and over again, "Vive les sections! Vive le bon ordre! Vive la Justice! Vive Marseille! Vive La République!"[4]

The entire citizenry joined this flurry of oath taking. Another occasion was the Bastille Day celebrations. The town constructed an altar to the

[1] AC Aubagne, *registre des délibérations,* f. 166v, session of 28 May 1793.

[2] ADBR, L 1959, *Comité général des 32 sections de Marseille. Séance du 23 mai 1793.* Ibid., same to *citoyen président,* Marseille, 31 May 1793. Ibid., L 1974, Comité général [d'Aubagne] to comité général de Marseille, 7 June 1793.

[3] AC Aubagne, *registre des délibérations,* f. 168v, session of 26 June 1793.

[4] Ibid., Extrait du registre des délibérations du comité général des sections de la ville d'Aubagne, 9 June 1793.

patrie on the Grand' rue near the large fountain. There at six in the evening the municipal officers, the General Committee, the battalions of the National Guard, the clergy, and ordinary citizens took an oath of loyalty to the nation and renewed the oath to not recognize the captive Convention.[5]

On August 11, a small force from Aubagne attempting to join the Marseille Departmental Army was dissipated in a small skirmish at nearby Roquevaire. That was also the date of the last meeting of the Federalist municipal council. On 25 August, Marseille itself fell to a force commanded by General Carteaux, and Aubagne was occupied a few days later. The Federalist interlude, as it is frequently called, was over.

Yet Federalism in Aubagne or elsewhere illustrated the nature of anti-Jacobin governance. It accepted the heritage of 1789. Indeed as they constantly proclaimed, the cutoff date was 31 May 1793. This meant they were revolutionaries not only in relation to the Old Regime but also in terms of accepting deviations from normal, peacetime government.

Anti-Jacobinism in Aubagne was not a restoration. Of the thirty men on the Federalist municipal council and General Council that chose it, only four had been members of the town council in 1788. Of those elected in February 1790, only five were restored in 1793. In short, the Federalists were largely new to local politics. But they were not new to the town. Many of the surnames are familiar, and many of them were related to men who had experience with local office: the Martinots, for example; or the Martels, who were related to the premier noble family of the town, the Seigneurets. Even when they were not, many had solid roots in the town. Federalist councillor François David's father had been married in Aubagne in 1721, seventy years before his son's great adventure. Several others – Honoré Paul, the solicitor, or François Robert, the notary – were born elsewhere but had married Aubagne women forty years before.

For all that the anti-Jacobins were in power a short time – a little over two months – they were aggressive about two things: municipal finances and repression. At first sight, restoring order to the municipal ledgers might not seem the highest priority given the parlous military situation in which they found themselves, but the fact that finance was the first sustained issue the new councillors discussed says a great deal about their aims. Almost immediately, they announced that the books were in

---

[5] Ibid., f. 175, session of 13 July 1793. There is no record of the 1792 celebrations, but the clergy did participate in those of 1791 (Ibid., f. 16, session of 14 July 1791). There was a religious element to the 14 July 1792 celebrations in Marseille (*JdM*, 13 July 1792).

disarray and that the budget shortfall was about 25,000 livres. This was a huge amount of money.

To be sure, the hot denunciations of accounting irregularities masked the old issue of governance. The wrong kind of people had taken over in 1792. Malfeasance and incompetence were the inevitable result.[6] To show they meant business, they sequestered all the real property, cash, and valuables of the old municipal officers. They were responsible for "the damages and interest that resulted from the vandalism, arson, pillaging, and assaults they authorized even though they had the means to prevent them."[7]

Repression was the other major activity. The Sections' goal was "to make available means that exclude any impunity for crimes that are essential to repress [to achieve] the total ruin of intrigue and anarchy." The Sections accepted jurisdiction of the Popular Tribunal in Marseille for all crimes related to "arbitrary acts and forced contributions."[8] Although none of the cases appears to have reached the Tribunal before the collapse of the Sections, they made a good start. How many people they arrested is not known, although some prominent Jacobins were, like the former procureur Charles Boeuf, Domergue, Dominique Pichou, Nicholas Gury, and then mayor Jean-Baptiste Camoin.

But this is only a hint of what they did. After the fall of the Sections, the Jacobins produced long lists of those persecuted under the Federalists and the lists contain hundreds of names from Aubagne.[9] Such large lists lack detail and do not discriminate between degrees of persecution but there are other documents that suggest the repression was extensive. For instance, one interrogation register is named the fifth cahier and another is numbered the twenty-seventh folio, fair numbers given the short duration of the Federalists on the local scene. Unfortunately, their records fell into the hands of the terrorist *comité de surveillance* and the archives of this body have not survived.

The remaining documentation indicates there were two main lines of inquiry. The first was an allegation that in March 1792, about a half

---

[6] AC Aubagne, *registre des déliberations*, f. 174, session of 23 July 1793.

[7] Ibid., ff. 175–7, sessions of 16, 23, and 28 July 1793.

[8] ADBR, L 1974, Comité général d'Aubagne to Comité général des 32 sections de Marseille, n.d.

[9] Ibid., L 334bis, *Répertoire alphabétique des patriotes victimes des fédéralistes section-naires, auxquels il a été accordé des indemnités*. Because the lists are so undiscriminating, they have not been used in compiling the lists of Jacobins that were analyzed in the appendix.

dozen bourgeois were rounded up and held hostage in the town hall until they and their friends outside could come up with 8,000 livres to secure their release. The timing would coincide with the town's equipping of the Aubagne legion's march on Arles.

Some witnesses claimed money was extorted from them. Thus, Marguerite de Guin deposed that in March 1792, "someone placed a mannequin on the Grand' rue, and paraded it around the entire town and to which they threatened by public rumor to hang all the honest men of the town." She also claimed that Etienne Suzan and Victor Amiel told her that if she did not come up with 1,000 livres she would be sorry.[10] Interestingly, Suzan later became a terrorist municipal officer and still later the gang murdered Amiel.

Marguerite de Guin was not the only witness to threats and hostage taking. Jacques Bastigne recalled that the previous March, Dr. Moussard who was being held in the town hall along with "several other bourgeois," sent him a note asking him to give what he could. He gave an assignat of 500 livres and afterward, "an infinity of people who rejoiced at these atrocities, came to take him from his house to force him to go with them and dance a farandole in all the streets of the town and that this lasted until an hour past midnight."[11] One of the depositions claimed that the Jacobins' true aim in this incident was to redistribute property to the poor. According to Marie Barthélemy, Charles Boeuf proclaimed from the tribune of the club that he had been named subsistence commissioner to "go around to the citizens of the town to make them contribute to the relief of the needy poor," and that if these citizens said "they no longer had any money to give us, then we have to demand their heads."[12]

The second line of investigation involved threats against the town elite. These were always linked to extreme and crude class hatred toward the bourgeois. Thus Jean-André Valentin, the son of a simple peasant, complained that national guardsmen took his weapon and called him "a bugger, a pathetic good for nothing [and their leader said], 'I want to find the men of violence like you and we will see what will happen.'"[13] But the threats did not always have to be so indirect. At the time of the

[10] Ibid., L 3115, Extrait de dénonciation de Marguerite de Guin, épouse de Etienne Martin contre Domergue patriote au comité infernal de [sic] sections d'Aubagne, n.d.

[11] Ibid., Extrait de dénonciation du comité infernal de cette ville d'Aubagne du citoyen Rastignac contre le citoyen Domergue et autres, n.d.

[12] Ibid., *Procès-verbal* of 24 June 1793.

[13] Ibid., Dénonciation de Jean-André Valentin patriote contre Jean Rainaud, ainé, 23 Nivôse An II – 12 January 1794.

celebration of the death of Louis XVI, in January or February 1793, the municipality gathered all the priests together to oblige them to take an oath of recognition of the Republic. Dominique Pichou waved his sword in the air and shouted out to the assembled crowd, "They have taken the oath but without it, they wouldn't leave here." The priest then led the crowd into the church to sing the psalm *In exitu israel* – the irony must have been intended – and while the priest was giving the benediction, Pichou stood behind him with his sword behind his neck, saying to one of his companions, "Let's get it over with, we ought to kill him," and he said they ought to do it now.[14]

Others described equally lurid outbursts. Thus Antoine Moulard was accused of saying before his fervently patriotic friends, "We have to support *la patrie*, we have to take out our swords, kill all these good for nothing bourgeois," while saying to his brother-in-law Victor Amiel, "If you don't do it, I'll slit your throat."[15]

Claire Monier claimed that Dominique Pichou and Rey *dit* Bourrasque, threatened her brother. He "is a doomed man" said Pichou, "He will be hanged anywhere he is found because he acted against *la patrie*." Monier declared that her brother had run afoul of men like Pichou because he was too honest to join with them in their "continual vexations and atrocities which they inflict on the [honest men]." Later Pichou and Rey approached her and demanded she produce a letter that proved that "Citoyenne Sivan mère" was dead – obviously, the innkeeper's wife and the pest her stepsons had complained of earlier. The context of all this is mysterious, but Rey's excitement was not. He refused to believe Monier knew nothing about any letter, and he could barely contain his wild gestures and arm waving. He needed the letter, he said, because if she is dead "we'll have a great fête, with a grand farandole, and we'll put you at the head."[16]

Joseph Guillermy, the mason and future killer, escaped death at the hands of the Jacobins several times.[17] The first occurred when Jean-Baptiste Camoin, the commander of the Aubagne legion's expedition to Arles, put out the story that he, Guillermy, was responsible for the imprisonment of the national guardsmen following the Velaux Affair. While

---

[14] Ibid., Extrait des dénonciation [sic] du citoyen Augustin Seigneuret faite au comité infernal des sections contre Pichou.

[15] Ibid., Extrait de dénonciation de Claire Monier contre Moulard, père, patriote, 15 July 1793.

[16] Ibid., Extrait du comité infernale des section d'Aubagne, 10 June 1793.

[17] Ibid., Extrait du 3e cahier des dénonciations du comité infernal des sections de cette commune d'Aubagne, 1 July 1793.

he was dining at the café Rousserie, he got word that some of Camoin's more gullible followers were coming to hang him. Once out on the Grand' rue, he ran into seven or eight individuals, among whom were a pair of harvesters, who called him a rogue, and shouted that he ought to be hanged. When they tried to pull the lamppost down, Guillermy escaped. On another occasion, he ran into Marcel Brun, who had frequently threatened to do him in, along with a few others on the Grand' rue. They called him a worthless scum and a brigand, removed his overcoat, and were setting to hang him when he escaped.[18] He had several other close calls in the summer of 1792, but the most frightening experience happened to his father. On the day Pons Arnaud was lynched, Rey *dit* Barrasque, who had always sworn to kill him, and others, came to get him at the café Rousserie, grabbed him by the stomach, and amid a shower of epithets, said, "Worthless scum, you, get on your knees, come kiss the feet of the worthless scum we have just hanged." He got to his knees and to his horror, found that they were forcing him to kiss the rope soaked in Arnaud's blood. During this grisly event, they said to him, "If we get your son, the way we have you, we'll cut him to pieces." They then released him. The next day, Guillermy himself was at a nearby *bastide* when the elder Poutet, Louis Jourdan, and some others arrived. They dragged the woman of the house off "to Mass." They told him that if he was still there when they returned that evening, they would hang him. The following March, Sicard *dit* Pot de Vin, and Joseph Amiel went to his house and told him to hand over 1,000 livres in the following thirty minutes, otherwise they would hang him. In May, Pichou and Pierre Blanc went to his house looking for him, tore his bedsheets, wrecked his paintings, called his wife a slut, and threatened to do to him what they had done to his pictures. Finally Guillermy related that the Widow Messie waylaid him on the street and said to him, "All the bourgeois of Aubagne have to be hanged because they are all rogues," and addressing him directly, "And you bugger, we won't spare you, so long as we do not hang, we will always be in the same condition." At the same time Pierre Martinot, the retired curé, passed by and she said, "If we could get this rogue, we would hang him, just like all the others."

In some people's minds then, there was a social dimension to such violent threats. There were other links too. Etienne Suzan, the municipal officer who implicated Pichou and others in incitement to kill the bourgeois

---

[18] This is my translation of the word *marrias*, a word of Provençal origin. I wish to thank Régis Bertrand for his very thorough inquiry into the meaning of *marrias*.

the previous August apparently renewed the threats later. He claimed that
the feast of Saint-Apolonie "was a boisterous fête and that to celebrate it
well, it would be necessary to hang at least a dozen [bourgeois]."[19]

It is nearly impossible to verify such stories in detail. Yet the testimony
before the Sections frequently refers to events that actually did take place,
like the hangings. Clearly Guillermy used the Arnaud hanging as a way
of dating events and referred to them as if everyone knew about them.
Suzan also admitted to the existence of a highly incendiary letter against
the bourgeois of the town and said that his colleagues had signed it.

More broadly, the depositions reinforce each other on the issues of the
forced contributions and the violent threats.[20] The extortion and forced
contributions evidently date from the efforts to prepare for the expedition
of Arles in March 1792. Furthermore, it is hard to imagine that the events
of 1792 on the Jacobin side occurred without some very strong language
to accompany them. Although the exact words might have been distorted
or exaggerated, the depositions agree that this language was hostile, and
that it had a social content, specifically a crude set of threats against the
bourgeois of the town.

The arrests and interrogations in Aubagne were part of a wider system. Once the local committees had processed the cases, the accused
found their way to the Popular Tribunal in Marseille. The investigations
in Aubagne never got that far, but the justice that would have awaited the
Jacobins of Aubagne was a revolutionary justice, one that they endorsed.
Moreover, the anti-Jacobins of Aubagne were small cogs in an insurrectionary movement that denied the legitimacy of the Convention and that
aimed to replace it with a new legislative body. Such ordinary men were
being drawn into a vast adventure.

Federalism in Marseille

On 12 June, the General Committee of the Thirty-Two sections of Marseille declared their program.[21] They were marching to Paris to liberate the capital and the Convention from an anarchistic faction. The

---

[19] Ibid., L 3556, *procès-verbal* against Etienne Suzan, 22 July 1793.

[20] On the other hand, an inquiry into all types of contributions, forced or voluntary, found
only two instances of contributions, one to raise money for the march on Paris that led
to 10 August, and another for volunteers for the army. The first raised 2,000 livres;
the second, 7,000 livres. Both were public and voluntary (AC Aubagne, *registre de
correspondance,* to *agent national du district,* 4 Pluviôse An III – 23 January 1795).

[21] *Manifeste. Marseille aux Républicains français* (Marseille: Jouve, [1793]). BM Marseille
5352. See also *Comité général des 32 sections de Marseille. Extrait des Registres des
Délibérations de la Section 24, séante dans l'Eglise du Bon-Pasteur. Séance du 11 juin*

Montagnards' goal was to place Philippe Egalité on the throne, the "most corrupt man of his century; a man overwhelmed with debts; rich in opprobrium, in villainy and in cowardice." Free men throughout the country had to defend the Republic against the outrage to popular sovereignty on 31 May. Consequently, Marseille declared itself in a legal state of resistance to oppression. Also, the Convention no longer represented the nation. Instead, anarchy, disorganization, and chaos dominated. "The domineering faction in Paris inspires the Republic to employ armed force against this ever imperious and abusive city." All able-bodied men must rise "en masse, to annihilate the factious in their lair, while the Marseillais who wish to end the Revolution they began call to their side every citizen burning to be worthy of the human race." Furthermore, the Popular Tribunal, "endowed with the confidence of the People," was acting against the conspirators within the city. It needed no other justification than "the most imperative of laws, the law of circumstances... [to mete out] the most prompt justice." The justification for the march on Paris, as well as the assumption of the right to administer justice, was thus revolutionary, independent of formal law, a justification terrorists too would make.

Once again, Marseille was inspiring the nation. "Let us march," declared the manifesto, "May the law enter Paris with us! And if you don't know the way, follow the drops of blood of your brothers, they will lead you to the edge of these walls, where murderous pestilence, bloody plots and devouring hoarding, all originate. There is the source of our misery."

Marseille and its brothers throughout the nation were in a state of insurrection whose purpose was to restore the law and respect for persons and property. The insurrection in Paris left the insurgents with no alternative than to resist oppression and restore usurped rights. Because of 31 May, no legal representation existed, only a "mutilated... truncated, corrupted [and] subjugated" Convention, "dominated by a tyranny of a city that has become a lair of the factious."[22]

The oath not to recognize anything the Convention did after 31 May had as its logical corollary the refusal to recognize the so-called Jacobin

---

1793, *l'an second de la République Française une et indivisible* (Marseille: Jouve, 1793), ibid., Xd3233....

[22] *Déclaration de l'assemblée électorale du Département des Bouches-du-Rhône à tous les François* (Marseille: Brébion, 1793). BM Marseille Xd3491 also ADBR, L 278. See also *Discours prononcé par le Président de l'Assemblée électorale du Département des Bouches-du-Rhône, sur l'Autel de la Patrie, le 14 juillet 1793, l'an second de la République françoise* (Marseille: Brébion, 1793), BM Marseille Xd3495 and ADBR, L 278.

Constitution of 1793. Even so, officials hesitated. Only after pressure from the General Committee of the Thirty-Two sections and after a long debate did the Department decide not to forward the Constitution to the Districts and Communes. Consistency trumped all other arguments. One of those, advanced by Granet, the brother of the Montagnard deputy, was thoroughly democratic: refusal to forward it deprived the citizenry of a chance to revise it.[23] The District of Marseille disagreed with the Department. It proposed that the Constitution be submitted to the people, but the General Committee retaliated by purging the District. A partial purge of the Department followed.[24] Although the Electoral Assembly renewed all levels of administration just two weeks later, the incident showed that power had shifted from formal administrators to the Sections themselves.

Yet this was not the end of the aggravating issue of the Constitution. At the end of July, the procurator of the department, Siméon, deplored the recourse to violence, as he would when he resumed his position in 1795. He proposed submitting the Constitution of 1793 to the Sections as a gesture of conciliation with the Convention. The Trois Corps tabled this idea in favor of a discussion on how to resist oppression.[25] Yet the Constitution of 1793, which the Convention itself never implemented, remained a thorn in the Sections' side throughout their ascendancy. Many of the demonstrations against the General Committee raised the issue, although the arguments in favor of implementing the Constitution did not always imply a pro-Jacobin position. Indeed, accepting the Constitution was a way of getting rid of the Convention so that the new legislature could amend that very Constitution. The General Committee warned that such thinking would only entrench the views of Danton, Robespierre, and the imitators of Marat, "that these false republicans seek to perpetuate trouble and anarchy only to maintain themselves in the absolute and tyrannical government they have arrogated to themselves."[26]

With the Convention's army preoccupied in defending the Alps, the anti-Jacobins had plenty of time to organize their army. The grand plan was to organize a whole series of departmental armies centered on Caen, Rennes, Limoges, Bordeaux, and elsewhere to converge on Paris and

---

[23] AN AF II 90, plaq 663, "... procès-verbal de l'administration du département des Bouches-du-Rhône," 2 July 1793.

[24] Paul R. Hanson, *The Jacobin Republic under Fire: The Federalist Revolt in the French Revolution* (University Park: Pennsylvania State University Press, 2003), 206.

[25] ADBR, L 48, f. 249v, 27 August 1793.

[26] AM Marseille, 13D 44, *Avis aux François*, 17 August 1793.

liberate the Convention. Marseilles was supposed to be one of these centers. Other departmental armies from the Southeast, Castries, Montpellier, and Toulouse would rendezvous at Marseille. They would represent the rising of the entire French people "exercising themselves the most sacred of duties, resistance to oppression."[27] None of these armies got very far, but the Marseille army set out with great enthusiasm. At any one time, it was never very large – somewhere between five hundred and three thousand men – but the national guardsmen who set out to overthrow the monarchy the previous August were equally few. The difference was that the Departmental Army of 1793 was very hard to organize and direct. Each city provided its own volunteers, who were mostly civilians rather than trained soldiers, and each city contributed its own commissioners to coordinate strategy, arrange supplies, and so on. At the beginning, this was a march of so many city-states. The Marseillais also detoured via Arles to reinforce the Chiffoniste municipality that had just taken power. This wasted several precious days.[28] They moved on to Noves where detachments from the Department of the Gard, Arles, Aix-en-Provence, and L'Isle joined them. This force then occupied Avignon on 6 July, after scaring off an army of brigands near the crossing of the Durance at Barbentane.[29] Amid this first victory, reinforcements from the Gard abandoned the citadel of Saint-Esprit. Soldiers scattered because the Department of the Hérault dragged its feet while those of the Isère, Ardèche, and Drôme supported the Convention. This left only the city of Nîmes to fend for itself.[30]

Then an advance guard that reached Orange panicked when it heard that a small force of about two thousand men under General Carteaux

[27] ADBR, L 128, "Circulaire aux départemens... relative à une assemblée centrale à Marseille," 16 July 1793. Hanson, *The Jacobin Republic under Fire*, 29.

[28] See the analysis of Joseph-Etienne Michel, *Histoire de l'armée départementale des Bouches-du-Rhône, de l'entrée des escadres des puissances coalisées dans Toulon et de leur sortie de cette place; précédé d'une introduction sur l'origine des troubles du Midi, sur leur durée, et les moyens de les faire cesser* (Paris: Du Pont, An V – 1797), 79–80. Unless otherwise indicated, this is the principal source for the military history of the period. On Federalism in Arles, see Fr. Trophime Masse, *Pétition à la Convention Nationale du 15 Juillet 1793* ([1793]), BM Marseille 5670.

[29] *Comité général des 32 Sections de Marseille... Copie de la Lettre des Commissaires civils des sections de Marseille près le Bataillon, écrite au Comité général* (Marseille: Jouve, 1793), BM Marseille Xd3251 *Comité général des 32 sections de Marseille... Copie de la Lettre écrite au Comité général, par le Citoyen Roussellet, Commandant général du Bataillon des Sections de Marseille* (Marseille: Brébion, 1793). Ibid., Xd3230.

[30] ADBR, L 1994, comité général des sections de Nîmes to comité général des 32 Sections [?], n.d., received 20 July 1793.

was approaching. Fearing Carteaux could cut off their retreat, the Marseille army thus withdrew from Avignon. Unfortunately, the Jacobins of Avignon began their reprisals against local collaborators too soon. When the Marseillais suddenly reoccupied the city, they and their allies slaughtered the Jacobins in the streets. They may have taken over sixty lives, several of them perpetrators of the Glacière massacre of 1791, victims of their own style of vigilante politics.[31] But confusing orders from the General Committee in Marseille and Carteaux's artillery provoked the abandonment of Avignon a second time on 25 July. Commissioners from Marseille also fled, so the attempt to establish a line of defense along the left bank of the Durance collapsed. This failure of leadership panicked the soldiers who scattered. "All paths from the Durance to Marseille were covered with soldiers running with unimaginable speed," one of the anti-Jacobin leaders wrote later.[32]

The retreat from Avignon was a major strategic defeat. It meant that a juncture with the Federalist forces at Lyon would never occur. The news arrived in Marseille on 27 July and provoked emergency measures very like those measures of revolutionary government that the Convention adopted a few months later for France as a whole. The Trois Corps replaced its general who had resigned with Villeneuve, a colonel in the Old Regime army. In addition, forty-eight battalions of the Marseille National Guard, about four thousand men, were to march to the Durance via Aix to reinforce the Departmental Army. Finally, four commissioners, very like the Convention's representatives on mission, were to supervise this larger army.

On the local front, the Trois Corps and the Sections adopted increasingly authoritarian measures. On the night of 20–21 July, some Jacobin hotheads had tried to stir up trouble in a couple of Sections and surrounded the meeting place of the General Committee to demand the release of their comrades. This small disturbance brought a draconian response. The Department rushed out a poster denouncing the demonstrators as outsiders, infamous agents of the Convention, "vile, paid agents of this Mountain, this assembly of tigers . . . they wanted the renewal of these

---

[31] J.-S. Rovère to Convention, 3 August 1793 in Aulard, *RACSP*, v, 458. René Moulinas, *Histoire de la révolution d'Avignon* (Avignon : Aubanel, 1986), 283.

[32] Michel, *Histoire de l'armée départementale des Bouches-du-Rhône*, 87. S. Vialla, *Marseille Révolutionnaire. L'armée-Nation (1789–1793)* (Paris, 1910), 401–31. See also ADBR, L 1994, Castelanet and Peloux to General Committee of 32 Sections, 27 July 1793.

bloody times of proscriptions and murders."[33] The Trois Corps decided the next day to establish the Committee of Public Security. This body received extraordinary powers "to take any measure of general security it judges necessary."[34]

The Committee of Public Security claimed the disturbances were the result of a "liberty destroying plot" designed to aid General Carteaux's conquest of the city. Consequently, the Committee proposed to the Sections that they establish a Military Tribunal to deal with cases of subversion, its judges chosen by the Sections.[35] This was much less cumbersome than the Popular Tribunal because there was no jury and procedures were rapid. In practice, the Military Tribunal punished the demonstrators of 21 July and women protesting the high cost of food with prison sentences ranging from six months' detention to twelve years in irons.[36] No one, of course, had the right of appeal, as this was revolutionary justice.

The establishment of the Military Tribunal showed that the *sectionnaires* were becoming impatient with the Popular Tribunal. On the day the Trois Corps passed the emergency measures to cope with the deteriorating military situation, it also merged the two chambers of the Popular Tribunal into one and called for more rapidity in rendering judgments. Although defendants retained defense counsel until the end, unlike the revolutionary tribunals to come, the anti-Jacobins were going down the same road of emphasizing the exemplary nature of punishments rather than due process for the accused. The judges protested these innovations, yet there was little they could do about the changes.

[33] AM Marseille 13D 43, *Proclamation et arrêté De l'Administration provisoire du Département des Bouches-du-Rhône, Du 21 juillet 1793.*

[34] ADBR, L 48, f. 243, 22 July 1793.

[35] Ibid., L 1976, Committee on Public Security to Section 6, 25 July 1793. Guibal, *Le mouvement fédéraliste en Provence*, 220–5.

[36] AM Marseille 13D 43, judgment of 23 July 1793 of Jean-Baptiste Félix to eight years in irons for participating in the demonstration against the General Committee. Ibid., judgment of 30 July 1793 of Jacques Ebrard to six months detention for saying Marseille should welcome General Carteaux's soldiers. Ibid., 13D 44, judgment of 3 August 1793 condemning Joseph Chastanier to three years detention for having proposed in his section on 20 July that the troops in Avignon be recalled. ADBR, L 485, judgment of 9 August 1793 condemning Marie Colette Lacroix to six months detention for protesting high food prices on the 2 August along with other women. Judgment of 12 August 1793 condemning Jean-Baptiste Carbonel to one year's detention for having said that the sansculottes will once again be on top. Judgment of 14 August 1793 condemning "Liberté" Taneron to twelve years in irons for having praised the hangings and urging their renewal, for having stirred up trouble against the General Committee, and for "discours incendiaires et désorganisateurs."

On 3 July, they condemned Louis Barthélemy, a former administrator of the Department and Jacobin militant. Apparently, he had tried to use his official position to extort revenge against two sets of individuals he had tried earlier to sue. Much more serious was the charge that he had contributed to the "Committee of blood" formed at Salon to reverse the sovereignty of the Sections, substitute the empire of anarchy for the power of the People, raise the throne of the wicked and the intriguers on the smoking ruins of the city. The purpose was to consummate the massacres that would satiate the sabers of the blind dupes of their extravagant projects."[37] His defense that the Popular Tribunal had no jurisdiction because the Convention had outlawed it naturally was not successful.

The Popular Tribunal also dealt with the other outrages at Salon earlier in the year. In the end, the Tribunal condemned six individuals from Salon to death for their participation in the lynchings. Around a dozen or so others were sentenced to prison in irons.[38]

In three separate judgments dating from late July to the very eve of the downfall of the Sections at the end of August, the Popular Tribunal sentenced eleven individuals to death for the lynchings in Aix-en-Provence.[39] But this was not enough for the local politicians. Just as the anti-Jacobin enterprise was collapsing, the Trois Corps authorized the judges to assemble in any number that pleased them so that the innocent would not be detained any longer and "the guilty be punished according to law."[40]

Beside its activity in proposing the Military Tribunal, the Committee of Public Security urged the Sections' *comités de surveillance* to greater zeal. The Jacobin municipality had established these in early March during the mobilization against the external and internal enemies. Now, in early August, they targeted the enemies of the Sections. The Committee ordered them not to hesitate "to denounce the traitors, the agitators, [and] the anarchists who need to be contained by prompt and rigorous punishments."[41]

The General Committee of the Sections also reminded the population of the enemy within who wanted to start a civil war. "Besotted with

---

[37] AM Marseille 13D 43, *Jugement du Tribunal Populaire de Jugement*, 3 July 1793.

[38] ADBR, L 3106, judgments of 28 July, and 3 and 12 August 1793.

[39] Paul-Albert Robert, *La Justice des sections marseillaises. Le tribunal populaire 1792–1793* (Paris: A. Rousseau, 1913), 146–56.

[40] ADBR, L 48 ff 282 and 282v.

[41] Ibid., L 1950, letter to president of Section 6, 5 August 1793. See also ibid., "Avis du Comité de Sûreté publique aux perturbateurs," 4 August 1793.

blood," said the Committee, "they wish to renew among us the bloody scenes our city witnessed for so long. . . . [They] mislead you to make you the blind instruments of their vengeance and cupidity."[42] Such warnings were part of a vaster campaign to keep public morale high, a restatement of the logic behind the insurrection against the Convention and its local acolytes. Thus, the municipal officers organized a fête in honor of 10 August, where officialdom would renew its oath of loyalty to the Republic and where it swore to arrest anyone who promoted the restoration of the monarchy.[43] Finally, at the suggestion of several sections, the General Committee supported an improvised procession on 15 August to implore the protection of the Virgin and the saints and to give thanks for the support of Toulon in the struggle.[44] Appeals to the Almighty were not signs of anti-Jacobin desperation; the Jacobin municipality had associated the Church with national fêtes earlier.

Meanwhile, following the withdrawal from Avignon, Villeneuve tried to regroup his forces at Aix-en-Provence. Reinforcements were on the way, detachments from Aubagne, Roquevaire, and La Ciotat; customs officers from Marseille; regular troops from Toulon who had gone over to the anti-Jacobin side; various artillery units in addition to the forty-eight battalions from Marseille. Yet the withdrawal allowed Carteaux and the Convention's forces to cross the Durance themselves and occupy Saint-Rémy and Salon. Villeneuve in turn faked an attack on Saint-Rémy and Orgon and on 9 August took the village of Cadenet. This raised morale so much that schoolboys from the college at Aix flew to join the anti-Jacobins, and the General Committee in Marseille rejected quasi-official approaches for mediation from officers in the Convention's army. The high spirits did not last long, however. On the 11 August, some six thousand national guardsmen from the Districts of Apt and Carpentras engaged the Departmental Army in a brief artillery battle. This broke the morale of the anti-Jacobins who deserted in great numbers.[45] An attempt to hold the line on the roads outside Salon failed when troops panicked again. This time they fled all the way to Marseille, blaming their leadership and spreading panic in the population.

---

[42] *Le Comité général des 32 sections de Marseille à ses Commettans* (Marseille: Rochebrun et Mazet, 1793), BM Marseille Xd3520/3.

[43] AM Marseille, 13D 44, *Fête Républicaine pour le 10 août*, 7 August 1793.

[44] Georges Guibal, *Le mouvement fédéraliste en Provence en 1793* (Paris: Plon-Nourrit et cie, 1908) 265.

[45] Ibid., 246–59.

While Carteaux delayed the attack on Marseille until reinforcements could arrive, the Trois Corps scrambled hard to recover. On 13 August, it established the Committee of General Security with five members "with unlimited powers for the common safety." This was the second time the Sections had established a special committee with exceptional powers. It was no more effective. On 19 August, they ordered all able-bodied citizens to rise en masse and to remain in permanent readiness. They closed the Bourse, theaters, casinos, dance halls, and cafés, and they limited opening hours for food shops.[46] None of this had any effect. Armed forces in the city dissolved and National Guard battalions failed to show up for roll call.[47] Undaunted, the General Committee decided that "circumstances required" more draconian measures against Jacobin sympathizers. On 20 August, it expelled them from the city. Any remaining who expressed their opinions "will be arrested as suspects, and judged in [twenty-four] hours by the Military Tribunal as disturbers of public order and enemies of *la patrie.*"[48]

As the Convention's forces were approaching the mountain passes around the city, the Sections began a negotiation with the English fleet. These contacts had begun a month earlier with discussions of a prisoner exchange. As the Convention's blockade of food supplies into the city tightened and as the military situation allowed them to control the land routes, the Sections asked the English to permit the shipment of grain that the city had in Genoa. According to Section 23, this was the only way to escape the "cruel dilemma" of either perishing under the Convention's "murderous iron" or dying of hunger.[49] Yet the price was high. Lord Hood, the British admiral, acting entirely on his own, required that the Marseillais proclaim Louis XVII. Whether the General Committee ever agreed to the demand, as opposed to certain individuals claiming to act

---

[46] ADBR, L 48, f. 275, session of 13 August; f. 281, session of 19 August 1793. The members of the new committee were Pelloux and Castellanet, both former members of the Constituent Assembly and leaders of Section 4; Jean Abeille, who later claimed to have negotiated the surrender of Marseille to the Royal Navy; Pierre Laugier, a judge on the Popular Tribunal; and Raymond, *fils aîné.*

[47] Michel, *Histoire de l'armée départementale des Bouches-du-Rhône,* 217–21.

[48] AM Marseille 13D 44, *Proclamation du Comité de Sûreté Générale,* 20 August 1793.

[49] William Scott, *Terror and Repression in Revolutionary Marseilles* (New York: Barnes & Noble Books, 1973), 120–2, is particularly good on the question of food supply. "Extrait *parte in qua* de la deliberation de la section n° 23," 19 August 1793, in *Pétition au nom de la section onze de Marseille, des patriotes qui s'y sont réunis dans les journées des 23 et 24 août dernier* (Paris: Impr. nationale, An II [1794]), 21–2, in AN AF II 9, plaq. 668, p. 10. Endorsed by sections 1, 8, and 9.

for them, is moot because Carteaux captured Marseille before they could conclude the negotiations.[50]

Any approach to the British was intolerable to some. On the 23 August, a ship entered the harbor to drop off the French prisoners. As a result, a meeting of Section 11 at the Eglise des Prêcheurs near the port protested, not only against the contact with the implacable enemy but also in favor of letting Carteaux's forces enter the city. Fighting soon broke out. The combatants exchanged artillery fire around the port.

Some members of the Sections had already realized that defeat was practically inevitable. What would the Jacobins do if they regained power? Some said they would exact a terrible vengeance. Section 4 proclaimed that the citizens had to arm themselves to exact a rapid justice on the prisons either by speeding up the trials or transporting others to Toulon. This would boost the morale of the Sections' fighters. Perhaps so, but it was as close to a demand for a prison massacre as it was possible to imagine. The insurgents of Section 11 believed such an event was possible and so they conceived an audacious plan to kidnap the members of the General Committee and hold them hostage to guarantee the safety of the prisoners in Fort Saint-Jean. Nothing came of it because the *sectionnaires* fled their meeting hall and events overtook them.[51]

On 24 August, mortars launched from the Canebière tore some bricks and roof tiles off the Eglise des Prêcheurs. This compelled the 400–500 protesters from Section 11 and their families to flee toward the village of Allauch, pursued by some angry sailors. At the same time Carteaux attacked the Departmental Army outside the city, which produced another panic. Artillerymen threw their pieces into the ravines, hurled their arms and baggage into the vineyards nearby, and set off their barrels of

---

[50] The Convention proclaimed these negotiations treason but the evidence Jean-Bon Saint-André, *rapporteur* of the Committee of Public Safety, produced is not at all conclusive that the Marseillais were going to proclaim Louis XVII, nor is the evidence in Hood's papers. See *Rapport sur la trahison de Toulon, au nom du Comité de salut public*. ([Paris]: Impr. par ordre de la Convention nationale, 1793), esp. 81–91. John Holland Rose, *Lord Hood and the Defence of Toulon* (Cambridge: Cambridge University Press, 1922), 16–22, 123–6. The usual evidence for this, a letter ostensibly written on 25 August by one of the negotiating team (Jean Abeille, *Notes et pièces officielles relatives aux évènemens de Marseille et de Toulon, en 1793* [Paris: (L.-P. Setier), 1815], 12–14), may have been altered. It is quite different than the letter reprinted in Rose's monograph (p. 123). The subject merits more investigation. There is a handy summary of the issues regarding treason and royalism in Toulon in William S. Cormack, *Revolution and Political Conflict in the French Navy, 1789–1794* (Cambridge: Cambridge University Press, 1995), 175–80.

[51] *Pétition au nom de la section onze de Marseille*, pp. 25–6.

powder. The explosions in the nearby mountains produced even more
panic in the city. Soldiers stumbled into Marseille itself exhausted and
covered with dust. The rich fled to their country houses; many working
people gathered their finest linens and left the city to camp under the stars
for a few days along the small rivers nearby; riderless horses clopped
through the streets; and from the high points of the city during the
moonlight, one could see the approaching republican army. An earth-
quake, said Lautard, a probable eyewitness, would not have frightened
people more.[52] That evening Jacobins got out of the prisons and roamed
the streets celebrating.

On 25 August, Carteaux entered the city without firing a shot.

Many of the *sectionnaires* fled to Toulon, perhaps as many as two
thousand gathered outside the city walls. Close to a thousand soldiers
of the Departmental Army also fled to Toulon. Because they were subject to the outlawry decree, they urged resistance at all costs once the
Toulon authorities admitted them. As he had with Marseille, Hood then
offered the Sections of Toulon military protection and food if they proclaimed Louis XVII. The Sections very reluctantly agreed. No doubt well
aware that the outlaw decree offered them no way of saving themselves,
they surrendered. France's Mediterranean naval port and its ships fell
to thousands of British, Spanish, and Neapolitan sailors and soldiers on
28 August.

As an insurrectionary movement that aimed to overthrow an established government, anti-Jacobinism took a risk that the violence it invoked
could be limited to its political aims of the defense of the rule of law. Yet
in the end, some of their supporters were imagining justice with rapid
judicial procedures, something close to vigilantism. They were not very
different than their leaders in this respect. They too wanted to accelerate
the procedures of the Popular Tribunal and to bring their enemies' political activities under the jurisdiction of the Military Tribunal. Moreover,
the failure to punish the atrocities some soldiers in the Departmental Army
committed at Avignon revived the partisan conception of justice that the
Federalists had condemned in the Jacobins. These atrocities passed almost
unnoticed.

As an insurrection, Federalist governance was incapable of simply restoring the pre-Jacobin past. Because Jacobins and anti-Jacobins
accepted a great deal of the revolutionary heritage, it was impossible to

---

[52] *Esquisses historiques. Marseille depuis 1789 jusqu'en 1815; par un vieux Marseillais*
(Marseille: Impr. de M. Olive, 1844), i, 276–7.

locate where the immediate past had gone wrong. Anti-Jacobinism in both Marseille and Aubagne, and no doubt elsewhere, drew on forms and styles of governance that were unheard of. This required a mobilization of the population that was also unprecedented along with an appeal to new men who had not participated in office during the Old Regime and the early Revolution. As the voting in early 1792 in Aubagne had shown, embittered factionalism widened the political arena. At the same time, Federalist governance was an improvisation that resorted to increasingly authoritarian measures as the military situation deteriorated. The various emergency committees were all empowered to act without reference to legal procedures. In smaller places like Aubagne, the insurrectionary mentality permitted an uninhibited continuation of the faction fight that had begun much earlier. The large number of arrests and the drafting of witness statements for use by the Marseille tribunals brought that fight to a new extreme. The failure of Federalism and the measures it adopted showed how difficult it would be for anyone to return to normal governance.

7

Terror in a Small Town

Aubagne

After the defeat of Federalism in Marseille and its evaporation in
Aubagne, authorities faced the problem of how to organize repression. By
September 1793, the law had criminalized a great deal of political activity: armed insurrection or attendance at a counterrevolutionary assembly
(Law of 19 March 1793), being an official of a Federalist institution,
taking the oath not to recognize the laws of the Convention passed after
31 May, being a witness before an illegal tribunal, denouncing patriots, signing passports, and so on (Law of 5 July 1793). The Law of
19 June applied to officials of major Federalist civilian institutions. Thus
for Marseille, all officials of the Popular Tribunal of Marseille, the General Committee of the Thirty-Two Sections, officers of the Sections, and
the Trois Corps were liable.[1] For Aubagne, former members of the Sectional Committees, the *comité de surveillance*, and the municipality were
targets for punishment.

Justice in the Terror

Revolutionary justice was supposed to be shocking and rapid. Its main
features were the denial of an appeal and the requirement that executions
occur twenty-four hours after the verdict. Revolutionary jurisprudence
also eliminated most procedural protections for the accused. The institution of a *jury d'accusation*, or grand jury, in which the state had to
present the preliminaries of its case, did not apply. Revolutionary justice also eliminated the long process of gathering information about a

[1] Text of Law of 19 June 1793 in *AP*, lxvi, 704.

particular crime that was so common in the Old Regime or in the early years of the Revolution. The standard of proof could be quite simple. The outlawry decree prejudged the question of guilt so that all a court needed to do was establish the accused's identity. This applied to all Federalists, however minor their role. Furthermore, the court was satisfied with a signature of the accused on a document that emanated from an illegal institution. This explains why trials were so short. The goal of revolutionary jurisprudence was rapid punishment, the better to deter. Even those who evaded the outlawry decree faced a telescoped justice that sacrificed due process rights. The accused never knew the details of the charges against them when they appeared in court, no attorney was ever present, no one offered rebuttal evidence, the accused never called defense witnesses, and the judges ignored arguments that invoked mitigating circumstances.

The Convention itself set the parameters of repression very wide. A special decree of 4 September ordered the representatives on mission to take "the most prompt and severe measures to have the authors and accomplices of the counter-revolution of Marseille punished [for their] violence and murder committed against the person of the republicans of these regions." The rebels' heirs would also be punished in that their property was also to be confiscated and distributed to worthy patriots. The decree thus established two important elements for the future. It imposed a political criterion for the redistribution of property. In this respect, St. Just's famous Ventôse Laws of March 1794 had a precedent. Second, the earlier laws on repression were specific in defining illegal acts and who was punishable; the decree of 4 September enlarged the scope for local decision making about the guilty and their punishment.[2] Liberty, they explained,

is just, and grateful but unfortunately, she must also be severe. Therefore, we must punish the assassins of the people; the property of the rebels must compensate for the losses of the republicans. The Law promises it. We know that you will execute it with prudence and firmness. With the unlimited powers conferred on you, you will not encounter any difficulty that your zeal cannot surmount.[3]

---

[2] *Décret de la Convention Nationale du 4 Septembre 1793, l'an second de la République française... Qui charge les Représentants du Peuple dans le Département des Bouches du Rhône de faire punir les auteurs et complices de la rebellion des contrerévolutionnaires de Marseille, et qui ordonne la confiscation de leurs biens* (Paris: Impr. nat. exécutive du Louvre, an IIe de la République, [1793]), BM Marseille 1882.

[3] CSP to Rovere and Poultier, 3 September 1793, in Aulard, *RACSP*, vi, 267–8. But as late as 25 September, some representatives were complaining that measures against Marseille were not severe enough (Ibid., vii, 68).

The elder Robespierre, as the President of the Convention, elaborated, "Let the traitors breathe their last, let us appease the ghosts of the murdered patriots, purify Marseille, avenge Liberty and solidify them against the crimes of these cowardly enemies!"[4]

Finally, the Ministry of Justice authorized a draconian interpretation of the Law of 19 June punishing participation in Federalist institutions, one that affected many individuals from Aubagne. The text of the law itself seemed to suggest that witnesses before Federalist judicial authorities would fall into the category of lesser offenders, but the ministry demanded that they too be subject to the harshest penalties. The fact that this was a retrospective application of the law did not matter, the ministry said, because the Federalists had prevented the law from being published in the rebel areas.[5] What witnesses knew of the law when they testified before the Sections' general committees was therefore irrelevant.

The representatives on mission launched the institutional framework for the Terror at the end of August. On 28 August, they established the new Revolutionary Criminal Tribunal for the Bouches-du-Rhône, with appointed, not elected, judges; no right of appeal; and no jury. That very day, the new judges condemned two officials of the Popular Tribunal to death.[6] The day before, the representatives authorized the Department to arrest anyone who "appeared dangerous to the solidification of the Republican system."[7] This was a remarkable anticipation of the Law of Suspects the Convention passed on 17 September, a law that permitted the arrest of anyone dangerous to liberty.

The legal apparatus that was available for punishment was, therefore, very flexible. Moreover, authorities in the Convention, the Committee of Public Safety, and the Ministry of Justice were signaling that almost anything was permissible, so long as it produced results. Terror in the Bouches-du-Rhône operated in this context. However much they might have dreamed of smiting their enemies in imaginative ways, locals were not able to act without inspiration from higher up. Frequently, the representatives on mission gave that lead.

---

[4] Session of 31 August 1793 in *AP*, lxxiii, 349.
[5] Paul Gaffarel, *Histoire de Marseille sous la Révolution* (Marseille: Comité du Vieux-Marseille, 1932–7), 188. The date of the poster announcing this was 8 September 1793. For a more benign view of the operation of Terror in Marseille, see Paul R. Hanson, *The Jacobin Republic under Fire: The Federalist Revolt in the French Revolution* (University Park: Pennsylvania State University Press, 2003), 223–6.
[6] Gaffarel, *Histoire de Marseille sous la Révolution*, 185–6.
[7] AN, AF II 90, *Arrêté* of Saliceti [*sic*], Albitte, Gasparin, and Escudier, 27 August 1793.

Moreover, revolutionary courts were exceptional in the true sense: revolutionaries expected many things of them that they did not expect of ordinary courts. Their judges were supposed to be very special people, men of a severe and pitiless character, men whose focus was on the salvation of the *patrie*. The minutiae of cases were not their concern. Revolutionary courts were political institutions, and as such, their role was controversial from the beginning – and has been ever since.

Revolutionary justice was not normal justice. The historiography of revolutionary justice says otherwise. Donald Greer, whose classic appeared seventy years ago, is still authoritative in expressing the ordinariness of revolutionary justice. Greer was not the first to excuse it, but his book carried a lot of weight, perhaps because it reflected received opinion so well. While he recognized there were injustices and excesses, he claimed that "the vast majority [of the accused] were guilty of the charges brought against them."[8] In other words, revolutionary justice achieved the same result regular justice would have achieved. He continued, "It is the right and duty of governments to put down revolts and to punish treason and espionage. . . . [W]e must agree that repression was a necessity in 1793 and 1794. . . . In the circumstances no government could have maintained itself without very severe measures of repression."[9] An imperiled government had the legitimate right to defend itself against rebels and enemies. Thus, Greer normalized the Terror.

Once we accept the banalization of revolutionary justice, we can move on to other, more palatable aspects of the Terror. But perhaps we should pause. One of the advantages of using a small town like Aubagne as a test case is that it is possible to fit Terror into a local context. Even if the Convention intended the Terror to be a part of the strategy of national defense, this paradigm is quite inappropriate at the local level. The victims of the Terror in Aubagne were in no way military threats. Too many were women, too many of the men were past military age, and too few had probably ever had military training. Instead, the local terror was a continuation of faction, where the Jacobin side had the legal right to inflict a huge amount of damage on the other. The question then is not to justify and excuse but to measure how effective this local terror was.

---

[8] Donald Greer, *The Incidence of the Terror during the French Revolution; A Statistical Interpretation*, Harvard Historical Monographs 8 (Cambridge, Mass.: Harvard University Press, 1935), 120.
[9] Ibid., 124, 127.

Greer's description of Terror as defense emphasizes the legitimacy, patriotism and even nobility of repression. This is a remarkably bland way to describe it for any part of the country where its "incidence," to use Greer's antiseptic term, was high. There was nothing measured about Terror in such regions. Terror in the southeast was far more complex and interesting than this suggests. One of the most important factors that made Terror interesting and extraordinary was the treason of Toulon.

Toulon

Toulon was the perfect treason of the Jacobin imagination. Not only was there the sellout to foreigners in the name of a restoration of the monarchy, Jacobins could represent the traitors as deceitful. They had disguised themselves as patriots, the better to deceive, to lead the simpleminded and the naive over the precipice. The surrender to the foreigner threw off the mask to reveal the repulsive face of treason and counterrevolution beneath. Such people could expect no mercy.

Until its recapture on 19 December, the Jacobins devoted huge amounts of energy to the siege of Toulon. Much of this was a standard military mobilization, but it was not exciting enough. What made the imagination race was the old idea of a mass mobilization of the entire people, a "holy insurrection." The Popular Society of Aix-en-Provence declared itself

impatient to see Toulon, the infamous Toulon in ashes, [and] has deliberated to rise *en masse* and march on this rebel city.... [The sansculottes of Aix] are going to depart, strike, annihilate and triumph. The society hopes that all the defenders of the *patrie* will follow its example, then they will grind its enemies to dust. Republicans do not swear [oaths] in vain: they will cease to live or they will exterminate the tyrants.[10]

Toulon also focused the language, the concepts, and the debate over the strategy of Terror. The language, of course, was at a very high level of excitement. The terrorists of Aix, for example, did not wish merely to defeat and punish the enemy, not merely to defend themselves against treason and foreign invasion, as Greer would have it; they wanted to crush, grind, and exterminate the enemy. The preferred method was the mass rising and the mass annihilation, not the cumbersome machinery of courts and procedures. All the terrorists endorsed utter defeat and

---

[10] Address of 12 frimaire An II – 3 December 1793 to Paris Jacobins in *Journal de la Montagne*, 25 Frimaire An II – 16 December 1793.

eschewed negotiation with the enemy. In early September, conceptions of mass annihilation were potentially at odds with official strategies of mobilization and vengeance. This conflict was very similar to those that divided Jacobins and anti-Jacobins before the Federalist revolt. They would reopen by the end of the year.

At first, almost everyone agreed on the importance of avoiding an Old Regime obsession with forms of legal procedure. Throughout the nation, revolutionaries agreed that ordinary people were frequently the dupes of social superiors. This justified leniency. Stubborn opposition, however, led revolutionaries to categorize entire peoples and regions as guilty. The solution in such cases was mass resettlement of the guilty to politically sunnier climates of the Republic; mass immigration of the politically healthy to infected regions; or finally, most chilling of all, outright massacre. Like the West, the Midi witnessed this debate, one that was never entirely settled, throughout the Terror. But even if there was no resolution, insofar as there was a tendency, it was toward more severe punishments, not moderation. Moreover, this was a debate in which the National Convention intervened, mostly to encourage greater terror.

The debate over leniency had a short life. The representative Albitte thought the decree of 4 September too harsh and demanded its abrogation. Albitte congratulated the Convention for its *grandes mesures* that would revive "the Republican spirit of this unfortunate city, which was the well spring of the counterrevolutionary torrent that would submerge the southern departments and overwhelm the infamous city of Toulon." Nevertheless, the decree of 4 September was "too severe and too extensive." The truth is that if one punished all the guilty in Marseille and in the Bouches-du-Rhône, at least three-quarters of the population would disappear. Either by mistake, fear, or weakness, almost everyone swore the anti-revolutionary oath, took up arms against the Republican army, were *sectionnaires*, or gave testimony to the bloody tribunal of Marseille. Punishing only genuine leaders would also have the political advantage of calming the base of operations in the ongoing siege of Toulon.[11]

Imagining Terror

Albitte's position was rare, however. Others contended that severe repression might be equally necessary to prevent the civil war from spreading. Lack of severity could encourage opponents. The representatives to the

[11] Letter to CSP, 12 September 1793 in Aulard, *RACSP*, vi, 457.

Army of Italy, Robespierre the younger and Ricord, argued that the Federalists should be "annihilated" while it was still easy. Also, it was shameful and dishonorable that a factious handful of brigands should check the Republic.[12] A week later, they urged that "Lyon, Marseille, and Toulon be immediately reduced to submission, and that the reunited French family find again all its energy to dissipate the crowned brigands."[13]

The younger Robespierre and Ricord were arguing for a relentless pursuit of the war, but others signaled that severe repression would be necessary to appease public opinion. The representative Rovère granted revolutionary powers to the Criminal Tribunal at Avignon in order to forestall the wrath of persecuted patriots. Referring to imprisoned Federalists, he claimed that "if their criminal heads do not fall beneath the blade of the law; if they are transferred out of Avignon, we declare to you that containing the patriots will be difficult after all the suffering they have endured for the past four years."[14] Of course, the representatives agreed with suffering patriots everywhere. "It is time," Rovère and Poultier wrote, "that the National Convention and the Committee of Public Safety put in our hands the means to extirpate this race of cannibals."[15] According to the representative Barras, who along with Fréron would have a decisive influence on Marseille and therefore on Aubagne, "Indulgence would lose the Republic; all its enemies must disappear and the land of liberty must be inhabited only by its apostles."[16] Language that spoke of a race of cannibals and of eliminating all enemies went well beyond the distinction between leaders and led. Because Federalism had "gangrened" everyone, far more extreme measures were justified. Without *grandes mesures*, Rovère and Poultier claimed there was a risk of losing public opinion.[17]

Throughout the region, representatives saw the damage that just a few months of Federalist rule had done to the public spiritedness of even the patriots. Thus at Arles, the representative Pomme l'Américain reported

---

[12] Letter to CSP, 16 August 1793, in ibid., 11.
[13] Letter to same, 23 August 1793, in ibid., 66.
[14] Letter to same, 2 August 1793, in ibid., v, 457.
[15] Letter to same, 16 August 1793, in ibid., vi, 9.
[16] Letter to same, 6 September 1793, in ibid., vi, 322. For an argument that Fréron was more an indulgent than an ultra, see Michel Vovelle, "Représentants en Mission et mouvement populaire en Provence sous la Révolution français: Du nouveau sur Fréron?" *Provence historique* 23, n° fasc 93–4 (1973), 463–83. For Barras's later assessment of his colleague Fréron – an effeminate writer who needed alcohol to shore up his nerve – see his memoirs, *Mémoires de Barras, membre du Directoire* (Paris: Hachette, 1895), 104–5.
[17] Letter to same, 8 September 1793, in Aulard, *RACSP*, vi, 366–70.

that while the club's sentiments were above reproach, "it had not yet recovered from the state of stupor where the fright of the counterrevolutionary army had thrown it."[18] Earlier, Marseille feared Carteaux because the people believed his army was composed "only of brigands, put in motion by cannibals (that's us [the representatives on mission])." Even when the army's behavior assuaged such fears, Marseille was "in an alarming stupor; even the patriots do not stroll about and if this city were left to itself, it would soon be delivered over to new misfortunes and perhaps to the English."[19] The occupying army found the streets nearly deserted, cannon sabotaged and abandoned on the public squares, and bullet scars on the public buildings. People scurried by one another on the streets, barely glancing to one side.[20] Terror alone could electrify a public that had surrendered to torpor.

Programmatic statements about the Terror coincided with the demands of the siege of Toulon. Marseille and its hinterland quickly became a base area for the siege. Thus everyone scoured the city for cannon. Shops set to work to make blue uniforms. The city became a "vast arsenal" with foundries turning out cannon and guns for the army besieging Toulon. Workers stripped churches and châteaux for copper and iron. They salvaged the tombs of the counts and countesses of Provence, dungeons, and feudal monuments for materials.[21] Enormous efforts were directed to finding food as the demands of war and the deteriorating assignat eroded the market. Representatives made overtures to naval officers and sailors who had not yet declared their loyalty to the rebel fleet at Toulon. They released nearly three hundred individuals whom the *sectionnaires* had imprisoned (many in the closing days of the siege). They restored former Jacobin administrators. They filled vacant positions by appointment, not election. The city witnessed yet another round of disarming and rearming along lines of political loyalty. The Club soon reopened in a solemn ceremony.

Despite much excited talk, repression was fairly restrained at the beginning. Authorities arrested only prominent leaders and seized the property

[18] Letter to CSP, 26 September 1793, in ibid., vii, 76.
[19] Barras and Fréron to CSP, 30 August, Barras to CSP, 6 September 1793, in ibid., vi, 183, 320.
[20] Carteaux to Minister of War [?], 25 August 1793, in *AP*, lxxiii, 262, session of 31 August 1793.
[21] Edmond Poupé, *Lettres de Barras et de Fréron en mission dans le Midi* (Draguignan: Impr. de Latil frères, 1910), 38. AN AF II 90, *arrêté* of 5e jour, 2e mois An II – 26 October 1793.

of known outlaws. They left the misled alone.[22] Revolutionary justice also advanced slowly. It conformed to Albitte's desire to concentrate on outstanding leaders and to ignore their dupes. Thus, in the first two months of its existence, from the end of August to the end of October 1793, the Revolutionary Tribunal of the Bouches-du-Rhône passed death sentences on thirty-nine people, all but seven of them residents of Marseille. Those convicted were officials or judges of the Popular Tribunal, the Sections' Military Tribunal, a member of the General Committee of the Thirty-Two Sections of Marseille, and illegal municipal officers of Marseille, or elsewhere.[23] As revolutionary tribunals went, this was a slow start but it was nonetheless already far more severe than the Federalist Popular Tribunal had ever been. Over a longer period, 15 May–24 August, the Popular Tribunal had condemned sixteen people to death. Even at the beginning, revolutionary justice was not a symmetrical retaliation.[24]

Demands for a much more dazzling expression of popular justice soon arose. The restored popular societies or Jacobin clubs had their own strategies for repression and how to achieve victory over Toulon and the foreign tyrants. In early September, a grand congress of seventy-one clubs representing nine departments met at Valence in the department of the Drôme to proclaim a program for the future. Although Marseille and Saint-Rémy were the only clubs from the Bouches-du-Rhône, the influence of the Congress throughout the region would be enormous. They continued advocating the ideas of spontaneous and continuous popular revolution that had made outsiders so uneasy since 1792.[25]

Like popular societies and official bodies throughout the nation, they urged the Convention to "stay at its post" until the danger to the *patrie* had ceased. This was an indirect way to urge that the Constitution of 1793 not be implemented. In effect, the Constitution had been a useful device to sow division among the Federalists, as it had been at Marseille and

---

[22] Escudier, Saliceti, Albitte, Gasparin to CSP 28 August 1793, in Aulard, *RACSP*, vi, 158–61.

[23] ADBR, L 3122, "Liste générale des individus condamnés à la peine de mort par le tribunal criminel révolutionnaire du département des Bouches-du-Rhône ... "

[24] Charles Berriat Saint-Prix, "La Justice révolutionnaire en France, 17 août 1792, 12 prairial An III," *Le Cabinet historique* (July–August 1866), 184–5. For a detailed comparison with the difficulties of establishing the revolutionary tribunal at Feurs in the Loire, see Colin Lucas, *The Structure of the Terror; The Example of Javogues and the Loire* (London: Oxford University Press, 1973), 241–9.

[25] ADBR, 156 E AC Roquevaire 2I 4, *Procès-verbal de l'assemblée de 71 sociétés populaires tenue à Valence ... (7–9 septembre 1793)* (Marseille: Impr. de Moisy, 1793).

perhaps Aubagne, but now was not the time to establish a constitutional, legal regime. Ordinary laws were "insufficient in a time of troubles," they said, while a revolutionary regime would accelerate and solidify the return to the rule of law. As if to anticipate an argument about the perils of this step, they proclaimed that authority corrupted the men who held it, that traitors who had once been patriots had from the beginning of the Revolution, abused the confidence of the people, "but the popular societies are incorruptible." Moreover, the Republic should seize and distribute the agricultural surplus to relieve the poor. They congratulated the Convention on the recently adopted controls on grain prices and demanded they be extended to essential manufactured products. People would accept the consequent deprivation joyfully because the people were not selfish and would work happily for the future: "The people demand only bread and iron." The Convention should give popular societies the right to designate "implacable enemies of the Revolution" whom they would imprison. Revenues of their properties could support them and their families. Authority should revoke all *certificats de civisme* and issue new ones only to those who had the clubs' approval. The Clubs would therefore have final authority on who could vote, who could hold public employment, and who could receive state pensions.

"We call these measures, 'the grand national medicine,'" they concluded. "It will purge the communes and the administrations of the counter-revolutionaries that infect them; the people, delivered of the impediments which prevent them from expressing their natural energy, will deploy their forces to their greatest extent and they will soon repel the enemy from the land of Liberty." To reflect this liberated energy, they decided to raise the Légion des Montagnards, a new revolutionary army. The clubs would recruit these very special soldiers from their members who were older than draft age. Their first duty would be to join in the siege of Toulon, but that was not all. The revolutionary force would "carry terror into the ranks of the enemy, spread enlightenment into the armies," and "annihilate the cowardly calumnies of the Aristocrats, the Moderates, and the Corrupt."[26] Besides the Légion des Montagnards, cohorts of "missionaries of liberty" would fan out over the countryside to

---

[26] *Teneur de l'autorisation du représentant du peuple Boisset pour la formation de la Légion des Volontaires Montagnards* (Marseille: Mossy, An II (1793)). BM Marseille 7289. See also BM Avignon, pce 190, *arrêté des Bouches-du-Rhône*, 15 September 1793 naming Guillaume Carles commissioner of the battalion and urging the formation of similar battalions elsewhere. See also report to the Club at Aix in ADBR, L 2028, f. 181, session of 21 September 1793.

struggle against fanaticism and Federalism, and to cast the all-seeing eye of surveillance on official institutions. In the same breath, they announced that whenever enemies oppressed a single patriot, the neighboring popular society would travel to the spot,

en masse to repress, to annihilate those audacious enough to oppose the development of liberty and reason. . . . [And] just as they must cherish the true republicans, so they must abhor, with this burning irascibility that defines the energetic man, these hypocritical worshipers of the laws, these false friends of the people, these ambitious and narrow-minded Federalists, so they must also desire their prompt and exemplary punishment. Hasten then you interpreters of the voice of the people to declare these ridiculous pygmies outlaws.[27]

The Congress of Clubs at Valence thus staked their claims more boldly than the Brothers had in the spring. They demanded total regional governance. This was not entirely new. The Marseille Jacobins had sketched these ambitions the previous March when they demanded a war tax on the rich, a special revolutionary tribunal, a generalized disarming, and the arrest of political enemies. By September, these ambitions were much clearer. The restored Jacobins eschewed the rule of law; claimed infallibility and incorruptibility for themselves; demanded the right to define political existence and the right to designate enemies; and finally, the right to punish them. Further, an oppressed patriot need not appeal to the courts or authority for protection and redress but to his political allies nearby, who would inflict punishment immediately. They swore to defend to the last drop of blood "all oppressed patriots, and before the universe, we declare all patriots under the protection of Jacobins everywhere in the Republic."[28] Again, the dream of a mighty rush to smite enemies in a single satisfying stroke dazzled the Jacobins. The cry to administer the "grand national medicine," to outlaw the "ridiculous pygmies," overlapped with popular conceptions of justice in 1792. Vigilantism continued in different forms.

Moreover, the Clubs' demands posed a major challenge to the Convention's notion of authority. For the national body, power emanated from the top down through the representatives on mission who were emanations of the single sovereign embodied in the Convention in Paris. The challenge was thus similar to that of the spring of 1793 when the Sections opposed the Jacobins. At that time, the Convention and the representatives had sided with the Club. With the anti-Jacobins

[27] *AP*, lxxiv, 498–500, session of 19 September 1793.
[28] ADBR, 156E AC Roquevaire 2I 4, *Procès-verbal de l'assemblée de 71 sociétés populaires tenue à Valence . . .* " 18.

eliminated, authority had to decide how to deal with well-organized extremists whose demands for vengeance were deeply unrealistic and destabilizing. The representatives did not automatically oppose the clubs. Partly this was because some representatives too wanted an uninhibited repression of some sort and partly because such enthusiasm was welcome. Yet there were limits, as one dramatic and consequential clash with between Fréron and the Club in Marseille in December showed. That clash brought Fréron's successor, Etienne Maignet, to create a form of repression and a style of Terror that even the wildest extremists could endorse.

The Clubs were not the only voices proclaiming what needed to be done. Parisians from the radical Cordeliers Club at the Valence Congress stayed on to agitate. The ministries in Paris also had their own agents roaming the region. One of them, from the Ministry of Foreign Affairs, a self-styled Brutus, complained of the inability to "republicanize" Marseille. He and his fellow "commissioners" wanted to arrest suspects on their own. He observed, "Here [in Aix-en-Provence] the guillotine is going to play on the barristers of the former Parlement; several hundred heads legally cut off in each town will do the greatest good."[29]

Such freebooting commissioners were shocking even to representatives who had themselves said shocking things. Thus Rovère and Poultier denounced one of them sent by a general from the Army of the Pyrenees for having "ignited a great part of this Department [Gard] by his ferocious preaching, for having the imprudence and extravagance to enter the city of Nîmes and give orders, like a vizier, to the administration of the department and defy our powers." Another, a Cordelier from Paris named Sébastian Lacroix, harangued the people of Avignon. Waving a dagger for emphasis, he invited them to massacre all suspect persons. The slowness in executing the laws of the Convention was an obstacle to the progress of liberty, he said. The two representatives sensed the counter-revolution in all this, although it was only standard vigilantism. Anticipating a famous speech Robespierre made a few months later about the extremes in politics joining up, they denounced suspects before 10 August who now wore the mask of the most exaggerated sansculottism. Such men spread terror and directed the misled people to every excess, the better to discredit the Revolution.[30]

---

[29] Cited in Henri Alexandre Wallon, *Les représentants du peuple en mission et la justice révolutionnaire dans les départements en l'an II (1793–1794)* (Paris: Hachette et cie, 1889), iii, 41.

[30] Letter of 15 October 1793, in Aulard, *RACSP*, vii, 437–98. Lacroix was later executed in Paris as a *hébertiste*.

Unfortunately, the Committee of Public Safety itself contributed to this chorus of competing strategies. They gave one of their agents, Marc-Antoine Jullien, a teenage fanatic, a commission to support the revolutionary effort along the Atlantic coast from Saint-Malo to Bayonne and to return via Marseille, Avignon, and Lyon. Although he was supposed to support the representatives, he frequently sided with local extremists against them, and because of his close relations with Robespierre, he had clout. When the Committee thought the better of such commissions and revoked them, it exempted Jullien whose tormenting of authority continued until the end of the Terror.[31]

When he discussed the same period and a similar phenomenon in Paris, Albert Soboul saw a middle-class radical authority – the Convention, the Committee of Public Safety– that resisted popular initiatives. This opposition provided the dramatic tension that propelled his narrative. Yet such a simple polarity does not readily apply here. The Convention and the Committee were constantly urging a vigorous repression on the representatives and on local bodies in the provinces. It never restrained extremism. Moreover, pressure from below on otherwise reluctant authority is not a helpful conceptual framework for understanding Terror here. Questions of the definition of *middle class* and *popular* aside, the Bouches-du-Rhône and the Southeast generally witnessed a multiplicity of competing voices over terrorist strategy, not a duality. Some radical voices originated from authority, some from marginal outsiders. Moreover, some marginal outsiders soon joined higher authority, without, by any means, losing their hard edge. Finally, terrorist language could be strategic as well as programmatic. Individuals could move between a discourse of demanding punishment only for ringleaders and aggressive punishment for all irrespective of the degree of guilt as the occasion suited. Yet this was only paradoxical, not contradictory. Protecting the innocent or forgiving the misled was always part of Jacobin ideology. Jacobins could invoke doing so to criticize the incompetence or vindictiveness of someone else's

---

[31] Ibid., vi, p 397, 10 September 1793. For the flavor of his thinking, see his letter to the Jacobins (*Journal de la Montagne* 94, 4 September 1793), extreme revolutionary measures, instead of the palliatives that were adopted, would have prevented the outbreak of counterrevolution in the Midi: "and the people, better enlightened, would not be the victim of those who would mislead it and lose it while affecting to serve it. Inaction, indulgence and weakness have made gobs of blood flow; let us be active and vigilant, firm and severe; let us be cruel for the sake of humanity [*soyons cruels par calcul d'humanité* (italicized in text)]." It is somehow fitting that Jullien became an early supporter of Bonaparte, editing the sycophantic propaganda sheet, the *Bulletin of the Army of Italy*.

repressive strategy. Highlighting the specter of enfeebled innocence did not mean that the speaker had become an advocate of moderationism.

One illustration of this would be the representatives on mission. Albitte was alone in demanding a restricted, defined repression. The others who passed through Marseille or who were active nearby wanted *grandes mesures*, justice that was quicker, more awesome, more intimidating. This was the line Barras and Fréron took. They criticized Albitte for being too slow to attack Toulon in the first days of the treason; they claimed that he was too soft on the rich, that he failed to seize huge quantities of weapons that were available that had since disappeared, that he botched the disarming of enemies, and that he had reimbursed actors at the Grand Théâtre for putting on counterrevolutionary plays during the time of the Sections while they had sponsored "Brutus" free at the liberation. If this were not malice, it was inexcusable carelessness; it was a mystery why anyone listened to his babbling talk and his boasting.[32] Albitte misconceived his approach. They told the Committee:

Force will be indispensable for a long time in the southern departments. A part of the unexpected success that we have obtained here is due to inflexible severity; we need arch-revolutionary men here.... Patriotism here is like a body in a coma that has to be recalled to life. Revolutionary means are the only ones that are practical and the only cures we know how to administer.[33]

Albitte should have treated Marseille like the Convention treated Lyon: demolish it totally after exacting a forever memorable repression, one that people would recall for centuries. "No more pity," wrote Fréron:

I see that they are modifying the most revolutionary decrees, ones that are perfect for freezing our interior and exterior enemies with fear. They fulminated against Longwy, Verdun and Lyon and these excommunications resembled those of the popes. It will not be like that at Toulon; it would not have been like that at Marseille if we had entered it with a victorious army. Albitte let an opportunity escape that will never return.[34]

Indeed, it was not "like that" at Toulon. Immediately after the recapture of Toulon on 19 December, the victors shot eight hundred people without trial. Although many ringleaders of the rebellion escaped on Spanish and British ships (where the British interned them on Gibraltar), a revolutionary tribunal set to work on the remainder. Because Lyon had

---

[32] Fréron to Robespierre, 20 October 1793, in Aulard, *RACSP*, vii, 532–6.
[33] Barras and Fréron to CSP, 29 October 1793, in Aulard, *RACSP*, viii, 115.
[34] Letter to Bayle, 23 Brumaire An II – 13 November 1793, in Poupé, *Lettres de Barras et de Fréron*, 47.

become "Ville-Affranchie," Barras and Fréron experimented with a new name for Toulon. They settled on "Port de la Montagne," after rejecting "Infamous City." Such drastic measures showed they would not let another opportunity slip by.

Securing the unruly base at Marseille was far more difficult. The problem arose with a Republican Congress at Marseille in early October that followed up on the previous one in Valence.[35] This time the Congress hosted no fewer than 1,500 delegates from 360 societies from all over the Southeast. From the beginning, members of the Marseille Club dominated the agenda. "For too long and too often," the organizers claimed, "a criminal moderation and a criminal indulgence have left the aristocracy to weave its hidden plots.... Rise up then, People of the southern departments. Let us crush the last head of the Federalist hydra. Let us imprison the entire French aristocracy."[36]

The thrust of their resolutions was to entrench the clubs deep within the body politic. The Ministry of the Interior would subsidize annual regional congresses of the clubs; the clubs would inspect the organization of military supply, evaluate the confidence soldiers had in their generals, decide whether the officers had proper *certificats de civisme*; the Convention would authorize the clubs to evaluate the work of the departments and districts; and the Convention, which would have the inspection reports, would punish any prevaricating administrator with death.

By mid-October, the Club and the Congress had merged. Both agreed to hold single night sessions from then on.[37] This gave the Marseille Club an obvious regional influence it had exercised only sporadically before. The Congress even established its own *comité de surveillance*. Moreover,

---

[35] For the congress in general, see Jacques Guilhaumou, "Le Congrès républicain des sociétés populaires de Marseille (3 octobre–21 novembre 1793)," *AhRf* 265 (1986), 533–7, and his "Le Congrès républicain des sociétés populaires des départements méridionaux de Marseille (octobre–novembre 1793): programme et mots d'ordre" (paper presented at the 111e Congrès national des sociétés savantes, Poitiers, 1986), 39–57. Also, *Précis des opérations des Sociétés populaires des départements méridionaux réunies en assemblée générale à Marseille. Séances depuis le 12 de Vendémiaire jusqu'au 12 de Brumaire, l'an second de la République française, une et indivisible* [1793] in ADBR, L 2076. Isoard later took credit for most of these ideas, see *Vie politique de François Isoard, de Marseille* (Marseille: Impr. révolutionnaire d'Auguste Mossy, 1793), in ibid. Finally, *Adresse des Sociétés populaires du Midi, réunies à Marseille, à la Convention Nationale* ([1793]), demanding the trial or deportation of Philippe Egalité, in BM Marseille 1676.

[36] ADBR, 156E AC Roquevaire 2I 4, Poster headed *Frères et amis*, 12 September 1793, signed Isoard, Président [one of the Republican missionaries deeply implicated in the Salon affair] Lewase, Leclerc, Morin, Loys, Beneche *fils*, Bergier, Secrétaires.

[37] *Journal de Marseille*, 85, 4 Brumaire An II – 25 October 1793.

the Légion des Montagnards gave the clubs armed forces of its own. The Legion's commander styled it the "daughter of the Popular Societies."[38] At one point the Congress took another approach and declared itself a revolutionary army and demanded the administration arm it.

Crisis of Authority

The Congress worried the representatives. At first, they fretted that intriguers would take advantage of the esteem of the popular societies to usurp authority.[39] But the early activities of the Congress must have been reassuring. The presence of the delegates rejuvenated the Marseille Club, and, as they said themselves, the delegates extirpated the remains of Federalism with their own bare hands.[40] According to their supporters, they spiked several plots, arrested some suspects, disarmed others who were dangerous or useless, discussed the eternal question of subsistence, contributed to the war effort, awaited the punishment of the leading scoundrels, and swore not to disburse until they had "exterminated" Toulon.[41]

On 30 October, a delegation from the Congress claiming to represent four hundred societies appeared before the Jacobins in Paris. They complained about the moderationism of all the representatives on mission in the region. Only Barras and Fréron were exempt. Only they had risen to the "height of principles and were acting *révolutionnairement.*" The speaker, Alexandre Ricord, a former editor of the fiery *Journal des Départements meridionnaux* and now procurator-syndic of the Department of Bouches-du-Rhône, expressed his shock at the absence of energy in Paris. The Revolutionary Tribunal of Paris had become an "ordinary court, that there had to be witnesses and forms to judge Brissot when he ought to be shot right away." The tribunal at Marseille had sometimes

---

38 *Légion de la Montagne. Le Sans-Culotte Chastel, Chef de brigade, commandant la Légion de la Montagne, à tous ses Frères, les Membres des Sociétés populaires de la République . . .* (Marseille: Mossy, An II [1793]), 1. BM Marseille 7289.

39 Barras and Fréron to CSP, 27 October 1793 in Aulard, *RACSP*, viii, 72. Also Albitte to same, 6 November 1793 in ibid., 366.

40 *AP*, lxxvi, 655, session of 17 October 1793.

41 *Journal de la Montagne*, 14 Brumaire An II – 4 November 1793 See also ibid., 24 Brumaire An II – 14 November 1793, where they claim to be only a center of light, action, and influence, frightening only to the timid. The club still supported Barras and Fréron on 25 Brumaire An II – 15 November 1793 (see its address in ibid., 6 Frimaire An II – 22 November 1793). But by 2 Frimaire, some in Marseille were denouncing the *civisme* of Fréron, denouncing him as an aristocrat, envious of domination, a satrap who spent lavishly, who shunned the company of patriots. Letter of 2 Frimaire, in ibid., 16 frimaire – 6 December 1793.

186 Murder in Aubagne

ordered such shootings (this assertion was false) and it had "done the greatest good." He disapproved of the decree ordering Lyon to be razed; instead the invading army should have turned three-quarters of it to ruins. That is what ought to happen at Toulon. If authorities treat the fops and dandies leniently, they will only begin again. The Revolutionary Tribunal should hasten the judgment of the guilty. Then, once more illustrating that the dazzling vision of the simultaneous cleansing blow still made the Jacobin imagination race, he exclaimed, "Purge Paris of the aristocrats that infect it, we take charge of making holy insurrections in the Midi, have patriots march to the relief of Toulon, and we swear that we will return this city to the Republic [thunderous applause]."[42]

Such talk outraged the Committee of Public Safety. The Congress had usurped powers and challenged national authority. The Committee reproached the Congress for raising its own armed force; sending commissioners to the departments; sending other commissioners to the army before Toulon, where they interfered with military operations; and second-guessing decrees of the Convention itself.[43] Ricord's impudent address to the Jacobins could only have aggravated the situation. The Committee ordered that troops be removed from the siege of Toulon and that an imposing garrison be stationed in Marseille because "underground maneuvers" aimed "to rekindle the spirit of rebellion and treason that delivered for a time this town to the enemies of the Republic."[44] Fréron had not yet come to this conclusion even as late as mid-November. He lauded the societies' good intentions but still worried about the possibility of mistakes.[45]

This changed abruptly between 2 and 8 Frimaire (22 and 28 November). Fréron heard reports from reliable Jacobins that extremists were planning a massacre of prisoners once the representatives were out of

[42] Journal de la Montagne, 8, 9, 10 Brumaire An II – 29, 30, 31 November 1793 reporting on sessions of 6 and 8 Brumaire. The 8 Brumaire issue reported the Société populaire of Tarascon complaining of being oppressed by the representative Poultier. Maillet was president of the Société populaire; Giraud, vice president; Micoulin, Doydier, and Turcan were secretaries. Ibid., 12 Frimaire An II – 2 December 1793. See also Journal républicain de Marseille, 22 Vendémiaire An II – 13 October 1793, 65–6.

[43] Paul Cadroy, Rapport du représentant du peuple Cadroy, sur ses diverses missions dans les départements méridionaux / impr. par ordre de la Convention nationale (Paris: [Impr. nationale], [An IV, 1795]), 47–8, citing the report of the representative Ricord.

[44] Decree of 4 November 1793 in Aulard, RACSP, viii, 222.

[45] Letter to Botot, 23 Brumaire – 13 November in Poupé, Lettres de Barras et de Fréron, 45. But he clearly felt the need to justify himself by citing his revolutionary pedigree in a letter of 13 Brumaire to the commune of Paris (Journal de la Montagne, 23 Brumaire An II – 13 November 1793).

town. They would "bathe themselves in the blood of all the prisoners.... And engorge themselves with the gold taken from the odds and ends of their still palpitating cadavers." The battalions of sansculottes destined for the siege of Toulon would do the job to protect their families from the prisoners before departing. Fréron himself saw the parallel with identical stories at the time of the September Massacres in Paris in 1792. Another variant was that the extremists would kill the representatives and then put out the story that Barras and Fréron themselves had ordered the prison massacres.

The consequences of this new mayhem would be enormous. Men seduced with "George's guineas" would fatally weaken the efforts against Toulon. The English would spread everywhere, and the Spanish would be able to establish a corridor that would link their home country to the Mediterranean littoral. Even more fantastic, delegates to the Congress talked about organizing simultaneous massacres in the prisons at Aix-en-Provence and Marseille. When the mayor of Aix refused to go along, Isoard, the delegate of the Congress, said that "the varnish of moderationism would harm him."[46] These were extraordinary stories but they were also consistent with the broad policies on repression that the extremists had endorsed at the Valence Congress and elsewhere. They were the logical consequence of the axiom of mass annihilation.

Of course, there was a difference between the extravagant language of repression and its institutionalization in the Marseille revolutionary tribunal on the one hand and a cold-blooded prison massacre on the other. For many months an emotional and exuberant language of repression covered these differences. No doubt, many speakers thought they understood one another, but rhetorical excess could not paper over the differences forever. The gulf between the Terror on the extremists' behalf or at their initiative was always fundamental.

Fréron launched a preemptive strike. He accused the extremists of incompetence, moderationism, and corruption. Politically, he tried to

---

[46] AN AF II 90, *Proclamation. Les Représentants du Peuple près les armées et les départemens méridionaux à toutes les communes du Midi*, 3 Pluviôse An II – 22 January 1794. ADBR, L 3037, *Jugement rendu par le tribunal criminel du département des Bouches-du-Rhône, qui condamne à la peine de mort Louis-François Dominique Isoard...du 2 vendémiaire de l'an quatrième Républicain*, 12–3. Cadroy, *Rapport... sur ses diverses missions dans les départements méridionaux*, 49, 60–1. The prisoners themselves had heard these stories and began to arm themselves with anything they could manufacture, to block corridors in the prisons, and to lay booby traps (Lautard, *Esquisses historiques. Marseille depuis 1789 jusqu'en 1815*, i, 330).

purge them. Thus, he reproached the Marseille *comité de surveillance* for arresting and releasing the wrong people: harmless old women who never left their neighborhoods, former intendants of the Old Regime, rich merchants who promised to import grain from Africa in return for their release, and so on. Worse still, the committee was corrupt. It released the "fat boars" for money payments and imprisoned many hundreds of simple artisans who were mere dupes.[47]

Fréron also tried to weaken the Jacobin power base in the city. He persuaded the delegates to dissolve the Congress. He later claimed this confounded the extremists who had hoped to use the Congress as a cover to spread the responsibility for the prison massacres so widely that investigation would be impossible. On 8 Frimaire (28 November), the representatives put Marseille in a state of siege, effectively giving the military greater police powers over the city.[48]

The declaration of the state of siege outraged the Club and the municipality. The Club went into a night session where someone proposed arresting the representatives Barras, Fréron, the younger Robespierre, and Ricord (not to be confused with Ricord the journalist). Someone else tried to induce the commander of the garrison to disobey the representatives's orders to march on Toulon. Some also claimed that this was the perfect time to assault the prisons. Maillet, one of the judges of the Revolutionary Tribunal, led a large delegation in the middle of the night to demand Barras explain himself. Another group of eight armed men escorted one of the military commanders to the Club at two o'clock in the morning, where he had to defend his revolutionary pedigree. On 2-3 December, the town council tried to raise the dockworkers and the

---

[47] Unless otherwise stated the material in the following three paragraphs comes from three letters from Fréron to Bayle, 22 Frimaire – 12 December; 16 Nivôse An II – 5 January 1794; 19 Nivôse An II – 8 January 1794 in Poupé, *Lettres de Barras et de Fréron*, 66–81, 120–6, 134–6. Another example of the use of the trope of misled patriot comes in a letter from Barras, Fréron et al. to Poultier and Rovere, 17 October 1793 in *Journal républicain de Marseille*, 22 Vendémiaire An II – 13 October 1793, asking for the release of Marseille patriots in prison in Avignon for marching with the Federalist army on the ground they were mostly artisans, "that is, men of the most respectable, credulous and unfortunate class." They should be transferred to Marseille where "the tribunal composed of Montagnards, almost all imprisoned and proscribed by the sections, will know how to distinguish the guilty from the innocent, the wicked from the misled men, playthings of intrigue." But Fréron and Barras later said all Marseillais including the dockers, artisans, and poor were guilty (see their letter to CSP, 14 Pluviôse An II – 2 February 1794, in Poupé, *Lettres de Barras et de Fréron*, 159).

[48] H. G. Brown, *Ending the French Revolution: Violence, Justice, and Repression from the Terror to Napoleon* (Charlottesville: University of Virginia Press, 2006), 201.

country people in the outskirts of town; ordered the arrest of the officer who proclaimed the siege; and ordered an army of sansculottes, probably the Légion des Montagnards, which was still recruiting in Marseille under the aegis of the Club, to disobey the representatives' order to march to Toulon.[49] The city council also played politics with bread prices. They lowered the controlled price of bread by 20 percent and quickly reminded people that this action proved who was more sympathetic to the working-man's difficulties. For the representatives, these were demagogic attempts to rouse the people at a time everyone knew that supplies to the city were at risk. Worse, the councillors even refused a summons to meet with the four representatives. They relented only to be welcomed with the representatives insulting them as Federalists and counterrevolutionaries. A new theme became increasingly common, that exaggerated patriotism was a mask for its opposite.[50] Privately, Barras attributed this unruliness to English gold. The ever-devious Pitt intended to subsidize extremism in the popular societies to effect the counterrevolution. Barras intended to forestall any further adventures by taking *grandes mesures*.[51]

Marseille: Sans-Nom

The *grandes mesures* included replacing the municipality with an appointed municipal commission on 15 Frimaire (5 December). While they reserved most places for well-known local Jacobins, they awarded a third of the positions to men from outside the city. At the same time, they purged the *comité de surveillance*. There was no question of an election to either body, and if any appointee refused to serve, he was to be treated as a suspect, that is he could be imprisoned until the war was over. To compete with the municipality's demagoguery over bread prices, they established a charity bureau and promised to extirpate begging.[52]

The Club retaliated by going into a secret session, refusing to purge itself of unreliable elements, and by refusing to recruit new members

---

49 AN AF II 90 and W 329, Barras to Fouquier-Tinville, 2 Pluviôse An II – 21 January 1794. Also AN W 329, Montmeau, *adjudant-général chef de Brigade* to Citoyen Lapoype, *général de division, commandant la place*, n.d. Ibid., *acte d'accusation*, 29 Pluviôse An II – 17 February 1794. Richard Cobb, *Les armées révolutionnaires; instrument de la Terreur dans les départements, avril 1793 (floréal an II)* (Paris: Mouton, 1961), 232–3, 274–5.
50 Barras to Moise Bayle, n.d., in Poupé, *Lettres de Barras et de Fréron*, 56–7.
51 Same to same, 20 Frimaire – 10 December, in ibid., 60–1.
52 AN AF II 90, *arrêté* of Fréron, Barras, Robespierre jᵉ, and Ricord, 15 Frimaire An II – 5 December 1793; second *arrêté* by same, 19 Frimaire An II – 9 December 1793.

democratically. It also sent off a delegate to Paris to complain of the representatives' moderationism. All this only convinced Fréron that a handful of intriguers who dominated the naive, uneducated members of the Club was collaborating with the foreigners at Toulon. A combined allied attack on the besiegers' positions in the midst of this crisis was interpreted as evidence of coordination. Some claimed that flares went up from the suburbs of Marseille as a signal for the English attack. Finally, the Jacobins administered the city badly. No one controlled passports at the gates, rubbish was everywhere, gaming houses proliferated, people called one another *Monsieur*, and prostitutes infected the soldiers.

Worse still, the representatives had to goad Marseille, the Club, and its minions into celebrating the capture of Toulon.[53] Yet Fréron was too isolated to arrest the handful of intriguers he felt was responsible for this deplorable state of affairs. The *patriotes d'industrie*, as Fréron called them, the professional revolutionaries, were credible in the eyes of the uneducated sansculotte because of their skill at deploying the language of patriotism for sinister ends. They cynically boasted about their time in the dungeons to which the *sectionnaires* had hurled them as proof of their sacrifices.

Consequently, the representatives tried to outflank the Club. They ordered several thousand draftees out of the city, thus depriving the Club of a source of armed force. On 17–18 Nivôse (6–7 January), they, along with Ricord and Salicetti, issued a "terrible decree," as they called it: they ordered the demolition of buildings, frequently churches, that had served as meeting halls for the sections. The exception would be the meeting hall of the brave Section 11. On the site of the others, a pole would be erected declaring the spot infamous. They transferred the Revolutionary Tribunal to Aix-en-Provence, where it would revert to being a Criminal Tribunal, and replaced it with a Military Tribunal. They ordered another round of disarming, now directed at Jacobins. If any arms were found later during domiciliary visits, the home's owner would be declared a suspect, that is, interned.

Finally, and most spectacularly of all, they renamed Marseille Sans-Nom, or "no name." Marseille merited this punishment because it had been the first to raise the banner of Federalism, had spread it to surrounding communities, and had pillaged and sacked towns that resisted her armies. The most recent protest over the state of siege proved the city was incorrigible. Both Marseille and Toulon had plotted to surrender

---

[53] Ricord, Barras, Fréron, Saliceti to CSP in Aulard, *RACSP*, x, 79.

to the English, and only Carteaux's prompt rescue had saved another treason.[54] This was a deliberate conflation of the hated Federalists and the Jacobin extremists. Needless to say, the Club was appalled.

On 22 January, Fréron and Barras ordered the arrest of the two principal judges of the Revolutionary Tribunal, Maillet and Giraud. Both were major clubbists, but most significant both had been leading officials of the Republican Congress. They must have planned the abortive prison massacres in December and perhaps, the murder of Barras and Fréron themselves. The accusation of failing to judge *révolutionnairement*, of being soft on the friends of the disgraced Barbaroux, was, therefore, only a part of the agenda, as the arrest warrant made clear. It accused them of being involved in the "recent troubles" at Marseille; accused them of being too lenient with major Federalists; and alluded to bribes that nobles and big wholesalers paid to stay out of prison.[55]

Most representatives on mission in this period of high terror ran into trouble, not because of their extremism but frequently because other extremists disagreed with their strategies. Barras and Fréron were prime examples. The Club wanted a settling of accounts within the city before moving onto Toulon; the representatives wanted to flatten Toulon above everything else.

How and why the two representatives ran afoul of the Committee of Public Safety is another matter, nor is it entirely clear why the Committee took sudden offense after it had already endorsed some of the *grandes mesures*. On 22 Frimaire (12 December), Barère condemned the recent actions of the Club. This included its protest at the state of siege, its attempt to arrest the officer who delivered the order, its defiance of the representatives' orders to send the revolutionary army to Toulon, and so on. He also blamed this defiance on a handful of intriguers who had subverted the good intentions of the Club. He implicitly condemned earlier representatives for not declaring the state of siege immediately upon Carteaux's victory in late August. In other words, the Committee not only condemned the faction in the Club but also accepted Fréron's interpretation that the Club was acting for what he oddly called the "Anglican

54 *Journal de la Montagne*, 18 Pluviôse An II – 6 February 1794. On the new Criminal Tribunal see *procès-verbal du 6 ventôse An II* – 24 February 1794, in AD BR L 3012. For the decree on the tribunals themselves, see *ibid.*, 2Mi 530, *arrêté* of 17 Nivôse An II – 6 January 1794, also in AN AF II 90. On 3 Pluviôse An II (22 January 1794), they corrected an oversight and ordered the demolition of the building "in which the infamous so-called Popular Tribunal held its sessions" (Ibid.).

55 Gaffarel, *Histoire de Marseille sous la Revolution*, 203.

Federalists."[56] On Barère's recommendation, the Convention ordered the arrest of the troublemakers.

Yet between Barère's speech and early January 1794, something went wrong. There had always been talk about Fréron and Barras, especially that they enjoyed the pleasures of the table overmuch at a time when everyone else had to live frugally. There was also a fantastic story, based on a poorly forged letter, that they were in league with the English to transfer part of Provence to the hereditary enemy. While they soon proved that this accusation was absurd, they were incredulous that the Committee of Public Safety and the Jacobins in Paris paid any attention to it. They also thought the false letter contributed to the failure of the Committee of Public Safety to give them sufficient credit for their heroic role in the capture of Toulon.[57]

Worse was to come. Despite Barère's speech, two days after they received the decree of 17 Nivôse changing the city's name to Sans-Nom, the Committee of Public Safety reversed itself. They condemned the representatives' actions. The Committee questioned the wisdom of demolishing buildings that would have included the Hôtel de Ville, when their sale would bolster the national treasury. Transferring the Revolutionary Tribunal to Aix appeared to reward a town that in the Old Regime swarmed with the legal chicaneries of obscurantist courts and that had recently raised the Federalist standard. Above all, the name change was totally misguided. It punished an entire city whose contributions to the Revolution were immeasurable. The constant struggle for liberty from the beginning, the role on 10 August, the Jacobin rebellion in Section 11 at the end of August 1793 as Carteaux's army approached, largely redeemed the city. Marseille just did not compare with the other Federalist cities. Nothing good could be said about Lyon and Toulon, and the punishment was excessive compared with that meted out to Bordeaux and Caen.[58]

The Committee was reacting to the pressure of the Bouches-du-Rhône delegation to the Convention. As soon as they heard of the decree, the delegates protested. Instead of the blanket condemnation of the entire city that Fréron and Barras had launched, they invoked the common figure

---

[56] *Rapport au nom du Comité de Salut Public, sur la Commune de Marseille, par B. Barère, dans la Séance du 22 frimaire* . . . (Paris: Impr. nat., [1793]). BM Marseille 5328.

[57] Gaffarel, *Histoire de Marseille sous la Revolution*, 207–8. Aulard, *RACSP*, ix, 558; Poupé, *Lettres de Barras et de Fréron*, 182–3; Barras and Fréron to CSP, 16 Nivôse – 5 January in Aulard, *RACSP*, x, 80–2.

[58] Letter to Barras and Fréron, 4 Pluviôse An II – 23 January 1794 in Aulard, *RACSP*, x, 400–3. Billaud-Varenne and Collot d'Herbois signed the copy in AN AF II 91 (undated).

of speech of misled people. The cause of the Federalist rebellion was the result of "a wicked minority who abused a part of the people and who adroitly took advantage of its burning, but unenlightened patriotism, to doom it and to drag other communes along."[59]

The Club aligned itself with the deputies. Although he arrived well after the Committee's condemnation, their delegate to Paris, Pierre Loys, a major figure in the Marseille Congress, spoke to the Paris Jacobins, claiming that for the previous two months Fréron had persecuted patriots in Marseille worse than the Federalists had. On the pretext they were ultrarevolutionaries, they were subject to unspeakable cruelties, victims of a "vast plot." Since the recapture of the city, the representatives had ignored them. Albitte had refused to order mass arrests, representatives had quarreled among themselves, a hidden hand had tried to stir up trouble between the people and the garrison, the declaration of the state of siege had frightened everyone, representatives had arrested eighty-six patriots and two sent before the Revolutionary Tribunal in Paris, patriots had been disarmed and the town hall barely saved from vandalism. Not a word about the inflammatory actions of some in the Republican Congress, not a word about defiance of orders to go to Toulon or the alleged plots against the lives of prisoners and the representatives. Not a word either about the name change to Sans-Nom.[60]

The Committee's reproach of Barras and Fréron was quite specious as demolitions, transfers, or improvised creations of courts as well as name changes were part of the repertoire of terrorist government. Lyon, or "Ville Affranchie," would be the best example. Stigmatizing whole populations, as the Committee did in its own letter of reproach when it mentioned Aix-en-Provence, was also common, for example, with the Vendée. Nor did the Committee object to the transfer of the Revolutionary Tribunal to another place. It preferred Salon because it had a more acceptable record as a hotbed of patriotism. On the other hand, emphasizing the name change avoided any discussion of the role of the Club in the region's recent history. It allowed everyone involved but especially the city and therefore the Club, to appropriate the great early days of the

[59] *Lettre de Moyse Bayle, représentant du peuple, à son collègue Barrère (11 pluviôse.)* (n.p. [Paris]: Impr. des amis de la liberté et de l'égalité, l'an second de la république), 9–10. AN AF II 90.

[60] *Journal de la Montagne,* 19, 20 Pluviôse An II – 7, 8 February 1794, session of 18 Pluviôse An II – 6 February 1794. Robespierre then intervened to request that no action be taken until the claims of both sides were sorted out. More from Loys in *Loys à Camille Desmoulins, sur les affaires de Marseille* (Paris: Impr. de Pelletié, [1794]). ADBR, L 2076.

Revolution for themselves, to dismiss Federalism as a vile aberration, and to absolve the Club of provoking opposition throughout the region. Underlying all this was the reason the Committee gave to Barras's and Fréron's successor, Etienne Maignet, for disapproving the decrees of 17–18 Nivôse: without being specific, it cited the "evil that can result from a possibly dangerous precipitation [in the execution of the decrees] and to remedy it by all the means of wisdom and prudence that are in your power."[61] In other words, the Committee was anticipating the sensibilities of the Club.

No one in this debate had any dispute with repression. For instance, the clubs in the region boisterously attested to Maillet's and Giraud's revolutionary pedigrees. The Club at Sans-Nom anointed them "martyrs of liberty." The brothers went on to explain that while a judge could make errors, "he is not accountable for his opinion every time he is strong in his conscience." The Club at Arles endorsed the address from their brothers in Marseille, claimed from direct experience that Giraud was one of the "first Apostles and Martyrs of the Revolution," and found it impossible to imagine "that he could have deviated from the true principles of the Revolution."[62]

The Revolutionary Tribunal in Paris agreed. It acquitted Maillet and Giraud on 5 Ventôse (23 February). The accused argued they were innocent of the charges of corruption and arbitrariness that Fréron and Barras had leveled. But they appealed to political criteria, not the evidence. Their long pedigree in the Revolution, their struggles against the Chiffonistes in Arles, against Barbaroux, and against the *appelants*, were guarantees of rectitude. Also, as judges, they had rendered five hundred decisions (more than one hundred a month, therefore), meted out death sentences to 162 people (actually 154), and condemned 200 people to the galleys at Port de la Montagne (Toulon).[63] Their activities were clearly up to the mark.

---

[61] To Maignet, 10 Pluviôse An II – 29 January 1794 in Aulard, *RACSP*, x, 517 and AN AF II 91. Paul Gaffarel argues for the importance of upsetting the delegation and "public opinion" in Marseille, but this has to mean the club ("Marseille sans-nom [Nivôse–Pluviôse An II]," *Rf* 60 [1911], 193–215).

[62] ADBR, AC Roquevaire 2I 4, "Adresse de la Société Populaire de [la] Commune Sans-nom, ci-devant Marseille, à la Convention Nationale," 19 Pluviôse An II – 7 February 1794. BM Arles, MS 664 n° 11, *Copie de la lettre écrite par les Monaidiers d'Arles, à la Société des Amis de l'Egalité & de la Liberté, séants aux ci-devant Jacobins, à Paris, en date du 8 pluviôse. Arles 24 Germinal, an Second de la République, une et indivisible.*

[63] *Mémoire justificatif des citoyens Augustin Maillet, président; et Joseph Giraud, accusateur public, près le tribunal criminel révolutionnaire des Bouches-du-Rhône, séant à Marseille* (Paris: Galletti, [1794]), BM Marseille 5827.

The Revolutionary Tribunal in Paris not only acquitted these indefatigable jurists but also gave them civic crowns and the fraternal kiss. In case anyone missed the message, Maillet was allowed to address the Convention. He rehearsed the long travails of many fellow patriots in prison during the Federalist episode; explained Fréron's and Barras's hostility as the result of a bribe from "the most refined aristocracy"; congratulated the Revolutionary Tribunal as terrible only for conspirators; and informed the deputies that a huge crowd in the courtroom had greeted their acquittal with applause and weeping. The President of the Convention congratulated them in turn for emerging "pure" from their ordeal and welcomed them into the arms of the people who "bathed you with its tears, delicious tears, consoling testimony for the Citizen who can still say to himself, 'I have not ceased to be worthy of public confidence.'"[64] The Convention then granted their request to resume their functions. The Paris Jacobins and the Cordeliers Club also fêted them. The rebuke to the Barras and Fréron was total.[65]

The other sign of the acceptance of severe repression in governing circles in Paris was the absence of any commentary on the successor to the Revolutionary Tribunal, the Military Tribunal. This court moved the degrading of due process rights to a new low. As was common with other provincial revolutionary tribunals, there was no jury and no appeal. There was no public prosecutor either. The judges themselves doubled as the prosecutors. One of them was Leroy *dit* Brutus, the itinerant agent of one of the ministries in Paris who had earlier talked about having the guillotine "play" on the heads of the barristers at Aix. Once they settled in, the judges informed the Paris Commune that the guillotine was functioning daily: "The more the guillotine plays, the more the Republic solidifies itself. The blood of the wicked, the enemies of the *patrie*, waters

---

[64] The quotation is from a reproduction of the minutes of the Convention in "Arrêté de l'administration du District d'Aix, 17 ventôse, [7 March] an Second de la République française, une et indivisible," which was printed and dispersed as widely as possible, which suggests a lot of support outside Marseille (ADBR, L 3012). See reports on the acquittal, and the rounds of visits to the Jacobins and Cordeliers in *Gazette nationale ou le Moniteur universel*, issues of 11, 12, 21 Ventôse An II – 1, 2, 11 March 1794. See also ADBR AC Roquevaire 2I 4, Maillet and Giraud's "Copie de la lettre adressée aux Citoyens composant la Société Populaire & Républicaine de Marseille," 11 Ventôse An II – 1 March 1794 with endorsements from the Club and the Bouches-du-Rhône delegation to the Convention.

[65] *Journal de la Montagne*, 7, 9, 10 Ventôse An II – 25, 27, 28 February 1794. Club and Convention sessions of 8 Ventôse An II – 26 February 1794. A copy of the actual decree ordering reinstatement is in ADBR, L 3012, dated 8 Ventôse An II – 26 February 1794.

the furrows of the South, their corpses fertilize the fields; the earth is thirsty for these monsters.... It's going well, it will go even better in a while." The Paris Council applauded when they heard that those who did not love the National Convention and the "holy Mountain" would vanish.[66] In ten sessions this tribunal condemned 120 people to death. The judges conducted the brief trials seated at a table piled with weapons. They announced the verdicts from the balcony of the Palais de Justice to the accused who were already in carts down below ready to be transported to the Canebière, where the guillotine stood. People swarmed around the carts shouting as they heard the verdicts.[67]

Fréron was delighted with the Tribunal's work. It gave the lie to the rumors the representatives wished to save the great guilty ones; on the contrary,

> they fall like hail under the blade of the law...In a week, the Military Commission has done more hard work than the [Revolutionary Tribunal] in four months.... Tomorrow three wholesalers will also dance the Carmagnole. We are focused on them because they are the true authors of the rebellion of the Midi, but they [Isoard and the Jacobins] have resolved to save [them].[68]

Nor did Maignet have any serious objection to the Military Tribunal. He criticized the all-Parisian composition of the judges because it slowed the processing of cases. He intended to remedy this not by naming local judges, but by calling a meeting with the existing judges and the *comité de surveillance*. They would group those "guilty" of the same crime to then appear at the same trial. This would save time and give justice a "greater character."[69] Indeed, Maignet was so pleased with the Military

---

[66] Cited in C. Lourde, *Histoire de la Révolution à Marseille et en Provence: de 1789 au Consulat* (Marseille: Laffitte, 1974), 355. Letter in full in *Gazette nationale ou le Moniteur universel*, 750, issue of 6 Germinal (24 March) reporting on the Commune's session of 3 Germinal. Partially summarized in *Journal de la Montagne*, 5 germinal An II – 25 March 1794, session Paris Commune of 3 Germinal An II – 23 March 1794. Brutus later became one of Barras's secretaries when he was a Director (Cobb, *Les armées révolutionnaires*, 881). Some of the nominations of the judges are in ADBR, L 3128, dated 1 Pluviôse An II – 20 January 1794.

[67] Lautard, *Esquisses historiques. Marseille depuis 1789 jusqu'en 1815*, i, 331–4, 368–72. Wallon, *Justice révolutionnaire dans les départements*, iii, 77–8.

[68] Fréron to Bayle, 6 Pluviôse An II – 25 January 1794, in Poupé, *Lettres de Barras et de Fréron*, 147–8.

[69] To CSP, 21 Pluviôse An II – 9 February 1794. Aulard, *RACSP*, xi, 34. He formalized this in his *arrêté* of 22 Pluviôse An II – 10 February 1794, in Etienne Maignet, *Recueil des arrêtés du représentant du peuple Maignet, envoyé dans le département des Bouches-du-Rhône, commencé le vingt un pluviose an 2me de la République française, et fini le 29 thermidor même année* ([1794]), BM Avignon 4° 3862. Hereafter cited as "Maignet

Tribunal that he ordered it to transfer its operations to Avignon to judge prisoners there rather than grant revolutionary powers to the Criminal Tribunal of the Vaucluse.[70]

The Convention's restoration of Maillet and Giraud nullified this project. Their exoneration implied the restoration of the Revolutionary Tribunal at Marseille instead. At the same time, the judges of the Military Tribunal resigned after going on strike for two weeks. They were quarreling with the *comité de surveillance* of Marseille over acquittals with the usual charges of indulgence and moderationism being directed at the Tribunal.[71] Maignet restored the Revolutionary Tribunal on 23 Ventôse (13 March). No one endorsed the *comité de surveillance's* criticism of the work of the Military Tribunal. Rather, Maignet recognized that the restored judges "had never ceased to merit public confidence and to return to their hands the blade of the law which they will use on the heads of all the guilty with the speed of a thunderbolt."[72]

Maignet had one important insight into what had gone wrong in Marseille while the rest of his labored analysis showed he barely differed from Barras and Fréron.[73] He too recognized that the difference was over how to inflict punishment and who would do it, the same debate that had raged throughout the revolutionary network for months. He criticized Barras and Fréron for claiming that the whole city was guilty and therefore everyone in it merited punishment.

Yet Maignet was not conciliatory to those outside the narrow circle of the Club, far from it. Like many radicals of the Terror, Maignet had no patience for half measures. He warned patriots against those who said the proper remedies were "too violent," who would wish "that we stop amputations that alone can save the body politic! Look, look where these half measures have led us, these vacillations, these uncertainties

collection" (MS copy in ADBR, L 3128). He added staff to the Tribunal because of the importance of the "greatest interest in sending promptly all the traitors who have rebelled against the sovereignty of the people and the unity of the Republic to the scaffold." (Ibid., L 3127, *arrêté* of 16 Germinal An II – 5 April 1794).

[70] *Arrêté* of 30 Pluviôse An II – 18 February 1794 in BM Avignon MS 3028, n° 11.

[71] Maignet to CSP, 23 Ventôse – 13 March 1794, in Aulard, *RACSP*, xi, 688–9.

[72] Maignet collection, *arrêté* 18, 23 Ventôse – 13 March mss. copies in ADBR, L 3012 and L 3127.

[73] On the mission in general, see Jacques Guilhaumou and Martine Lapied, "La mission Maignet," *AhRf*, no. 300 (1995), 283–94. Also Paul Gaffarel, "La mission de Maignet dans les Bouches-du-Rhône et en Vaucluse," *Annales de la faculté des lettres d'Aix* vi (1912), 1–100, and René Belin, *Un Représentant du Peuple en mission dans ses rapports avec la Convention et le Comité de Salut public. Etienne Maignet, membre de la Convention nationale* ... (Ambert: Impr. Migeon, 1921).

that a [concern for] humanity has made us take! Eh! Has not enough patriot blood flowed, patriots whom this false clemency slaughtered?"[74] Earlier, he jotted a list of what needed to be done: "An entire department to regenerate, measures of general security [have] become urgent, some powerful guilty ones to have to guillotine, a crowd of others to have to arrest." Amnesty was unthinkable, he continued, "The guillotine will strike down at least [fifty] counterrevolutionary heads today, and all will be perfectly tranquil.... [Arrests] are continuous; we purge a neighborhood every night; [five hundred] people are already arrested, and everything is calm."[75] Arrests were now continuous, he reported with satisfaction, with patrols constantly on the streets. "The guillotine expedited yesterday and today forty-three wicked people who left nearly 30 million [livres in confiscated property] to the Republic."[76]

Civic Order of Terror

The major symbolic move towards reconciliation between the representatives and the Club was the restoration of the name *Marseille* on 24 Pluviôse (12 February).[77] There followed the restoration of the Revolutionary Tribunal with all of its former members returned to their places. In addition, Maignet not only halted the destruction of the town hall but also promised funds for its restoration. The room where the infamous Section 18 had met was to be sealed up and was never again to be used as a meeting place. A placard would be placed on the main entry door overlooking the harbor bearing the inscription:

Here the Federalists of Section 18 agitated to cause the counter-revolution;

They are no more:

Patriots, flee these places that crime inhabited.[78]

---

[74] *Proclamation de représentant du peuple, envoyé dans les Départemens des Bouches-du-Rhône et de Vaucluse*, 16 Ventôse An II – 6 March 1794 Maignet collection, n° 11.

[75] To CSP, 7 Ventôse An II – 25 February 1794 in Aulard, *RACSP*, xi, 406–7.

[76] To CSP, 10 Ventôse An II – 28 February 1794 Aulard, *RACSP*, xi, 472.

[77] Decree in Aulard, *RACSP*, xi, 93. See also CSP to Maignet, ibid., 273 explaining the restoration was being done over Barras's and Fréron's protests and ordering their recall, because patriots should not be punished for the actions of others.

[78] *Arrêté* of 13 Ventôse An II – 3 March 1794 Maignet collection n° 15. The room was eventually sold as national property at the end of 1794 (Auguis and Serres to CSP, 5 Frimaire An III – 25 November 1794, in Aulard, *RACSP*, xviii, 342).

Maignet also replaced the Municipal Commission, which he claimed lacked energy, with a town council. He appointed it, after consultation with officials, the *comité de surveillance* and the Club. None of the new members had been councillors in the pre-Federalist municipality. Later still, he authorized the rearming of citizens. That is, only members of the Popular Society or holders of *certificats de civisme*, a card only the Club granted, could own weapons. The *comité de surveillance* would produce lists of rearmed citizens. Anyone owning a weapon without a proper card would be subject to the death penalty.[79] In other words, the Jacobins whom Fréron had disarmed were to get their weapons back.

Thus, with the restoration of the name *Marseille*, the restoration of the Jacobin dominated Revolutionary Tribunal, the rearming only of people the Club had vetted, the restoration of the municipality, the halting of the destruction of buildings and the promise of repairs to the town hall, the stigmatization of the hated Federalist strongholds, and so on, Maignet implicitly endorsed the Club. Marseille, therefore, would not go the way of Lyon with its name change, its colonization by outsiders, and its demolitions.

Maignet also claimed symbolic and rhetorical dominion for the Jacobins. Like Fréron and others, he created antimonuments, markers of impure territory. The sterilization of the room where Section 18 met was an example. Another was a parade (1 Germinal, or 21 March, the first day of the Republican spring) that symbolized unity with the Club. Papier-mâché Mountains and Bastilles; floats depicting Hercules dragging the corpse of Federalism; singers and actors dancing around the Liberty Tree; trumpeters, drummers, and young women waving tricolor ribbons, and so on claimed all the moments of the Revolution for the Jacobins. The parade began at the town hall, and snaked by the Temple of Reason, the former Eglise des Prêcheurs, where Section 11 had sparked the anti-Federalist Jacobin rebellion the previous August. Maignet gave a speech there denouncing fanaticism, that is, Christianity. It ended four hours later at the Place du 10 Août, formerly (and presently) the Allées de Meilhon. From the late afternoon onward, people feasted and danced the farandole. The only people who represented themselves in the procession were the soldiers who paraded without arms, presumably because the garrison had sided with the departed representatives against the Jacobins; the Club;

---

[79] *Arrêté* of 23 Ventôse An II – 13 March 1794, Maignet collection n° 19.

various officials; and Maignet, who came last presumably to represent his, or the Convention's importance.[80] The promenade reclaimed the city for the entire population, in realty for the victors over Federalism. The parade depicted this hideous monstrosity as entirely outside urban life. Earlier representatives, like Albitte, had claimed that most Marseillais were Federalists. Maignet's speech at the Temple of Reason emphasized fraternity and stigmatized enemies after excluding them from the polity.[81]

Maignet also claimed the history of Marseille during the Revolution for the Jacobins. This was the most important restoration of all. The Temple of Reason was also a site of a battle, a museum of sorts for outside visitors to receive instruction in recent events. It was a sacred site where the Republican community affirmed itself. It was also a temple where each *décade*, the Republican day of rest, officials would read out the Constitution and the Declaration of the Rights of Man. Thus 1789 culminated here. At the same time, the temple commemorated a rupture, the defeat of superstition promoted by an avaricious priesthood and the return of the French to nature.[82] The two, of course, were connected because the significance of this battle and many others was the triumph of ignorance over obscurantism. This rupture in time, from Old Regime to Revolution, from ignorance to philosophy, from fanaticism to reason, belonged to the patriots. Specific events linking the dead and the living belonged to them as well. The spirits of the dead comrades, killed on 10 August and during the liberation of August 1793 looked down on the living and called them to the highest sacrifices.[83] Maignet developed a passion for the recent history of the region, especially for the development of Federalism.[84] It would help him understand how that history took a wrong turn and how to guide it back to its true course.

---

[80] Poupé, *Lettres de Barras et de Fréron*, 203–4, letter of 5 Germinal (23 March). On the general context of this fête, see Michel Vovelle, *Les métamorphoses de la fête en Provence de 1750 à 1820* (Paris: Aubier/Flammarion, 1976), esp. 126–7.

[81] "Discours prononcé par le représentant du peuple Maignet Dans le Temple de la Raison, Lors de la Fête de la Fraternité & du Triomphe de la Philosophie, célébrée à Marseille le 1er germinal," in Maignet collection n° 22.

[82] *Arrêté* of 24 Ventôse An II – 14 March 1794, Maignet collection n° 20. See also Catherine M. Bell, *Ritual: perspectives and dimensions* (New York: Oxford University Press, 1997), 157–9, 248–9.

[83] "Discours prononcé...Dans le Temple de la Raison," Maignet collection, pp. 6–7.

[84] See his letter of 28 Pluviôse An II – 1 February, to the administrators of the District of Avignon, in AD Vaucluse, 1L 135.

Terror in Aubagne

Events in Marseille and the rest of the Department mattered because Aubagne did not experience the Revolution in isolation. By the time the story resumes, struggles in Marseille opened the way for an extreme terror. Albitte's recommendation of death only to the leaders was on nobody's agenda at the end of 1793. The Convention, the Committee of Public Safety, the representatives, and the club movement throughout the region all agreed that repression should be widespread. They had differed on how spontaneous and how much popular initiative there was to be. In that sense, the defeat of Barras and Fréron settled little. With Maignet's mission, however, a new opportunity arose that permitted those demanding a severe repression to coordinate their efforts and no longer work at cross-purposes. The compromise among the factions was that officialdom, particularly Maignet, would sponsor a terror with no inhibitions. This is what the clubs had wanted all along.

On 1 September 1793, the citizens of Aubagne assembled in the chapel of the White Penitents – the patriots' penitent chapel – and accepted the new Jacobin constitution by a vote of 365 to 0, although, of course, the Convention had already suspended this constitution. The municipality that took office the previous January assumed control again. Thus, some familiar faces reappeared on the local scene: Camoin as mayor, Domergue and Suzan as municipal officers, Gury as *secrétaire-greffier*, and so on.[85] Yet this was no simple restoration. Although details are lacking, enough has survived from Aubagne and from other small cities to show that the autumn of 1793 would be dramatically different.

The absence of a detailed record in the Council minutes, the absence of the minutes of the Club and of the *comité de surveillance*, create the impression that from the reinstallation of the Jacobin municipality on 1 September until the arrival of Maignet, nothing much happened.[86] Yet this would be quite misleading. A formal terror was a long time coming because Jacobins in Aubagne frequently looked to Marseille for a lead, but

[85] AN F¹ᶜIII Bouches-du-Rhône 8, procès-verbal du 1ᵉʳ septembre 1793 for the referendum results, and ibid., Extrait du registre des délibérations de la commune d'Aubagne, 1 septembre 1793 for the reinstallation of the municipality.

[86] The *agent national* of the District of Marseilles noted the existence of the Club in Aubagne during the Terror (ibid., L 1015, 11, letter to Maignet, 3 Ventôse An II – 22 February 1794). The Club also conducted a *scrutin épuratoire* or self-purging: ibid., L 1034, *compte décadaire*, 12 Germinal An II – 1 April 1794.

while the siege of Toulon continued and while the Jacobins of Marseille fought with Fréron and Barras, there was little time to extend the Terror to outlying localities, even to ones as close as Aubagne.

Nevertheless, a vigorous, informal terror, one paralleled in the experience of other towns, exploded almost everywhere from the beginning. In early September, the town council of Aubagne reported that many former Federalists had taken refuge in Toulon, taking five hundred military muskets with them. They also heard that someone had disarmed 130 local people, so presumably at least that many were also under arrest. Many more arrests would follow. The council was also preparing to join the local *levée en masse* against Toulon and so asked General Carteaux to supply them with three hundred muskets.[87] In the previous spring the Jacobins' *comité de prudence* had wanted to arrest just a handful of opponents. The year before the council had sent a half dozen young men to march on the Tuileries. The period of informal terror was supposed to be far more repressive and witness a far greater mobilization than anyone had envisioned before. Moreover, this informal terror would reach into new areas. Foreign residents in Aubagne were to present their passports, and the National Guard was to be reorganized, *républicainnement,* so that only citizens known for their "firmness and patriotism" would be admitted. While this purge was taking place, the council proposed to raise its own little army, "a company of elite republicans, who [would] execute the law, while marching to the orders of the municipality." This would be drawn from men beyond draft age and the company would number one hundred men.[88] Because the other things the municipality was doing – managing the subsistence crisis and national property, mostly – did not require much coercion, the revolutionary army of Aubagne must have been destined to arrest, guard, and transport prisoners. The inspiration for this was clearly the creation of the Légion des Montagnards by the Valence Congress and the representative Boisset. Moreover, many activities would have a social dimension. Throughout the autumn, the council prepared to inventory émigré property. At the end of the year, it appointed commissioners to draw up the rolls for a forced loan on the rich.[89]

---

[87] AC Aubagne, *registre des délibérations*, ff. 1v–2, session of 1 September 1793.

[88] Ibid., ff. 2–3, session of 2 September 1793.

[89] Ibid., f. 14, session of 22 Frimaire An II – 12 December 1794. One of these commissioners was Louis Poutet, later a victim of the murder gang. Shortly after, the council authorised the hiring of four assistants, all of them leading militants, including Dominique Pichou, to complete this operation (ibid., f. 23v, session of 5 Ventôse An II – 23 February 1794).

Finally, to celebrate the capture of Toulon, the council voted to obtain a quantity of grain to distribute to the poor.[90]

Nonetheless, however enthusiastic the Club and the council were, there were limits to what they could do by themselves. Quarrels in Marseille slowed the pace of executions. Despite the very large number of arrests, the Revolutionary Tribunal in Marseille meted out the first death sentence to a *sectionnaire* of Aubagne on 8 November 1793, more than two months after the restoration of the Jacobin municipality. Two other sentences followed over the next three months. All the other executions of Aubaniens came after Maignet restored the Revolutionary Tribunal in Ventôse (March 1794).[91] The meager results for the early months of the Terror suggest that many Federalists had taken refuge elsewhere. They would also substantiate Fréron's assertion that earlier representatives and generals had let the great guilty ones escape.

The experience of other towns confirms the hypothesis of an initial confusion followed by a formal institutionalization. Such an extension of the field of vision beyond Aubagne shows that there was also more to the Terror than the operation of formal institutions. For terrorists, the entire experience after September was one of high excitement. For them, the period of what historians call anarchic terror, roughly from September to December 1793, may have been the most authentic, perhaps even the most satisfying.

At Marseille in September, for example, enthusiasts undertook their own house-to-house searches. The municipality denounced these arbitrary acts and rather quaintly reminded fellow citizens that "revolutionary measures require morals and public probity."[92] Following the Federalist collapse, the interim town council at Aix-en-Provence established no fewer than three *comités de surveillance*, each with different powers. While two eventually ebbed away, the last one survived throughout the Terror, with heavy representation from the Club, its members never elected, and with almost no interference from the representatives on mission. Nonetheless, the institutional confusion did nothing to impede the shower of arrests at the beginning. In September and October, the committees arrested nearly 190 people.[93] At Salon, which the murders in the previous March had torn apart, a regular *comité de surveillance*, one

[90] Ibid., f. 18v., session of 17 Nivôse An II – 6 January 1794.

[91] Ibid., L 3122, *Liste generale....*

[92] AM Marseille, 13D 46, *Proclamation de la municipalité de Marseille," 9e jour de la 1re décade du second mois de la seconde année de la République* – 30 September 1793.

[93] Grimaldi, *Comité de surveillance d'Aix-en-Provence*, 36–41, 58–9, 119.

authorized by the Law of Suspects, arrested eighty-two people, twenty-one of them women, in a one week period in mid-October. It would appear that many Salon Federalists did not have the opportunity to flee, perhaps because Carteaux's army captured the little town so quickly. That would explain why the committee sent twenty-nine former members of the local sectional committee, no less, to the Revolutionary Tribunal in Marseille in mid-November.[94]

Establishing a regular *comité de surveillance* was the way to link small communities with the larger terrorist apparatus. Under the Law of 14 Frimaire, the organizational untidiness of the early Terror gave way to formal institutions. So whoever was doing the arresting in places like Aubagne in the autumn of 1793, the municipality or a committee of the club, had to surrender the power of arrest to a *comité de surveillance*.

The Law of 17 September 1793, the infamous Law of Suspects, gave the *comités de surveillance* a new injection of energy everywhere in France. This was a very broadly drafted law that permitted the arrest or internment of anyone who was an "enemy of liberty," a "supporter of tyranny," or a Federalist. The committees defined who fitted these categories themselves. The law provided no formal mechanism of appeal of their decisions. Yet the committees were far more than just the preventive institutions that the Law of Suspects specified. On 22 Pluviôse (10 February), Maignet ordered the committees to produce lists of suspects and their alleged crimes. The committees would forward these lists to the Military Commission for further processing. These papers were frequently the only material that the revolutionary tribunals considered. A person whom the tribunals found innocent would not necessarily be released. They could be held without charge as a suspect. So too could the wealthy who had not made a sufficient sacrifice for the Revolution. It was presumably for the committees to decide what amount was sufficient.[95] In other words, the *comités de surveillance* were essential to the functioning of the revolutionary tribunals. The power to denounce and arrest was the power to inflict ultimate harm on factional rivals.

The original committees were supposed to have been elected monthly but, by the winter of the Year II, most, including that of Aubagne, had

---

94 ADBR, L 1856, *comité de surveillance* of Salon register, sessions dated 13 through 19 October, 26 Brumaire An II – 17 November 1793. Of those sent to Marseille, three were executed.

95 *Arrêté du Représentant du Peuple, Envoyé dans les Départemens des Bouches-du-Rhône & de Vaucluse du 22 Pluviôse [10 February 1794], l'an second de la République, une et indivisible*, in Maignet collection n° 4. Largely repeated in his decree of 29 Ventôse An II – 19 March 1794 in ibid., n° 21. Same decree in form of a poster in ADBR, L 1039.

a permanent membership. At one point, the committee in Aubagne said there were nine members but two were always absent, one because he was a municipal officer and another because he had a job at nearby La Ciotat.[96] Turnover was minimal. Three people signed the earliest letter from the committee, on 3 Nivôse (23 December 1793), but only one of them became a permanent member.[97] By the end of Ventôse (mid-March), the committee acquired a nearly permanent membership that scarcely changed until the committee dissolved. Five individuals signed most of the fifty-odd post-Ventôse letters from the committee that have survived, while another four individuals signed letters off and on throughout the history of the committee.

Most of them were already prominent in town politics. One of them was Jean-Baptiste Camoin, leader of the anti-*piquet* forces in 1790–1, commander of the marauding expedition of the National Guard to Velaux in the spring of 1792, and occasional mayor and municipal officer. Another member was Sivan, a founding member of the Jacobin club in the spring of 1791 and at times a municipal officer. Two other assiduous members, Louis Poutet, an agricultural laborer, and Nicolas Debenet, a locksmith, were prominent Jacobins from an early date; the *égorgeurs* later murdered both of them in 1795. Other members of the committee had the good sense to flee to Marseille, Toulon, or Nice. One list of refugees contains the names of all the core members of the committee.[98]

If the committee had links through the club, it also had links through the pre-Federalist municipality. True, some prominent members of the municipality like Domergue, Pichou, Freze, and others were never members of the *comité de surveillance* but there was some overlap all the same. Castelin, Jean-Pierre Tessier, and Antoine Nicolas were members of both institutions. Some members of the restored municipality – like Camoin himself, Jean-Baptiste Baudin, and Vincent Olive – were also members of the committee.[99] In other words, the fact that so many of its members had a past in local politics necessarily affected how the committee defined its mission. For the Jacobins of Aubagne, their past and their mission included a war upon the bourgeois, a political struggle for control of the town between them and the established families. The Law of

96 *Ibid.*, L 1060, letter to District of Marseilles [?], 15 Prairial An II – 3 June 1794.

97 Ibid., L 3111, letter to *accusateur public*, 3 Nivôse An II – 23 December 1793.

98 AN F7 7171, Copie de la lettre écrite par le citoyen Ramel, médecin au commissaire du Directoire exécutif du département des Bouches-du-Rhône, 22 Pluviôse An V – 10 February 1797.

99 See the list in ibid., F¹ᶜIII Bouches-du-Rhône 8, Extrait du registre des délibérations de la commune d'Aubagne, 1 September 1793.

Suspects and Maignet's linking of suspects to the revolutionary tribunals gave them powerful weapons to settle this issue once and for all. The Aubagne committee understood this role very well. As the committee put it, "Our principal task has been to discover the counter-revolutionaries of this commune and to send them immediately to the military commission established at *Sans-Nom* [i.e., Marseille] . . . we have given almost all our attention to their discovery because the solidification of the Republic demands it."[100]

Solidification was a new way to fulfill an older aim of eliminating enemies. This was an aim that might have surprised members of the Convention in Paris, for whom terror was a device to defend the country and punish transgressors. In many places like Aubagne, locals translated the national idiom of terror into a local context. Thus, just as the local terrorists had graduated from earlier faction fights, so too had their enemies. Suspects and émigrés, for example, were drawn disproportionately from the well-off bourgeoisie. A very large proportion of these were proscribed for their participation in the Federalist revolt, but even where these men had fled, the terrorists imprisoned their women folk. Almost without noticing, the Law of Suspects had become a law of hostages.[101]

The arrests of suspects, Federalists, political enemies of all sorts, and their relatives, as well as the seizure of the émigrés' property, were the mundane aspects of the Terror in Aubagne. The sensational part, the part that has made the Terror infamous, was revolutionary justice. Seventeen people from Aubagne were condemned to death during the Terror. One, Claire Monier, had her sentence postponed because she was pregnant. She became involved with the murder gang several years later.[102] The largest batch of Aubaniens came up for trial before the restored Revolutionary Tribunal. They also came to trial after Maignet's decree organizing trials

---

[100] ADBR, L 1060, letter to "citoyens administrateurs," 24 Pluviôse An II – 12 February 1794.

[101] See my "Etude des cas: le comité de surveillance d'Aubagne," *Rives nord–méditerranéennes*18 (2004), 113–22.

[102] This underlines the importance of confirming whether these death sentences were truly carried out but the sources are lacking: the civil registers of Marseille never mention death by execution, which suggests there must have been a special register for the prisons that, like most the prison records for Marseille from this period, have not survived. On Monier's case, see AN F7 7160, "Extrait du greffe du tribunal criminel des Bouches-du-Rhône," 13 Vendémiaire An III – 4 October 1794, and ibid., D III 30, her husband's petition for clemency undated but received 21 Thermidor An II – 8 August 1794. Both she and her equally anti-Jacobin husband, Dominique Donde, died of old age during the Empire.

by accusation rather than by case. This meant that what held the accused in common on any particular session was not a specific event, say, the same counterrevolutionary act like holding office in a particular town at a particular time – normal justice, in other words – but a common accusation in unrelated cases. This practice greatly accelerated justice in Marseille. After the restoration of the Revolutionary Tribunal in Marseille, the number of death sentences and acquittals tripled over what they had been the previous autumn. In other words, each trial was taking less and less time. In the case of the Aubaniens tried on 5 Floréal (14 April 1794), the court tried twenty-one people between eleven in the morning and five-thirty in the afternoon, which, assuming no breaks, meant that each defendant received less than twenty minutes of the court's time.[103] The judges condemned eleven people to death, all but two of them from Aubagne. They acquitted five; none was from Aubagne.

Speed added to the theatrical quality of a revolutionary trial. Judges routinely expressed the outrage of the entire community toward the defendant, not for what he or she had done, but for every contentious action the accused had committed since the beginning of the Revolurion. To take one example among many, the President of the Tribunal railed at Jean-Jacques Rastègues, a bourgeois from Aubagne: "You, Rastègues, you have shown yourself to be an excellent counterrevolutionary, moderate in the moments of the Revolution, and crazed [*énragé*] in the time of the sections. You deposed against patriots."[104] Such upbraiding might explain why the accused were so laconic, why so few offered a vigorous self-defense: the defendants undoubtedly knew they had little chance. Consider, for example, the trial of Jean Duperret, aged seventy-three, a rentier accused of having gathered and distributed in secret all kinds of "fanatic" [i.e., religious] literature, including a papal bull. The court tried him on 23 Germinal (12 April 1794) along with ten others. His interrogation was purely about political loyalty. Thus, the President of the Tribunal asked:

What have you done for the Revolution?

Reply: Only what an old man overwhelmed with infirmities can do.... I have always been submissive to authority and I do it out of duty. I lead a very retired life.

The court found Duperret guilty and sentenced him to death.[105]

---

[103] ADBR, L 3119, session of 5 Floréal (24 April).
[104] Ibid., L 3119, session of 5 Floréal (24 April).
[105] Ibid., L 3118, trial of 23 Germinal (12 April 1794).

Most of the other accused were equally passive. Many were even willing to admit their guilt, though they attempted to mitigate it. Thus Antoine-Barthélemy Le Comte, a former sea captain, was accused of being a member of the Federalist municipality, of having raised money to equip nine volunteers to march to Avignon, and of having participated in the sequestration of the property of the former municipal officers. He admitted doing these things but claimed he did them "to obey the will of the people [and] persuaded that we would be replaced in a week," as someone had promised. When asked if he knew he was rebelling against the law, he gave a very revealing answer: "The country people believe more in the wisdom [*lumières*] of those of the towns – they are scarcely able to discern the danger and we believed we were doing the right thing by obeying the orders coming from Marseille.... [Besides], the *comité* [*général*] gave its orders to the commune which carried them out."[106] In other words, Le Comte appears to have been claiming that the Federalists were reasserting their "natural" leadership of the countryside.

"We poor folks of Aubagne," declared Jean-Tropès Landon, a former chancellor at Tunis and now a retired rentier. "We had to bend [before the superior force of the Federalists of Marseille].... I was a sheep who followed the herd." Images that distanced the accused from the act were common. Landon also compared himself to a piece of wood borne along by the torrent.[107]

Accelerating verdicts and highlighting the theatrical quality of punishment made trials more administrative than judicial procedures. On 25–6 Ventôse (15–16 March), for example, the judges condemned all eleven defendants to death. On 19 Germinal (8 April), they condemned no one to death and acquitted six of the eight defendants.[108] In other words, these imbalances between acquittals and condemnations suggest that someone had decided the outcomes in advance.

Moreover, increasing the rate of condemnations required authorities to criminalize some trivial activities. By the late winter of 1793–4, the tribunal had condemned most of the "fat boars," to borrow Fréron's terminology. In Lyon when the tribunals had emptied the prisons, the number of executions dropped. Not so in Marseille. Terror began to

---

[106] Ibid., L 3113, dossier Le Compte, denunciation of 8 November 1793.

[107] Idid., L 3114, interrogation before the court, 17 Frimaire An II – December 7, 1793. Ibid., L 3129, petition of Antoine Bestagne, cultivateur, n.d., used the same metaphor but was condemned anyway, possibly because while he claimed to have been forced into the Departmental Army, he did not name those who compelled him.

[108] Ibid., L 3123, various lists.

widen its scope and so charges became increasingly vague. Thus during the session of 25 Germinal (14 April), Honoré Bense, a cultivator and sometime municipal officer of Aubagne, was acquitted of unspecified counterrevolutionary crimes. Bense was fortunate. So was Marie-Therese Aubert of Marseille, who was also acquitted, but then discerning her crimes in the first place was hard: not always showing zeal for the Revolution; "complained several times about the Maximum [on prices]; at the time of the Sections, she joined other women to applaud criminal executions." Ange-Henri Ferroul, a notary's clerk also from Marseille, was less lucky in that he was to be imprisoned until the war's end. He had "claimed that a workshop cannot remain without a head; and that consequently we need a king...and he bet that all the revolutionaries would be guillotined." Part of Antoine-Hippolite L'Hérmite's crime was to have been living in Lyon when he was caught or not fleeing it during the Federalist rebellion. Yet he was also a noble, a councillor in the Parlement of Aix-en-Provence, who "never pronounced for the Revolution. He left his home where he could have been useful to his fellow citizens, if it had pleased him. [Instead], he inhabited a city that was habitually in a counter-revolution. He was indifferent [*tranquille*] before the *incivisme* of those he visited. He has not given his fortune, his talents, [or] his conduct for the progress of liberty." For all this, the court sentenced L'Hérmite to death.[109] The Revolutionary Tribunal was executing people who had not fled retribution, people who probably thought their own role did not merit much attention. Yet the logic of relentless and pitiless repression could not possibly overlook them. A final example among many: Antoine Chevalier, executed for accompanying the victims of the Popular Tribunal to the scaffold, doing a drumroll to drown out their last words, and arousing those who attacked heroic Section 11.[110]

As it turned out, the verdicts against the nine Aubaniens of 5 Floréal (24 April) were the last in which the Revolutionary Tribunal of Marseille pronounced any death sentences. The Tribunal soon ceased operations altogether when the Law of 19 Floréal (8 May) abolished all the provincial revolutionary tribunals and transferred their cases to the Paris Tribunal.

Far from being the end of judicial terror, the Law of 19 Floréal was an opportunity for a fresh start. This was the Popular Commission of

---

[109] Ibid., L 3127, "Jugement du Tribunal Criminel révolutionnaire du département des Bouches-du-Rhône," 25 Germinal An II – 14 April 1794.

[110] AM Marseille, 2I 165, *Troisième tableau des individus jugés à mort par le tribunal criminel révolutionnaire des Bouches-du-Rhône* (Marseille: Impr Jouve & Compagnie, An II), 13.

Orange. The Commission was the first of what the government intended to be a new generation of revolutionary tribunals. Maignet himself initiated it. He persuaded the Committee of Public Safety to establish it in the Midi because Paris was too far away. It would be too difficult to transport the fifteen thousand people who needed to be executed to cleanse the region. Moreover, a tribunal was effective only if it worked before the eyes of the guilty onlookers.[111] The Popular Commission of Orange was the only provincial revolutionary tribunal that the Committee of Public Safety established directly. Like other revolutionary tribunals, there was no appeal. It also codified existing practice that an accused did not have to have committed a specific act. Instead, the decree refined the category of political enemy: the enemy of the Revolution, a category first mentioned in the outlawry decree of 27 March 1793. The rest of the Floréal decree went on to define such a person and specify the modalities of judgment:

The enemies of the Revolution are those who by whatever methods and under whatever mask they have been disguising themselves, have sought to block or slow the march of the Revolution and to prevent the Republic from consolidating itself.

The penalty due to this crime is death. The proof required for a condemnation is all the information of whatever nature that could convince a reasonable man who loves liberty.

The rule of the verdicts is the conscience of the judges, enlightened by the love of justice and love of country.[112]

The Popular Commission of Orange had jurisdiction over the Vaucluse and the Bouches-du-Rhône. One person from Aubagne actually has a file in the Commission's papers.[113] The court never tried him but he was not supposed to be the only accused. The Commission was also intending to put suspects on trial, that is, people who were often arrested for preventive reasons or who were, in the case of Aubagne, relatives of émigrés. An enemy of the Revolution, therefore, was a very broad category. This would explain why lists of suspects from Aubagne appear in the papers of

---

[111] Letter to Couthon, 4 Floréal An II – 23 April 1794, in Aulard, *RACSP*, xiii, 20–1.

[112] AD Vaucluse, 8L 1, "Instruction de la Commission Populaire établie à Orange par l'arrêté du Comité de Salut Public, du 20 floréal l'an 2ᵉ de la République française une et in^dble." Signed by Billaud-Varennes, Couthon, Carnot, and Robespierre.

[113] Ibid., 8L 103, dossier Antoine Tourneau. He was the father of a leading Marseille Jacobin, a native of Aubagne. The father was a member of the General Committee of the Sections of Aubagne, who was captured returning home for some reason after his initial flight. He claimed he joined the sections only to save his son who was then under arrest.

the Commission. Fortunately for those involved, the fall of Robespierre in Paris on 9 Thermidor saved them. The Committee of Public Safety abolished the Popular Commission on 13 Thermidor. The atmosphere in Paris had changed dramatically with the downfall of the Robespierre clique. Three of the four who signed the original decree establishing the Commission on 20 Floréal – Collot d'Herbois, Billaud Varennes, and Carnot – signed the abolition decree. The fourth, Robespierre, of course, was dead. At almost the same time, Maignet ordered the release of hundreds of people from prison.[114] Parisian politics had a huge effect on faraway Provence. The *journée* of 9 Thermidor would be one of the most decisive of the Revolution.

The Terror never accomplished the goals of many of its proponents. If it was ever related to the defense of the country in this region, the Jacobins had accomplished this goal long before. As for punishing enemies, the Terror was scandalously ineffective, despite truncated justice and despite the blurring of distinctions among accused, suspects, and hostages. Aubagne was quite typical of this failure. Of the 109 people in Aubagne who held some sort of office during the Federalist insurrection, only four were executed. In fact, the terrorist apparatus was not particularly effective in Aubagne. The others who were sentenced to death were truly marginal to Federalism. The teacher Marie-Roch Barthélemy, for instance, was "one of the primary motors of the rebellion, he usurped the place of a public functionary," that is, the post office. Two others who were on the borderline of rebellion were women who were condemned for denouncing patriots, while a handful of men were condemned for doing the same. The remainder fell victim to the extraordinarily vague accusations that the public prosecutor launched in the second phase of the Revolutionary Tribunal's history.

Repeating this exercise for Marseille confirms that judicial terror did not punish many *grands coupables*. One obvious measure is how successful the Revolutionary Tribunal was at executing judges from the Popular Tribunal. After all, this court was the heart of anti-Jacobin repression, and all its judges were legally outlaws thanks to the Law of 19 June 1793. Theoretically after the reinstatement of the Popular Tribunal on 3 June, a reinstatement that defied the Convention, there should have been forty-eight judges. It is known how many judges of the "tribunal

---

[114] Ibid., 8L 2, ff. 3–3v., minutes of the Popular Commission, session of 18 Thermidor – 5 August 1794. BM Arles, MS 664, n° 32, Maignet *arrêté* regarding the release of prisoners in Arles, 6 Fructidor An II – 23 August 1794.

of blood," as the Jacobins liked to call it, were sentenced to death: ten.[115] The record was even more astonishing with the political institutions of organized anti-Jacobinism. On 23 July 1793, the Trois Corps held a large meeting that authorized the conscription of all single men aged up to age forty-five for the Departmental Army. There were present twenty-seven representatives of the General Committee of the Thirty-Two Sections and thirty-one from the individual sections. Of these fifty-eight individuals, all of them at the core of anti-Jacobinism, only one was executed.[116]

Reflections

Had the Terror continued, it might have been different. Even more radical social consequences might have occurred; the mass arrests and executions that Maignet envisaged might have been even more tragic. Terror, never a single essence that a single definition can capture, had been evolving throughout the period. At the end, the direction was toward more spoliation and more death. Unlike other parts of the country, there was no easing of repression, no harbingers of the relaxation to come after the fall of Robespierre. While the Terror had always been harsh, it had also moved through stages, both in Aubagne and in the region. The purge of the Jacobins in the summer of 1793 was greatly unsettling. Following the defeat of the Federalists, the institutional disarray and the initial confusion had opened a rhetorical space in which local Jacobins and representatives on mission engaged in a noisy dialogue about all aspects of the agenda. The entire revolutionary spectrum agreed on a vast repression. Differences were differences among extremists over who was in charge and over the targeting of enemies. Toulon's treason highlighted these differences between the representatives and the congresses of clubs, but the defeat of the infamous city did not end them. The dispute was more fundamental. The clubs dreamed of a mass assault on enemies with their own armed force, the Légion des Montagnards, and with their own *comités de surveillance*. The local initiatives of the autumn of 1793 in

---

[115] Paul-Albert Robert, *La Justice des sections marseillaises. Le tribunal populaire 1792–1793* (Paris: A. Rousseau, 1913), 193. Unaccountably, Robert left Pierre Languier, the president of the *tribunal d'accusation*, off his list. Although the number of functioning judges in the *tribunal d'accusation* is not known, several surviving verdicts of the *tribunal de jugement* (ADBR, L 483) dating from early August 1793, mention that twenty-three to twenty-four judges of that chamber were present.

[116] Ibid., L 48 meeting of 23 July 1793, 244–5.

which militants operated in a vacuum and could define and arrest enemies were the apogee of this idea of autonomous revolution.

For the representatives on mission, such spontaneity was welcome so long as the militants focused on Toulon or directed their repressive energies toward the Revolutionary Tribunal in Marseille. It was altogether different if the clubs sponsored vigilantism. For the Committee of Public Safety and for the representatives on the spot, such actions were intolerable. Despite the difficulties, Fréron's coup against the club movement was successful. Although the militants could shed tears of joy when the Paris Revolutionary Tribunal exonerated Maillet and Girard, the clubs' independence had ended. The restoration of Marseille was cosmetic. After that, no one acted on the fiery rhetoric of the simultaneous extermination of enemies. The Légion des Montagnards and the clubs' *comités de surveillance* quietly disappeared.

Maignet compensated for this loss of initiative from below by dazzling the militants with more ambitious goals and new methods. His operational vision of the Terror was bureaucratic, and so there would be no return to autonomy. Maignet was no moderate either and his strategic vision of the Terror required the cooperation of the clubs. His endorsement of the Military Tribunal, his efforts to speed trials along, and his establishment of *comités de surveillance* everywhere all show him as one of the most radical representatives of the period. His criticism of the clubs was minor and rare because they were a part of his strategy of extirpating immorality through violence. This agenda was the most radical of all. The terms of reference of the Popular Commission of Orange were also so broad that they permitted arresting authorities, all of them club members, a huge scope to pursue enemies. The court's dealing with the accused in large batches and its rapid verdicts channeled the militants' vigilante instincts. Moreover, when municipalities like Aubagne began seizing enemies' property and preparing its distribution to the worthy poor, Maignet was charting a course into a huge social revolution. Terror exercised on behalf of the clubs rather than at their initiative might have been a satisfactory trade-off in such circumstances.

Once the promise of Maignet's social revolution ended after the fall of Robespierre, the vigilante reflex returned but the consequence was utterly disastrous.

8

The Revolution of the Antiterrorists

Vengeance, Massacre, and Justice

Many unjust arrests dictated by resentment prove that men are not moderate in either party. The malevolent had done a lot of harm by atrocities; the good do it for revenge. The human race rarely knows how to maintain *un juste milieu.*

– Procureur syndic of the department of Bouches-du-Rhône to same
of district of Salon, 13 Prairial year III – 1 June 1795

The aftermath of the fall of Robespierre on 9 Thermidor, Year II, is usually treated as a depressing slide into vindictive violence and sickening corruption. One of the signs of this was the emergence of murder gangs throughout the Southeast. The gangs themselves are supposed to have been composed of draft dodgers, returned émigrés, former suspects, and relatives of victims of the guillotine. They were called either Companies of Jesus or Companies of the Sun. When their goal was not ignominious revenge for the Terror, they are usually labelled "royalist." They thrived because of the complicity of sympathetic authorities who succeeded the local terrorists. New teams of representatives on mission purged the terrorists, and the new men were often victims of the Jacobins or their sworn enemies. Whatever the politics of these replacements, they were rarely very loyal to the Republic and many of them were secret royalists. The victims of the murder gangs were usually former terrorists, who could be murdered in any number of gruesome ways. The most spectacular was the prison massacre. There were any number of these in the period, at Aix-en-Provence, Lyon, Marseille, Tarascon, Bourg-en-Bresse, Sisteron, Saint-Etienne, and elsewhere. Another manifestation was the attack on a column of prisoners being transferred from one jail to another. Local authorities frequently alerted the gangs while the escort conveniently melted away. The gang could then accomplish its work, often with the assistance of bystanders. There were dozens of such incidents, but among the most spectacular were those of Nîmes and Orange. Finally, there was the murder of individuals who for one reason or another had not fled or who had failed to protect themselves. Michel Vovelle has counted over 400 such murders, an impressive number since the killers did not have the support of the state, as the Jacobins did in the Year II.[1]

Revenge for the Terror and complicity from authorities is the basic analytic framework of any discussion of the White Terror of the Years III through V (1795–7). The inhabitants of Aubagne witnessed all three versions of the White Terror: the massacre of prisoners being transferred, the assault on the actual jail and the murder of those being held, and finally the individual murder. The little city also witnessed other outrages, like mass assault and outright mass robbery of neighboring villages. Furthermore, whether related to the gang or not, highways surrounding the town were infested with brigands for many years into the Empire. Bonaparte himself had his belongings stolen on the outskirts of Aubagne on his return from Egypt in 1799, and people remembered the burning of a mannequin of the victorious general on the town square for many years afterward.

Jacobins, the primary victims of the gangs, of course, had their own explanation of the White Terror and historians have taken over much of it. Nor was the Jacobin version entirely wrong. But by focusing almost exclusively on revenge for the Terror as the sole motive and on complicity of authority as the political precondition for the murders, the Jacobins left many things out.

The White Terror did not occur in the historical and political vacuum that the Jacobins assumed. In the case of Aubagne, and no doubt elsewhere, the murders of the post-Thermidorian period flowed from the factional politics of the town that preceded the Terror. Furthermore, the White Terror was not entirely a return of the anti-Jacobins, or at least the same anti-Jacobins, to power, so that the metaphor that contemporaries liked to use of the swinging pendulum was not entirely exact. Rather than return to power thirsting for revenge, many former Federalists simply

---

[1] Michel Vovelle, "Massacreurs et massacrés. Aspects sociaux de la contre-révolution en Provence, après Thermidor," in *Les Résistances à la Révolution: actes du Colloque de Rennes, 17–21 Septembre 1985*, ed. François Lebrun and Roger Dupuy (Paris: Imago, 1987), 142.

withdrew from local struggles altogether. The *bande d'Aubagne* certainly
flourished in an atmosphere of complicity and revenge, but it also thrived
because of the collapse of authority, because the civic order was severely
damaged, and because the gang had support beyond the complicity of corrupt officials. This allowed for some very unsavory characters to emerge,
men who dominated the public square through murder.

The process by which this came about was not a direct or inevitable
consequence of the end of the Terror. The Thermidorians wanted to
rid the country of men whom they considered bloodthirsty cutthroats.
The terrorists would also have to account for their actions, but ideally,
this accounting would avoid the excesses of the Terror. Retribution and
punishment would be a measured, judicial process, one that respected the
forms enshrined in the Penal Code of 1791.

This turned out to be an impossible standard. Their own equivocation
and the high expectations of their followers for a ruthless and severe
justice overwhelmed the Thermidorians. The Thermidorians and their
followers became anti-Jacobins who reflexively employed terrorist methods. They even invoked similar justifications for their actions. The spectacular crisis that the suppression of Jacobinism provoked resembled the
responses that the Jacobins had displayed earlier in 1792–4, when their
own levels of excitement were so high. By the late winter of the Year III,
it was clear that the Thermidorians had not met their goals of suppression and punishment of the Jacobins. Despite the success against the
clubs, their frustration and rage were immense. They feared that regular
justice was too slow or would be too indulgent. Disillusion with formal
justice produced an eerily familiar result: vigilantism and a deplorable
willingness on the part of authorities to look the other way. The doctrines of popular justice were turned against the terrorists. This was
the atmosphere that permitted the *bande d'Aubagne* to get away with
murder.

Thermidor in Limbo

The fall of Robespierre eventually brought about the total defeat of
Jacobinism in Marseille and the Bouches-du-Rhône. What the Federalists
and Fréron had failed to do, the Thermidorian representatives on mission brought about with spectacular success. The few months between
the fall of Robespierre in Paris and the armed demonstration in Marseille
on 5 Vendémiaire (26 September 1794) was a liminal period in which

contending parties struggled to decide the significance of 9 Thermidor.[2] While the Convention showed its hostility to extremists in the provinces very early, the radicals in the Midi advocated not an end to the Terror, but a revival of violent repression.

Within the Convention itself and elsewhere in the country, the initial reaction to the fall of the Robespierre clique was to celebrate and assume that things would continue as before. At Marseille, Jacobins did indeed celebrate the fall of the dictator but saw an opportunity not to continue, but to accelerate and extend the Terror. On the day the news from Paris arrived, the District of Marseille requested that the Convention establish a new revolutionary tribunal modeled on that of Orange which "will rid us promptly of these enemies of the *patrie*" who "infect the air of our southern departments with their impure breath."[3]

The Club too celebrated the fall of the dictator, although its policy prescriptions were rather generic. Its first address mixed caution and bravado. The Club promised to be ever present to defend liberty as it had on 10 August. It urged Parisians to continue to fight the interior enemy. It repeated, as it often had, that there could be no safety for the French so long as foreign tyrants, under whatever mask they wore, continued to exist. It denounced the new monsters, the false patriots, and usurpers. Finally, they vowed to exterminate the friends of tyrants. Significantly, two of the signatories were judges and officials on the former Revolutionary Tribunal, Maillet and Chompré.[4]

If the Club's language was general, the *comité de surveillance* could not have been more specific. The committee had discovered evidence of a possible prison plot. A woman from Aix-en-Provence had tried to smuggle 356 old lottery tickets each emblazoned with a royal fleur-de-lis into the prison near the Palais de Justice. Jacobins knew what this was: a *signe de ralliement*, a sign the detainees could use to recognize one another. A *signe de ralliement* was therefore a signal of a plot stirring. Even so,

[2] I have learned much from Bronisaw Baczko, *Ending the Terror: The French Revolution after Robespierre* (Cambridge: Cambridge University Press; Éditions de la maison des sciences de l'homme, 1994).

[3] AM Marseille, 13D 55, *Adresse à la Convention nationale par les administrateurs du district de Marseille et agent national*, 18 Thermidor An II – 5 August 1794. In an address of 6 Fructidor An II (23 August 1794), the District demanded the deportation of all interior enemies (AN W 86, folder titled "Société populaire," doc. 38).

[4] *Journal de la Montagne*, 1 Fructidor An II – 18 August 1794. Address of 18 Thermidor An II – 5 August 1794 to the people of Paris.

the committee claimed sarcastically, the prisons were not being emptied fast enough "to vomit into society the wicked who would not exist if the revolutionary tribunals had not been suspended. In their frenzy, they [the prisoners] are counting on a pardon, a general amnesty, on an absolute forgetting of their crimes." But they are plotting new crimes as well. "They are deploying the most perfidious means to lead from moderationism to counter-revolution."

The only solution to this turbulence in the prisons was to restore the revolutionary tribunals. "By terror and fear [they] have always constrained men who know only how to conspire against . . . all the friends of liberty." In a final soaring peroration, the committee wrote, "We know more than ever, that if justice toward the innocents is a timeless duty to be applied everywhere, the most male, the most repressive severity, must always be by its side and deliver irons and death to all the conspirators."[5] The tribunals that were so praiseworthy were, of course, the Revolutionary Tribunal of Marseille in its second phase and the Popular Commission of Orange. Anything less than their implacable severity guaranteed a rebirth of moderationism and, in a theme that would recur, prison plots. While the *comité de surveillance* had exposed the lottery ticket plot, "the prisoners are looking for a way to revolt."[6] One consequence of moderationism, then, was a revival of the idea of preemptive, expedited justice.

Jacobins in the Southeast were out of phase, once again, with national rhythms. Far from wilting before the moderate winds blowing from the north, they defended their positions bluntly. Thus, while his enemies in the Convention were attacking Maignet for his atrocities, many clubs and officials leaped to his defense.[7]

---

[5] *Le comité de surveillance et révolutionnaire de la commune de Marseille à la CN*, n.d., in *AP*, xcvi, 229–30, session of 18 Fructidor An II – 4 September 1794. See also AM Marseille 13D 56, *Administration du district de Marseille à la Convention nationale*, 6 Fructidor An II – 23 August 1794.

[6] *Journal de la Montagne*, 13 Fructidor An II – 30 August 1794, club session of 11 Fructidor An II – 28 August 1794. The club at Saint-Rémy also expressed fears of prisoners and linked them to the growing moderationism in the Convention: after expressing their alarms at the slide to moderation, they wrote, "The enemies of the *patrie*, who never sleep, are beginning to come alive with pride, even in prison, they even dare to insult patriots and threaten them with a terrible vengeance. Will they be the conquerors? No, we will never believe it" (Address, n.d., to Jacobins of Paris in *Journal de la Montagne*, 18 Fructidor An II – 4 September 1794).

[7] For a defense of Maignet's actions in repressing the Jourdan faction in Avignon, see the address of the SP of Tarascon to the Convention , in ibid., 22 Fructidor An II – 8 September 1794, also in *AP*, xcvii, 49–50; of Avignon and Allauch in *AP*, xcv, 471, session of 9 Fructidor An II – 26 August 1794; of Eyragues in ibid., xcviii, 174, session of

The Club at Aix soon caught the drift of events. At first, it congratulated the Convention for its "male firmness" in overthrowing Robespierre
and quickly removed the plaster bust of the dictator from its gallery of
great men. It also swore fealty to the "Holy Mountain" and "hatred and
war on moderationism." The Club defended itself from the conspirators
who survived Robespierre, "the impure debris of all the factions." The
Club had never been the dictator's accomplice. All the same, its principles
were unwavering. Within a few weeks, however, it claimed, "Moderationism has dared throw off its mask; the aristocracy raises its hideous
head." But people were daring to express their disapproval of the Club,
much to the brothers' indignation. "Corrupt men deluded women who
carried themselves en masse to applaud the triumph of crime. They have
treated energetic patriots as men of blood." In fact, Maignet's "just and
salutary measure" of ordering the arrest and internment of all priests and
nobles was imperative against "the leeches and the vampires still engorged
with the blood of the people." The solution was obvious: "Judge without
delay all the conspirators; be just and impassable like the law, but as firm
as the rock on which you are installed, severe and inflexible like Brutus.
Justice will support, will avenge innocence; but the perfidious moderates,
the aristocrats, the vainglorious, the despots, let the thunderbolts of the
Mountain, launched all at once, pulverize them in an instant."[8] Amid
the denunciations of moderationism, the appalled reaction to aristocrats'
strutting about the streets, the deplorable release of prisoners, and with
it the worrying suspicion that all this was no accident – after all, even

---

9 Vendémiaire An III – 30 September 1794; of the Club of Salon to the Paris Jacobins in
Journal de la Montagne, 27 Fructidor An II – 13 September 1794, session of 25 Fructidor
An II – 11 September 1794; of the Club of Apt (Vaucluse) to the Convention of 10
Fructidor An II – 27 August 1794, in ibid., 28 Fructidor An II – 14 September 1794, also
in *AP*, xcvii, 148–9; of the Club at Aix-en-Provence, in ADBR, L 2031, 166, session of 16
Fructidor An II – 2 September 1794; and finally, of Marseille in *Journal de la Montagne*,
29 Fructidor An II – 15 September 1794, Paris Jacobins, session of 27 Fructidor An II – 13
September 1794, in which a club spokesperson declares that with Maignet's arrival, "We
breathed at last, he took us in his arms." Maignet was attacked for not being extremist
enough. The mayor of Aix-en-Provence appeared before the deputies to denounce him for
continuing the work of the "wicked Robespierre" for oppressing patriots in the Vaucluse,
but this is the only discordant note (*Journal de la Montagne*, 9 Fructidor An II – 26 August
1794 reporting on session of Convention of 8 Fructidor An II (25 August 1794). For his
popularity among the clubs in the Vaucluse, see Pierre Vaillandet, "Après le 9 Thermidor:
les débuts de la Terreur blanche en Vaucluse," *AhRf*, 5 (1928), 111–2.

[8] Speech of a delegation from the SP of Aix-en-Provence, session of 20 Fructidor An II – 6
September 1794 in *AP*, xcvi, 316. See also their address (n.d.) in ibid. xcvii, 56 (session of
24 Fructidor An II – 10 September 1794) against "fops wearing the mask of patriotism,"
a sure sign that hostile opinion was beginning to express itself.

Maignet was releasing dozens of prisoners just before his recall – someone in the Club spoke the unspeakable: the lamppost. At first the Club tried to deny that anyone had called for a lynching. But the alarm that swept through the town, which after all, had witnessed five episodes of hangings in 1792–3, had to be confronted. It said the statement had a different context. The word *lanterne*, or lantern, had arisen in the context of the reviving aristocracy whose face was radiating light. Perhaps this might have baffled some and satisfied others, but the Club's elaboration must have ruined the effect. It claimed that if the Aristocracy attacked the Convention, the only way to save the *patrie* would be to begin the Revolution again; there would be only one way to save the *patrie*, "it would be to begin the game of the *lanterne* [lamppost, or lantern] again." Authority concluded that the Club had indeed endorsed vigilantism and so closed it down. The response was an armed invasion of the town through the Porte Notre-Dame from the rural areas. This forced the reopening of the Club.[9]

The little club at Aubagne also showed the same brave defiance. After congratulating the Convention for confounding the new Cromwells, the new Catalinas, whose blood had just watered the Liberty Tree, they went on to warn of the ever necessary requirement to be vigilant against the winds of aristocracy, royalism, Federalism, and moderationism. Just as all the other local societies had done, that of Aubagne demanded the continuation of the "just rigor that in all times had saved the Republic." "Strike with the blade of the law," they insisted, "with the revolutionary thunderbolt, all the agents, all the perpetrators of the thousand and one conspiracies that have threatened and still threaten the liberty of the people." Innocence would be guaranteed, of course, but "let the revolutionary tribunals, promptly organized, strike all the guilty, and let Liberty at last see only ever more her energetic defenders and her true friends on the land consecrated to her. *Vive la Montagne! Vive la République!*"[10]

From the moment they detected the dangerous veering off course, the Jacobins had begun to protest. Their solution was the restoration of the revolutionary tribunals or even to advocate direct action. Some speakers at the Club meetings in Marseille in Fructidor quickly raised the rhetorical temperature even more. Thus Tournau, one of the missionaries to

---

[9] ADBR, L 2031 pp. 161–2, session of 15 Fructidor An II – 1 September 1794. AM Toulon, L 325, *Procès-verbal de ce qui s'est passé dans la commune D'Aix, le 19 Fructidor An II.*

[10] *Journal de la Montagne*, 25 Fructidor An II – 11 September 1794, session of Convention of 24 Fructidor An II – 10 September 1794. Also in *AP*, xcvi, p. 50.

Manosque in 1792, spoke of the growing danger for patriots and concluded, "Let us offer a mass of defenses; being all brothers, we owe each other the most active support." Tournau may have been calling only for more solidarity, but Baissière went much further. "The popular societies are inviolable," he claimed. "If they attempt attacks against large and energetic popular societies, so much for the wicked, they will all perish. Should they have the audacity to attack our society, we will bury them beneath the ruins of the Mountain." The assembly greeted this with thunderous applause, crying out, "Death or Liberty."[11] At the Club's invitation, the brothers in Aix-en-Provence unanimously took a similar oath, "If a single patriot from the Midi is incarcerated or vexed, we will regard this as an act against all the patriots of [Aix and Marseille] and we will rise up en masse to fly to the aid of a single oppressed patriot."[12] The oath could have been copied from that of the Congress of Popular Societies in Marseille, just one year before. Some in the Club in Marseille had clearly begun to think beyond the Convention's possible refusal to restore the Terror. A delegation from the Club to the brothers in Paris on 25 Fructidor (11 September) implied that extralegal action was a possibility. It was not a calumny against the national representation, the delegates said, to observe, "Patriots have replaced aristocrats in the prisons." It was the responsibility of the popular societies to defend persecuted patriots. The spokesperson of the delegation concluded defiantly: "The Midi will be happy, the patriot will be peaceful in his cottage, only when liberty triumphs, only when revolutionary government exists in all its vigor, only when we crush the head of the last reptile who wants to gnaw at the Liberty Tree, only when the aristocracy turns its humiliated face from the Jacobins."[13] Another speaker declared, "The only way to have liberty triumph and repel the death that threatens [us], is to crush [our] oppressors from one end of France to the other."[14]

Still another address from the Club denounced those who "wished to turn for their profit the sublime revolution that struck the tyrant Robespierre and his accomplices dead. We swear to be deaf to the cries of this false pity that will infallibly drag the Republic to new

[11] *Tribune de la Société populaire de Marseille*, 21 Fructidor An II – 7 September 1794.
[12] ADBR, L 2031 pp. 167–8, session of 17 Fructidor An II – 3 September 1794.
[13] *Journal de la Montagne*, 27 Fructidor An II – 13 September 1794, n° 136, 1115, club session of 25 Fructidor – 11 September 1794.
[14] Ibid., 29 Fructidor An II – 15 September 1794, Paris Jacobins, session of 27 Fructidor An II – 13 September 1794.

misfortunes. We must be inexorable toward traitors."[15] Finally, the
municipality denounced "the aristocracy of moderationism and selfishness" and observed that "the blade of the law suspended over their heads
awaits them."[16] Despite the incessant proclamations of loyalty to the
Convention, such heady language required everyone to contribute to the
relentless struggle. Given past history, the patriots would triumph once
again. They could recall the glorious battles they had won, so the fight
would continue. For them, the situation paralleled the spring of 1793
when the moderate anti-Jacobins took advantage to effect the full-blown
Federalist counterrevolution.

Discussion about what to do about this dreadful reversal had probably
begun in Marseille even before the addresses of the Club, the *comité de
surveillance*, and the subsequent delegation had reached Paris. The Club
had decided to explain to the new representatives, Auguis and Serres,
the proper relationship between the national representation and local
militants. Both representatives were moderates. Auguis had voted for a
referendum to decide Louis XVI's fate, Serres to impeach Marat. Among
militants, this made them virtual counterrevolutionaries. All previous
representatives had been Montagnards. For the Convention to have sent
men like these to the region was bound to be provocative, especially
given the rising anxieties about the direction of events. Prosecutors later
claimed that the Club's aggressive behavior toward the representatives
was designed to make them abandon their mission and leave.[17] Perhaps
so, after all, they had done something like this in the spring of 1793 to
the representatives Bayle and Boisset.

Be that as it may, about ten members of the club, armed with dag-
gers and guns, met the representatives at Aix-en-Provence. They brazenly
told the representatives of the sovereign people that they could act only
with "the advice and under the surveillance of the members of the Club."
The near defiance of the representatives continued after their arrival in
Marseille. When they spoke at the Club, members responded by stomping their feet, clapping their hands and with yells "which resembled the
growls of tigers and the furious cries of a troop of conspirators." At
one celebration at the end of the Republican calendar in September,

[15] Ibid. 30 Fructidor An II –16 September 1794, address to Paris Jacobins, n.d., session of
29 Fructidor An II – 15 September 1794
[16] AM Marseille, 4D 3, letter to National Convention, 1 Sansculottide An II – 17 September
1794.
[17] ADBR, L 3041, *acte d'accusation*, 27 Brumaire An III – 17 November 1794.

the clubbists packed the Temple of Reason with angry supporters who insulted and threatened the representatives' supporters. The Temple of Reason, of course, was a holy site where the glorious Section 11 had begun the Jacobin rebellion against the Federalists in August 1793. The Club had fêted Maignet here a few months earlier. Now the Temple was filled with its tempestuous partisans, who insulted and threatened those who came to cheer the representatives.[18]

Marseille had also become a refuge for all sorts of former terrorists who had already been purged elsewhere or who already felt threatened. The city became an oasis because its terrorist administration remained intact. Serres and Auguis reported, "There exist in the commune of Marseille men of a wickedness, of a depravity and a boldness without equal.... We are certain that at Marseille the mass is good as it is in the department, but the terror has frozen every soul. The 9 Thermidor has produced nothing here for the pure and virtuous Republican."[19] The shift in the representatives' stance toward the Club was glaring. Where Maignet had considered the Club an ally, his successors considered its leaders arrogant and corrupt enemies. By early September, disturbances at Aix-en-Provence and Marseille were especially upsetting the representatives on mission, all the more so in that the garrison numbered only six thousand. The commander was also unreliable in several ways: he was a partisan Jacobin, deaf, and approaching senility. Both the Club and the new representatives were preparing for a trial of strength. The Club was sending emissaries to their allies in the smaller towns and villages. These agitations resembled the Republican missions of 1792 and 1793, and for many, they were equally threatening. The representatives spoke of the need "to strike a great blow" but despaired that "we are lacking all means."[20] For Goupilleau on mission in the Vaucluse, these agitators were "sectarians of the infamous Robespierre who cry moderationism when one dispenses justice, and who believe that the Revolution

---

[18] Serres and Auguis to CSP, 6 Vendémiaire An III – 27 September 1794, in Aulard, *RACSP*, xvii, 108; repr. in *AP*, xcviii, 261. See their speech of 27 Fructidor (13 September) to the Club in which their reference to representing 25 million Frenchmen may have been an allusive rebuttal to the Club's demand for dual sovereignty in AM Marseille, 13D 56.

[19] Serres and Auguis, 24 Fructidor An II – 10 September 1794, in Aulard, *RACSP*, xvi, 629.

[20] Ibid., 628. See their speech to the Marseille Club of 27 Fructidor An II – 13 September 1794 in *Journal de la Montagne*, 5 Sansculottides An II – 21 September 1794, which gives no hint of what they were saying in private to the Committee of Public Safety.

is made only for them and who believe that, in order to be a [R]epublican, terror in general must be eternal and that it's only a question of pillaging, dilapidating, and massacring with impunity."[21]

Thermidor in Marseille

But if each side was preparing for a trial of strength, it was the Jacobins who were the more confident. Because the Convention would not restore the revolutionary tribunals to halt the giddy slide to moderationism, patriots would have to deal with the prisoners directly. The vigilante reflex thus returned in late August 1794, just over two years after the hangings in Marseille. It was the third alleged plot to slaughter prisoners following those of March and December 1793. Serres and Auguis claimed the plan this time was nothing less than the slaughter of all the anti-Jacobins or suspects still in prison in the city. One of the ringleaders, Reynier, a former secretary of the Revolutionary Tribunal, wrote a letter that his recipient soon turned over to authorities. It was extraordinarily indiscreet. All had been well, he said, until moderationism in the Convention produced counterrevolutionary laws that led to the release of two hundred "wicked" from the prisons of Marseille. But a great mass of patriots remained intact "forming a cluster [*faisceau*] with the administrative bodies and the popular society, [that is] waiting only for a signal that will consolidate the Republic, by making all there is that is impure in Marseille disappear by a new 2 and 3 September [an allusion to the Massacres of September 1792 of prisoners in Paris]." Reynier not only spelled out the coming massacre but also gave a timetable. "We are on the eve of striking great blows," he informed his correspondent. "My ferocity against the public enemy is terrible, and as this moment is not long off, I give you my word that at the end of the month I will be by your side."[22] Whatever the ultimate plan, the Reynier letter could not be dismissed as an unfounded rant by a lone fanatic. Auguis and Serres had him arrested. As he was being transferred to Paris for trial, 150 men, with hats pulled over their faces and armed with sabers and pistols, leaped from the ditches at a spot

---

[21] Goupilleau to CSP, 26 Fructidor An II – 12 September 1794, in Aulard, *RACSP*, xvi, 657.

[22] Letter dated 9 Fructidor An II – 26 August 1794, to national agent of commune of Chabeuil (Drôme) reproduced in *Gazette nationale ou le Moniteur universel*, 3 Vendémiaire An III – 24 September 1794. Reynier was a former brother in the *Frères des écoles chrétiens* of the Old Regime and he was writing to explain why he would be delayed in arriving for a teaching post.

on the outskirts of Marseille some time after three in the morning. They overpowered the small escort and released Reynier. The representatives suspected that the concierge of the prison was part of the rescue plot.

The plot may have had wider ramifications as well. Certainly, the Club continued to send emissaries to sister clubs in the region, perhaps suggesting plans were afoot to repeat the scheme of March 1793 whereby outsiders would help restore the Marseille Club's prominence in the city. At least one outside club gave real support to Marseille's efforts. The Club at Aubagne intercepted a thousand reliable soldiers sent from Toulon to Marseille as reinforcements against the prison plot. The brothers told them that they were being sent to do the work of the aristocrats, "to oppress the patriots and obey the scoundrels who wanted the counter-revolution." After Reynier's arrest, someone in the Club of Marseille, probably Auguste Mossy, a leading member since 1790, reiterated the old axiom of solidarity: "When they attack a true patriot [*un patriot chaud*], we have to rise en masse, that if we don't, little by little, they will destroy us." Someone even hinted that Auguis and Serres should be declared traitors for having suggested that members of the club defrauded the public purse. The deaf and senile commander of the garrison tried to persuade the representatives to rescind the measures they had already taken to defend the city. They quickly removed him, but dangerous rumors continued. There was a story that the patriots of Marseille were preparing a march to deliver Paris from its oppressors. Some said that Jacobins would attempt to seize the arms stored in Fort Jean by sneaking in through underground passageways.[23]

The rescue of Reynier gave the representatives the excuse they were looking for to take action against the Jacobin power base. They purged the

---

[23] Speeches and letters in *Journal de la Montagne*, 2 Vendémiaire An III – 23 September 1794, also ibid., 3 Vendémiaire An II – 24 September 1794. Their version of Reynier's letter is truncated and so I have preferred the version given in the *Moniteur* above and in *AP*, xcvii, 330-1. Some militants had given up on the Jacobins in the Convention. The municipality of Marseille wrote in an address, "Mountain, nursemaid of republican virtues, they say you exist no longer! We cannot believe it. However, if that is true, be assured your virtues will flourish among us always" (*Journal de la Montagne*, address to Convention, n.d., issue of 5 Vendémiaire An III – 26 September 1794, reporting on session of 4 Vendémiaire An III – 25 September 1794 (different version based on a different newspaper in *AP*, xcviii, 54). See also Auguis and Serres to CSP, 27, 28 Fructidor, 1er Jour des Sanculottides An II– 13, 14, and 17 September 1794, in Aulard, *RACSP*, xvi, 688-90, 715-7, 767-8. See also *AP*, xcvii, 339-40. Also their letter to the deputation of the Bouches-du-Rhône in, 2e Jour Sanculottide – 18 September 1794, in ibid., 385. For the Mossy quote AN W 86, dossier "Enlèvement de Reynier," n° 16, interrogation of Pierre Crup, 28 Vendémiaire An III – 19 October 1794.

municipality, closed the Club, seized its papers, and arrested twenty-eight of the worst agitators. When soldiers came to arrest him, Carles, former commissioner of the Légion des Montagnards and then president of the Club, climbed on to the roof of his house, harangued the soldiers below, and then hurled himself four stories to his death. The Convention declared Reynier an outlaw and ordered the arrest of the military commander of Marseille and an investigation into the conspiracy by the Revolutionary Tribunal in Paris.[24]

Up to this point, the resemblance to the earlier struggle between Fréron and the Club was uncanny. This clash had culminated in the arrests of the leaders of the Marseille Congress and the judges of the Revolutionary Tribunal in December 1793. The insurrection the militants had hoped to provoke never occurred. The difference just nine months later, in Vendémiaire Year III, was that the arrests, sometimes of the same men, set off an armed demonstration. No doubt the reason was that the demonstration occurred in a context of growing despair over the prospects for a vigorous repression of enemies. A spontaneous protest thus erupted when the representatives installed the new municipality on 5 Sansculottide (21 September). A demonstration of about six hundred people gathered in front of the town hall, roamed the nearby streets, and burst into the council chamber. They were singing "couplets arranged in the Provençal idiom." They insulted the representatives by calling them *appelants* and claimed that the new councillors were only provisional and that they would go to the guillotine. Some even threatened to hang them, a real possibility as past experience showed.[25] This demonstration failed to dislodge the new municipality or win the release of the prisoners, so another trial of strength was bound to occur. Angry talk and inflammatory songs over the next few days kept the patrons of favorite cafés excited. Such talk threatened the representatives with "the tumbrels and they would pass through the window." None other than Maillet, Giraud, and Chompré from the Revolutionary Tribunal of Marseille and Isoard, a Republican

[24] CSP to Auguis and Serres, 5ᵉ Sansculottides An II – 21 September 1794, Auguis and Serres to CSP, 5 Vendémiaire An III – 26 September 1794, in Aulard, *RACSP*, xvii, 4, n⁰ 1; 94–5.

[25] Les officiers municipaux de la commune de Marseille à la CN, 7 Vendémiaire An III – 28 September 1794, in *AP*, xcviii, 265–6. *Proclamation 4 Sansculottide An II – 20 September 1794*, in AM Marseille, 13D 56, gives the list of appointees. Of those with an occupation, most were artisans or petty merchants. ADBR, L 3041, *acte d'accusation*, 27 Brumaire An III – 17 November 1794. AM Marseille, 13D 56, *Proclamation par les représentants du peuple ... 3 Vendémiaire An III – 24 September 1794.*

missionary of 1792 and a participant in the planned massacres of March and December 1793, had been meeting in the café Français – the very café the radicals had used in 1789 – to discuss what to do.[26] Whether what happened next fulfilled their plan is another matter.

During the night of 4–5 Vendémiaire, the Convention's decree outlawing Reynier and ordering the arrest of his rescuers arrived. Late in the morning of 5 Vendémiaire, crowds milled about the entrance of Fort Jean demanding the release of the Jacobins, but the guards dispersed them. Soon, some women started a farandole. The dancers wound their way from the promenades, past the Autel de la Patrie at one end of the Canebière, then continued in the direction of the port to the Place Brutus near the Grande Théâtre, close to where the representatives were lodging. The dance was a community event, composed of men, women, children, and soldiers. It swelled as it picked up laborers along the way, many of whom joined because they thought the crowd intended to request that the representatives reopen the Club. Other participants intended to be more aggressive. By midafternoon, a crowd of 1,200, linked arm in arm five across, surrounded the Hôtel de la Patrie where Serres and Auguis were dining. Many demonstrators were packing pistols and sabers. Some shouted coarse insults, and others revolutionary slogans like "Vive la Montagne!" sometimes in French, sometimes in the unique Marseille Provençal accent. A few women threatened the representatives with the guillotine by the motions of their raised arms. Many others demanded the Jacobin leaders be released. A turner, André Maxion from the Porte d'Aix, armed with a saber and two pistols, broke into the dining room and demanded that the Jacobin leaders be freed from Fort Jean. Along with threats if they were not satisfied immediately, these demands, as always, overrode the formal law the representatives upheld. One daredevil assaulted Auguis, shoved a pistol against his chest, and tore his shirt. The representatives even descended into the street with their own pistols. They shouted that the crowd should retire, that they always had the right of petition. Moments later Serres retreated to a first-floor window and tried to harangue a jeering crowd about the majesty of the law. Some furious individuals hurled insults back and even threatened to hang them because the people were sovereign.

---

[26] AN W 86, *Extrait du registre du comité de surveillance révolutionnaire du District de Marseille*, 26 Vendémiaire An III – 17 October 1794, which also gives a list of regulars at the café Français. ADBR, L 3037, *Jugement rendu par le tribunal criminel du département des Bouches-du-Rhône, qui condamne à la peine de mort Louis-François Dominique Isoard du 2 Vendémiaire de l'an quatrième Républicain.*

That one exchange between the upper window and the street, amid all the tumult and threats, summarized the entire local revolution. Here again were two different conceptions of law and justice.[27] As in Aubagne in September 1792, the crowd was trying to force authority to do its bidding. The representatives were supposed to defer to a higher authority, the people, who would exercise justice directly. As the turner from the Porte d'Aix announced when he burst into the dining room, "We are the sovereign people [*Voici le peuple souverain*]." He later admitted to saying that "the people wanted the prisoners."[28] Another text has him also saying, "the people, which is here, will not be refused."[29] Some rioters reverted to another part of the script of 1792 when they threatened to make the representatives "dance the carmagnole."

By dusk, soldiers had restored order. They had to clear even rooftops of adjacent buildings of demonstrators who were stomping about trying to break into the representatives' hotel. Authorities arrested few rioters, however, because gendarmes and soldiers had actually joined the armed demonstration. The courts did punish some ringleaders. In an ironic reversion to revolutionary justice, the representatives sent all the accused to one form or another of a revolutionary court. Because the gendarmes were part of the military, and because they had sided with "crime and wickedness," the Military Tribunal tried them. In a single session on 7 Vendémiaire at Fort Saint-Nicolas, it condemned five to death, including the turner Maxion, and three gendarmes.[30] And, in a touch that would

---

[27] Two letters of Auguis and Serres to CSP, 6, 7 Vendémiaire An III –27, 28 September 1794 in Aulard, *RACSP*, xvii, 108–13; also repr in *AP*, xcviii, 260–3. See their report: *Rapport fait à la Convention nationale, par les représentans du peuple Auguis & Serres, sur leur mission dans les départemens des Vouches-du-Rhône, du Var & de l'Ardèche* (Paris: De l'Imprimerie nationale, Ventôse, l'an III). NYPL *KVR 8589. See also Jacques Guilhaumou, "L'affaire de Marseille: l'émeute du 5 Vendémiaire An III, analyse de discours," in *Le tournant de l'an III: réaction et terreur blanche dans la France révolutionnaire*, ed. Michel Vovelle (Paris: Éditions du CTHS, 1997), 557–68. Michael L. Kennedy, *The Jacobin Club of Marseilles, 1790–1794* (Ithaca, N.Y.: Cornell University Press, 1973), 145–8. G. Martinet, "Les débuts de la réaction thermidorienne à Marseille: l'émeute du 5 Vendémiaire An III," in *Actes du 90e congrès national des sociétés savantes. Nice 1965*, I, 149–66 (Paris: Impr. nationale), 1965. *Procès-verbal du 5 Vendémiaire An III –26 September 1794*, in *Gazette nationale ou le Moniteur universel*, 15 Vendémiaire An III – 6 October 1794, reporting on session of Convention of 12 Vendémiaire An III – 3 October 1794. The definitive, and more accessible text of the *procès-verbal* of 5 Vendémiaire is in *AP*, xcviii, 263–4. Copy in AN W 86, Liasse B n° 5.

[28] ADBR, L 3131, interrogation of Henry Marion, 28, portefaix, 7 Vendémiaire An III – 28 September 1794.

[29] Ibid., L 3041, *acte d'accusation*, 27 Brumaire An III – 17 November 1795.

[30] C. Lourde, *Histoire de la Révolution à Marseille et en Provence: de 1789 au Consulat* (Marseille: Laffitte, 1974), 380–1.

have delighted the most excitable sansculotte of the Year II, one of the condemned even cried out "Vive les Anglais!" on the scaffold, or so it was said.[31] There were no witnesses for the defense; the accused never argued mitigating circumstances; and the witnesses against them were all soldiers who gave incredibly laconic statements that the accused did not challenge.[32] This was a nearly perfect reversion to the reviled justice of the Year II, with the exception that during the Terror, witness statements were rare. In another crisis, the Thermidorians would revert to revolutionary justice.

The representatives also sent the twenty-eight accused of rescuing Reynier to the Revolutionary Tribunal in Paris, which, of course, also judged without appeal. The remaining twenty accused of being part of the Vendémiaire demonstration were sent to the Criminal Tribunal of the Bouches-du-Rhône. For this special case, it would also judge without appeal.[33] Although they could never prove it, many in authority were certain that those who rescued Reynier were also behind the armed demonstration.

Toward a New Vigilantism

Anti-Jacobin inhabitants of Marseille treated the defeat of the Jacobins as deliverance. During a parade to the Temple of Reason – again one recalls Maignet's promenade of a few months before to the same place – Serres and Auguis described "immense crowds, an emotional and grateful people, shouting blessings on the National Convention that had just delivered them from the hell of the wicked conspirators." Once at the Temple, "We impressed upon the people the enormity of the crimes of the criminal *journée* of 5 [V]endémiaire, but we assured them that we knew how to discover the truly guilty and that the pure man who was beyond reproach, would enjoy the tranquility of virtue." As with Maignet's ceremony and with the same tender expressions toward the innocent, this one emphasized a unity restored, a general rallying, once more, around the Convention. At a similar ceremony at the newly reopened Club that evening, there were identical pledges of unity. Members and the galleries

---

[31] Auguis and Serres to CSP, 8 Vendémiaire An III – 29 September 1794 in Aulard, *RACSP*, xvii, 148–50.

[32] ADBR, L 3131, trial dossier, 7 Vendémiaire An III – 28 September 1794. AM Marseille, 13D 57, *Jugement rendu par la commission militaire établie à Marseille*, 7 Vendémiaire An III – 28 September 1794.

[33] Auguis and Serres to CSP, 6 Brumaire An III – 27 October 1794, in Aulard, *RACSP*, xvii, 654–5.

swore their horror and repugnance for the scoundrels and the intriguers. Once again, expelling the wicked and the deviant restored and reinforced the community.[34]

The Jacobin defeat following 5 Vendémiaire was far from total, however. The Club and its sympathizers were too large and their relations with affiliates outside, like Aubagne, were too close, for the arrest of a few dozen leaders to destroy the organization. Anti-Jacobins thus expected the judicial apparatus to continue the struggle against their enemies. Yet this was a frustrating exercise. The Thermidorians had renounced speedy justice, and they expected the citizenry to contain its impatience for results.[35] But the longer they deferred the trials of former terrorists, the less impact it would have on the Jacobins. Thus a gulf slowly began to open up between the representatives on mission and ordinary anti-Jacobins. Always irrepressible anyway, Jacobins took heart and began to express themselves more boldly. This was feeble enough, as the Jacobin press had disappeared, the leadership was disrupted, and the "regenerated" society in Marseille was hostile to extremists. Nonetheless, any sign of Jacobin activity was intolerable to their enemies. Soon, they began to imagine the most lurid plots and describe them in macabre language. No matter that this language was frequently a caricature of the immediate past; it reflected the contemporary practice of framing opponents and rewriting recent history. Jacobins were no longer sturdy patriots, implacable in their severity. Instead, their history was that of death, destruction, pillage, rapine, and ruin.[36] As justice ground on, fear of terrorists actually grew and the scope of their potential malice increased. So the desire for vengeance for past wrongs and future transgressions led to extralegal

[34] Same to same, letters of 11, 12, and 20 Vendémiaire An III – 2, 3, and 11 October 1794, in ibid. pp. 190–1, 208–9, 369–70. See also the "regenerated," i.e., purged, Club's address to the Convention (*AP*, xcvii, 359–60, n.d., session of 16 Vendémiaire An III – 7 October 1794), emphasizing loyalty and praise for the representatives and claiming sovereignty rested with the Convention. See also ibid., 402, session of 17 Vendémiaire An III – 8 October 1794, address of the purged Department, n.d.

[35] See the proclamation of 24 Frimaire (14 December 1794) of the representative of the people Jean Espert in his *Rapport fait à la Convention nationale / par Espert, représentant du peuple, sur sa mission dans les départemens du Var & des Bouches-du-Rhône, suivi des pièces y relatives* (Paris: de l'Imprimerie nationale, 1795), 140–3. BM Arles AA 45709 M and BM Marseille 5830.

[36] See AM Marseille, 13D 57, *Les administrateurs du département des Bouches-du-Rhône à la Convention nationale*, 8 Vendémiaire An III – 29 September 1794, and *Discours prononce à la Société populaire de Marseille... par les représentants Auguis et Serres...* 10 Vendémiaire An III – 1 October 1794 in which both agree that from the beginning of the Revolution, the terrorists wished only to dominate.

solutions. Eventually, even the representatives and other officials tilted in that direction as well.

While the justices of the peace throughout the department began gathering evidence against the terrorists, the most important trial, that of the defendants of 5 Vendémiaire, stumbled. On 15 Nivôse (4 January), the defendants and a crowd of Jacobin sympathizers disrupted the trial of twenty accused. This forced authorities to transfer the seat of the Criminal Tribunal to Aix-en-Provence, thus delaying the trial.

Consequently, the strategy of using the courts failed to dazzle opinion in the streets. Emboldened Jacobins allegedly predicted that the nightmare would be over in a month, that a bloodbath was coming, and so on. Every night, revelers meandered through the streets crying out, "Vive la Montagne! Vive les Jacobins!" A fistfight at a café between Jacobin sympathizers and soldiers broke out on the anniversary of the execution of Louis XVI – the same battalion that had fought against the demonstrators of 5 Vendémiaire. Once, some artillerymen swooped down on a café seeking a fight with the Jacobins, only to have one soldier killed and five severely wounded. Two days later, someone struck an officer on the street with a saber. The military commander of Marseille warned that those shouting Montagnard slogans would be arrested, but to no avail.[37] Authority shuddered at far-fetched reports that Jacobin fanatics were threatening to play boule with the heads of their future victims, or that they were saying, "We will [soon] have blood up to our knees."[38]

The Jacobin revival had spread to Toulon as well. The working people in the arsenal remained impassioned Jacobin supporters. The representatives on mission blamed outside agitators for provoking seditious outbursts like "Vive la Montagne!" They also accused them of predicting the return of the "system of blood." But Jacobinism was more deeply rooted

---

[37] Mariette to Rovère and Durand-Maillane, 8 Pluviôse An III – 27 January 1795, in A. B. J. Guffroy, *Rapport sur la situation de Marseille le 8 pluviôse, fait le 16 pluviôse, au nom du Comité de sûreté générale* (Paris: Impr. Nationale, III [1795]), 8–12. The French Revolution research collection; 7.478. "Grillon, adjudant général, commandant temporaire de la place de Marseille en état de siège, à ses concitoyens," 22 Nivôse An III – 11 January 1795 cited in Espert, *Rapport... sur sa mission*, 15. Also Espert's *arrêté* of 4 Nivôse An III (24 December 1794), in ibid., 146–9. See also Poultier to Convention nationale, 26 Germinal An III – 15 April 1795 in Aulard *RACSP*, xxii, 141–3.

[38] J. Mariette to Rovère and Durand-Maillane, 28 Nivôse An III – 17 January 1795, in Jean-Baptiste Clauzel, *Convention nationale. Rapport fait au nom des comités de salut public et de sûreté générale, sur les troubles de Marseille, par Clauzel; le 7 pluviôse, l'an III de la république une et indivisible* (Paris: Impr. nationale, An III [1795]), 14–17. The French Revolution research collection; 7.762.

than this. On 20 Ventôse (11 March), a crowd beat a handful of émigrés to death despite their military escort and went on to the Hospice Esprit to finish the job.[39]

Most Jacobins of Aix-en-Provence scattered into the surrounding villages. They were impossible to hunt down without gun battles. They terrorized the rural municipalities with talk that on their return, heads would roll around the streets. At Jouques, near Aix, a rumor got around that the brothers in Paris had risen and killed three thousand aristocrats. At a celebration at the local cabaret, people threatened that the next time no aristocrats would survive.[40]

Such reports, embellished as they frequently were, only increased the determination of the Thermidorian Convention to defeat terrorists and Jacobins. Apart from his equivocal actions toward the murder gangs, another new representative, Cadroy, expressed the principles of high-level anti-Jacobinism very clearly. Marseille and the southern departments as a whole had to silence hatred and vengeance. There could be no dual authority. The Convention alone was the source of law and justice. The Jacobins' seditious slogans and tumultuous gatherings undermine public order. Do the Jacobins, he asked, "wish to restore the reign of Roberbière [*sic*] in waking up terrorism?... Terror is the arm of tyrants."[41] As he expressed it later, he arrived "in the southern departments with the duty and the desire to cure the scabs that the brigands, the so-called patriots, had vividly opened on the French people."[42] Moreover, the method would require the aggressive participation of the entire citizenry, not just the administrative apparatus. "Certainly," he wrote, "when the wicked have armed themselves against *la patrie*, it is permitted to swear their total extinction. This is the oath of any good citizen."[43] Cadroy was inviting

---

[39] AM Toulon, L 115, *Arrêté* of Mariette, Chambon, and F. J. Ritter, 19 Ventôse An III – 10 March 1795. Ibid., L 370, *procès-verbal de la commission municipale*, 20 Ventôse An III – 11 March 1795.

[40] Gaston Bizos, "Le District d'Aix du 23 Vendémiaire an III au 15 Brumaire an IV, de sur [*sic*] le registre de correspondance de l'agent national du district," Rf 13 (1887), 6–8.

[41] ADBR, L 1044, Cadroy to *agent national du district de Marseille*, 26 Nivôse An III – 15 January 1795.

[42] Paul Cadroy, *Rapport du représentant du peuple Cadroy, sur ses diverses missions dans les départements méridionaux / impr. par ordre de la Convention nationale* (Paris: [Impr. nationale], [an IV, 1795]), 5. The French Revolution research collection; 7.748.

[43] Paul Cadroy, *Arrêtés et correspondance avec le Comité de salut public, du représentant du peuple Cadroy, en mission dans le département du Rhône: 23 floréal–29 prairial an III / imprimé en vertu du décret du 25 vendémiaire [par la] Convention nationale* ([Paris]: [de l'Impr. nationale], [an III, 1795]), 36. The French Revolution research collection; 6.2.2617.

an aroused citizenry to eliminate its enemies, justifying, in advance, a vigilante justice. From a very early point, therefore, the restoration of legitimate order might have had to go beyond the law. Calling forth the citizenry in a mass action was the second occasion in which the Thermidorians reverted to revolutionary justice. The first had been to send those arrested after the Vendémiaire demonstration to courts that tried without appeal. As the rolling up of the Jacobin apparatus in the clubs and administration advanced, these devices would acquire greater appeal.

Fears of the wicked justified the purge that had begun soon after 5 Vendémiaire. This purge was very extensive throughout the Southeast. The representatives for the Bouches-du-Rhône and the Var, Cadroy and Espert, set about a systematic clearing out of administrations of districts, municipalities, and courts.[44] The experience of Aubagne was exceptionally turbulent. Maignet had already sacked a handful of terrorists from the municipality on 24 Messidor for failing to obey the decrees on grain requisitions, but he had replaced the slackers with perfectly meritorious Jacobins. Following 5 Vendémiaire in Marseille, however, Auguis and Serres replaced these individuals with new municipal officers.[45]

These purges are important because the historians frequently claim that the new officers were émigrés, suspects, former Federalists, and so on. They then assert that because they were victims of the Terror, they took revenge, perhaps by encouraging the murder gangs. In the case of Aubagne at any rate, the first Thermidorian municipality was not particularly sinister. One of the newcomers was Félix Aufran, one of the anti-*piquet* leaders of 1789–90. The only émigré was Joseph Christin. His relations were interesting. His sister was a former suspect and she was married to Mathieu Rousserie, the café owner. One of the most interesting illustrations of these relationships was another new councillor, Dominique Donde, a tanner. For some reason, Donde appears on none of the surviving émigré or prisoner lists, but he was certainly well known for his anti-Jacobin associations. He was married to Claire

44 Espert to CSP, 24 Nivôse An III – 13 January 1795, in Aulard, *RACSP*, xix, 474. Paul Gaffarel, "Les massacres royalistes dans le département des Bouches-du-Rhône aux premiers mois de 1795. Episode de la réaction thermidorienne," *Annales de la Faculté des Lettres d'Aix* 3, no. 1–2 (1909), 2n1. For a comparison with Aix-en-Provence and its surrounding communes, see Bizos, "Le District d'Aix du 23 vendémiaire an III au 15 brumaire an IV," 3–5. Christiane Derobert-Ratel, *Institutions et vie municipale à Aix-en-Provence sous la Révolution: 1789–an VIII* (Aix-en-Provence: Edisud, 1981), 134–6, where the purge appears to have been total, without, however, excluding working people.
45 AM Marseille 13D 51, *arrêté* of 24 Messidor An II – 12 July 1794. AC Aubagne, *registre des délibérations*, f. 67v, *arrêté* of 7 Brumaire An III – 28 October 1794.

Monier, the woman who was spared execution in the Year II because she was pregnant. Both had a history of oppositional activity that predated the Terror. Claire was also the daughter of André Monier, who was a member of the Federalist municipality. Her two brothers were officers of the Federalist neighborhood committees. All three of the Monier men would be indicted as members of the gang. Both Claire and her husband, Dominique, would also be indicted for their activities on behalf of the gang. The reprisal element was now part of local politics.

The second Thermidorian municipality showed an even clearer tendency in this direction. The representative Cadroy selected it on 5 Germinal, Year III (25 March 1795).[46] If his appointments to the council of Aubagne were typical, towns throughout the region were becoming militantly anti-Jacobin. Cadroy sacked five of Auguis's and Serres's appointments – none of whom had anti-Jacobin records and appointed eight individuals, including the justice of the peace. Of these, six had been émigrés. All but one of these six had been members of the Federalist municipality or the General Committee of the Sections. Another man, Joseph Guillermy, a mason, was neither an émigré nor a Federalist official, but the Revolutionary Tribunal of Marseille had sentenced him to prison, and he had been active in some of the more threatening anti-Jacobin demonstrations of the spring and summer of 1792. A few months later, Guillermy was using his official position to advance murder. The Cadroy municipality, then, was very sinister in its associations.

Its outlook was equally ominous. In an address to the Convention about a week before the first murders, it denounced the Jacobins' "cries for death," their desire "to devastate our property," and their goal to "snatch our existence that had just barely escaped their furies." The council continued, "The whole of society is interested in vengeance for virtue that was oppressed for too long, [and] in the restoration of justice so long unknown. Give to the former a necessary satisfaction in order to encourage it; and to the latter all the serenity that circumstances require. Divide your energy proportionately between our impatience and our needs."[47] A restoration of justice thus required compensation for the Jacobins' fury and devastation. Although the council was looking for the Convention to satisfy the need for vengeance, one can imagine that those who denounced their enemies in such violent terms would accept vengeance in whatever form it took. As they said, their impatience was great.

---

[46] Ibid., f. 189v, *arrêté* of 5 Germinal An III – 25 March 1795.
[47] Ibid., f. 255-5v, Adresse du conseil général de la commune d'Aubagne à la Convention, 14 Prairial An III – 2 June 1795.

This council, with its background and vindictive attitudes was in charge when the first murders took place later that month of June 1795. Indeed, the justice of the peace who should have investigated these murders but who apparently did very little was François Robert. He had also been a member of the General Committee of the Sections in 1793.

The new councillors had a distinct past in the town's anti-Jacobin politics. A few had been municipal officers earlier in the Revolution, but of the twenty appointments, thirteen had been municipal officers in the Old Regime. The Thermidorian appointments were a restoration of a pre-1789 group. But this was not particularly a restoration of the town's elite.[48] The average *contribution mobilière* payment was about 10 livres, well above the 6 livres of the terrorist council that resumed office in September 1793. Although both groups landed in the top quartile of taxpayers, both fell below the mean and median payment of the top quartile itself (19 livres and 11 livres, respectively). Thus, both the terrorist and the Thermidorian councillors were much better off than their fellow citizens but not particularly close to the town's richest taxpayers.

The local Jacobins had to withdraw from politics. The affair of 5 Vendémiaire in Marseille was crucial. The Club had tried to aid the extremists in Marseille in the prison plot by preventing the arrival of reinforcements from Toulon. Specifically, the action of J.-B. Camoin, former Jacobin mayor and former administrator of the department of the Bouches-du-Rhône, provided a handy excuse. The representatives strongly suspected he had a role in the rescue of Reynier and in the events in Marseille. Moreover, he marched into the Club of Aubagne on 30 Brumaire (20 November) with an escort of thirty armed men and delivered an inflammatory, "liberty destroying" speech. Because no one in the Club protested, Auguis and Serres dissolved the Club.[49] A few weeks later, the Aubagne council received a letter from the *comité de surveillance* of Nice about the arrest of four individuals from Aubagne who had arrived without passports.[50] They had fled to avoid the representatives' order to arrest them for their part in the "conspiracy" of Marseille. Most of them had a high profile in local Jacobin politics: François Rey *dit* Bourrasque,

48 Less traditional, therefore, than in the Loire. See Colin Lucas, "Violence thermidorienne et société traditionnelle: l'exemple du Forez," *Cahiers d'histoire* 24, no. 4 (1979), 3–43.

49 AC Aubagne, 2D 150, *arrêté* of 2 Frimaire An III – 22 November 1794. Ibid., *registre des délibérations*, f. 120, session of 24 Frimaire An III – 14 December 1794.

50 Ibid., bundle titled "Différentes correspondances, 1790–An III," "Extrait en partie du registre des délibérations et arrêtés du comité de surveillance du district de Nice," 12 Frimaire An III – 2 December 1794, plus the interrogations of the four individuals, various dates.

guardsman in the Légion d'Aubagne that attacked the château of Velaux, and a sergeant in the forces that besieged Toulon in 1793; Joseph Guillen, a former member of the *comité de surveillance*; Dominique Pichou, who led the 1789 demonstration; and Joseph Aillard, a carter with an indeterminate political past. Later, they arrested Nicolas Gury, former secretary of the Jacobin municipality and secretary of the Club. The letter from Nice was important for two reasons: it initiated a long process by which the Thermidorean municipality eventually retrieved the fugitives. Gury and Rey were then murdered on the outskirts of Aubagne in July 1795 despite their official escort. The letter from Nice also showed that some former Jacobins had fled in order to seek protection in the ranks of the Army of Italy. Jacobinism in Aubagne had effectively fallen apart.

Many Jacobins fled because they feared arrest. Some may have fled even earlier because almost as soon as the terrorist regime eroded in the summer of 1794, reports of vigilante justice against Jacobins began to circulate. Almost immediately after it heard the news of Thermidor, the District of Orange in the Vaucluse informed the municipality of rumors that certain ill-intentioned people were plotting to seize the guillotine at night for their own nefarious purposes. They advised removing the blade. The following February, a furious crowd at Avignon nearly clubbed to death a former judge of the Popular Tribunal of Orange. When he attempted to swim to safety over the Rhône, they killed him with a harpoon.[51]

It did not take outright violence to show how much the atmosphere had changed. The municipality of Aubagne petitioned to have the model mountain in the Temple of Liberty removed. But feelings ran ahead of the council. At the end of January, "a crowd of people and children" destroyed the model mountain and the statue of liberty. Although they cried, "Vive la République! Vive la Convention!" these were anti-Jacobin slogans. In any case, the municipality dismissed the "zeal of a few puerile souls" who meant no harm.[52]

Politics in the terrible, cold winter of the Year III were not healthy. From the summer of 1794 onward, the Jacobins dreamed of a vast settling of accounts, the great simultaneous purge. This would involve not only the revolutionary courts that had worked so well in the latter months

---

[51] Vaillandet, "Débuts de la Terreur blanche en Vaucluse," 113.

[52] AC Aubagne, *registre de correspondance*, letter to *agent national* of District, 26 Nivôse An III – 15 January 1795. ADBR, L 1044, municipality to national agent of district, 11 Pluviôse An III – 30 January 1795; copy in AC *registre de correspondance*. In their letter of 26 Pluviôse An III – 14 February 1795, the municipality claimed a gust of wind blew the statue of liberty from its pedestal.

of the Terror but also direct action if that failed. The new teams of representatives knew from the beginning that repression would have to be forceful. Yet many of those who welcomed the fall of the dictator wanted to go further than purges and arrests. Despite its triumph following 5 Vendémiaire both in Marseille and throughout the department, the post-terrorist regime was in crisis. At one level this showed in the inability to persuade its supporters that measured and traditional justice would be sufficient to punish the terrorists. At another level, the failure to deliver this justice frustrated even antiterrorist representatives on mission. The Jacobins' loss of their political bases in the clubs and committees was insufficient to satisfy the fear and hatred of their enemies. The continuing challenge from the Jacobins and especially the rising in Toulon in late Floréal forced almost everyone in the anti-Jacobin coalition to draw on models of exceptional justice. Courts judging without appeal had been the terrorists' response to the post-Federalist crisis earlier. By the spring of 1795, more and more Thermidorians yearned to adopt revolutionary justice too. Now it would be directed at the Jacobins.

Massacre at Aix-en-Provence, 22 Floréal (11 May 1795)
The massacres were the result of the progressive loss of confidence in authorities and especially in the ability of the courts to mete out appropriate punishment.

Even before the massacre, local politics in Aix-en-Provence turned violent. Sometime in the late spring, two leading Jacobins, one of whom was a former member of the *comité de surveillance*, were found bludgeoned to death in the nearby countryside. A third individual was badly beaten because he bellowed Montagnard slogans at the theater. The situation was bad enough that the representatives on mission had to issue a proclamation warning the citizens of Aix against taking justice into their own hands. It had no effect. A few days later, a crowd fell on a father and son, both former terrorists, as they were being escorted to prison and beat them to death.[53]

After delays of many months, the trial of those arrested after the Vendémiaire rising in Marseille got under way in Aix. The trial attracted huge crowds of spectators, many from elsewhere. As the accused were

[53] Bizos, "Le District d'Aix du 23 vendémiaire an III au 15 brumaire an IV," 11. "Proclamation des représentants du peuple Mariette et Chambon, envoyés dans les départements des Bouches-du-Rhône et du Var, aux citoyens de la commune d'Aix," in Chambon, *Première partie, Sur sa mission dans les départements des Bouches-du-Rhône, du Var et du Vaucluse*, 26–7, 29.

moved each day from the prison to the courthouse, they taunted the onlookers in the street who responded with predictable outrage. Once inside the courtroom, the accused disrupted proceedings and tried to intimidate witnesses. One of the accused, a woman, boasted that she had had many people guillotined and she would do it again in the future. Some said the accused had formed a club in the prison itself to keep their rage well stoked. Practiced orators in this peculiar club predicted that when they were released, it would take only two or three hours to make rivers of blood flow and to burn Aix to the ground.[54]

Wild tales swept the town that the trial would turn out well for the accused. The court was too indulgent. The accused would get off. Hotheads were determined to see justice done. A dozen adventurers journeyed from Marseille the night before the massacre to stir things up or perhaps attack the prisoners, as others had in 1789, 1790, 1792, and 1793. Some would participate in the massacre at Fort Jean in Marseille the next month.[55] Authorities in Aix thus had plenty of warning that the prisoners were in danger. But they had little force available to keep order. The National Guard had been disarmed since 1793. There were too few soldiers to control an outraged crowd.

The early session of the trial of 22 Floréal had gone well, but throughout the morning and well into the afternoon, an increasingly restless crowd milled about the promenades. When trial proceedings resumed in the afternoon, spectators pelted the prisoners with rocks as they were escorted from the prison to the court. After that session finished, the accused were returned to the prison. At around four in the afternoon, a band of individuals seized two cannon at the town hall; another crowd demanded "in the name of the people" that the municipality arm them. Others attempted to seize the powder stores. In the later afternoon, a crowd finally overwhelmed the guard, broke into the prison, and began killing the prisoners. The crowds had also taken over the town, placing cannon at strategic cross streets, including along the present-day Cours Mirabeau. The town councillors tried but failed to enter the prison. Overwhelmed by the immense crowd, they ordered the troops to withdraw. Their work done as night fell, the killers withdrew, leaving behind twenty-nine victims but sparing seventy-eight others. All but one of the accused

---

[54] ADBR, L 242, pp. 13–15, *procureur syndic du département des Bouches-du-Rhône* to CSP, 23 Floréal An III – 12 May 1795.

[55] AD Gard, L 3151, depositions of Joseph Vitou and Joseph Reybaud, 29 Pluviôse An IV – 17 February 1796.

in the trial of 5 Vendémiaire had been murdered. They also set fire to the prison, but it was quickly extinguished. The victims included a former judge on Fréron's Military Tribunal of the Year II and a member of the *comité de surveillance* of Marseille.[56] As in Lyon, the killers selected their victims. As in Lyon, too, the crowd thought of itself as applying a more appropriate justice than the courts. Like all descriptions of the outrages of the period, authorities never identified the faces in the crowd.

Toulon Rising and Its Aftermath, 28 Floréal–4 Prairial (17–23 May 1795)

The Toulon rising reflected the long-standing Jacobin axiom about flying to the defense of their beleaguered comrades. It did not differ in any significant way from the dozens of similar marches the Jacobins of Marseille and other cities had undertaken earlier. This time, however, the result was a disaster.[57]

By mid-May 1795, Jacobins in Toulon had had enough. The murders of their brothers in the street and the tacit acceptance of returned émigrés were intolerable. Besides, outrages like the massacre at Aix-en-Provence and the persecutions of patriots at Arles and Marseille had to stop. When rumors spread that the imprisoned patriots in Marseille were being slaughtered, they determined to rescue their oppressed brothers. A demonstration, acting in the name of the "sovereign people," successfully forced authorities to release Jacobin prisoners held in Fort Lamalague and to surrender weapons. The representative Brunel killed himself for having permitted this. Another representative, Niou, took refuge on a warship in the harbor. Some soldiers in the garrison, some sailors, and most

---

[56] Various reports in Louis Marie Stanislas Fréron, *Mémoire historique sur la réaction royale, et sur les massacres du Midi* (Paris: Baudouin frères, 1824), 201–13. AM, Aix-en-Provence LL 81, ff. 241–2v, "Rapport de la commission municipale d'Aix sur les évènements des 21 et 22 floréal," 23 Floréal An III – 12 May 1795.For a list of those killed, see Etat-civil d'Aix-en-Provence, p. 396, 24 Floreal An III – 13 May 1795. This source is available on line.

[57] Malcolm Crook, *Toulon in War and Revolution: From the Ancien Régime to the Restoration, 1750–1820, War, Armed Forces, and Society* (Manchester: Manchester University Press, 1991), 167–72. Malcolm Crook, "La dernière insurrection jacobine du midi: la révolte de Toulon en Floréal/Prairial an III" (paper presented at the Actes du 113e et 114e Congrès national des Sociétés savantes [Strasbourg, 5–9 avril 1988 et Paris 3–9 avril 1989]), (Paris: Éditions du C.T.H.S., 1991), 363–71. Edmond Poupé, "Le Département du Var, 1790–an VIII," *Bulletin de la Société d'études scientifiques et archéologiques de Draguignan* Tome XL. Mémoires 38 (1934–5), 379–402. Frédéric Masson, *La révolte de Toulon en prairial an III* (Paris: Librairie des bibliophiles, 1875).

dangerous of all, some workers in the arsenal went over to the rebels. There may have been as many as eight thousand insurgents.

A band of patriots made its way to a reputed émigré hideout in nearby Solliès, disarmed the village and its neighbors, and escorted several émigrés back to Toulon. Some prisoners were carrying small pieces of paper on which "Vive Louis XVII!" was written, a sure rallying signal in the Jacobin worldview. They were turned over to a representative who had remained behind, and he promised a quick trial. Liberating prisoners and arresting enemies fit the justification of spontaneous mass action. It continued with the seizure of the city. The insurgents closed the gates, mounted cannon, and tried to seduce the garrison at La Ciotat by claiming to be the sole defenders of the Jacobin Constitution of 1793.[58]

Throughout the region, Thermidorians responded to the news of the Jacobin uprising at Toulon with a vast counterrising of their own. On 1 Prairial (20 May), the representative Chambon mobilized the population against the Toulon rebels and their allies nearby. He issued a stirring proclamation urging all citizens to resist. He ordered house-to-house searches to find people the municipality considered suspect. Those whose papers were not in order were to be imprisoned. All the municipalities in the Bouches-du-Rhône and the Var were to imprison anyone who after 9 Thermidor had expressed, "by words, the desire to reestablish the system of terror and blood, so justly proscribed, and abhorred." Such individuals were also to be disarmed. Moreover, all citizens were to assist authorities in the execution of this decree. This was an obvious invitation for the anti-Jacobins to arrest their enemies.[59] In other words, Chambon had revived the Law of Suspects in slightly different form. Finally, he ordered local authorities to prepare "the good citizens to march if necessary at the first signal."[60]

---

[58] "Les représentants à Marseille" au Comité de salut public, 1 prairial An III – 20 May 1795, in Aulard, *RACSP*, xxiii, 397–8. Jean-Michel Chambon-Latour, *Chambon, représentant du peuple français, député du département du Gard, à la Convention nationale... Seconde partie, sur les opérations de sa mission relative à la reddition de Toulon* ([Paris]: Imprimerie nationale, Brumaire An IV [November 1795]), 1–5.

[59] Chambon *arrêté* of 1 Prairial An III –20 May 1795, in Chambon, *Sur les opérations de sa mission relative à la reddition de Toulon*, 14–15.

[60] Chambon to CSP, 6 Prairial An III – 25 May 1795, in Aulard, *RACSP*, xxiii, 544–5. Chambon and Cadroy to CSP, 6 Prairial An III – 26 May 1795, in ibid., 555. The proclamation is in Chambon, *Sur les opérations de sa mission relative à la reddition de Toulon*, 22. ADBR, L 242, f. 22, procureur syndic des Bouches-du-Rhône to Chambon, 4 Prairial An III – 23 May 1795.

The decree had an electric effect. An official in the Vaucluse asked for verification of the news of the Toulon rising so that "the good citizens can act together, combine their means, and form a mass that will crush the enemies of the patrie." As it turned out, in Avignon, the call for a mobilization stirred a pro-Jacobin working-class quarter whose inhabitants proposed to relieve their oppressed brethren in Lyon. The good citizens feared that the departure of forces to Toulon would permit the terrorists to run amok. Jacobin partisans shouted, "A bas les muscadins! Les aristocrates à la lanterne! Vive la montagne!"[61] In Orange, stories flew that the "cannibals" had already dug the graves that would gobble up the "good citizens."[62] But if the Jacobins were rising in the Var and Vaucluse, elsewhere the mobilization produced a massive anti-Jacobin surge. At Aubagne, for example, sixty-six members of the National Guard marched to Toulon thrilled with "the desire to share the glory." But significantly, the National Guard companies of the *terroir* were unreliable. They might join with the Toulon Jacobins hiding in the mountains surrounding the town. Together they were a threat to "homes."[63] Thus, despite the purges and the flight of their leaders, the country people outside the town proper retained the Jacobin loyalties they had acquired in 1791.

At Aix-en-Provence, the rising of the good citizens was exceptional. As soon as the councillors received Chambon's decree, they secured the prisons, closed the town gates, mobilized the National Guard, disarmed Montagnards, and distributed arms to good citizens. They all assembled on the *grande promenade* (the Cours Mirabeau) ready to march at four in the morning, but not before authorities and freelancers arrested thirty-seven known "suspects." Most of these had been arrested illegally but only a few were released. About 150 guardsmen and some 400 good citizens marched "against the enemies of the *patrie* and of humanity." But before they arrived at the rallying point at Aubagne, the fighting was

---

[61] René Moulinas, *Histoire de la révolution d'Avignon* ([Avignon]: Aubanel, c. 1986), 342. See Cadroy to CSP, 29 Prairial An III – 17 June 1795 in Aulard, *RACSP*, xxiv, 464. BM Avignon, MS 1673, [?] to Goupilleau and Poultier, n.d.

[62] Goupilleau de Montaigu to Rovère, 12 Prairial An III – 31 May 1795 in *Documents sur la Révolution dans le Vaucluse. Correspondance intime du conventionnel Rovère avec Goupilleau (de Montaigu), en mission dans le Midi, après la Terreur (1794–1795)*, ed. Marcel Giraud-Mangin Michel Jouve (Nîmes: Debroas, 1908), 189.

[63] AC Aubagne, *registre de correspondance*, municipality to "Rep^r du peuple sous les murs de Toulon," 10 Prairial An III – 29 May 1795.

over. They returned about ten days later to celebrate "the victory of virtue over crime."[64]

The countermobilization of the "good citizens" from all over the region camped at Aubagne before moving on to the decisive battle. Chambon and other representatives estimated that ten thousand such volunteers from as far away as Nîmes and Avignon flocked to fight alongside the regular army.[65] Despite these massive numbers, the Toulon army of Jacobins quickly overpowered the advance posts of the "army of citizens." It appeared their aim was to march on Aix and Marseille to "avenge the blood of their brothers.... They propose also to do in all the fugitives of 1793."[66] They also meant to rectify the recent turn of events in Marseille. The patriots of Toulon "complain of the daily murders at Marseille; the arbitrary imprisonments and the protection the [returned] émigrés receive."[67] Once that was accomplished, they would march to liberate Paris, gathering with them, as a hostile witness declared, "all the most corrupt beings all the way." Or as the representative Chiappe, who spent some time as the rebels' prisoner, explained, they would gather an army along the route, "slaughter the good citizens, set the men of blood free, and thus form a considerable army."[68] The revival of the aim of a vast national march of liberation of oppressed brothers shines through even this pejorative description.

The opposing sides met near the village of Beausset on the road from Toulon to Aubagne on 4 Prairial. The little army of three thousand Jacobins with their dozen pieces of artillery succumbed after five hours of combat to a combined government force of regular army and local national guardsmen who numbered only 1,200. The government lost less than a half dozen men while the rebels left forty-five dead on the field of battle and many more wounded or killed following the ferocious pursuit of the cavalry. The government captured 360 prisoners. As the government army entered Toulon that night, many feared that the National

[64] ADBR, L 558, pp. 38–9, District circular to municipalities advising the arrest and/or disarming of "gens suspects," n.d.

[65] Chambon, Chiappe, Niou, Guerin, Isnard, and Cadroy to CSP, 12 Prairial An III – 31 May 1795, in Aulard, *RACSP*, xxiii, 767–70.

[66] ADBR, L 242, 22, procureur syndic du département des Bouches-du-Rhône to same of Vaucluse, 6 Prairial An III – 25 May 1795.

[67] Guérin and Poultier to commandant temporaire de Marseille, 4 Prairial An III – 23 May 1795, in Chambon, *Sur les opérations de sa mission relative à la reddition de Toulon*, 17. See also the Jacobin petition dated 3 Prairial An III – 22 May 1795, in ibid., 36–7.

[68] Two letters of Chiappe to Chambon, 2, 4 Prairial An III – in Chambon, *Sur les opérations de sa mission relative à la reddition de Toulon*, 43–5.

Guard would take reprisals, but this did not happen. Instead the rebels surrendered their arms peacefully at the town hall. Although many fled, the Military Commission that was established to try them had enough prisoners "to give a grand example and finally assure the tranquility of the Midi."[69] At least one of the worst aspects of the recapture of Toulon in December 1793, the shooting without trial of eight hundred prisoners had been avoided. But the ramifications of the Toulon rising were just beginning.

Massacre at Fort Jean, Marseille, 17 Prairial (5 June 1795)

All the prison massacres that followed the rising in Toulon were reprisals or pretexts for the anti-Jacobins to exercise justice for themselves. This included the first murders at Aubagne that began at the same time. The prison massacres therefore help to understand the murders.

The massacre at Marseille was the bloodiest of them all but it did not occur in a void. A gang of killers based on a couple of cafés near the eastern end of the Canebière had emerged earlier. Their first operation was the murder of a soldier as early as December 1794. Although the links among gang members needs a thorough investigation, many of the murderers had killed on the streets of Marseille before the massacre, had journeyed to Aix-en-Provence to participate in the massacre there, and had exploited the opening of the Jacobin rising in Toulon to wreck havoc in Fort Jean in Marseille. Killers in Marseille knew killers in Aix and Aubagne, but how deep these relations were is unclear. They also had relations with the city's *comité de surveillance* in that several of the killers acted as agents in arresting known Jacobins. Many of them were also members or even officers of the National Guard. Thus, they had access to weapons, a quasi-official authority, and information about their opponents that they might not have had otherwise. It was these renegade militia units that Jacobins called "Companies of the Sun," a name that soon caught fire with the Jacobins. None of the accused killers was a prominent Federalist in 1793, but a few had been soldiers in the Departmental Army that had tried to defend the city against Carteaux in August 1793.[70] A similar process was

[69] Reports in *Journal des hommes libres* 4, 19 Prairial An III – 7 June 1795 and ADBR, L 242, f. 34v, letter to proc. syn, dept. of Drôme, 18 Prairial An III – 6 June 1795. Ibid., L 1297, Department to District of Salon, 12 Prairial An III – 31 May 1795. Chambon, *Sur les opérations de sa mission relative à la reddition de Toulon*, 6–7. Pacthod to Chambon, 5 Prairial An III – 24 May 1795, in ibid., 22–4.

[70] ADBR, L 3048, acte d'accusation contre Benoît Lafont, Auguste Pelard et Pierre-Luc Ferréol, 22 Nivôse An V – 11 January 1797. AD Gard, L 3151, declaration of Antoine Gardin, 22 Ventôse An IV – 12 March 1797.

occurring in Aubagne at the same time. The mantle of anti-Jacobinism was passing from men who professed a respect for the rule of law in 1793 and in the aftermath of 9 Thermidor to a small but exceptionally vicious number of groups whom the Thermidorians found nearly impossible to contain, let alone punish. That failure ruined the chances for a restoration of constitutional government in the region.

More than a dozen murders occurred in Marseille in the three weeks before the massacre. Many of them took place in broad daylight on main streets, mostly near the port. The killings were as public as could be imagined, at the entrance to the theatre, on the doorstep of the victims' homes in front of their families, just opposite the flour-weighing post, and so on. A gang murdered three men and a woman near Notre-Dame de la Garde, the highest point in the city. A half dozen young men killed a woman on the Rue de l'Ancienne Comédie with sabers and robbed the corpse. One particularly unfortunate individual was left for dead on the street, but when the killers heard he had survived and had made his way home, they bounded up four flights of stairs in his building and hacked him to death with their sabers in front of his screaming children, neighbors, and the surgeon. Another victim was the wife of the former president of the Revolutionary Tribunal, Mme Maillet. She was murdered in plain view of many witnesses on the Rue Longue-des-Capucins. No one dared remove her body until nightfall. The desire for revenge and expunging was particularly clear in the murder of Sicard Poitevin, a shoemaker and captain in the National Guard, killed with a massive blow to the head and then shot in mid-May 1795 on the promenades at the eastern end of the Canebière. He had arrested the father of one of the assailants and vainly pleaded with his killer that no harm had come to him. The killers apparently said to passersby, "We have to purge this street, we have the captain and soon we'll have the sergeant." One of the killers was from Aubagne; the victim may have been as well.[71]

According to Lautard, the streets of Marseille in this period were more dangerous than the woods at night. He witnessed one killing near the Canebière in which an assailant ran up and shot a prisoner in the head despite an escort of four soldiers, as if he had just destroyed a mad dog. An acquaintance who also saw the murder said, "Take it easy, M[onsieur]

---

[71] *Journal des hommes libres* 96, 369, 21 Fructidor An III – 7 September 1795. Also, ibid., 626, no. 83, 8 Fructidor An III –25 August 1795. Gaffarel, "Massacres royalistes dans le département des Bouches-du-Rhône," 9–11. Fréron, *Mémoire historique . . . sur les massacres du Midi*, 96–100. AD Gard, L 3152, declarations of Jean Vessière, Magdeleine St. Paul, and Thérèse Arnaud, 22 Nivôse An IV – 11 January 1797.

L... it's only one less wicked person."[72] The justices of the peace could find no one willing to give evidence in these murders.

Some authorities were aware of these signs of danger for the prisoners in Fort Jean. Two weeks before the massacre, concerned District authorities and the commander of the fort closed off certain avenues leading to the outer walls. They also repaired moats that gave too-easy access to the interior of the fort.[73] But the Toulon affair overwhelmed everything.

As soon as they received Chambon's decree of 1 Prairial, authorities in Marseille and even "good citizens" acting on their own, arrested a very large number of Jacobins, both men and women – preemptive measures against a simultaneous rising as their comrades approached. Many of them were thrown into Fort Jean. Chambon himself visited the neighborhoods of Marseille to encourage volunteers and encourage the arrest of suspect citizens. As the number of prisoners grew, the fort was largely stripped of troops for the expedition to Toulon. Inexperienced national guardsmen replaced them. In the inquiry that followed the massacre, prisoners invariably referred to them as "Enfants du Soleil." Very likely these guards allowed the killers to enter the fort, and they may have participated in the massacre too. Furthermore, the commander of the fort and his secretary were both ferocious anti-Jacobins. The evidence is unclear about whether they participated in the massacre itself – several prisoners said the secretary of the fort, Manoly, was a leader of the Company of the Sun – but both did taunt the prisoners with macabre forecasts of their future that acquired a sinister light after the massacre.[74]

Weak leadership and inadequate defenses made the obvious excitement of the Jacobins about the march of their comrades from Toulon all the more threatening.[75] The anti-Jacobins were terrified. The size of the Toulon army grew by the hour in the popular imagination. People recalled Carteaux's invasion in August 1793 and the fears of massacre

---

[72] Laurent Lautard, *Esquisses historiques. Marseille depuis 1789 jusqu'en 1815; par un vieux Marseillais*, 2 vols. (Marseille: Impr. de M. Olive, 1844), i, 425.

[73] ADBR, L 242, 69–72, Siméon, procureur général syndic du département des Bouches-du-Rhône to Comité de sûreté générale, 22 Messidor An III – 10 July 1795.

[74] "Extrait d'une lettre écrite des prisons de Nice, le 23 frimaire an 4°, de la République, au représentant du peuple Fréron, par le citoyen Pagez, ex-commandant temporaire du fort Jean," in Fréron, *Mémoire historique... sur les massacres du Midi*, 191–4. Prisoner testimony on pp. 152–67.

[75] ADBR, L 1045, L'agent national de la commune de La Cadière to Gandre, commandant de la place à la Ciotat, 6 Prairial An III – 25 May 1795. AD Vaucluse, 1L 135, Extrait reg delibs de l'admin mun du canton d'Orange, 5 Prairial An III – 24 May 1795. There are similar complaints from authorities in Carpentras and Avignon.

and pillage from that time were revived. As in' 1793, people fled to the country, the bourgeoisie taking their money bags and jewelry to safeguard them against certain plunder. At Aix-en-Provence, a panic-stricken crowd surrounded the hotel of the representative Isnard and demanded arms. Isnard appeared on the balcony and shouted back, "What! You have no arms, you say? Unearth the remains of your forefathers and use their bones [as weapons]." Also at Aix, the representative Cadroy give a thrilling speech from the height of the altar of the *patrie*, after which the crowd "swore to exterminate the wicked who dared revolt against the national representation."[76] Like the Jacobins, the Thermidorians believed in raising the armed people to smite their enemies.

The massacre started around five in the afternoon on 17 Prairial (5 June). Despite the authorities' precautions, the killers, perhaps about forty of them, got into the prison with no resistance.[77] The return of the troops from Toulon earlier in the afternoon distracted officialdom. Spectators lined the roads to Marseille to watch. An undetermined group tried to assault or even kill the shackled prisoners as they shuffled through Aubagne. Once at Marseille, the antiterrorists fêted the troops deliriously because their fears had earlier been so intense. The troops' commander received a laurel wreath from the municipality at a ceremony by the Porte de Rome. Despite or because of the celebration, some suspected Jacobins were murdered in the streets while the event was occurring. Even though the coup against the fort was well timed, some killers had to steel their nerves with eau-de-vie.[78]

Once inside, they tore open the dungeons and began killing the prisoners with guns, sabers, and heavy clubs. They considered every prisoner guilty. One of the killers, holding a bloody saber in one hand and a handkerchief in the other, hollered, "Don't let anyone escape!" Another killer taunted a prisoner with, "Montagnard, tell Marat to come and save you." One of the killers brought his huge ferocious dog with him,

---

[76] Lautard, *Marseille depuis 1789 jusqu'en 1815*, ii, 10–12, and 12n1 for the Isnard quote. Slightly different version of the famous quote in Fréron, *Mémoire historique...sur les massacres du Midi*, 371. According to the laconic version of the municipality of Aix, Isnard merely promised arms to an immense crowd below his balcony (AM, Aix-en-Provence, LL 81, *registre des délibérations*, f. 254, procès-verbal du 6 Prairial An III – 25 May 1795).

[77] ADBR, L 3048, interrogation of François Pages, *commandant du fort*, 26 Floréal An IV – 15 May 1796, where the interrogator lists forty suspected killers while asking Pages whether he knew them.

[78] Declaration of Gabrielle Tissière, 21 Brumaire An IV – 11 November 1796, in Fréron, *Mémoire historique...sur les massacres du Midi*, 151–3.

imaginatively named Mastiff [*Dogue*]. The dog also attacked the prisoners. Many prisoners pathetically tried to shield themselves with their mattresses. One feigned death. Others hid in piles of straw. Some tried to barricade themselves inside their dungeons, so the killers blew off the doors with cannon fire or brought up wet burning straw and sulfur, which was then stuffed through the bars on the cell doors. The black noxious smoke forced those inside to come out. One prisoner was able to fight back by smashing his assailant in the face with a bottle and seizing his ax, but such exploits were inevitably rare. Amid the screams and agony, amid the shouting and bellowing, amid the fierce barks of the dog, amid the fire and foul smoke, some prisoners shrieked desperately for help through the cell windows to the outside. But these were eight feet above the floor of the cells, and the fort itself overlooked the port on one side and was separated from the land by a moat on the other. The noise of the cannon blasts attracted a sizable crowd outside the prison, but someone had pulled up the drawbridge, so rescue was impossible. Finally, four hours after the affair began, Cadroy, Isnard, and Chambon arrived. This ended the spree. The military commander of the city arrested a handful of killers on the spot. Others strode out of the prison in triumph. They sang, "Victory is ours!" and fanned out to the streets taunting passersby and heading to other prisons where they were repulsed.[79] One killer later bragged about his exploits and participated in another murder on the streets a short while later.[80] Those arrested were released three days later and left the prison, singing and celebrating.

The day after the massacre, three justices of the peace drew up a gruesome inventory. They found thirty bodies under a trellis, all of them killed with sharp instruments, many of them so badly beaten they were unrecognizable. They found more corpses along the arches, and after climbing to the central courtyard of the fort, they found another thirty-eight near two dungeons. The doors of these cells were scorched. Some of the bodies inside were charred. This would have been the spot where

---

[79] *Journal des hommes libres* 96, 369, 21 Fructidor An III – 7 August 1795. C. Lourde, *Histoire de la Révolution à Marseille et en Provence: de 1789 au Consulat* (Marseille: Laffitte, 1974), 400–8. Lautard, *Marseille depuis 1789 jusqu'en 1815*, ii, 17–22, which is heavily dependent on the memoirs of the *duc* de Montpensier. Cadroy, *Rapport du représentant du peuple Cadroy, sur ses diverses missions*, 24–5. There was another attempt on the prison on 20 Messidor (8 July). Authorities took it so seriously that they warned the prisoners they might have to defend themselves, opened the dungeons, and distributed weapons (*Journal des hommes libres* 51, 103–4, 6 Thermidor An III – 24 July 1795).

[80] ADBR, L 3048, acte d'accusation.

the killers had blown off the door with cannon fire. As many as fifteen of the victims were still alive, barely breathing and unable to talk. They were transported to the nearby Hôpital de l'Humanité, where a few later succumbed to their wounds.[81] Two flat-bottomed boats in the harbor were filled with corpses. Estimates vary greatly about the number of victims, but there were certainly over one hundred. At least one was a veteran of the march to the Tuileries in August 1792. Three were from Aubagne.[82]

Massacres at Tarascon, 6 Prairial and 3 Messidor (25 May and 21 June 1795)

After the destruction of a few liberty trees in the late spring of 1795, the good citizens of Arles and Tarascon drove the Jacobins into the hot flat-lands of the Crau or into the marshes of the Camargue, where these "apostles of anarchy" lived in isolated hunters' cabins. They remained tireless agitators. According to Cadroy, "It's there they made it a duty to preach blood and carnage, disorder and the most shameful *maratism*."[83] The terrorists' continuous plotting required *grandes mesures* for public safety, including disarming and arrest.[84] The army and National Guard rounded them up and threw them in prison. One particularly interesting catch was a former cathedral canon and his wife. The soldiers often had to endure the catcalls from the onlookers who had given the Jacobins refuge.

[81] "Extrait du dépt de l'état civil. des citoyens de celle maison commune de Marseille," 18 Prairial An III – Fréron, *Mémoire historique... sur les massacres du Midi*, 125–7.

[82] Stephen Clay, "Le massacre du Fort Jean: un épisode de la Terreur blanche à Marseille," in *Le tournant de l'an III: réaction et terreur blanche dans la France révolutionnaire*, ed. Michel Vovelle (Paris, 1997), 577–8. There are 107 names in the two lists ("Liste des prisonniers morts au Fort-Jean..." 18 Prairial An III – 6 June 1795, and "État nominatif des morts au fort Jean le jour de l'événement qui est arrivé le dix-sept Prairial..." 9 Messidor An III – 27 June 1795 in Fréron, *Mémoire historique... sur les massacres du Midi*, 128–30. There is a manuscript list by the justices of the peace of Marseille dated 23 Messidor An III – 11 July 1795, in AN F⁷ 7130. The three from Aubagne were Jean-Baptiste Paumond, Joseph Ferrand, both of whom are identified as from Aubagne, and Probasse Savau. There is some confusion about this, however. This might be Probace Sivan, who was so deeply involved in the events leading up to Jourdan's murder in September 1792. On the other hand, Probace Sivan was later arrested as a deserter (AC Aubagne, bundle titled "Justice et repression," Interrogation of 21 Frimaire An VI – 11 December 1797) so that it may have been his brother who was murdered. Both Paumond and Probace Sivan were also members of the terrorist *comité de surveillance*.

[83] Cadroy, *Rapport du représentant du peuple Cadroy, sur ses diverses missions*, 57.

[84] ADBR, L 1517, f. 166, meeting of 6 Floréal An III (25 April 1795) of District of Tarascon. Printed version in ibid., L 1549.

The trigger for the first massacre at Tarascon was the news of the Toulon rising. The representatives Chambon's and Guerin's proclamation of 1 Prairial enlisting the entire population in the annihilation of terrorism had a huge effect. The immediate response was a popular rising, a "tumultuous torrent" that arbitrarily and violently arrested over one hundred former terrorists, men and women, who were then thrown into the dungeons of the château. At the same time, anger boiled at the slowness of the trials of the former terrorists who were in prison already. The immediate event may have been a rumor that the rebels from Toulon were on the verge of invading Arles, only a stone's throw downriver from Tarascon. A rumor swirled that terrorists were on their way to rescue the prisoners.[85] As with the other massacres, authorities had some indication of the danger. In the case of Tarascon, the municipal officers complained of the great number of Jacobin prisoners in the château and the inadequacy of the defenses.[86] No one could spare any reinforcements. The councillors were also on a permanent watch in the town hall.

As in the cases of Aix-en-Provence and Marseille, the château's defenses were ineffective. Sometime after two in the morning on the night of 5–6 prairial (24–5 May 1795), a huge crowd of 200–300 people, often with blackened faces or disguised as women, besieged the château. They duped the sentinels into believing they were an escort delivering prisoners. Once inside, the assailants took the garrison prisoner and shouted that they would shoot the first one to make a noise. Some of the guards even joined the attackers. One killer claimed they were the municipality, department, district, Convention, and tribunal rolled into one, a claim, in other words, of direct sovereignty. They killed all the prisoners in the second and third dungeons. This suggests some prior knowledge of whom they were looking for. Some victims were dragged still alive by their feet up to the battlements and hurled into the Rhône ninety meters below. A killer told a prisoner, "Look up there, you are not in good health, but you will leap." One victim actually threw himself off the battlements into the river while trying to escape and miraculously survived. As he struggled to shore, another killer in a boat murdered him. In all, there were twenty-four victims, including the married cathedral canon.[87]

[85] BM Arles MS 668, n° 14, District of Salon to District of Arles, 7 Prairial An III – 26 May 1795, promising reinforcements for the defense of Arles.

[86] Ibid., n° 5, District of Tarascon to District of Arles, 3 Prairial An III – 22 May 1795.

[87] For general accounts, see the three reports in Fréron, *Mémoire historique . . . sur les massacres du Midi*, 213–22; and the somewhat jumbled narrative in Gaffarel, "Massacres royalistes dans le département des Bouches-du-Rhône," pp. 20–22. ADBR, L 3051,

Killers tried to repeat the massacres at Aix and at Marseille, but only at Tarascon was the second attempt successful. Despite doubling the guard around the château and increased vigilance in general, somehow the killers got in. Even worse, the municipal officers had advance warning of a plot originating in the nearby villages "to slaughter the prisoners of their respective communes detained in the fort" at Tarascon. Tragically, they did not take the rumor seriously enough. On the night of 2 Messidor (20 June 1795), the prisoners also had advance warning that the killers would return, so they barricaded themselves in their cells. They refused to open them even to the municipal officers who came to satisfy themselves that all was well. Sometime around three in the morning, after the municipal officers had left, crowds from the communes surrounding Tarascon burst into the prison, forced the barricades, overwhelmed the guard, and seized the keys to the cell doors. They killed those inside who had been arrested for "excesses for which they had made themselves guilty during the reign of Terror." Once again the bodies were hauled up to the battlements and thrown onto the rocks of the riverbed below. Early the next morning, a group of women out to market, saw one of the killers strolling along, a pistol in one hand and a still-bloody saber in the other. Later that afternoon, a mother and her fifteen-year-old daughter were slaughtered on the street. There were twenty-three victims, including the two women. Several bodies washed ashore at Arles a few days later.[88]

There was even a third attempt on the night of 23 Thermidor (9–10 August). Some planning went into this one too. Some would-be killers got into the château while others waited in a large skiff on the river below the walls. One of them shouted up into the night, "What are you doing up there? ... [T]he water is ready, throw us these good for nothing sansculottes!" A fellow conspirator yelled back from the battlements, "Just a

declaration of Dominique l'Hérmite, 21 Ventôse An VII – 11 March 1799. Disguising oneself as a woman occurred from time to time in European risings and symbolized a world out of joint, a monstrous transformation from nurture to menace. Ibid. L 3004, commissaire du directoire exécutif près le tribunal correctionnel du Tarascon-sur-Rhône to same près les tribunaux civil et criminel du département des Bouches-du-Rhône, 25 Fructidor An VI – 11 September 1798. Also AM Tarascon, *état civil*, item 201, twenty-four names.

[88] Fréron, *Mémoire historique... sur les massacres du Midi*, 223–7. Copies in BM Avignon, MS 1673, and in AM Tarascon, folder titled "La Révolution française à Tarascon."*Journal des hommes libres*, n° 36, 21 Messidor An III – 9 July 1795. AN F⁷ 7130, procureur-syndic of District of Tarascon to CGS, 8 Messidor An III – 26 June 1795. ADBR, L 1518, ff. 21v–22v, "Tarascon. Délibération de la dite commune... des détenus attaqués pour la 2ᵉ fois dans la nuit du 2 au 3 messidor," 4 Messidor An III – 22 June 1795.

small moment." Yet that moment never came because the prisoners barricaded themselves in their cells with mattresses until late morning. Their wives had rushed to the representatives who were staying at Saint-Rémy. Only when they arrived did they feel safe to appear. One prisoner, in a part of the dungeon called ironically the *salle de la comédie,* later said he recognized the voices of several of his neighbors.[89] Although the project collapsed, the intent to kill enemies and damage their families was clear. In high summer, the river was low so anyone who survived the enormous fall, if that was even possible, would have been killed on the exposed rocks. The men on the water were there to tow the bodies into the middle of the river where the heavy currents would carry them off. The night was clear and the moon was in its last quarter, so moving about the river and retrieving the bodies would have been fairly easy for experienced boatmen. But the wider goal lay elsewhere. The disappearance of the corpses would prolong the agony of the victims' families while the anti-Jacobin community would expunge the presence even in death of their enemies.

The outrages at Tarascon epitomize the importance of faction throughout the period. Rivalry between two families for much of the period divided the small city. Clearly townspeople took sides.[90] But other small towns and villages were also deeply involved, and the prison was attacked because it housed men and women who had made themselves thoroughly objectionable. Indeed, in the second massacre, outraged neighbors from Saint-Rémy, Graveson, Chateaurenard, Barbentane, and other places attacked former Jacobins from their communities, not Jacobins from Tarascon. As the municipality of Tarascon expressed it, "Crazed armed outsiders, dominated by fury and vengeance" carried out the second massacre.[91] Without a detailed analysis of occupations and tax assessments, it is impossible to be precise, but the lists of accused killers

---

[89] ADBR, L 3051, question to Barthélemy Dumas, 29 Ventôse An VII – 19 March 1799 and *dénonciation civique,* of Blanc Roman 19 Thermidor An VI – 6 August 1798. Ibid., L 1518, ff. 39–39v, "Procès-verbal au sujet du bruit que [*illeg.*] les détenus dans le fort de cette commune," 23 Thermidor An III – 10 August 1795, where authorities interpreted the tumult among the prisoners as a prison break and huge crowds gathered around the prison. See also Pierre Toussaint Durand de Maillane, *Histoire de la Convention nationale: suivie d'un fragment historique sur le 31 mai.* Collection des mémoires relatifs à la révolution française; v. 27 (Paris: Baudouin frères, 1825), 280–6.

[90] AN F7 7171, General Melle, "Tableau de la situation des Bouches-du-Rhône," n.d. [An VI].

[91] AM, Tarascon, 1D 3, session of 4 Messidor An III – 22 June 1795. According to "Premier massacre au chateau…" in BM Avignon, MS 1675, all but one of the twenty-four

contain plenty of people in the more humble trades: wigmakers, rope makers, shoemakers, laborers, cultivators, and so on.[92] As in Aubagne, anti-
Jacobinism had a significant amount of popular support. Jacobins and
anti-Jacobins were neighbors who did not differ from each other very
much.

Another characteristic of the massacres was how little ideology
counted, certainly not the ideology so often attributed to the killers. There
is no sign of royalism and royalist sympathies among the killers, here or
elsewhere. Although the inquiry into the massacres began very late, in the
Years VI and VII, royalism was still illegal, and expressing sympathy for
it would have caught authorities' attention. Nor was there any indication
of the existence of the paramilitary Companies of the Sun or Jesus, or
that any of the accused were returned émigrés. The Jacobins claimed all
these things motivated both the prison massacres and the gang killings,
but this was an all-too-convenient way of explaining the events. Instead,
the features of the massacres and later the killings was the localism and
the factionalism.[93]

Contemporary Understandings

Contemporaries assumed that forces in the shadows had planned these
horrendous catastrophes long in advance and that the conspiracy had
huge ramifications. For instance, rumors flew that the Compagnie de
Soleil shared guard duty with the regular detail at Fort Jean in Marseille;
that killers involved in the massacre in Lyon journeyed to Marseille to
participate; that the plotters had dug graves and filled them with lime three
weeks in advance; that the baker who supplied bread to the prisoners
knew beforehand not to bother with any deliveries for 18 Prairial, the

---

victims were from Tarascon, while in the list of victims of the second massacre, only
four of twenty-three were from Tarascon.

[92] For a preliminary approach, see the comparison between Jacobins and anti-Jacobins in
Tarascon in Colin Lucas, "Résistances populaires à la Révolution dans le sud-est," in
*Mouvements populaires et conscience sociale: XVIe–XIXe siècles: actes du colloque de
Paris, 24–26 mai 1984*, ed. Jean Nicolas (Paris: Maloine, 1985), 477.

[93] This is also the conclusion of René Moulinas after his examination of a number of incidents, but especially the spectacular massacre of prisoners on the road from Orange
to Pont Saint-Esprit ("Le département du Vaucluse en 1795: la contre-révolution
en marche?" in *Le tournant de l'an III: réaction et terreur blanche dans la France
révolutionnaire*, ed. Michel Vovelle (Paris: Editions du CTHS, 1997), 529–38. Another
sign of this localism was that two of the accused in this massacre were women, and the
men were in humble trades, with necessarily restricted contacts (AD Vaucluse, 7L 65,
"Procédure contre Blayet ainé, d'Orange prévenu d'assassinats et de rébellion contre la
République)."

day after the massacre; and so on.[94] It was evidently hard to accept the possibility that audacity and luck created the opening for the prison massacre – hard to accept, too, that an organized independent Compagnie de Soleil at Marseille may have barely existed.[95] But perhaps accepting that the massacres and the subsequent activities of the murder gangs were dependent on contingency, or that they were a reflection of the venomous desires of part of badly fractured communities, or that they had popular support may be even harder.

Conspiracy theories, of course, were part of the revolutionary generation's way of explaining adverse outcomes. Fréron developed the most famous of these conspiracy theories to explain the massacres. Jacobin that he was, the scale of the conspiracy was truly staggering. The bloodlettings of the Midi were nothing less than a vast plan masterminded in London, Rome, and Vienna to undermine the Revolution.[96] This grisly plot included morally corrupt officials, returned émigrés, and refractory priests who sanctified the murder of Republicans. More specifically, its agent at Marseille was the representative Cadroy, who not only let the massacres happen but also encouraged the killers and protected them from arrest.[97] Cadroy, of course, angrily denied all this, especially the well-known story that he permitted the massacres to continue well after he knew they had begun.[98]

Like his accusation in December 1793 that the Jacobins in Marseille were grubbing after English guineas and gold, Fréron's charges were

---

[94] "Pâris d'Arles, ex-président du département des Bouches-du-Rhône, au citoyen Fréron, commissaire du gouvernement, envoyé dans les départemens méridionaux," 28 Brumaire An IV – 18 November 1795, in Fréron, *Mémoire historique ... sur les massacres du Midi*, 137–46.

[95] ADBR, L 242, f. 71, *procureur syndic du département des Bouches-du-Rhône* to CGS, 22 Messidor An III – 10 July 1795. Ibid., f. 144v., same to *comité de législation*, 1 Vendémiaire An IV – 22 September 1795.

[96] Fréron, *Mémoire historique ... sur les massacres du Midi*, 37–8.

[97] "Note des déclarations faites devant le jury d'accusation le dix germinal courant mois l'an IV, par le citoyen Jean-Jacques le Cesne, capitaine des grenadiers du premier bataillon de Loir-et-Cher, en garnison à Marseille ... " and "Note des déclarations faites devant le jury d'accusation, le dix germinal, présent mois, par le citoyen Uris Bruno, volontaire au premier bataillon de Loir-et-Cher, en garnison à Marseille ... " in Fréron, *Mémoire historique ... sur les massacres du Midi*, 132–7.

[98] Paul Cadroy, *Cadroy, membre du Conseil des Cinq-Cents, à ses collègues, sur le mémoire de Fréron* (Paris: Impr. nationale, Thermidor An IV [1796]), 9. Apparently Cadroy and Isnard arrived in the prison while the killers were still at work and the fires from the cannon blasts were still going, but they ordered Pages, the fort's commander, to halt the killing and gave him their swords (ADBR, L 3048, interrogation of François Pages, *commandant du fort*, 29 Floréal An IV – 18 May 1796.

certainly inventive. Far fetched as his interpretations were, they shared features of the nightmares of other Jacobins. Indeed, many local Jacobins at the time were convinced that complicity explained everything, and so their interpretation is very much a part of the documentary record that remains in the archives, a trap for present-day historians. Other deputies believed this too. Marie-Joseph Chénier issued two reports on the massacres and gang killings that were short on detail but long on interpretation. According to him, the prison massacres at Lyon and elsewhere were the responsibility of returned émigrés and former terrorists who wished to mask their old atrocities by committing new ones. Above all, the vast majority of the citizens of Lyon had nothing to do with them. As for the gangs, these were composed of draft dodgers, returned émigrés, refractory priests, and "wicked vagabonds sold out to any party provided there are crimes to commit."[99]

Many believed that the murders of terrorists were the work of the terrorists themselves. Cadroy claimed that the goal was to divert attention from the Toulon victory celebrations or to cover a prison escape that only his timely arrival on the scene forestalled.[100] The *comité de surveillance* and the municipality of Marseille endorsed this interpretation. They also claimed the terrorists had been killed while trying to escape.[101] Again this was identical to the excuses the terrorists gave for the massacres of their enemies at Salon in March 1793. Presumably the intent in both cases was to deflect attention from the real perpetrators, marginalize both the killers and their victims, and reduce the urgency of an investigation.

Fréron's and Chénier's representations of the massacres as the result of conspiracy were simply not believable. Their emphasis on complicity was also far too narrow. Both assumed that the mass of ordinary citizens was essentially good and had no part in the massacres. Indeed, for Chénier, they were the work of outsiders. Conspiracy theories, like Fréron's, denied ordinary people agency. This was a revival, of course, of

---

99 Marie-Joseph de Chénier, *Convention nationale. Rapport fait à la Convention nationale, au nom des Comités de salut public et de sûreté générale, par Marie-Joseph Chénier,... dans la séance du 6 messidor an III...*, n.p., n.d. BNF 8-LE 38 1507 and his *République française. Rapport fait à la Convention nationale, au nom des comités de salut public et de sûreté générale, par Marie-Joseph Chénier. Séance du 29 vendémiaire, l'an IVe de la république française une et indivisible.* Paris: Impr. de la république, n.d. BNF 8-LE 38 1507 for the quotation.

100 Cadroy, *Rapport du représentant du peuple Cadroy, sur ses diverses missions*, 42–3, 65.

101 ADBR, L 242, f. 70v, procureur syndic du département des Bouches-du-Rhône to CGS, 22 Messidor An III – 10 July 1795.

the old Jacobin trope of good people lulled to passivity by incompetent or disloyal administrators. The full picture, however, is much more interesting. The massacres occurred in a context, specifically in a political culture that made certain assumptions about judicial procedures, how these were legitimated, and how they related to the functioning of a democratic polity.

For the Thermidorians, as for the Jacobins, the mass mobilization of the population was fundamentally legitimate. Indeed, mobilization was an instrument of justice. From this, it followed that sovereign people could short-circuit judicial formalities – thus the demand from the Thermidorians, as from the Jacobins, for special courts.

Indeed, mass mobilization and the delivery of justice overlapped. The representative Blanqui spoke of thousands of volunteers who covered the roads to Toulon, and like any representative of the year II, he cried out for an end to clemency and impunity, and like any representative of the year II claimed that indulgence would be weakness.[102] Other representatives urged that the Convention satisfy the demand for vengeance against terrorists lest the people respond with vigilantism.[103] Yet these courts would be revolutionary courts, which, like their predecessors, would sacrifice process to quick results. For example, two representatives protested loudly that their colleague had established juries at Toulon to punish the rebels, but this "changes absolutely the nature of the tribunal" that was intended. "Public tranquility in the Midi depends entirely on a prompt judgment of these brigands."[104]

Public opinion demanded exceptional justice for exceptional crimes. On two occasions the procurator-syndic of the district of Marseille wrote to the representative Cadroy demanding a special tribunal for those imprisoned "as the most proper means to calm the effervescence." Two days before the massacre, he informed Cadroy "of the indignation at the slowness of justice."[105] Because regular procedures slowed the process down too much and could have even permitted the truly guilty to get

---

[102] Letter to National Convention, 15 Prairial An III – 3 June 1795, in Aulard, *RACSP*, xxiv, 34. See also Chiappe to same, 19 Prairial An III – 7 June 1795, in ibid., 149–51 for similar statements.

[103] Chambon, Rouyer, Despinassy, and Cadroy to CSP, 25 Prairial An III – 13 June 1795, in ibid., 347.

[104] Rouyer and Despinassy to CSP, 28 Prairial An III – 16 June 1795 in ibid., 430. See also Chambon to National Convention, 28 Messidor An III – 16 July 1795, in ibid., xxv, 481, for further justifications for expedited justice.

[105] ADBR, L 242, ff. 69–72, Siméon, procureur général syndic du département des Bouches-du-Rhône to Comité de sûreté générale, 22 Messidor An III – 10 July 1795.

off, a special court might be required. In any case, slow regular justice itself was not proportional to the offense, given what the terrorists had done. Thus, on the eve of the massacres in Aix, Chambon expressed his frustrations at how the trial of those arrested after 5 Vendémiaire was going. "Strike then with a great blow," he said. "These monsters must disappear forever from the Republic."[106]

The municipality of Marseille also saw a revolutionary form of justice as forestalling vigilantism. "Hurry, legislators," it told the Convention. "Make national justice gush forth, if you wish to avoid individual vengeance from overcoming it. Hurry to establish a competent tribunal against the crimes of the Terrorists, the drinkers of blood."[107]

Justifications

For some, vigilantism was not the opposite of justice but at the extreme end of a continuum of judicial options. One justification was that outrages from one side provoked vigilantism, or something very close to it, from the other. Thus, the administrators of the District of Tarascon worried about the continuing agitations of the Montagnards. They thundered with indignation against the pro-Jacobin rising of 12 Germinal (1 April) in Paris. "Why is it necessary, citizen legislators," they asked the Convention, "that an excessively slow justice gives them the time to prepare for murder and meditate crimes? . . . We cannot live among embezzlers of the public treasury, and the murderers of our brothers, and the assassins of our wives and children. . . . Stifle the sanguinary hydra!"[108] Although these officials called for judicial punishments, their impatience with regular procedure was obvious. Similarly, the procurator of the District of Marseille argued that the patience of law-abiding citizens had its limits. "If the wicked, the terrorists and the *buveurs de sang* . . . had not raised their arrogant heads and, using the most insidious pretexts, had not sought to stir us up in every way to destroy our unity and to doom us, the peaceful and tranquil citizens, obedient to the law, would not have been forced to purge the soil of the Republic of their most sworn enemies."[109]

---

[106] Letter to Convention, 21 floréal An III– 10 May 1795 in Aulard, *RACSP*, xxiii, 36.
[107] Address dated 4 prairial (23 May 1795) cited in Gaffarel, "Massacres royalistes dans le département des Bouches-du-Rhône," 24–5.
[108] ADBR, L 1517 f. 53, address to the Convention, 24 germinal An III – 13 April 1795.
[109] Le procureur-syndic du district, au procureur syndic du département des Bouches-du-Rhône, à Aix, 1 prairial An III – 20 May 1795, cited in Fréron, *Mémoire historique . . . sur les massacres du Midi*, 184.

In the minds of its apologists, direct justice was legitimate because it was an emanation of popular sovereignty. Thus according to the *comité de surveillance* of Marseille, the people had thrown off the yoke of the "sanguinary faction" and had awoken from its stupor. Still, "the court appeared to be paralyzed and without force. Each family wept for the death of a victim." Their hatred was excusable, and in any case, nothing could be done.[110] In other words, an aroused people had imposed justice directly. Theirs was a justifiable act of vengeance that official courts were incapable of providing.

The killers in Marseille also spoke. After their arrest, nineteen of them petitioned authorities in Paris to excuse their guilt. They complained of the blatant unfairness of not exempting them from the amnesty of the Year IV under which so many of "Robespierre's hangmen" had escaped their just deserts while they languished in prison. They claimed to have meted out justice the way the Convention really wanted. They blamed "atrociously perfidious insinuations" from royalists who incited "arbitrary acts that made humanity shudder." Such claims are fanciful but what rings true is the petitioners' assertion that in their eyes, the agenda that the government itself set after 9 Thermidor was not fulfilled. The retention of terrorist officials or their fellow travelers in office at the local level frustrated the Convention's wishes, they said. Doubtful as this was, they continued, "this sort of half justice and even more the boldness and the criminal threats of the satellites and the hangmen of the last tyrant put in motion all the passions, all the hatreds" of which royalist agents took advantage.[111] The failure of the courts and officialdom to render justice and the Jacobins' continual taunting justified the massacres. The killers did not think of themselves as royalists; instead, they claimed to know and to act on the true wishes of the Convention when local circumstances prevented their fulfillment. This was an assertion of judicial sovereignty and legitimation that was identical to what had been heard before.

The self-pitying language in this petition was also far from the brutal language many of the same men had used before their victims. The

---

[110] AN F7 3281, *comité de surveillance* of District of Marseille to CSP, 23 Prairial An III – 11 June 1795. For the reaction of the regenerated Club, see Stephen Clay, "Justice, vengeance et passé révolutionnaire: les crimes de la terreur blanche," *AhRf* 350 (2007), 126.

[111] AN, BB¹⁸ 174, petition of J.-B. Allegre, J. Brocard, etc., to Council of 500, 3 Pluviôse An IV – 22 January 1796. All those who signed were living in Marseille and all were working people: dockers, wigmakers, soap makers, and so on. The largest single category was clothing: eight of the nineteen.

language of cruelty could be taunting, menacing, sarcastic, or mordant, but whatever the variant, it always proclaimed the dominance of the speaker. There are many examples, as we have seen. And there are many more. Thus, just before the massacre at Fort Jean started, one of the prisoners complained to a guard that he and his companions had not had a shave in nearly three weeks. Don't worry, said the guard, "In a quarter of an hour, you will all be shaved."[112] Another killer told a group of terrified victims, "Wicked people, your turn has come, you will not escape, say your confiteor."[113] For the killers, the Montagnards, terrorists, drinkers of blood, despoilers of the public treasury, whatever they called them, were primordial evil. No one had to bother with explaining why they had to die. Killing them and even their families "to destroy their roots," as one of them said, was itself a great thing.[114] Jacobins were utterly malevolent. Thus, Luc Feriol, a clerk, rejected the accusation that he was one of the most ferocious *égorgeurs*: "Those who dare say such a thing," he replied indignantly, "are men unworthy of the name, who ache only for the destruction of honest men. They want to wipe out all those who during the Terror refused to join them to make incendiary motions at the Club and carry desolation and death into every family." He admitted to having been in the Federalist Departmental Army, to having worked for the Thermidorian *comité de surveillance*, to having joined the "good citizens" in the march against the Toulon uprising, but he denied participating in vigilante murder.[115] For men like this, the massacres were civic acts, therefore. No wonder they bragged about them and said they would do it again.

No wonder too that their petition showed them to be utterly bewildered that they were in prison. But they need not have worried. Probably because many of the witnesses developed endless excuses why they could not journey to Nîmes, where the bulk of the trial had been transferred, the charges against them were dismissed. One of them, Joseph Guillermy of Aubagne, went on to kill again. The court also dismissed the charges

---

[112] AD Gard, L 3151, declaration of Joseph Reybaud, 29 Pluviôse An IV – 17 February 1796.

[113] Ibid., "acte d'accusation contre Nicolas Grandvoinet," 28 Vendémiaire An V – 19 October 1796. Grandvoinet is also quoted as saying just after the massacre, "I have just been hunting Montagnards [*je viens de faire la chasse aux Montagnards*] and if everyone did their duty like me and if we had massacred all the wicked, prisoners and others, we would not have the pain of seeing them before our eyes" (Ibid., declaration of Magdeleine Abel, 24 Pluviôse An IV – 12 February 1796).

[114] Ibid., declaration of Jean Marcia, 16 Frimaire An IV – 6 December 1796.

[115] ADBR, L 3048, interrogation of 4 Thermidor An IV – 22 July 1796.

against the defendants in the trial of the Tarascon killers, all sixty-two of them. This decision was such a shock to local opinion that the government decided to keep the accused in prison, lest the public act on its outrage.[116] Once again, the disconnect between law and opinion manifested itself, as always to the detriment of law.

A few officials were appalled at such assertions legitimizing vigilantism. The public prosecutor of the Vaucluse condemned this violence and attacked those who wanted to draw "a veil" over it. Thus even the metaphors of 1792 were redeployed.[117] Other officials certainly deplored the violence too but frequently showed a benign understanding. While he certainly gives the impression of being a humane man, the procureur-syndic of the Department of the Bouches-du-Rhône, Siméon, could nonetheless express what must have been the point of view of the killers and their sympathizers. Indeed, he made excuses for them while fully realizing the dangers of extracurricular justice. He blamed the prison massacre at Aix-en-Provence on the "drinkers of blood" because "their insolence [toward the courts] provoked an indignation that knew no limits"[118]

A few months later, Siméon had taken a much more interesting point of view, less apologetic and more analytical, a view that perhaps was related to his vocation as a law professor of the faculty at Aix. Vigilantism, he said, had defiled local culture, and it would be nearly impossible to eradicate it without drastic measures. "The corruption of civic morals is such that in this regard, remedies are perhaps beyond the means of local authority."[119] Indeed, Siméon's gloom asserted a descent into barbarism: "The multiplicity of the massacres . . . proves how much we are familiarized with blood, and how much we are demoralized. It seems we have returned to a state of savage and cruel nature."[120]

The remedy was a kind of official terror: "The most extraordinary measures, the most extravagant [measures] appear to me to be the best. It is here we must eliminate [*comprimer*] terrorism of the so-called *honnêtes*

---

[116] Clay, "Le massacre du Fort Jean," 582–3. ADBR, L 3004, Commissaire du directoire exécutif près le tribunal correctionnel du Tarascon-sur-Rhône to same, près le tribunaux civil et criminel du département des BR, 15 Messidor An VI – 4 July 1798, 9 Fructidor An VI – 26 August 1798.

[117] Proclamation of 12 Prairial An III – 31 May 1795, in *Journal des hommes libres* 45, 30 Messidor An III – 18 July 1795.

[118] ADBR, L 1043, Letter to procureur-syndic of District of Marseille, 29 Floréal An III – 18 May 1795.

[119] Ibid., L 242, 59–60, two letters to CSP and CSG, 13 Messidor An III – 1 July 1795.

[120] Ibid., f. 71v, letter to CGS, 22 Messidor An III – 10 July 1795.

gens by the terrorism of the laws adapted to circumstances. It's here that arrests for suspicion and all the appropriate revolutionary forms would be just and sacred."[121]

The hatred for the Jacobins remained for a long time. Clearly for all that he was a humane and amusing man, Lautard retained such hatreds for his entire life. Half a century after the events, Lautard callously dismissed the victims of the massacre at Fort Jean as "Jacobins of the lowest rank [*Jacobins de bas étage*], whose only social distinction was the seal of terror on their forehead." In their lives they had done more harm than "caterpillars in a field of vegetation."[122]

Reflections

In the general literature, *Thermidor* is a shorthand way of saying that the Revolution cooled off or lost its momentum. The Thermidorian reaction in the Midi was hardly a cooling off. In fact, the period witnessed perhaps the most extensive and divisive popular mobilizations of the era. The principal theme of the period was the enormous difficulty of defeating Jacobinism. Up until Thermidor, the clubs had determined the trajectory, and their overthrow, to them and to us, appears sudden and unexpected – thus the impression that Thermidor was a sudden reversal of the Jacobin trajectory.

It was much more difficult than anyone had imagined to annihilate Jacobinism. If the Thermidorians believed at the beginning that all that needed to be done was to remove the many hideous faces of the hydra of the bloodthirsty former despotism, they soon learned that resistance would be formidable. Throughout the summer of 1794, clubs throughout the region, including Aubagne's, loudly protested the drift to moderationism and showed that not everyone endorsed the "revolution" of 9 Thermidor. These protests climaxed with the armed demonstration in Marseille on 5 Vendémiaire that challenged the Thermidorian representatives' authority. But the purge of the club at Marseille, the disappearance of clubs like those in Aubagne, and the flight of their members did not solve the problem of Jacobinism. Agitation remained at worrying levels. Above all, dissatisfaction among both the representatives and the anti-Jacobin rank and file at the slow pace of punishment led to demands for

---

[121] Ibid., 64, letter to procureur-syndic of district of Salon, 18 Messidor An III – 6 July 1795.

[122] Lautard, *Marseille depuis 1789 jusqu'en 1815*, ii, 22. Other killings, 27.

expedited justice or even vigilantism. Thus the prison massacres and the extraordinary mobilization in response to the rising of Toulon. Unlike 1792, the Year III witnessed mobilization by both sides of the political divide, mobilizations that had a very wide appeal throughout the region. Yet the mobilization of the anti-Jacobins revived concepts of direct justice that had first been developed by the Jacobins and that were now turned against them.

The result was a destruction of the civic order. The murder gangs were both a cause and a consequence of this destruction.

9

The *Bande d'Aubagne*

The first round of murders in Aubagne was an aftershock of the prison massacres elsewhere. Nor was Aubagne alone in suffering these tremors. Murders or prison massacres occurred in smaller centers like Polyzoan, Lambesc, Eygalières, Noves, Salon, Eyragues, Graveson, Barbentane, Senas, and Roquevaire. In the Basses-Alpes, there were murders of prominent republicans at Manosque and Sisteron.[1]

In the Vaucluse, there were dozens of shootings, stabbings, beatings, and even a decapitation in that terrible summer of the Year III. In Avignon, the trial of the judges of the Popular Commission of Orange inflamed opinion enormously. Every day, angry crowds gathered at the courthouse. Outraged spectators assaulted the prison that held the former judges. All were found guilty and guillotined on the Place du Palais on 8 Messidor (27 June). As their bodies were being transported to the cemetery, the crowd overwhelmed the escort and seized the corpses. They threw them into the Rhône because, in another example of the highly significant gesture of exclusions that dominated the legal and extralegal executions of the period, "the people did not wish the same earth to cover both the victims and their executioners." The Criminal Tribunal also sentenced a clerk of the Popular Commission to the pillory where the crowd seized and murdered him. They dragged his body through the streets as they had other corpses earlier, and then hurled it into the Rhône as well.[2]

[1] Louis Marie Stanislas Fréron, *Mémoire historique sur la réaction royale, et sur les massacres du Midi* (Paris: Baudouin frères, 1824), 40.

[2] René Moulinas, *Histoire de la révolution d'Avignon* (Avignon : Aubanel, 1986), 343–8. Pierre Vaillandet, "Le procès des juges de la Commission Populaire d'Orange," *AhRf* 6 (1929), 137–63.

Young toughs with white gloves pinned to their hats terrorized Avignon. They roamed the streets, broke the windows of known Republicans, and shouted, "No more patriots!" Elsewhere at Sorgues, Orange, and Montdragon, the Companies of Jesus and the Sun murdered dozens of Jacobins while authority turned a blind eye.[3]

Aubagne stands out in this tragic mayhem only for the rapidity of the series of murders. In about six weeks between the end of Prairial and 9 Thermidor, Year III, there were five incidents in which the gang killed former Jacobin militants in various gruesome ways.[4] Officials investigated none of these murders, fourteen in all, for some time afterward; no witnesses came forward, and higher officials did not press for a speedy resolution. When the inquiry finally did get under way, after the Jacobins took power following the coup of Fructidor, Year V, it confirmed what one might have expected, that the killers in all five incidents were usually the same individuals. The *Journal des hommes libres*, which reported vaguely on the killings at the time, said that the motives stretched back to events that had occurred between 1790 and 1792.[5] In other words, these were revenge killings, but some reasons also predated the Terror.

The massacres at Aubagne were the local version of the massacres in Aix-en-Provence, Tarascon, and Marseille. In Aubagne, all five incidents involved the killing of prisoners, most of whom were former Jacobins. Moreover, the massacres in Aubagne were an unintended consequence of the risings in Toulon, specifically Chambon's decree of 1 Prairial authorizing the imprisonment without charge of dangerous Jacobins. The result was a wave of arrests, not only in the big cities in the region but also in many of the smaller centers. In the case of Aubagne, all the prisoners were locals who usually had been arrested elsewhere. They were being transferred to prison in Aubagne or from Aubagne to Marseille when they were murdered. Chambon rescinded his decree on 3 Messidor citing the end of the emergency that originally justified it, but for the killers, the opportunity to act against their helpless enemies was too good to pass up.[6]

---

[3] *Journal des hommes libres* 70, 279–80, 15 Thermidor An III – 2 August 1795.

[4] Details on these cases from the trial records in ADBR, L 3049, *Procédures contre les auteurs de vols, assassinats, attroupements, etc., d'Aubagne, Cassis, Roquefort, et leurs environs, de l'An III à l'an VI*. And a printed version/ summary with no title in AN BB[18] 189.

[5] *Journal des hommes libres* 53, 212, 8 Thermidor An III – 26 July 1795.

[6] "Chambon, représentant du peuple envoyé dans les départements des Bouches-du-Rhône, du Var et de Vaucluse, aux autorités constituées de ces mêmes départements, et cetera 11 messidor An III [29 June 1795]," in Jean-Michel Chambon-Latour, *Chambon,*

The gang had erupted on the local scene with one of the most violent series of episodes anywhere in the Bouches-du-Rhône in the terrible summer of the year III. Afterward, it went quiet for over a year, no doubt because anyone who felt threatened immediately fled. But these local massacres were highly significant because they show the lethal combination of complicity and popular support that permitted the murders to occur. As Siméon, the procurator of the department, said of the spectacular urban massacres, the operative element was the existence of a culture that enthusiastically welcomed the killing of Jacobins because their deaths were merited; because the courts were too slow and too risky; and, no doubt, because it was more satisfying to do the job oneself.[7]

Murder of Debenet and Rey *dit* Bourrasque

On 20 Prairial, year III (8 June 1795), three days after the prison massacre in Marseille, Antoine Moulard, then a boy of fourteen, saw a number of prisoners tied to carts being paraded thorough town. Among the escorts were Étienne Venuse and the elder Rousserie, who was on horseback. They took the road to Marseille, and once they had gone beyond the Bras d'Or Inn, they murdered Debenet and Rey *dit* Bourrasque, with merciless blows from their sabers and bayonets. The escorts were, in fact, part of the National Guard of Aubagne, and among them were some familiar names from earlier struggles: the elder Rousserie, the café owner; Guillermy, the mason who had participated in the anti-Jacobin demonstrations of 1792 and who had massacred prisoners in Fort Jean just three days before; and Joseph Monier, a member of the Donde-Monier clan. As for the prisoners, Debenet had been a locksmith and member of the terrorist *comité de surveillance*, while Rey had marched on Arles in 1792 with the Légion d'Aubagne and had sacked the château of Velaux. He had also celebrated the hanging of Pons Arnaud.

There was no investigation of this outrage for another two and a half years.

---

représentant du peuple français, député du département du Gard, à la Convention nationale...: Seconde partie, sur les opérations de sa mission relative à la reddition de Toulon ([Paris]: Imprimerie nationale, Brumaire An IV [November 1795]), 52.

7 There is a list of the victims that helps establish the chronology in AN BB[18] 176, "Tableau des citoyens de notre commune qui ont été assassinés dans Aubagne ou dans son territoire et à quelle époque" signed by the Jacobin municipal officers and dated 18 Germinal An IV – 7 April 1796.

Murder of Jullien and His Sons

On 3 Messidor, year III (21 June 1795) an armed escort from Aubagne journeyed to Brignolles in the Var to retrieve Jullien and his two sons where they had taken refuge. As the party reached the Pont de l'Étoile, the escorts shot their prisoners. These are the murders that opened our story, and as it turned out, there were a lot of witnesses to at least some of the events that led up to them. The only report for over two years on the incident, however, was the affidavit of the *officier de santé* of Roquevaire, who could not even identify the victims. The Julliens, however, were well known. The father had denounced the hanging victim Jourdan in 1792, had denounced anti-Jacobin activity in the spring of 1793, and finally had become a member of the terrorist municipality. Fifteen men were charged with these murders, and as with the Debenet-Rey murders, they included some individuals who were core members of the gang: Jauffret the cook; Barthélemy the elder *dit* La Machine; and the baker who would be charged with every murder that occurred over the next three years, Antoine Michel *dit* Calade. When the gang retired to the café Rousserie to celebrate, the cook Jauffret presented the ear of Jullien *père* to Father Martinot, his former employer. The retired priest examined it, and returned it to Jauffret, who then put it in his pocket for safekeeping.

Murder of Jean-Baptiste Domergue, 4 Messidor, Year III (22 June 1795)

Domergue was the most outstanding of the Aubagne victims. His election as mayor in 1791–2 had set off the events leading to the Olive Festival, which had revealed the politicization of the factions. Domergue had remained a leading Jacobin and municipal officer until the summer of 1794. Once again, no one summoned the many witnesses to the murder until years after the events. In the year VI, Antoine Moulard, who was also an important witness in the Debenet-Rey murders, deposed that three years earlier he had seen around a dozen young men escorting Domergue, including Christophe Janselme, Maurin ainé, and Joseph Caillot, along the Toulon road. They were singing the Thermidorian hymn, the "Réveil du Peuple." A few hours later, Moulard learned that Domergue had been killed on the grounds of the Bertrand ceramics works. Another witness came forward to say that Domergue had been taken to the Aubagne

prison, accompanied by a large crowd at the head of which was Joseph
Guillermy, the elder, a killer in the previous two incidents, and now
identified, of all things, as a special commissioner of the representatives
of the people at Marseille, Chambon, and Guérin.[8] After removing him
from the prison, they took Domergue to the house of the Justice of the
Peace Robert, then to the Bertrand ceramics works, where he was killed.
He was buried on the property of the émigré and bourgeois Louis Mille.
Robert had been *juge de paix* at the time of the Jourdan murder in 1792.
On both occasions, the crowd removed the future victim from custody,
took him to Robert in a simulated gesture of judicial procedure, and then
killed him.

According to Louis Pignol, a confessed member of the gang, some of
the killers brought their stilettos with them to make sure. Jauffret the
cook was there. So was Rousserie, along with his son. So were Claire
Monier's brothers and the priest Martinot. One of the Isnard clan, a
relative of Claire Monier's, was screaming encouragement to the murderers and wildly exclaiming that they should go after all the Republicans.
According to Auguste Farren, another confessed gang member, the person
who actually killed Domergue was a young woman, the elder daughter
of one Dominique Moussard.[9] She stabbed him to death with a stiletto
while the other killers looked on, screaming and bellowing, drowning out
Domergue's dying agonies.

Domergue's murder is also important because the people of Aubagne
still know about it. They say his corpse was stuffed down a well on the
summer estate of the bishop of Marseille and later dragged out by wild
dogs. Contemporary testimony is different, but the collective memory
is not entirely wrong. It has simply conflated two incidents, Domergue's
murder and that of Jean-Baptiste Achard, which occurred two years later.
His body was thrown into the bishop's well, not Domergue's. One witness
heard about this from François Lieutard, *homme de loi*, one of the leaders
who paid the assassins.

---

[8] AC Aubagne, *registre de correspondance*, letter to "représent du peuple envoyés dans
les dépts du var et des bouches du Rhône," 19 Prairial An III. The letter complains
that Guillermy is too busy "discovering and arresting the malevolent" in surrounding
communes to fulfill his duties as a municipal officer.

[9] It might be Aimée Moussard who denounced several of the future victims of the gang
as extorting contributions in 1792 and with threatening her brother with hanging, by
erecting a gallows in front of their house on the Grand' Rue in 1792 (ADBR, L 3064,
"Extrait des registres du comité de surveillance du district de Marseille," 5 Floréal An
III – 24 April 1795).

Murders of Poutet, Baylle, Verdagne, Autier, and Olivier *dit* l'Évêque

The murders demonstrate the issue of complicity extraordinarily clearly. The victims had been transferred to the prison of Aubagne from the prison in Toulon. They may have been captured following the battle near Le Beausset that defeated the Jacobin rising in Toulon. At the same time, the military commission that tried these rebels had some difficulty in getting up and running, and in any case, it did not punish all that many prisoners.[10] It may well be then, that the killers in Aubagne were determined to make vengeance certain.

On the night of 14 Messidor, Guillermy, still acting as a commissioner of a representative of the people stationed in Marseille, and Venuse, a major in the National Guard of Aubagne, appeared before the doors of the jail with a requisition to transfer some prisoners. Guillermy himself had signed it in his capacity as a municipal officer. So had the *agent national*, unnamed in the indictment, but certainly Honoré Paul, soon to be the *juge de paix* charged with investigating subsequent murders.

The National Guard detachment arrived around midnight. This was, of course, an unusual time to retrieve anyone, but the pretext was that they were taking advantage of the cool night air. And the procession took a side road, they claimed, to avoid the dust of the main highway. In fact, it permitted the gang to murder five of the seven prisoners – two escaped – and bury them in an outlying place still known as Camp Major. In all, twenty-one men were charged with being part of this ghastly escort. At least a dozen of them had participated in ten murders in less than a month. Except for Louis Poutet who had been a member of the *comité de surveillance*, the other victims had not held office during the Terror or before, although one or two had marched on the expedition to Velaux. Baylle was the surgeon who had denounced the comings and goings of the anti-Jacobins in 1792. The Thermidorian municipality had accused one of Poutet's sons with involvement in the hangings.

Murder of Victor Amiel, Nicolas Gury, Jean-François Étienne, and Louis Bonifay, 9 Thermidor, Year III (27 July 1795)

Victor Amiel, Nicolas Gury, Jean-François Étienne, and Louis Bonifay were part of a small colony of refugees from Aubagne that had made

---

[10] Edmond Poupé, "La répression de la révolte terroriste de Toulon, fin floréal An III," *Var historique* l (1924), 1–32.

their way to Nice, where several had joined the Army of Italy or the navy. Authorities in Nice had little sympathy for them, however, and they had begun cooperating with the municipality of Aubagne, which had been demanding their return for some months.[11]

The victims were all fairly minor figures. Gury was the most prominent among them. He was a founding member of the club and onetime recording secretary-archivist of the Jacobin municipality, but the other three were never members of the terrorist institutions or the municipalities. All three, however, had been members of the National Guard sent to Arles in the spring of 1792 and had been were arrested for their attack on the château of Velaux. Since then, two of them had joined the regular army. Moreover, the municipality had accused Amiel, Étienne, and Bonifay with demanding forced contributions from the anti-Jacobins in 1792 and with involvement in the hangings.

In early July, the municipality of Aubagne ordered their arrest and sent several National Guards to retrieve them. Among them were at least eight members of the gang, some of whom had killed well-known Jacobins before – Michel *dit* Calade; Venuse, the National Guard officer; Poucel *dit* Ferry; and so on. Some were participating in their fourteenth murder of that year. Although they could have killed their prisoners anywhere along the way and easily could have disposed of the bodies along the savage coast or in the forbidding mountains and gorges of the interior, they waited until they reached the outskirts of Aubagne to do the job. At least here, they could count on a negligent local administration that would look the other way, something that could not be counted upon further east. As they reached the Pont Sicardon, just on the outskirts of Aubagne, the guards beat and shot their prisoners.[12]

The judicial inquiry into the *bande d'Aubagne* that began in the year VI revealed how witnesses needed protection before they could come forward. In the case of these killings, there were a number of credible witnesses who saw and heard a great deal. The case could have been closed much earlier if the killers had feared the authority of the municipality and the *juge de paix*.

---

[11] AC Aubagne, *registre de correspondance*, letter to municipality of Nice, 20 Frimaire An III – 10 December 1794; letter to comité revolutionnaire du district de Marseille, 1 Nivôse An III – 21 December 1794. AD Alpes-Maritimes, L 993, "Liste des malveillant [sic] de la commune d'Aubagne refugiés à Nice ou aux environs...," n.d., but evidently late May or early June 1795. The list contains twenty-five names.

[12] Aside from the trial record, the *Journal des hommes libres* published a useful account in its number of 22 Thermidor An III – 9 August 1795.

Marianne Cayolle saw the actual killings about as closely as anyone could. She had spent three months in jail earlier in the spring. Once she was released, she feared she would be arrested again and so fled to the mountains behind Aubagne. She lived in the wild, but one night, 9 Thermidor of year III, as it happened, her hunger became too agonizing. She cautiously approached a *bastide*, where she heard some singing coming from the road to Marseille. She recognized Rousserie's voice. Others were escorting the prisoners. The moon was exceptionally bright so she hid behind a large oak. Someone croaked to no one in particular, "We piss on the ass of *la patrie*." She heard several shots and someone shouted, "On your knees!" Someone else, probably a prisoner, cried, "Ay, ay, ay." Then someone took off after a prisoner who escaped. Finally, the gang returned to Aubagne. Because the moon was so bright, she stayed behind the oak for some time, torn with indecision. Her knees buckling with fright, she made her way to Marseille.

On returning to Aubagne, she was indeed arrested but quickly released. That same evening, young men came to her house to kill her, she thought, broke down the door, rampaged about the house, ripped her bed linens, and stole 56 ecus, forty pounds of coffee, fifty pounds of sugar, and two new serviettes. Someone told her later that the robbers were, among others, François Freze *dit* Glouglou; Antoine Michel *dit* Calade; and François Faren. One of the gang members later told her that they were acting on a requisition signed by the municipal officers Christin Bonasse and Dominique Donde.

Three other witnesses saw the murders from different hiding spots. Colomb was returning that night from Marseille, when, near the Pont Sicardon, he saw a group of armed men escorting four bound prisoners. He hid among the vines. François Lau was returning home from Toulon and took refuge under the bridge. Louis Olivier *dit* Lou Veirier, also hid among the vines. All three witnesses saw prisoners and escorts leave the main road and head down a track. Lau heard Feraud, a mason from Roquevaire, say, "Come, follow me, I am going to lead you to their tomb." Once they thought they were out of sight, the escorts began beating the prisoners, one of them so hard the assailant broke his saber. This unleashed a round of gunshots. The murderers then left, except for Feraud, who beat one of the victims with a hammer.

The accused, of course, had a completely different story. Jean-Pierre Lion agreed that he had escorted the prisoners from Nice, but once they halted at Saint-Zachairie for dinner, around forty armed and masked men fell on them and grabbed their prisoners. Lion then went home and apparently never spoke to anyone officially about the incident for another three years.

Jacobins were right to insist that the complicity of official bodies was essential to this killing spree. In each of the five cases, the failures and occasional encouragement of the municipality and the National Guard and the fecklessness of the *juge de paix* were astonishing. Nor did superior administrative bodies demand local officials do their duty. Fourteen murders in five separate incidents, and not a word appeared in the correspondence of the representatives on mission. In fact, the responsibility of higher authorities in facilitating the murders was very great. The representatives Chambon's and Guérin's appointment of Guillermy as their special commissioner occurred before he had killed anyone, but his use of these special powers continued after many must have known or suspected his involvement in the gang. Guillermy was later tried and acquitted of being part of the gang that broke into Fort Jean and massacred the prisoners on 17 Prairial of year III.[13] He was probably in Marseille in the first place as an escort of the prisoners captured after the battle of Le Beausset and certainly after he received his commission. At the very least the representatives were shockingly negligent. But the department's role was arguably criminal as well. After all, by later appointing Guillermy, an accused murderer in the Fort Jean massacre and a suspected leader of the murder gang as *commissaire du directoire exécutif* to the municipality of Aubagne, they were in effect condoning and absolving his actions. The municipality was also deeply compromised in the Jullien murders and no doubt others. Once they had discovered the father and his two sons had fled to Brignolles, they wrote to their counterparts to demand their arrest. They would be sending six of their own national guardsmen to escort them home to Aubagne, they said. As we know, the escort murdered them instead.[14] One might imagine that this demand would have opened the municipal officers to a formal charge of conspiracy to commit murder. Unfortunately, we can only speculate that the only reason it was never made was because of the incompetence of the prosecution.

A year after the murders, an official of the newly restored Jacobin administration also explained how this complicity worked. During what

---

[13] AC Aubagne, bundle titled "Justice et repression," judgment of the Criminal Tribunal of the Gard, 10 Frimaire An V – 30 November 1796.

[14] Ibid., *registre de correspondance*, letter to "officiers municipaux de brignolle," 30 Prairial An III – 18 June 1795.

was already being called the *réaction royale* of the year III, it would have been too much to expect the *juge de paix* to investigate the murders, he wrote, because "he himself drank and ate every day with the same men. At the time of the slaughters, he was also the *agent national*. He took no steps to prevent the atrocities that were committed in our commune, on the contrary, he provoked them."[15] He even informed the killers of who had denounced them. The commissioner in Aix concurred: "The *juges de paix* [of the canton of Aubagne] have generally neglected to investigate those responsible for the killings and the witnesses to these horrible events do not dare denounce them."[16] The municipality also claimed that during the "reign of the assassins," the *juge de paix* issued requisitions to remove five miserable prisoners at midnight, who were murdered in the Deydiere quarter. "In a word, he is a partisan of the royalists and the cannibal cutthroats."[17]

Protection went further up. According to the department, partisan judges tainted the entire judicial apparatus. Referring to the judges on the Criminal Tribunal, the administrators claimed, "So many crimes would not have been committed in the past six months by obscure men if powerful men had not protected or led them." The public prosecutor had been forced to resign because he was an émigré, but "it's a double who replaces him, a straw man[,] a true assumed name has been appointed by the Criminal Tribunal to occupy his place while he obtains his definitive removal" from the émigré list.[18] Complicity also reached into the administrative structures. "The horrible children of Jesus and the Sun" escape the notice of administrative bodies and the judiciary because they are "worthy imitators of the conspirators... [who] paralyze the action of the laws: using technicalities [*à la faveur des formes*] monsters covered with the blood and sludge of crime are returned to society. Emboldened by their impunity, they raise the hopes of their numerous accomplices and dream of new crimes every day."[19]

But reading through the evidence, there was more than just reckless negligence or active encouragement. As the department suggested, local

---

[15] AN BB[18] 176, Lacombe-Villard to commissaire du directoire exécutif près le tribunal criminel des Bouches-du-Rhône (copy), 8 Prairial An IV – 7 May 1796.

[16] Ibid., Commissaire du directoire exécutif pres le tribunal criminel des Bouches-du-Rhône to Ministère de la Justice, 11 Prairial An IV – 10 May 1796.

[17] Ibid., BB[18] 178, letter to same, 21 Messidor An IV – 9 July 1796.

[18] ADBR, L 173, f. 12, Administration centrale to Ministre de la Justice, 3 Germinal An IV – 23 March 1796.

[19] *Ibid.*, L 174, f. 9, letter to same, 4 Germinal An IV – 24 March 1796.

officials could avoid their obligations or collude with killers because there was substantial support for them. A culture of vengeance had taken hold among the anti-Jacobins that permitted murderers like Guillermy, Michel *dit* Calade, and Venuse to walk the streets of Aubagne untroubled for years after their horrible attacks.[20]

One sign of this broader collusion was the role of the National Guard. Every one of the five killing rampages involved the National Guard and some of its officers. This was not an accident. "Certains propos" in the club forced the representatives Auguis and Serres to order a general disarmament in both the town and *terroir* of Aubagne on 2 Frimaire of year III, 22 November 1794. The disarming of the remaining Jacobins was an important step. The Jacobins who were murdered were unarmed prisoners, and this made it easier to arrest them when the time came. The more significant step, however, was the reorganization and rearming of the National Guard. The officers swore their oaths in the Temple of Reason on 20 Ventôse of year III, 10 March 1795, before a reportedly large cheering crowd.[21] The new National Guard was the public face of the anti-Jacobin municipality, one that the council was certain would be "very vigilant sentinels who will hunt down our cannibals," that is, the former terrorists.[22] The vigilant sentinels, the future killers, thus had access to whatever firearms the municipality had available and the authority to claim and escort prisoners.[23]

But once again, the Thermidorian National Guard was not a restoration any more than the municipality was. Of the thirty-three officers in the new guard whose names are known, at most seven were onetime officials in the Federalist institutions of the summer of 1793. At most only four had fled after the Federalist adventure and had had to petition for

[20] A similar allegation in "Noms des égorgeurs de la commune d'Aix, département des Bouches-du-Rhône," in *Journal des hommes libres*, 3 Vendémiaire An IV – 24 September 1795. Also, AN BB[18] 189, Commissaire du tribunal criminel des Bouches-du-Rhône to Ministre de la Justice, 26 Fructidor An VIII – 12 September 1799, reporting on the robbery of the tax office at Peyrolles and the murder of an official's daughter. "Les habitants de la commune n'ont fait aucune résistance, l'on assure qu'ils n'ont pas même interrompu leurs travaux."

[21] AC Aubagne, registre de correspondance, letters to the commandant de la place in Marseille, 4 Pluviôse An III – 23 January 1795; 20 Ventôse An III – 10 March 1795.

[22] Ibid., letter to the "comandant [du] détachment en mission dans nos contrées," 21 Ventôse An III – 11 March 1795.

[23] The National Guard was probably never that well armed. Despite an order to release weapons to them (AM Marseille, A 27, *arrêté* of Chambon of 5 Prairial An III – 24 May 1795), to judge from the weapons used in the killing, the National Guard had few firearms.

certificates of residence.[24] The military face of the Thermidorian reaction in Aubagne was composed of men who had not been particularly prominent in past struggles. This does not mean, however, that they had no past at all in earlier faction fights. Some like the mason Guillermy did. Some like Guillermy and Étienne Venuse would soon become killers. The changed circumstances of the year III required a different kind of individual, a particularly vicious kind, from the "normal" politics of 1791–3.

The informal collusion or indifference of official bodies like the municipality and the National Guard resembled the situation surrounding the hangings of 1792. The rationale that justice was inadequate or too slow was also common to both situations. But the differences are even more striking. Vigilante justice in 1792 was public, designed to enforce conformity on political enemies or simple onlookers. Vigilante justice in 1795 was clandestine, often undertaken at night on the outskirts of town far from the Grand' Rue where the hangings had occurred, out of sight of witnesses who could be expected to be asleep – although, incredibly, there were a lot of people out and about in the small hours. The motive was not informal exemplary justice as it was in 1792. Rather, the killers were motivated by vengeance, a retributive justice that was not guaranteed otherwise. Base as such a motive is often thought to be, there was a certain morality to it.[25] In general terms, it was intended to redress profound humiliation, recompense a deep mortification, and satisfy nearly uncontrollable anger. By inflicting pain on another, it compensated for an earlier loss and thus restored a rightness to the otherwise-intolerable situation.

In nearly every case, the victims must have suffered enormously. The killings were never sleek and economical; instead, they were prolonged and brutal, with innumerable blows of sabers, bayonets, cudgels, and even hammers before the victims were shot. The enraged killers did not inflict a graduated punishment based on positions the then-helpless Jacobins had held in the terrorist regime or the prominence they had during the club's ascendancy. The brutality was indiscriminate. Moreover, continuation

[24] AC Aubagne, 2D 150, "Verbal de l'organisation de la garde nationale d'Aubagne, bataillon de la ville," 18 Ventôse An III – 8 March 1795.

[25] On what follows, I have learned a great deal from Ralph Cintron, "Listening to What the Streets Say: Vengeance as Ideology?" In *Violence*, ed. Elizabeth Anne Stanko (Aldershot, UK/Burlington, Vt.: Ashgate/Dartmouth, 2002), 331–42; from Susan Jacoby, *Wild Justice: The Evolution of Revenge* (New York: Harper & Row, 1983), 17–36, 39–44, 46–8; and especially Jack Katz, *Seductions of Crime: Moral and Sensual Attractions in Doing Evil* (New York: Basic Books, 1988), 22–43.

of the killings from the beginning to the end of the cycle did not make the murderers less frenzied or less excited or less fearful about taking a life. The fury was always at a high pitch. This would explain also the celebration at the café Rousserie once the killings were over. Once inside the threshold of this perpetual site of opposition, the killers could release their excitement and bask in the evident admiration of those who had not been present. The incident of the cook showing the ear of Jullien *père* to his former employer, Father Martinot, the retired priest, was a trophy shown off to a social superior to win approval.[26] Clearly, the killers and their fellow celebrants thought they had done something worthwhile. They had punished their enemies.

Even in death, punishment continued. In June 1796, when the Jacobins were again running the municipality, the corpses of twelve of the fourteen victims were officially disinterred and buried elsewhere.[27] Thus for a year, the victims' families could not reclaim the remains of their relatives to provide them with a proper burial. The killers therefore had delivered a double punishment, something the courts could never do. That particular punishment was on the victims' families. By burying the victims without a funeral and intimidating anyone who tried to retrieve the corpses, the killers stretched the liminal period of mourning in a Christian culture to agonizing lengths. The rip in the familial fabric was impossible to repair, and the surviving family could not readjust to the social roles that the loss of the dead person required. Adjusting to the loss of the loved one was thus unobtainable. Domergue's daughter, for example, had her legal status as a minor recognized only with the appointment of a family council eight months after her father's murder.[28] Thus, the prolonged

[26] Body part trophy practices existed elsewhere. In addition to the *barbets* cited in the introduction, see AN BB[18] 888, Commissaire du directoire exécutif to minister of justice, 26 Messidor An IV – 14 July 1795: "le fameux Pasteur, le chef des assassins de nos contrées, si renommé par les nez qu'il coupoit aux victimes qui avoit le malheur de tomber sous ses coups..." For the phenomenon elsewhere, see Philippe Descola, *The Spears of Twilight: Life and Death in the Amazon Jungle* (New York: New Press, 1996), 273–8. On the Pasteur gang itself, there is a small folder of correspondence in AD Vaucluse, 7L 96, which includes a list of members and paymasters. It names fifty-seven individuals from L'Isle-sur-la-Sorge.

[27] ADBR, L 3557, "Verbal...aux propriétés...dans lesquelles il a été trouvé et reconnu divers cadavres, 23–25 Prairial An IV [11–13 June 1796]."

[28] Ibid., Verbal de nomination de tutrice de Marie Domergue, 18 Pluviôse An IV – 6 February 1796. Among the council members were her mother, Domergue's widow; her mother's brother, a priest; Camoin, Domergue's successor as mayor; and Antoine-Clément Blanc, a Jacobin municipal councillor. For the theoretical statements about liminality and death, see Victor Turner, *The Ritual Process: Structure and Anti-Structure*

ambiguity in the status of the victims' relatives demonstrated to everyone the marginalization of the Jacobins and their families. The killers thus had avenged the assaults the Jacobins had inflicted on the community at several levels, at the moment of death and in the tortuous aftermath. They had restored the wholeness of the community that mattered: their own.

The café and its macabre conviviality was emblematic of this anti-Jacobin community, that section of it that had the courage and energy to restore its honor and standing. Café society was almost exclusively male – Claire Monier was a celebrant sometimes though. It was apparently typical of masculine café sociability that was ubiquitous throughout Provence. But there were divisions among the men who frequented the cafés. The café Rousserie had always attracted like-minded anti-Jacobins from the beginning, and always the same people. The favorite Jacobin café was the Lion d'Or, no doubt equally male.

Yet the community either side defended had changed a great deal during six years of the Revolution. The Jacobins, of course, were underground or in flight but the traditional elite had changed a great deal too. The men who fêted the killers were a small group, no more than a dozen individuals. The rest of the old elite had either moved away or had withdrawn from local politics. One sign of this disaffection was participation in local elections. Of course this involved more than just the elite. The decline in participation was both a reflection of the gang's ability to intimidate and a reflection of the alienation of voters as a whole.

An examination of election results shows how damaged the political structures of the town had become over the revolutionary period (see the appendix, Table 6.1). The extraordinary decline in turnout after 1792, a decline of well over 200 percent, is remarkable. The recovery by the years V and VI was not a return to normal participation levels, as one of the opposing factions clearly stayed away each time. Indeed, after the December 1792 elections, the vigorous factional competition of the early Revolution gave way to lopsided results that reflected the dominance of

(Ithaca, N.Y.: Cornell University Press, 1977), 95–103, and Peter Metcalf and Richard Huntington, *Celebrations of Death: The Anthropology of Mortuary Ritual*, 2nd ed. (Cambridge: Cambridge University Press, 1991), 82. For similar practices of denying burial to victims in sixteenth-century Friuli, see Edward Muir, *Mad Blood Stirring: Vendetta & Factions in Friuli during the Renaissance* (Baltimore: Johns Hopkins University Press, 1993), 117. Because a lot of people knew about the murders, I am assuming the killers were able to use the sympathies of the municipal council to prevent any reburial or funeral.

one party. Moreover, the winners had achieved this dominance not by winning elections but by intimidating the other side. After the elections of January 1792, the Jacobins had resorted to crushing the freedom of assembly of their opponents by dispersing the participants at the Olive Festival and, in September, by failing to bring the murderers of their opponents to justice.

Three years without voting between the end of 1792 and 1795 probably also dampened the faith of the voters in the efficacy of elections. Revolutionary government in the year II was not simply a resort to temporary emergency powers that restored the political system to health after the emergency was over. In Aubagne, it had far more drastic consequences. With the flight or murder of Jacobins, the anti-Jacobins remained in power so long as outside authority in the department was supportive. Once the configuration of outside powers changed, so too did electoral outcomes generally. After the Terror, voters endorsed a council that supported higher authorities.

The Gang

The documentation about the gangs in the Midi usually reflects Jacobin convictions. According to them, the gangs were counterrevolutionary and royalist. They were well organized, and each gang was part of a broader network. Essentially criminal organizations composed of draft dodgers, émigrés, and brigands, the gangs thrived on the complicity of higher authority and the cowardice of the courts.

This picture is not so much wrong as incomplete. While gangs elsewhere may have had links with one another and even with foreign, mainly British, spies in Switzerland, there is no indication that the *bande d'Aubagne* had any relation with any of the gangs that operated elsewhere, even in the Bouches-du-Rhône.[29] Royalist gangs did exist. The most notorious was that of the marquis de Saint-Christol, which operated in northern Vaucluse. Some gangs even had a religious inspiration. One gang leader in the Drôme, for instance, predicted that "in eight days, everything will be finished. Those with nothing will have something, those who have something will have nothing."[30] No trace of such

---

[29] Warren Wilson, "Les journées populaires et la violence collective dans le Vaucluse rural après thermidor," *Canadian Journal of History* 28, no. 1 (1993), 41.

[30] Richard Maltby, "Le brigandage dans la Drôme." *Bulletin d'archéologie et statistique de la Drôme* 79 (1973), 116–34, and his "Protéstants, insurgés et sans-culottes dans la

millenarianism or even royalism surfaces in the documentation about Aubagne. Much, of course, depends on definitions. Royalism could mean simply anti-Jacobinism, in which case the gang was royalist. However, no leader of the gang endorsed the reactionary declarations of the Pretender, Louis XVIII, or his Declaration of Verona that promised an integral restoration of the Old Regime. Nor did the gang consistently call itself a Company of the Sun or a Company of Jesus. Louis Pignol, who ratted on his fellow gang members, did use the terms to describe the gang, but Auguste Monier said he did not know if he had joined the Company of the Sun. He thought he was a member of the National Guard. It appears that the terms were not common in Aubagne.[31] Gangs then differed from place to place. They took on different hues depending upon the predilections of the leadership or on the earlier history of the communities that produced them. The gang in Aubagne was viscerally anti-Jacobin, without deep royalist or religious overtones, and not linked in any serious way with other gangs.

The remaining documentation suggests a distinction between the *bande* and the gang. Prosecutors indicted sixty-seven people. This is probably a minimum, however, of the size of the outer group, or *bande*. The associations among this outer group appear to have been quite slight. No operation involved anything like these numbers. Many were accused of having participated in a single crime, and while this might be an artifact of the evidence that remains, it suggests that many members of the band were not associated with one another's activity. There were also some individuals who were not indicted for some reason. Perhaps authorities felt they could not have secured conviction with hearsay testimony. Historians' standards are not so high, and on a lowered standard, a number of individuals stand out: Georges Cartier, the notary, Federalist, and émigré; Honoré Paul, Federalist and justice of the peace; the lawyer Colomb; the innkeeper Sivan, one of whose sons was murdered during the Fort Jean massacre; and so on.

But the gang itself was a smaller group. Although the band was responsible for scores of acts of vandalism, pillage, robbery, and murder, authorities concentrated on about a dozen spectacular incidents, where,

Drôme, 1792–An II," ibid., 79 (1974), 209–21. René Moulinas, "Le département du Vaucluse en 1795: la contre-révolution en marche?" in *Le tournant de l'an III: réaction et terreur blanche dans la France révolutionnaire*, ed. Michel Vovelle (Paris: Éditions du CTHS, 1997), 529–38.

[31] Paul Gaffarel, "La bande d'Aubagne sous la Révolution," *Annales de Provence* 17 (1920), 8–9.

presumably, they thought they could present enough evidence to convict. These incidents always turn up the same people, somewhat more than a dozen in all: Michel *dit* Calade, Rousserie, Guillermy, and so on. The gang had a stable inner core while the band as a whole was a shifting penumbra of individuals.

The gang's crimes usually did not involve very much long-term planning and many of its operations were improvised crimes of opportunity. Where there are detailed narratives of the major events, it is clear that the killers sometimes left much to chance or could count on many of the witnesses to their outrages not coming forward. This raises the issues of intimidation and complicity. Contemporaries made much of this, but it is necessary to be careful because these sorts of explanations permitted Jacobins to retain their concept of a good, if temporarily silenced, populace. The Jacobins were not entirely wrong about this, of course. There are plenty of examples of officials failing to follow through on inquiries they had begun or of the failure to interrogate important witnesses. When the investigations into the *grande affaire d'Aubagne* finally commenced after Brumaire of year VI, officials apparently found few documents available to use as a basis for their own investigations. In case after case of political murder throughout the region, witnesses refused to name the culprits because they feared for their lives. In the case of the prison massacre at Aix-en-Provence in Floréal of year III, not even the prisoners who were spared dared denounce the killers. Yet intimidation and negligence were not insufficient explanations for what happened. In one particularly telling case of an investigation of two murders at Gémenos, right next to Aubagne, in mid-July 1795, none of the witnesses knew anything. The public prosecutor of the Criminal Tribunal attributed this to the pusillanimity of the witnesses, who feared the partiality of the justices of the peace and the juries in the criminal courts. But often the justices of the peace feared for themselves too.[32]

The Trial

The huge investigation that followed the opening of the dossier, the *instruction,* as this part of the process is called in French criminal procedure, yielded an extraordinary amount of information about the gang. More than a hundred witnesses gave statements, authorities interrogated at least a dozen accused, and two gang members even confessed.

---

[32] Fréron, *Mémoire historique... sur les massacres du Midi,* 168–80.

Nevertheless, prosecutors and subsequent historians faced major problems in understanding the *affaire*.

The prosecutors who drew up the trial dossier focused primarily on participants in the murder gang itself. They did not pursue issues of political ideology, the gang's structure, the relation to outside groups, or even the relation to the shadowy figures who sustained it. This was a reflection of the inquiry's origins in the Jacobin restoration of the Year VI. The *juge de paix,* Charles Boeuf, a zealot from 1792, concentrated on local perpetrators. This decision gives the impression that only one such gang existed in the entire Bouches-du-Rhône, as the archives contain no other trial record quite like this one. This conclusion would be entirely false, however, because there was plenty of violence, robbery, and murder throughout the region that in no way differs from what happened in Aubagne.[33] The huge bundle about the trial in the archives also circumscribes the gang in a way that historians would find unsatisfactory. Other tribunals punished men from Aubagne who may have been part of the gang's outer circle but who do not appear in the dossier itself. Moreover, brigandage and murder continued around the town before and after the trial.[34] Finally, the trial dossier adds little to the context in which the gang phenomenon appeared. Thus, the historian must look well beyond the trial record to recover the context and analyze the dossier itself for answers to questions about structure and complicity.

[33] BM Avignon, MS 3029, various lists of victims from Aubagne, Aix-en-Provence, Graveson, Chateaurenard, Senas, Saint-Rémy, and so on. This also includes a list of those murdered in the prison massacres at Tarascon. Also ibid., MS 3151, "Commune d'Eguilles. Cadre des événemens et genre de supplice que l'on a fait subir à divers malheureux de la ditte commune," 16 Nivôse An VI – 5 January 1798. One victim died in a clear case of torture. A wool carder, he had bought *biens nationaux.* AD Vaucluse, 7L 96, "Liste des assassinats commis dans le département de Vaucluse depuis le 18 fructidor an 5e, jusqu'au 5e brumaire an 6e," naming the gangs of Pasteur and Saint-Christol as responsible for eighteen murders over this six-week period. The document also claims the department was divided into four regions and directed from Avignon. Lots more on Pasteur, his escapes, and murders in ibid., 15L 35. Finally, references scattered throughout Colin Lucas, "Themes in Southern Violence after 9 Thermidor," in *Beyond the Terror: Essays in French Regional and Social History, 1794–1815,* ed. Gwynne Lewis and Colin Lucas (Cambridge: Cambridge University Press, 1983), 152–94.

[34] AN BB^3 7, "Jugement rendu par la commission militaire extraordinaire des départements des Bouches-du-Rhône, Vaucluse et Basses-Alpes, séante à Avignon, 18 ventôse An IX [8 March 1801]." AC Aubagne, *registre de correspondance,* letter to prefect, 26 Floréal An VIII – 15 May 1800; letter to prefect, 2 Floréal An IX – 21 April 1801, reporting two murders in the *terroir;* letter to défenseur officieux, 28 Vendémiaire An X – 19 October 1801.

Finally, the decision to bring the case to trial quickly after years of delay appears to have been related to the government's goal of ridding the country of brigandage. This scourge resurfaced in the summer of 1799, and while the Directory took some initial steps, Bonaparte's Consulate took ruthless measures. The victories at Marengo and Hohenlinden (1800) released troops for repression in the interior. A roving military commission tried brigands rapidly and without appeal.[35] The government also enacted the Law of 30 Pluviôse year IX (18 February 1801) that transferred cases like that of Aubagne to special tribunals.[36] Like the revolutionary tribunals of the year II, these functioned without juries and without appeal. Like the revolutionary tribunals, too, they meted out punishment extraordinarily quickly. The opportunity the new law created and the hiatus in the war on the frontiers appear to have prompted the decision to hurry the *affaire d'Aubagne* to trial. The difficulties in the case itself and the absence of many of the accused persuaded the government to turn the case over to a special tribunal in Aix-en-Provence.[37] But the prosecutors inherited a dossier that was disorganized and in which many of the depositions were years old. The new urgency meant that the old testimony was never verified. This would affect the frustrating outcome of the trial.

Prosecutors did have one extraordinarily fortunate piece of luck. Two gang members confessed, but their case shows how difficult a successful prosecution was. One of them was Louis Pignol, age twenty-three, a baker, probably the son of Pierre Pignol, also a baker. Louis admitted to much that was clearly illegal and that could have brought the most severe penalties, including execution. But he never admitted to murder. Nor did he ever admit to having been present when a murder had taken place. For historians with more relaxed standards than prosecutors, his testimony is pure gold, but it was too slippery for prosecutors.

Pignol had been arrested in Milan as a deserter from the Fourth Battalion of the Bouches-du-Rhône. He deserted because he feared arrest on suspicion of participating in the robberies and murders that had taken place in Aubagne. As well he might, because by his own admission he

---

[35] Maurice Agulhon, *La vie sociale en Provence intérieure au lendemain de la Révolution*, Bibliothèque d'histoire révolutionnaire. 3. ser., 12 (Paris: Société des études robespierristes, 1970), 378–93. Marcel Marion, *Le Brigandage pendant la Révolution*. (Paris: Impr.-libr. Plon, 1934).

[36] H. G. Brown, *Ending the French Revolution: Violence, Justice, and Repression from the Terror to Napoleon* (Charlottesville: University of Virginia Press, 2006), 326–30.

[37] AN BB³ 7, memorandum, n.d., titled "Affaire d'Aubagne."

knew a lot about the gang's activities. He had heard stories about a half dozen murders and who had done them, even though he said he was elsewhere when they occurred. He knew, for instance, who had journeyed to Nice to retrieve the four Jacobins imprisoned there and who killed them on the outskirts of Aubagne on 9 Thermidor, year III (27 July 1795). He gave some credible names and claimed to have heard that Pierre Gautier *dit* Figuière, in a disgusting phrase, "fit baiser son sabre audit citoyen Gury," one of the victims. He admitted to being a member of the Company of the Sun and Jesus, and that he had wandered the rough hill country behind Toulon under the command of the émigré Jean-Baptiste Jourdan. He asserted that the company of assassins had been paid for by the former curé Martinot, the wholesaler Blanchard, the innkeeper Sivan, the notary Berenger, the lawyer Colomb *fils*, the bourgeois Martin Deguin, and a naval officer in the Old Regime, Martel. All of these men were former émigrés, and most of them had been municipal officers before the Revolution. Pignol named the murderers of the Julliens in the Year III and of the four men murdered near Camp Major a week earlier. He said one of the killers was the mason, Joseph Guillermy, a municipal officer and special agent of one of the representatives on mission, who brought a pickax, casually slung over his shoulder, to the planning meeting at the café Rousserie. Pignol also knew a lot about the murder of Jean-Baptiste Domergue – his seizure from prison, the visit to the Justice of the Peace Robert, the murder near the ceramics works, and the burial on the property of the émigré Louis Mille.

Pignol's deposition continued for three days, and each time he understandably tried to minimize his responsibility. Nonetheless, he provided an enormous amount of detail. Above all, he was able to name other names. And it was almost always the same core of individuals who were responsible for the murders, the innumerable robberies of stagecoaches and ordinary citizens, the vandalism of houses and *bastides*, the raids on tax offices, and on the registry office, not to mention various assaults and countless threats.

Auguste Faren, a twenty-year-old tailor, was arrested with Pignol, and he too gave valuable testimony. He also admitted being a member of the Company of Jesus and of the Sun. Like Pignol, he was rarely present during the worst of the gang's attacks – he seems to have spent his time asleep during the nocturnal raids; in other words, he was absent most of the time. Or he lost his nerve just before an ambush on the stagecoach on the Toulon road and fled into the hills, hiding his face, lest someone see him and denounce him as a highway robber. Nonetheless, he had some valuable information. He added more names to the growing list of gang members, and above all, he corroborated Pignol on many details. It was the only information the prosecution could generate from inside the gang. When they were arrested, all the other accused denied any participation in the gang's outrages.

Unfortunately, they soon recanted their testimony, claiming the assistants of the *juge de paix* of Aubagne had threatened them. This was a major disaster for the prosecution because Pignol and Faren were the only links to many of the other accused, so the case against some of the minor figures vanished as well.[38]

The trial collapsed because more than twenty other witnesses whose written pretrial testimony implicated at least thirty people disavowed their declarations. Some said the *juge de paix*, Charles Boeuf, had inserted the names of the accused into their declarations on his own. Others insisted that his wife had done so. Boeuf's earlier career as an enthusiastic Jacobin at the time of the Olive Festival opened him to allegations of bias, but his lack of experience in managing a big case no doubt better explains the many procedural violations. Probably the worst such violation was the issuing of arrest warrants before deposing witnesses against the accused. All of the arrest warrants thus had to be reissued once the *directeur du jury* of Marseille took over the *instruction*. Moreover, the president of the Special Tribunal reproached the prosecution both in Aubagne and Marseille for adopting a cumbersome strategy for investigating the *affaire d'Aubagne*. Instead of grouping all the outrages together so that the gang as a whole could have been pursued, it would have been more economical to prosecute individual crimes. The decision to compile an omnibus dossier delayed the case for years. The Criminal Tribunal had shied away from taking it. The sheer size of the dossier was too intimidating and "the successive suspensions, annulments and new starts [were] always to the detriment of the evidence and the interests of justice."[39] Procedural complications were too overwhelming. Interestingly, judicial authorities never cited intimidation or bribery of witnesses as a problem, nor did they cite sympathies the jury may have had for the defendants, an issue that arose in similar trials elsewhere. The final straw was that most suspects remained at large. Or they were dead. Rey *dit* Mascaron and Antoine

---

[38] AN BB¹⁸ 189, Ailhaud, président du tribunal criminel et spécial du département des Bouches-du-Rhône to Ministre de la Justice, 26 Fructidor An IX – 12 September 1801.

[39] Ibid. Same to same, 2 Fructidor An IX – 19 August 1801, as well as the letter of 26 Fructidor cited earlier.

Michel *dit* Calade had been murdered in their hideout in the Basses-Alpes in the year VII. Joseph Guillermy had died in a military hospital in Marseille the same year. Venuse had been shot by firing squad in the Year VI.[40]

Thus, the Special Tribunal failed to satisfy the government's desire to use the *affaire* as a grand example in its continuing war on brigandage.

The Tribunal acquitted too many people. It imposed just six capital sentences. But only one of the accused, François Freze *dit* Glouglou was in custody, so only he was executed. The others, Michel *dit* Calade, Venuse, Rey, and Christin were also sentenced to death but only in absentia, as they were fugitives or dead. Pignol who had accused many other members of the gang but who withdrew his testimony, got twenty-two years in irons. Faren who corroborated much of Pignol's testimony but who also withdrew his testimony, got four years in irons. Four others drew prison sentences for theft. All the other accused, forty-nine of them, were acquitted. It was a deeply frustrating result. Killers, like Barthélémy *dit* La Machine, the Monier brothers, François Sicard *dit* René, and many others got off on outrageous technicalities. The prosecution had even failed to pursue the investigation into the supporters and paymasters of the gang so even these men escaped justice. Although the government could have retried the case, Fouché, the Minister of the General Police, decided that a new trial would be too threatening to public order.[41]

In any case, the government had no intention of respecting the verdict. It decided even before the trial started that the accused would continue to be imprisoned even after the verdict. This involved an imaginative stretch of the law, of course. In December 1800 (4 Nivôse year IX), Fouché informed the Prefect of the Bouches-du-Rhône that those suspected of armed robbery or of holding up stagecoaches fell under the jurisdiction of military tribunals. The government could hold these suspects indefinitely. Those whom prosecutors had released in a moment of weakness and whom the authorities considered guilty would also remain in captivity.[42] In other words, the government's judgment trumped verdicts.

The government must have known in advance what the outcome of the trial would be. Right after the tribunal had pronounced its verdict,

---

[40] Ibid., F7 7784, Vernet to Delacroix, 17 Fructidor An IX – 19 August 1801.

[41] Verdict in ADBR, 2U 39, 96–136, 14 Fructidor An IX – 31 August 1801. AN BB[18] 189, letter to minister of justice, 13 Frimaire An X – 3 December 1801.

[42] Ibid. Letter of 4 Nivôse An IX – 24 December 1800. Also Verdet, sous-préfet de l'arrondissement d'Aix-en Provence to Concierge des prisons, 14 Fructidor An IX – 31 August 1801.

soldiers invaded the courtroom itself and carted off all those whom the magistrates had just declared innocent. They were imprisoned in Fort Jean in Marseille for an indefinite period. The preparations for the trial had been so long that some were entering their fourth year in prison. Even then, such high-handedness could not have been very satisfactory because the government was holding only seven members of the gang. The others remained in hiding. Nonetheless, Charles Delacroix, the father of the painter and the Prefect of the Bouches-du-Rhône, justified this drastic act as a measure of public safety. The courtroom was not a sanctuary for criminals, he said. Fouché's letter had a retroactive effect: "The eye of the police is open on the past and on the future." It was "culpable indulgence" to try to return these people to society. The court's permissiveness had rekindled criminal hopes. The verdict "paralyzed the intentions of the government who sees no distinction of party or opinion when there is only perversity and wickedness."[43] Delacroix, a regicide and former representative on mission in the year II, thus invoked terrorist cadences to justify a reiteration of the Law of Suspects. Or perhaps a lettre de cachet of the Old Regime, as extraordinary circumstances justified the Law of Suspects, whereas Delacroix recognized that detaining the innocent from the *grande affaire d'Aubagne* was a type of administrative arrest.

Right to the end, the authorities conflicted over the nature and purpose of law and justice: process or public safety.

---

[43] Ibid., letter to minister of justice, 12 Vendémiaire An X – 3 October 1801. Similar procedure in the Var (Agulhon, *La vie sociale en Provence intérieure*, 394).

Conclusion

The discovery of the Julliens' bodies leads backward into Aubagne's recent past and outward to its sister towns and cities. The Julliens were victims of the factional politics that had flared up early in 1789. Factionalism in turn is the avenue toward an exploration of small-town violence during the Revolution. Reflections on the broader significance of this story have much to teach historians.

This study began as a microhistory. The purpose of the genre is to construct a paradigm that explains a larger problem by means of a single case study. In this instance, the example is the murders in a small town in Provence, while the larger problem is the interpretation of revolutionary violence in the years from 1789 to 1799. Yet the genre usually privileges a single source – abundant records from a trial, perhaps – and intuits the wider significance. Without the wider context that situates the case study, however, the step toward demonstrating the significance is risky. A researcher working from the trial of the members of the *bande d'Aubagne* alone might conclude that the violence of the Revolution was ultimately senseless. With an abundance of documentation on the region and especially on the role of Marseille, however, the researcher is bound to stumble on the phenomenon of violent democracy. This in turn means that violence in Aubagne and throughout Provence is comprehensible, but also that it was not paradigmatic of France as a whole.

The violence so common in this region had few counterparts elsewhere in the country. The West of France differed both in the circumstances of the Revolution and in the social structure in which revolutionary violence occurred. The casualties in the West were much higher because the *Vendée militaire* mobilized whole communities in huge military operations. In addition, the role of the Church in each region differed completely. The massive rejection of the oath to the Civil Constitution of the Clergy in much of the West meant that lay opposition to the revolutionary settlement focused on religious issues. By contrast, there was very little opposition to the Civil Constitution in the Southeast: the Bouches-du-Rhône was a region of massive oath taking, and all ten clerics in Aubagne swore the oath. Necessarily, opposition to the Jacobins there would take on another hue.[1] Finally, the revolutionary rearrangement of public and private systems of taxation differed because the social structure was not the same as in the West. There, the pivotal group was the tenants of medium-sized farms whose rents and taxes rose. Yet they got no compensation from the abolition or reforms of seigneurial dues, tithes, and taxes. In places like Aubagne, peasants and artisans were consumers who benefited from the reconfiguration of taxation toward direct payments.[2]

Another lesson, not a particularly new one, is the immense diversity of the experience of Revolution in France. In western France, the Revolution came to rural communities from the outside. In Aubagne, it began within the town and expanded outward, connecting to similar upheavals in the larger cities: to Marseille, of course, but also to Lyon and Paris. In all these places, revolutionaries spoke the language of direct democracy: the rights of initiative, recall, referendum, insurrection, and all the other ways of hedging against unfavorable election results. This common language suggests that the urban revolutionary event has a common root.[3] In Lyon, for instance, female police commissioners cited the legitimacy of the sovereign people to justify imposing fixed prices in the autumn of 1792. Throughout the following spring, the extremist Central Club of Lyon tired to set up a popularly elected revolutionary tribunal to get their enemies. And, of course, imaginations raced when someone suggested building a guillotine on a swivel attached to the rails of the Pont Morand over the Rhône, to dispatch these enemies even faster.[4]

---

[1] "Religion," in *Atlas de la Révolution française*, vol. 9, ed. Claude Langlois, Timothy Tackett, Michel Vovelle, Serge Bonin, and Madeleine Bonin (Paris: Éditions de l'EHESS, 1996), 32.

[2] See T. J. A. Le Goff and D. M. G. Sutherland, "The Social Origins of Counter-Revolution in Western France," *Past and Present* 99, no. 1 (1983), 65–87.

[3] Jack Censer, *Prelude to Power: The Parisian Radical Press, 1789–1791* (Baltimore: Johns Hopkins University Press, 1976), *passim*.

[4] Maurice Wahl, *Les Premières années de la Révolution à Lyon (1788–1792)* (Geneva: Mégariotis, 1978), 606–7. W. D. Edmonds, *Jacobinism and the Revolt of Lyon, 1789–1793* (Oxford, UK: Clarendon Press, 1989), 146–8. C. Riffaterre, *Le mouvement anti-jacobin et antiparisien à Lyon et dans le Rhône-et-Loire en 1793* (Lyon: A. Rey, 1912),

We usually think of direct democracy as a perfected version of representative democracy, a matter of better imparting the collective will of the citizen to the state. But for its proponents in the Revolution, direct democracy, with its menacing and bloody language, was a radically different substitute for representative government, not a device to influence or improve it.

There is a problem, of course, of where these doctrines of violent democracy originated. Nonetheless, it is not necessary to invoke the malign influence of eighteenth-century scribblers or a top-down model of the influence of ideas, as Alexis de Tocqueville argued in the nineteenth century or François Furet claimed in the twentieth. The potential for radical politics was there from the very beginning, in March 1789 in the riots in Marseille and Aubagne, and no doubt elsewhere. For ordinary people, there was a simple solution to the high food prices, unfair taxes, and vexing municipal fees on articles of subsistence: participatory government. Direct democracy would reform existing structures and remove the beneficiaries of invidious taxation from power. The Municipal Law of October 1789 and later the institution of direct taxes on land and wealth made local government accessible and taxes a lot less regressive. Such outcomes were already implicit in the program that peasant activists like Dominique Pichou of Aubagne articulated in March 1789. Although this grassroots rural program contained timeless themes that had occurred in other revolts at other times, the transformation of governing structures after 1789 made possible another kind of politics. Instead of the armed petition that was the only approach ordinary people could use to seek redress in the Old Regime, revolutionary government enlarged the field of politics to include legalized regular petitions, widespread voting, and freedom of assembly. The antifiscal and antifeudal platforms of the half dozen petitions the Jacobins of Aubagne submitted after June 1790 do not differ radically from demands that flared up from time to time in the Old Regime.[5] The difference was that they were one of several options available to the citizenry to promote their ideals. From the very beginning, the citizenry claimed or seized other characteristics of the sovereign like granting amnesty and inflicting punishment. In the midst of this creative, contested and destructive process, men like Pichou could follow a

---

8–14. A. Salomon de La Chapelle, *Histoire judiciaire de Lyon et des départments de Rhône-et-Loire et du Rhône depuis 1790; documents, relatifs aux tribunaux de district, de département & d'arrondissement* (Lyon: Librairie Générale H. Georg, 1880), vi–vii.

5 Yves Marie Bercé, *Histoire des croquants: Etude des soulèvements populaires au XVIIe siècle dans le sud-ouest de la France* (Geneva: Droz, 1974), 382–93.

step-by-step trajectory that began with leading demonstrations, and that continued with signing petitions, acquiring local office and then marching to Paris. He quickly became an anticlerical agitator, a terrorist official, and finally a fugitive at Nice. Along the way various authorities arrested him three times and many accused him of involvement in the hangings of 1792.

Some have argued that elections and the Jacobin clubs were apprenticeships in modern democratic sociability.[6] This may well be true for the less turbulent parts of the country but in the Midi, violent democracy actually stifled a promising start toward democracy. First patriot leaders, then the clubs, legitimized a popular sovereignty that could exercise judicial powers. This notion emerged after the massacres in Paris in 1789 too but only to slide into the shadows until September 1792.[7] But similar concepts materialized right after the d'Ambert and Beausset affairs in Marseille in 1790. Apologists justified the crowds' or fellow patriots' extreme behavior by citing the proximity of enemies, whether they were individuals like Joseph Jourdan in Aubagne in September 1792 or like the Chiffonistes in Arles, the papists in Avignon and the Comtat, or the Catholics in Nîmes. Patriots also contended that government and the courts were unreliable or pusillanimous. As in the much earlier religious riots, such failures of public authority justified unofficial action.[8] A doctrine of fraternity naturally emerged from these rationales that required patriots to attack directly and everywhere enemies of all sorts, a doctrine made real in the spectacular expeditions. The utopianism of the period, so obvious from 1792 onward, was a natural outcome of a violent politics that endorsed popular initiatives and mutual support. But violent politics by their nature produced high excitement that heightened tensions within the revolutionary fraternity. Patriots and

---

[6] Jean Boutier, Philippe Boutry, and Serge Bonin, eds., *Les sociétés politiques*, vol. 6, *Atlas de la Révolution française* (Paris: Éditions de l'EHESS, 1992), 12. Malcolm Crook, *Elections in the French Revolution: An Apprenticeship in Democracy, 1789–1799* (Cambridge: Cambridge University Press, 1996), *passim*. Suzanne Desan, "What's after Political Culture? Recent French Revolutionary Historiography," *French Historical Studies* 23, no. 1 (2000), 195. Serge Aberdam and Serge Bianchi, *Voter, élire pendant la Révolution française, 1789–1799: Guide pour la recherche* (Paris: Cths, 1999), 18–23.

[7] Raymonde Monnier, "Paris au printemps 1791: Les sociétés fraternelles et le problème de la souveraineté," *AhRf* (1992), 1–16. But the districts were passionate defenders of their police powers. See David Andress, "Neighborhood Policing in Paris from Old Regime to Revolution: the Exercise of Authority by the District de Saint-Roch, 1789–1791," *French Historical Studies*, 29 (2006), 231–60.

[8] Natalie Zemon Davis, "The Rites of Violence," in *Society and Culture in Early Modern France: Eight Essays* (Stanford, Calif.: Stanford University Press, 1975), 152–87.

crowds sometimes diverged on the desirability of vigilantism and always diverged on the ceremonial surrounding lynching. No one in the articulate classes endorsed the mutilations, display, humiliations, and exclusions.

Yet such practices had been a part of the popular repertoire of assault for centuries. As during the Revolution, beating an enemy to death was just the beginning. Stripping clothes, beheading, dragging corpses through the street, hanging headless corpses upside down, celebration with body parts as trophies, dancing farandoles, singing and self congratulation for inflicting true justice, discarding in defiled ground, tossing into rivers, mockery and chilling humor – all these things continued into the Revolution.[9] Of course, people in the Revolution imitated these practices from the courts and executioners before 1789 but the Revolution also transformed these habits in two ways. In the Old Regime, popular action expressed the values of a unified community; in the Revolution, communities were deeply divided. Such practices announced the willingness of one faction to defend itself, to intimidate or even destroy the other side, to purify the community, and to restore a mythic harmony. Second, once the political class in Paris converted to a policy of uninhibited repression during the summer of 1793, the men of the National Convention adopted a jurisprudence for the revolutionary tribunals that channeled the vigilante instinct. Paradoxically, this was the role intended for the Federalist Popular Tribunal in 1792–3 but this court was supposed to moderate violence from below. The Terror was different. Most of the representatives on mission but especially Maignet with his Popular Commission of Orange, declared that the scale of killing would be enormous. After Thermidor, the sudden lurch to moderationism in Paris revived threats of new vigilante massacres in Marseille, Aubagne, Aix-en-Provence, and Arles along with demands for a restoration of improved revolutionary tribunals.

It is difficult to assess how different the White Terrorists were. They shared the same horrific brutality of the Jacobins, the same willingness to humiliate, maim and kill the victim, and the same discarding of the body into the Rhone or into profane ground. The White Terrorists did not seek display in quite the same way. Although Domergue was paraded

---

[9] Yves Marie Bercé, *Croquants et nu-pieds: Les soulèvements paysans en France du XVIe au XIXe siècle* (Paris: Gallimard/Julliard, 1974), 75–82, 133. Bercé, *Histoire des croquants*, 327–42. Emmanuel Le Roy Ladurie, *Les Paysans de Languedoc* (Paris: S. E. V. P. E. N., 1966), i, 503–8. Denis Crouzet, "La violence au temps des troubles de religion (vers 1525–vers 1610)," *Histoire, Economie et Société* 8, no. 4 (1989), 507–25. Pascal Bastien, "Usage politique des corps et rituel de exécution publique à Paris, xviie–xviiie siècles," *Crime, Histoire & Sociétés* 6, no. 1 (2002), 31–56.

and scorned in the streets, most other victims were either killed behind prison walls or snatched from prison and killed in out of the way places. In some respects, the very anonymity of the murders may have punished the families more.

Revolutionary leaders found it hard to condemn violence the extremists incited or committed. Jacobin and Thermidorian politicians followed an unspoken rule of not reproaching crowds that supported their politics. But there was more to it. Most people know the story of how the political class condemned Barnave for his excuses for the crowds who murdered, maimed, and humiliated the bodies of Bertier de Sauvigny and Joseph Foulon in Paris in July 1789 ("Was this blood, then, so pure?"). Yet fewer people know that pamphlet opinion endorsed Barnave.[10] Such apologetics got support throughout the Revolution at the national and provincial levels. The passionate disputes in the Convention about the September Massacres of 1792 paralleled those occurring in the Midi at the same time. The participants made the same assertions, invoked the same metaphor of drawing a veil over events, and made the same excuses for violence in the past while in the same breath warning against future outrages. The failure to agree on a solution to the problem of vigilantism at the national and local levels made politics lethal.

This partisan concept of justice and the failure to support the rule of law produced a terror in 1793–4 that had only a peripheral relationship to national defense. The interpretation of terror as necessary and patriotic is the standard one among historians. They may be right that along the frontiers and against the *Vendée militaire* the exceptional improvised measures historians label "revolutionary government" were necessary. But the outright slaughter that was visited on the West in the name of revolutionary justice was not. After all, every revolutionary and military tribunal executed people who were already prisoners and who therefore posed no direct threat to the Republic. Federalists were not a threat to Republican institutions either, Toulon notwithstanding. The Federalists of Toulon acceded to Lord Hood's personal demand that they restore Louis XVII as the lesser evil because the Laws of 19 June and 5 July promised certain death for political opposition. Elsewhere,

[10] *Les tyrans anéantis, ou Foulon, ex-contrôleur général des finances, & l'intendant de Paris punis par la nation* (n.p.: [1789]). The French Revolution Research Collection: 6.2.920. *La botte de foin, ou Mort tragique du Sr Foulon, ministre de quarante-huit heures* (Paris: Chez Maradan, 1789) The French Revolution Research Collection: 6.2.916. See also Pierre Serna, "Le duel durant la Révolution, de la joute archaïque, au combat politique," *Historical Reflections/Réflexions historiques* 29 (2003), 409–31.

anti-Jacobinism was a defense of the rule of law against the Jacobins' call for a simultaneous, headlong mass rising to crush all enemies at a stroke.

In national discourse, Jacobins stigmatized their opponents as counterrevolutionaries, and the regional Jacobins assumed this way of talking without a thought. Whether these opponents deserved this qualification depends on the definition of *counterrevolution*, but one thing is evident: opponents of the Jacobins – whether they were the Chiffonistes of Arles; the *noirs* of Salon, Toulon, or Sisteron; or their counterparts in Aubagne, who never gave themselves a name –were factions in local politics before they became counterrevolutionaries. As a result, the Terror in regions like these was not about national defense but about winning the faction struggle once and for all by physically eliminating the adversaries. The crucial institution here was the *comité de surveillance*, all of whose members in the case of Aubagne, and no doubt elsewhere, were prominent Jacobins. They had practically unlimited powers of arrest with no formal mechanism of appeal. They were usually the only source of information about the people they sent to the revolutionary tribunals, there to be stripped, according to the Law of 19 June, of any rights to due process that the Penal Code of 1791 had given accused persons. In this way, the Terror became an ultimate, nuclear weapon in the hands of one of the local factions. Violence had already pushed politics off normal earlier, but the legal apparatus of the Terror permitted the unconditional pursuit of local enemies.

But the Terror failed to eliminate these local enemies. The result was the murder of the Julliens and their brothers in the Clubs. It also led to the illegal arrests in the courtroom of Aix-en-Provence in the Year IX of the remaining gang members, and so, in the larger world of French politics and power, to the consolidation of another kind of dictatorship.

Appendix

Aside from those sources cited at the bottom of the individual tables, the principal sources are as follows: Capitation: AD Bouches-du-Rhône 135E CC 40; Census: *Dénombrement de 1790; contribution mobilière de 1792:* AC Aubagne, unclassified, "Imposition mobilière de 1791." Godfather file: the *état civil* of Aubagne of the 1780s, births, now online at the AD Bouches-du-Rhône Website.

"Occupation" is a grouping of every occupation encountered in the documents. The codebook and the regrouping are available on request.

TABLE 1.1. *Occupation and Wealth of Jacobins in Aubagne, 1792*

Occupation	Percentage in Petition	Ratio Using Census	Mean *contribution mobilière*	Ratio
Peasants	75.6	1.7	5.31	1
Building	4.7	0.7	4.78	0.9
Clothing	4.1	0.3	5.18	0.9
Food and Drink	5.8	0.5	5.2	1
Transport	4.1	0.5	5.1	1
Professional-Official	2.9	0.6	10.1	0.6
Bourgeoisie	2.9	0.3	22.6	0.5
Total			5.38	0.7

Sources: AD Bouches-du-Rhône L 292, petitions of 20, 23 February 1792, Brumaire An IV. AN DXL 7, "Adresse de la Société des Amis de la Constitution, Sous le titre de frères antipolitiques, séante aux cidevant Cordeliers de la Ville d'Aubagne... à L'Assemblée Nationale," received 22 September 1792.

TABLE I.2. *Attendees at the* Fête des Olliviers, *February 1792*

Occupation	Percentage Attendees	Percentage in Capitation Roll	Ratio	Percentage in Census	Ratio
Peasant	14.6	30.1	0.5	57.3	0.25
Building	13.5	12.9	1	5.2	2.6
Clothing	10.1	12.7	0.8	9.2	1.1
Food and Drink	11.2	8.1	1.4	10	1.1
Transport	15.7	14.5	1	7.2	2.2
Professional-Official	18	12.7	1.4	6.8	2.6
Bourgeois	16.9	9.1	1.9	4.4	3.8

Sources: AC Aubagne, *registre des déliberations*, f. 60v–61v, *Liste des convives pour le repas d'union, le 12 du courant*, 12 February 1792.

TABLE I.3. *Wealth and Attendees at the* Fête des Olliviers

Mean *contribution mobilière*	Attendees	Population	Ratio
Peasants	4.8	5.3	0.9
Building	4.9	4.9	1
Clothing	6.9	5.2	1.3
Food and Drink	5.7	5.2	1.1
Transport	4.5	5.1	0.9
Professional-Official	25.5	10.1	2.5
Bourgeois	32.6	22.6	1.4
Total	17	8.1	2.1

Sources: AC Aubagne, *registre des déliberations*, f. 60v–61v, *Liste des convives pour le repas d'union, le 12 du courant*, 12 February 1792.

TABLE I.4a. *Occupational Categories of Olive Festival Attendees and Signers of Jacobin Petition, February 1792 (%)*

	Olive Festival (N = 120)	Jacobins (N = 172)
Agriculture	11.7	75.6
Building	11.7	4.7
Clothing	9.2	4.1
Food and Drink	13.3	5.8
Transport	11.7	4.1
Professional	9.2	2.9
Bourgeois	33.3	2.9

TABLE 1.4 b. *Residence: Olive Festival Attendees and Signers of Jacobin Petition, February 1792 (%)*

	Olive Festival (N = 76)	Jacobin (N = 173)
Section 1 (intra muros)	50	30.1
Section 2 (intra muros)	46.1	30.6
Section 3 (*terroir*)	3.9	39.3

TABLE 1.4 c. *Tax: Olive Festival Attendees and Signers of Jacobin Petition, February 1792 (livres)*

	Mean	Median
Olive Festival (N = 75)	17	7.3
Jacobin (N = 173)	5.4	4.5

TABLE 1.4 d. *Olive Festival Attendees and Signers of Jacobin Petition, February 1792 (tests of significance)*

Loyalty	Test	N	Value	Significance
Tax payment	T-test	248	6.7	0.0001
Occupation category	Chi-square	292	123.8	0.0001
Residence	Chi-square	249	32.5	0.0383

TABLE 1.4 e. *Binary Logistic: Olive Festival Attendees and Signers of Jacobin petition, February 1792, Classification Table*

		Predicted Loyalty		Percentage Correct
Observed		Jacobin	Olive	
Loyalty	Jacobin = 1	156	16	90.7
	Olive = 2	26	49	65.3
Overall Percentage				83

Variables in the Equation

		B	S.E.	Sig.
Step 1	OCC	−2.857	.488	.000
	SECT	.570	.722	.430
	TAX	.130	.045	.004
	Constant	−1.190	.732	0.104

Variable(s) entered on step 1: OCC (peasant = 0; nonpeasant = 1); SECT (town = 0; *terroir* = 1), tax (*contribution mobilière*).

TABLE 1.5. *Literacy and Political Loyalty (%)*

	Jacobin Militants	Jacobin February 1792 Petition	Jacobin August 1792 Petition	Republicans, Year IV	Population
Sign Yes	73.3	22.3	44.1	75	35.9
Sign No	26.7	77.7	55.9	25	64.1

Sources: Jacobins, a composite file that includes the municipal officers of 1793, the *comité de surveillance*, and the names of those who could be identified on the Velaux expedition (AD Bouches-du-Rhône 2Y 24, pp. 30–2: *registre commencé par baille concièrge des prisons nationale* [sic] *de cette ville d'ais* [sic]). Petition of February 1792: ibid., L 266; of August 1793: AN DXL 7, "Adresse de la Société des Amis de la Constitution, Sous le titre de frères antipolitiques, séante aux cidevant Cordeliers de la Ville d'Aubagne... à L'Assemblée Nationale," received 22 September 1792. Republicans: AD Bouches-du-Rhône L 266: petition of 5 Pluviôse An IV. Population: fathers in godfather file.

TABLE 1.6a. *Occupational Categories of Anti-Jacobin and Jacobin Municipal Officers, Summer 1793 (%)*

	Anti-Jacobins (N = 40)	Jacobins (N = 26)
Agriculture	17.5	57.7
Building	5	7.7
Clothing	0	3.8
Food and Drink	5	7.7
Transport	2.5	0
Professional	17.5	3.8
Bourgeois	52.5	19.2

Sources: Federalists: AD Vaucluse 8L 103, "Extrait du procès-verbal de la nomination de douze membres composant le comité général des trois sections d'Aubagne..." 3 June 1793. AD Bouches-du-Rhône 1Q 532, pp. 51–4, "Membres composants la municipalité mis hors la loi."
Terrorists: AN F^{IC}III Bouches-du-Rhône 8, *Extrait du registre des délibérations de la commune d'Aubagne*, 1 September 1793.

TABLE 1.6b. *Residence: Anti-Jacobin versus Jacobin Municipal Officers, Summer 1793 (%)*

	Anti-Jacobin (N = 36)	Jacobin (N = 26)
Section 1 (intra muros)	19.4	23.1
Section 2 (intra muros)	69.4	42.3
Section 3 (*terroir*)	11.1	34.6

TABLE 1.6c. *Tax: Anti-Jacobin versus*
Jacobin Municipal Officers, Summer 1793
(livres)

	Mean	Median
Anti-Jacobin (N = 30)	24.9	16.7
Jacobin (N = 26)	6.9	4.4

TABLE 1.6d. *Anti-Jacobin versus Jacobin Municipal Officers,*
Summer 1793 (tests of significance)

Loyalty	Test	N	Value	Significance
Tax payment	t-test	56	4.2	0.0001
Occupation category	Chi-square	66	17.1	0.009
Residence	Chi-square	62	6	0.05
Sign	Chi-square	61	10.2	0.001

TABLE 1.6e. *Binary Logistic: Effect of Tax Payment on*
Political Loyalties, Municipal Officers, Summer 1793,
Classification Table

		Predicted Loyalty		Percentage Correct
Observed		Federalist	Terrorist	
Loyalty	Federalist	21	9	70.0
	Terrorist	4	22	84.6
Overall Percentage				76.8

Variables in the Equation

		B	S.E.	Sig.
Step 1	Tax	−.165	.054	.002
	Constant	1.782	.596	.003

TABLE 1.7a. *Occupational Categories of Murder Gang and Terrorists (%)*

	Gang (N = 52)	Terrorists (N = 11)
Agriculture	9.6	27.3
Building	11.5	18.2
Clothing	19.2	0
Food and Drink	28.8	18.2
Transport	9.6	18.2
Professional	7.7	9.1
Bourgeois	13.5	9.1

Sources: Gang from the indictment in AD Bouches-du-Rhône 2U 39; *comité de surveillance* from the signatures in the denunciations in ibid., L 3112–9.

TABLE 1.7b. *Residence: Murder Gang and Terrorists (%)*

	Gang (N = 32)	Propensity Gang	Terrorists (N = 9)	Propensity Terrorists
Section 1 (intra muros)	37.5	*1.1*	22.2	*0.7*
Section 2 (intra muros)	50	*1.3*	44.4	*1.1*
Section 3 (*terroir*)	12.5	*0.5*	33.3	*1.3*

TABLE 1.7c. *Tax: Gang and Terrorists (livres)*

	Mean	Median
Gang	9.7	4.7
Terrorists	6.1	4.3

TABLE 1.7d. *Gang versus Terrorists (tests of significance)*

Loyalty	Test	N	Value	Significance
Tax payment	t-test	38	−0.937	0.36
Occupation category	Chi-square	63	5.8	0.446
Residence	Chi-square	41	2.3	0.315
Sign	Chi-square	46	2.9	0.09

TABLE 1.8. *Landed Revenues by Occupational Category in Aubagne, 1791*

Category	Percentage in Category	Mean Value	Median Value	Percentage Revenue by Category
Agriculture	59.1	231.1	136	44.3
Artisan	23.2	209.7	129	15.8
Bourgeois	14.6	762	357	36.2
Service/Clerks	2.7	215	176	1.9
Church	0.3	2016.3	853	1.8
Total		283.5	154.5	

TABLE 1.9. *Top Quartile Landed Revenues by Occupational Category in Aubagne, 1791*

Category	Percentage in Category	Mean Value	Median Value	Percentage Revenue by Category
Agriculture	52.1	605	456.5	38.6
Artisan	15.6	621.3	474	11.9
Bourgeois	29.2	1274.3	834.5	45.5
Service/Clerks	2.4	488.9	468	1.5
Church	0.7	2926.5	2926.5	2.5
Total		816	545.5	

Source: AC Aubagne (unclassified): *contribution foncière.*

TABLE 1.10. *Nonlanded Wealth in Aubagne, 1791*

Category	Percentage in Category	Mean Value of Tax	Median Value of Tax	Percentage Revenue by Category
Agriculture	52.9	5.1	4.2	34.8
Artisan	28.2	5.1	4.5	17.7
Bourgeois	15.5	22.6	14.8	43.2
Service/Clerks	3.4	10.1	5.6	4.2
Total		8.1	4.5	

Source: AC Aubagne (unclassified): *contribution mobilière.*

TABLE 2.1. *Aubagne's Budget in 1780 (in rounded livres)*

Revenues		Expenditures	
Lease of Mills, *piquet*, etc.	21,227	Royal taxes	42,686
Other leases, weighing fees	2,855	Provincial taxes	3,886
Previous surplus	10,683	Back taxes and interest	9,190
Occasional revenues	1,779	Honoraria and salaries	11,259
Taille	36,408	Legal fees	1,200
		Repairs and construction	7,845
Total	72,952		76,066

TABLE 6.1. *Election Returns in Aubagne 1790–9*

Election Date	Turnout	Jacobin	Anti-Jacobin
14 November 1790	105	64	51
14 November 1791	217	208	1
16 January 1792	432	226	205
31 December 1792	137	136	1
10 Brumaire An IV	94	0	92
1 Frimaire An IV	88	0	86
1 Germinal An V	?	10	330
1 Germinal An VI	189	179	?
1 Germinal An VII	179	146	?

Sources and Methods

Because the bibliography for this work is quite long, interested readers
can consult it at http://www.cambridge.org/9780521883047. Instead of
presenting a traditional bibliography, researchers might find it helpful
to have an explanation of the archival and library strategy I have pursued. As I explained in the preface, the research began with a more or
less accidental discovery of the *grande affaire d'Aubagne* in the archives,
specifically with AN F^{IC}III, Bouches-du-Rhône 6, "Notice historique sur
la commune d'Aubagne," n.d. [An IX]. This is an anonymous appeal to
Napoléon in favor of the defendants in the trial. This is an extremely elo-
quent but tendentious document that presents the local Jacobins as utterly
malicious in their assaults and murders but the murder gang's reprisals
as noble and justified. It takes quite some time to realize this as special
pleading, however, and by that time, I was already well into the trial
records, in particular the untitled printed version in ibid., BB^{18} 184, and
the manuscript version in ADBR, L 3049, *Procédures contre les auteurs
de vols, assassinats, attroupements, etc., d'Aubagne, Cassis, Roquefort,
et leurs environs, de l'An III à l'an VI.*

Despite their volume, however, the trial records do not address the
full story of Aubagne that led up to the trial. Moreover, they say nothing about the regional context. Indeed, considered alone, they leave the
impression that the events in Aubagne were *sui generis*, an assumption
some contemporaries made as well. The best way to begin this recon-
struction of the town's and the region's history is with the *registres des
déliberations* of the town. The Old Regime resisters have been deposited
in the ADBR, but those of the revolutionary decade consist of five
uncataloged registers currently held in the *mairie*. The other bundles

of Aubagne's archives have recently been moved from the Bibliothèque Marcel Pagnol, where I consulted many of them, to the town's archive at No. 6 Rue Mireille Lauze. The headings on the bundles have not changed.

For the regional context, the *registres des délibérations* of other municipalities are also essential. The minutes of Marseille's council becomes very uneven during the summer of 1793 because, one suspects, of the difficulty in establishing a normal municipality after Federalism, its replacement by Freron's municipal council, and the purges of the later Terror and Thermidor. Other municipalities like Arles, Aix-en-Provence, and Toulon before 1793 have a more continuous set of registers. The records of the municipalities, until they became cogs in the national war machine in 1795 and 1796, are essential for understanding how the new regime installed itself. They also contain copies of almost anything the councils considered important, deliberations on local emergencies, *procès-verbaux* on demonstrations and disturbances, elections, proclamations, and so on.

After that, information on, for example, riots, disturbances, elections, petitions, and so on, can be found anywhere in the archives of the administrative hierarchy. There is no alternative but to go through them all, but as the text demonstrates, administrators frequently believed that crowd actions were deplorable but not criminal. So they did not always open investigations. For example, records on the massacres in Marseille in the spring of 1792, or those in Aubagne in the late summer, ought to exist or be more abundant in the ADBR, but they do not. The AN provides some compensation in F7. Where the Popular Tribunal, or after Thermidor, the Criminal Tribunal, conducted an investigation, an overwhelming documentation survives for Aix-en-Provence (ADBR, L 3043, *Procédure contre les fauteurs, exécuteurs et complices des assassinats et enlèvements des prisonniers, commis à Aix (janvier-mars 1793)* and Salon (ibid., L 3044–7, *Affaire de Salon* in 2Mi 544, 2Mi 738, 2Mi 796–799). Otherwise, pickings can be thin as in Arles or Tarascon, or in the case of Toulon, the documents in the municipal archives appear to have been moved.

It is essential in any sociopolitical study to be able to establish lists of those who participated in the political process. Of course, there is almost never any such list in the archives so one must devise strategies for re-creating them. Because there are no archives for the Jacobin Club or *comité de surveillance* of Aubagne (nor for Marseille, but records exist for Aix and Arles), lists of militants must come from other sources: signatures on cover letters for the *comité de surveillance* in the papers of the Revolutionary Tribunal, or petitions (e.g., ibid., L 289), or the list of those arrested in the Velaux Affair of 1792 (ibid., 2Y 24, *registre commencé par baille concierge des prisons nationale* [*sic*] *de cette ville d'ais* [*sic*]). Opponents can be identified from the enemies list of those who attended the Olive Festival, from petitions, lists of suspects, trials in the Revolutionary Tribunal, and the indictment for the trial of Year IX (ibid., 2U 39, *Tribunal criminel spécial, actes d'accusation*, an IX). Both factions controlled the municipality at various times, so the names of councillors can be found in the election returns, which are usually, but not always (e.g., AC Aubagne, 2D 150, Elections, 1790–an VII), copied into the *registres des déliberations*. I did not use the lists that can be derived from the compensation awarded to victims of Federalism. The lists are suspiciously long and do not indicate the political activity that merited persecution.

Names are only the beginning, however. It is necessary to collect as much data about these individuals as possible. Where not indicated, occupations can usually be found by matching up the names with the census and tax records. The latter also notes tax payments, of course. I have also preferred the *contribution mobilière* of the Revolution for these data to the *capitation* of the Old Regime, because the latter capped the top payment at 20 livres. Census and tax records often indicate precise residence in the town. Signatures come from many sources, often scattered haphazardly throughout the archives, but the principal source was the *état civil*, now conveniently on line at http://www.archives13.fr/dorisuec/ jsp/system/win_main.jsp. This is also the source for studying marriage alliances and godparenting.

Index

CPSIA information can be obtained at www.ICGtesting.com
Printed in the USA
LVOW061756080612

285296LV00005B/81/P